Also edited by David Nichols

Ernie's War: The Best of Ernie Pyle's World War II Dispatches

ERNIE'S AMERICA

🏠 Random House New York

ERNIE'S AMERICA

The Best of Ernie Pyle's 1930s Travel Dispatches

Edited with an Introduction
by David Nichols

Foreword by Charles Kuralt

Grateful acknowledgment is made to the Scripps Howard Foundation for permission to
reprint columns written by Ernie Pyle as a roving correspondent for Scripps Howard
Newspaper Alliance and originally published by various Scripps Howard newspapers.
The columns are subject to certain copyrights © owned by the Scripps Howard
Foundation. All rights reserved. Certain revenue generated by sales of this work will be
donated to the Foundation, which sponsors an annual newspaper feature–writing
competition and scholarships for journalists in Ernie Pyle's name.

Library of Congress Cataloging-in-Publication Data

Pyle, Ernie, 1900–1945.
Ernie's America: the best of Ernie Pyle's 1930s travel
dispatches / edited with
an introduction by David Nichols; foreword
by Charles Kuralt.
p.   cm.
Bibliography: p.
Includes index.
ISBN 0-394-57572-5
1. United States—Description and travel—1920–1940.
2. United States—Social conditions—1933–1945.
3. Pyle, Ernie, 1900–1945—Journeys—United States.
I. Nichols, David. II. Title.
E169.P927   1989   917.304′916—dc20   89-3967

Manufactured in the United States of America
24689753
First Edition

Maps by Dual Image

Not so many years ago there was no simpler or more intelligible notion than that of going on a journey.

—Daniel J. Boorstin

Highways have made tangible the conviction that the truth about America, its heart and soul, collective and individual, is always to be found somewhere just over the horizon, somewhere around the next bend.

—Phil Patton

CONTENTS

FOREWORD
By Charles Kuralt

Many a good journalist has yielded to the urge to leave the newsroom and hit the road. I have a five-foot shelf of American wanderings. Calvin Trillin is there in a place of honor beside John Steinbeck and William Least Heat Moon. There are books by T. H. White and Harrison Salisbury, Alistair Cooke, Richard Reeves, lyrical James Agee, mythological Jack Kerouac, statistical John Gunther, geographical John McPhee. There are many others. There are a couple of my own.

Ernie Pyle was there first. He showed everybody else the way. He wrote plain pieces about plain people, never straining to find lofty significance in their lives, rarely analyzing them or trying to make them fit into a big picture. He was not a sociologist. He was a reporter.

He was a hell of a reporter, with an ear for the laconic remark that explained everything else. We remember him as a war reporter. *Ernie's America* reminds us that what made him so good at covering the war was there all along, the easy way he had of looking over a new place and understanding quickly how things were there, a way of standing in the corner and listening, a habit of putting himself into the other fellow's shoes.

By improving a scene here and juggling a quotation there, a writer can transmute reality into art. The reader can tell Ernie Pyle never did that. We don't see that his pieces are artistic. We do see that they are true.

He was admired in many American households in the thirties and forties. "Loved" is not too strong a word. I remember my father coming home from work and asking my mother where Ernie was today, her cue to hand him the afternoon paper, already turned to Ernie's column. I was only a kid, but out of curiosity, I started reading "Ernie's column" myself. Soon I felt I knew him. His life seemed rugged and romantic. He won his Pulitzer Prize in 1944, the year I was ten, the year I decided I wanted to be a reporter.

Twelve years later, the managing editor of the newspaper in North Carolina where I was working at my first job came over to my desk with a box in his hand.

"I didn't tell you," he said, "but I entered some of your columns for a writing prize. It's worth a thousand dollars, and I figured you could use it."

He handed me the box.

"You won it," he said, and stood there while I opened the box. There was a plaque inside. I recognized Ernie's face in bas-relief in bronze. His jaw looked as if it held a chaw of tobacco.

Most reporters win a few prizes in the course of their lives, plaques they accept and put in their closets. I still keep that one propped up on the bookshelf, the shelf with the traveling books.

"Ernie Pyle Memorial Award," it says. "Presented to Charles Kuralt of the *Charlotte News* for newspaper writing during the year 1956 most nearly exemplifying the style and craftsmanship for which Ernie Pyle was known."

Ernie is up there now, looking over my shoulder. He looks over the shoulder of everybody who writes about America.

ACKNOWLEDGMENTS

My greatest debt is to Mary Pat, who has heard it all before, but who still offers insights. Without the loving goodwill and patience of our three daughters—Katie, Meghan, and Erin—this project would have taken a lot longer than it did.

Random House executive editor Bob Loomis—soft-spoken, decorous—saw exciting possibilities from the start. He suggested an organizational scheme I wouldn't have thought of, and gently pulled me ashore in several instances. Helpful, too, was his congenial assistant, Barbé Hammer.

My interest in the Great Depression and in the war that followed derived from listening to my parents tell of their experiences during both. Both have been especially generous over the years with their remembrances—some pleasant, some painful—of those times. Both extended all manner of consideration to me and my young family during the time I worked on this book. My father proofread the manuscript and read and commented on the introduction.

David Stolberg—assistant general editorial manager of Scripps Howard Newspapers and vice president of the Scripps Howard Foundation—is a man of infectious enthusiasm. I thank him for his advocacy of the past several years, and for his help with the permissions.

Lydia Slaughter was my good-humored partner in the preparation of this book. She typed the manuscript, charitably endured the clutter of my basement office, and offered gratuitous and often useful commentary on the material. (Sample: "I really don't like this stuff about building airplanes. I don't particularly like airplanes.") Thanks as well to Phyllis Gunderson, who tackled the typing of a previous manuscript, learned her lesson, and this time sent Lydia my way.

I've been especially fortunate to have astute readers in John Jordan, Diane Salucci, and Edward Johnson. John, just beginning his bright academic career, was of inestimable assistance. He sent me books and articles, read and commented on the introduction, and tracked down facts and figures for footnotes. Diane, world-class grammarian and syntax mechanic, was a wonder on verb tenses, nonparallel constructions, and missing hyphens. Ted Johnson copyedited the manuscript top to bottom; his keen eye made this a better book.

Evelyn Hobson, curator of the Ernie Pyle State Historic Site at Dana, Indiana, and a longtime friend, was a great help to me as I researched Pyle's life and work. She set up interviews, hunted down information, had photographs copied—all, alas, on short notice. I've never met a public employee more devoted to her work, more enthusiastic about her subject matter. Helpful, too, were her associates Diana Pritchett and Esther Campbell. In Indianapolis, Dr. Lee Scott Theisen, executive director of the Indiana State Museum, and his assistant Cary Floyd quickly accommodated my several requests for materials.

Many people shared their memories of Ernie Pyle with me. I owe a special debt to Paige and Edna Cavanaugh of Orange, California, who twice sat for extensive interviews on their friendship with the Pyles and lent me photographs and other materials. My thanks to Ed and Leila Goforth, Herb and Charlotte Aikman, Nellie Hendrix, Marty Myers, and Dorothy Elder in Dana, Indiana. A salute to George Shaffer (who not only consented to an interview but also lent me many letters), George and Ruth Baldwin, and my hosts Carl and Rosemary Altepeter in Albuquerque; Bill Mauldin in Santa Fe; and Rosemary Miller in Washington, D.C.

Marty Shank transcribed the tapes of my interviews and helped with photocopying. She has a near-flawless ear for extracting sentences from the tangle of the spoken word. Marty also proofed galleys on the shortest of notice. Tim Nicholson copied audio and videotapes and put together a video clip with heroic speed.

Frances Wilhoit, head librarian at the Weil Journalism Library at Indiana University, Bloomington, arranged for photocopying of the Pyle columns and for the copying of photographs. Renee Risk, an organizational wonder, did the photocopying and made my job much easier. In Fort Wayne, Laura McCaffery of the Allen County Public Library helped me locate books and articles with dispatch.

Thank God for the CPT 9000—and for Terri Burgess, Connie Bussell, and Tom Karnes of Computer Systems Indiana. In what purports to be our new service-based economy, these three truly provide *service*. Terri, who taught me to use the computer (no mean feat), is a woman of infinite patience, good humor, and resourcefulness.

At Indiana Michigan Power, my thanks to Wayne Hasty, Roger Dyer (who rightly insisted the 9000 was *the* machine to buy), Denny Miser, Vanette Dylan, Jerry Reidy, and Dick Menge—patient people, all. Thanks as well to my former colleagues in the Public Affairs Department for their friendship and affability over nine memorable years.

Hats off to Matt Sarad (who always loved Pyle's travel stuff best), Eric Ashworth of Candida Donadio & Associates, Dr. Thomas Gross of Ohio Northern University School of Pharmacy, Alaska historian Perry Eaton of Anchorage, Harry Gann of Douglas Aircraft in Long Beach, Charles Kuralt of CBS News, historian Robert McElvaine of Millsaps College in Jackson, Mississippi, my brother Dan Nichols, my friends Bob Floyd and Skip Carsten, and Acme Bar's Edna Heckber, who still lends me her pen and who still always takes a check.

INTRODUCTION

Photo by Lordsburg, New Mexico, Chamber of Commerce

Rare is the American who has not dreamed of dropping whatever he is doing and hitting the road. The dream of unrestrained movement is a distinctly American one, an inheritance bequeathed to subsequent generations by those restless souls who populated the American continent. Travel—away from here, toward a vague and distant destination—is part of our national folklore.

Economic hardship has been a common inducement. Steinbeck's Okies traveled west on Route 66 toward what they hoped would be a better life. Others have had a more spiritual motive: the outer journey has been a mere symbol for the inner, the road a means of finding themselves. Still others have traveled to escape themselves, flight on the open road promising to postpone, if not forestall, some rigorous self-examination.

Motives aside, many are the Americans who could say with Huckleberry Finn, "I reckon I got to light out for the Territory," and do so, hoping in the American way for some transformation, only to be disappointed with the results. Such came to be the case with Ernie Pyle, who, hopeful and excited, set out from Washington, in late summer of 1935, on a big adventure.

Pyle's bosses at Scripps Howard Newspapers had relieved him of what had become an onerous routine—the managing editorship of the *Washington Daily News*—and were permitting him to go where he pleased and write about what he pleased. There was one stipulation: that he produce six pieces a week, each about a thousand words, for distribution to the twenty-four Scripps Howard papers. Driving a Ford coupe, Pyle and his wife, Jerry, took a leisurely journey through the Northeast and into Nova Scotia, Ontario, and Quebec provinces. Then they crossed back into the United States and traveled through Minnesota, Iowa, and Indiana.

During that time, my father, about to turn ten years old, followed Ernie and Jerry's every move in the pages of the Scripps Howard *Indianapolis Times,* now defunct but then very much alive and delivered to Coats' Garage at Templeton, Indiana, each afternoon by the Indianapolis-to-Chicago Greyhound bus. "Delivered" doesn't quite tell the story. Unfailingly, the driver merely slowed, opened the door, and heaved the rolled newspaper in the direction of the office door. If a curly-haired kid named George Nichols was there to catch it, fine. If not, the brown wrapper wouldn't keep the paper from being torn on the paving stones or soaked in a puddle. But he was usually there, waiting. Meeting the Greyhound assured George first crack at Ernie Pyle's column, which fascinated him. Pyle, after all, was on the move, visiting places my father could only dream of. Where had Pyle been today? What had he seen? With whom had he talked along the way?

The boyhood my father was living in Benton County, in and about the village of Templeton, was much like that Pyle had experienced a quarter century before in Vermillion County, Indiana, fifty miles to the southwest. Like Pyle as a boy and later as an adult, my father was hopelessly afflicted with wanderlust. He wanted to break away from his small town and see what there was to see beyond the corn prairie.

The *Indianapolis Times* subscription belonged to my grandparents, who daily read the news about what Roosevelt was up to, what new New Deal scheme was afoot to help people like themselves, people bent on working for a living but who found themselves frustrated and wary of the future. After digesting the news from Washington, my grandparents turned to Pyle's column, which ran under the standing head HOOSIER VAGABOND. While there's no record of what they thought of Pyle's pieces, they must have enjoyed them, because they kept reading. Whatever their quotient of wanderlust, my grandparents had a good deal more on their minds than travel. They had three children to feed and clothe, and times were tough.

My grandfather was a college history professor, recently out of work, a condition he shared with twenty-five percent of his working-age countrymen. (Another twenty-five percent were "underemployed.") Having looked for other jobs and received no offers, my grandfather had moved the family back to Templeton, his childhood home, where rents were cheap and the soil fertile. The family gardened in the summer and lived through the winter on the canned vegetables. A friendly grocer extended credit for meat and staples.

By the time Pyle finished his first trip as a roving reporter, eight weeks and six thousand miles after he began, the fall term at Templeton School was well under way, and my father and his wanderlust were imprisoned for another nine months in the small brick schoolhouse. When the winter term began, the relentless wind—"the wind of futility" Pyle had so evocatively described on his September pass through the Midwest—was bitter cold and dusting snow through the cornstalks at the edge of town. But by then Pyle was on another trip, this time through the South and Southwest and into Mexico. My father's only escape from school and Templeton and that cold wind of futility was each day's edition of the *Indianapolis Times.*

My father and his parents were but three of the thousands of readers who traveled vicariously with Ernie Pyle over the next seven years, following him to every state in the Union at least three times, crossing the American continent with him thirty-five times, journeying to Canada, Alaska, Hawaii, Mexico, Central and South America, and eventually to England in 1940, where Pyle wrote about the German bombings of London and other cities. On the one hand, it was a hard, relentless job, as Pyle often said in his column, but on the other, it was the acting out of a distinctly American fantasy. And while Pyle was sometimes at a loss to see this, readers like my father never were.

Reporter from home

It is impossible to reintroduce Ernie Pyle's largely forgotten travel writings without talking about Pyle the war correspondent. Pyle's journalistic reputation is justly based on his frontline dispatches during World War II, when he lived almost exclusively with the infantry in North Africa, Europe, and the Pacific. So sympathetic and affectionate was his portrait of the infantryman—so adept was he at articulating the frustrations, occasional elations, and constant home-yearnings of men whose lives were lived and lost at the whim of others—that his death assured him a permanent place in postwar mythology. It was a martyr's place, no less, because Pyle needn't have gone to war at all. A profound need to be useful in a time of national crisis was his reason for subjecting himself to dangers he admitted frightened him. When he was killed by a Japanese sniper on the island of Ie Shima, near Okinawa, in April of 1945, civilians and servicemen alike grieved as though they'd lost a personal friend.

Some of his wartime readers had never heard of Pyle before he showed up in North Africa and began filing dispatches datelined WITH THE AMERICAN FORCES IN ALGIERS. It may or may not have occurred to them to wonder how he had acquired the understanding of America and Americans so evident in his columns. But those who had read Pyle before the war knew exactly where those kernels of insight so liberally sprinkled in Pyle's dispatches came from. They knew they derived from years of travel in America before the war sent people off in all directions.

Pyle, in fact, was uniquely equipped to bring the reality of the war and the American men fighting it home to the American people. Few correspondents had traveled so widely in their native country, absorbing regional nuance and making the acquaintance of so many Americans. When Pyle arrived in a new war theater, he could readily describe the countryside in terms of its counterpart in the United States. When a soldier told him about his home, Pyle could resurrect a mental picture of the territory: he'd been there, likely as not more than once. Thus was Pyle able to link the prewar man with the soldier he had become, surrounded now by foreign people and cultures, existing day to day in a world turned upside down, his identity shored up by fond memories of home and a longing to return there.

Pyle's readers appreciated this. Physically insulated from the battles being fought in Europe and the Pacific—but not from home-front deprivations and long, hard hours of work in defense industries—those stateside had to exert considerable imagination to conceive of how these men were living (and dying) so far away, and Pyle's writing helped them do so. It also served to unite, albeit in print, those at war and those at home.

The Pyle pieces that follow will explain a great deal about how Pyle was able to do what he did so well during the war. Present here are the same reporting and writing skills that made him the most popular war correspondent in American newspapers: the intimate approach, the insistence on portraying the people behind the headlines, the physical description that enabled the reader to experience to the fullest what Pyle had experienced, the carefully selected detail. This is not the stuff of ordinary newspaper reporting, but it was the essence of Ernie Pyle's work.

The war changed Ernie Pyle, just as it changed the soldiers he wrote about. The man who wrote the travel dispatches collected here was big-hearted and compassionate; he was also hard-edged and hard-drinking, profane and irreverent. So was Pyle the war correspondent. But there was a difference. At war Pyle was a man connected with his times, engaged and tuned in and daily seeking to evoke such from his readers. During the thirties, Pyle was disengaged and tuned out, seeking to divert his readers' attention from what was bothering them—and him. And those things were not, as we'll see, one and the same.

The agenda

It's worth sorting out just who Ernie Pyle was and how he happened to be at large in America between 1935 and early 1942.

Pyle's roving-reporter pieces answered a need for lighter reading fare in some American newspapers at a critical time in the nation's history, but it would be a mistake to suggest that Pyle had perceived this need and had sought to fill it. Neither he nor his Scripps Howard superiors had given much thought to how they would "market" his work to those twenty-four Scripps Howard editors in places as disparate as New York and Indianapolis, Fort Worth and Knoxville, Albuquerque and Evansville. The Pyle travel column would be included with other material the company's feature service, Scripps Howard Newspaper Alliance, wired daily to the chain's papers, and would compete for space just as any other feature did.

Pyle's bosses were willing to shelve any concerns they had about this new enterprise and let him have his way for a while. His enthusiasm was infectious, and they knew that was generally an indicator of good things to come. They knew him to be a dependable and resourceful sort, a hard worker, and they didn't want to lose him. But lose him they would if they insisted he continue as managing editor of the *Washington Daily News*. For his part, Ernie wanted to give the roving column a try and see what would turn up. Regardless of how his pieces fared elsewhere in the chain, he knew they would run in the *Daily News*. And besides, his agenda was far more personal than professional. Though he saw the travel column as a challenge, he saw it even more as a means of escape.

Ernie's personal agenda wasn't enough, however. There had to be something more, and it came in the form of a public agenda supplied not by corporate headquarters in New York, nor by Scripps Howard Newspaper Alliance in Washington, but by the chain's editors in all those distant cities—and by their often-vocal subscribers. Returning from a meeting of Scripps Howard editors in June of 1936, Frank Ford, editor of the *Evansville Press*, wrote an encouraging letter to Ernie's parents, Will and Maria Pyle. The editors had discussed the travel column, Ford said, and "almost without exception the editors reported the same experience we have had on the *Press*. At first they used a few of the articles. Then readers started calling up and writing in about them, until they were practically forced to use them daily, regardless of how badly the space was needed for other things. Right now, on the *Press*, if we were to omit even one of them indignant subscribers would call in by the dozen." Ford added, "I think most of the editors would agree with me that Ernie's daily column is more widely read than anything else in the paper."

Ernie's column soon became a daily habit with many editors and their phone-calling and letter-writing readers, who saw his pieces as the perfect antidote to the "too-heavy grist of political, economic, and international news" of the day, as one editor put it. It was refreshing, this "gentle wholesomeness and wide-eyed country-boy absorption with homely but essential trivia," as another wrote. "Escape" was the operative word—escape for Pyle and for his readers, most of whom faced hard times.

There was a depression on, after all—the Great Depression, one of the biggest economic and social catastrophes in American history—and what to do about it was a source of bitter controversy. Americans' enthusiasm for politics has been at best inconstant, but in these years virtually everyone had an opinion about how to get the country moving again, and with good reason. This calamity had affected almost everyone, from the wealthiest industrialist to the poorest day laborer. After the prosperity of the 1920s, the 1930s had been a bitter shock: something had gone terribly wrong with the dream. Bitterness and anxiety were playing themselves out daily in newspapers nationwide.

Pyle knew all about this. The Depression had entered its third year and the American electorate's patience with President Herbert Hoover was all but shot when Pyle became managing editor of the *Daily News* in 1932, just as Hoover and Franklin Roosevelt were campaigning for the presidency. From his vantage point in the newsroom, Pyle saw the American people's hopes rise with Roosevelt in office, only to dip again when the economy failed to revive during the first years of the New Deal. He saw accounts of labor strife, bank closings, the rise of right- and left-wing pressures alike. He saw photographs of unemployed men standing in long lines, seeking work or a bowl of soup and a slice of bread—pictures of men in business suits selling apples for a nickel on street corners. And frankly, none of it interested him much. It was important stuff, of course, and it had to receive prominent play in the paper, but politics, economics, and all the attendant wrangling left him flat. So, for that matter, did newspaper management.

Only reluctantly had Pyle accepted the managing editorship. He had been Scripps Howard's aviation editor and columnist from 1928 through 1932. As a lifelong admirer of men of action, Pyle had been perfectly suited to convey to an equally admiring public news of the pilots, their "ships," and the fledgling airlines that employed both. He had thoroughly enjoyed his first attempt at personal journalism and his first experience with insider reporting—becoming intimately involved with a group of people and then explaining that group to outsiders, just as he would do with the infantry during the war. In those years he had developed a highly readable style, intimate and anecdotal, and the column had enjoyed extraordinary success in the *Daily News* and later in other Scripps Howard papers. Pyle's readers had been an expressive lot and had sent letters from all over the country when a column had especially touched them.

By 1932, aviation was no longer the rough-and-tumble business it had once been. Much of its early pioneering spirit had given way to a more businesslike approach, its randomness to regulation. The old romance was waning. Even so, Pyle had been reluctant to give it up, and even more reluctant to return to the copy desk, where he'd spent most of his early newspaper career. A facile copy editor and a good headline writer, he hated doing both. He had accepted the position because during the Depression it made sense to take a job his bosses badly wanted him to take.

His decision dismayed aviation readers. "Sorry to read you are leaving—seems like losing an old friend," wrote one. Another closed his letter with a cautionary note that proved prophetic. "Please don't forget the old aviation column, however," he wrote, "and also don't forget that work behind the desk without air is bad."

There followed three difficult years of trying to put out a daily newspaper on the tightest of budgets, haggling with upper management for meager pay increases for his staff only to have them taken away when the economy worsened. He had done a good job of it. In his three years as managing editor, Pyle had fired only one employee, an incompetent copyboy. A diplomat, he could extract hard work from his people under circumstances that tried everyone's patience. But working every day in the noisy, congested newsroom, breathing air thick with tobacco smoke, a fair portion of which was his, Pyle had longed for release. Work behind a desk without air truly *was* bad. So was hard drink, consumed at the regular intervals and in the fantastic quantities Ernie, Jerry, and their friends were accustomed to in these years.

This was an era when heavy drinking was as essential a part of being a newspaperman as speedy two-fingered typing. Ernie and Jerry had been drinking to excess for years, but his stint as managing editor had been an especially stressful time, and now they were drinking more than ever. Although both were alcoholics by 1935, Ernie's nights of "alcoholic insanity," as one *Daily News* associate called them, were offset by his having to be at work the next morning. Jerry had no such check on her drinking. She was a recluse, spending her days alone in their shabby apartment, reading books, writing poetry, playing the piano, having a drink or two at lunch—anything to take the edge off the despair she kept tacitly at bay.

Pyle worried about Jerry, and she about him. He feared he was a burned-out newspaper hack at age thirty-four. The job aged them both, Jerry no less than Ernie, for it was up to her to soothe his sagging emotions. When Pyle had been slow to recover from influenza in December of 1934, the *Daily News* had granted him a leave of absence, and he and Jerry had left Washington for an auto tour of the West and Southwest. The trip had been redemptive. Pyle returned to Washington convinced that travel had to figure prominently in his life, just as he'd thought it would during his years at Indiana University. He wrote a series of eleven articles about his trip for the paper, and one of his bosses said the pieces had "a Mark Twain quality that knocked my eye out." Ernie decided that never again could he allow his writing skills to go unsummoned.

Here, too, the trip had made him question his staying in Washington. It had been a good city to be young in, but those wide-open spaces out West exerted a powerful pull. The small towns were a welcome change, too. Washington had become too big, too busy, too congested with New Dealers trying to save the world. And he knew that as long as he stayed in the city, his social circle would continue to consist mostly of newspaper people, and that the drinking would go on and on. It was time for a change.

Such was Pyle's personal agenda in early August 1935, when, doubtless hungover after a rousing farewell party, he and Jerry locked their apartment door, put a few bags in the trunk of the car, and drove their Ford coupe out of Washington and onto the open road. Pyle had no way of knowing that his personal agenda would mesh nicely with the public agenda editors and their readers would set for him in the months and years to come. Nor would he have cared. For now, just getting out of town was enough.

No easy job

Americans born around the turn of the century had grown up with the automobile. Pyle was eight years old when Henry Ford introduced the Model T, an adolescent when Ford began mass-producing his car for the common man on an assembly line. By the time Pyle began his roving-reporter assignment, the automobile had gone a long way toward transforming American life and the American countryside.

Even a decade earlier, Pyle's travel assignment would have been a terrific hardship. Roads had been either haphazardly marked or not marked at all, their quality a study in diversity. Roadside accommodations had been bleak or nonexistent, and the cars themselves had been too uncomfortable for anything but local travel. Drivers had justly considered motoring a perilous undertaking. Traffic on any thoroughfare had been constantly assaulted by traffic on intersecting roads. Americans had just begun getting used to automobiles in any number, and drivers' safety habits still left much to be desired. Night driving of any distance had been especially dangerous.

By 1935 things were much improved, but driving long distances was still altogether more rigorous than it is today, all the more so in Pyle's case because of the frequency with which he traveled. Roads were still of uneven quality; interstates, with their limited access, were years in the future. Cars of the day were more comfortable than their predecessors but still lacked such amenities as automatic transmissions, air conditioning, and comfortable seats. Pyle was a short, skinny man, and after a long day of motoring cross-country, he often ached from the car's constant bumping over rough back roads. He never knew whether the hotel bed he would sleep in that night would be comfortable or as bumpy as that day's roads. Ernie and Jerry weren't fussy about food, and they were fortunate in this: the quality of roadside restaurants varied as widely as the quality of the roads themselves. And these were the least of their difficulties.

Having already sustained a daily column for almost four years, Ernie knew something of the difficulty of turning out an appealing piece on deadline. But this was harder by far than the aviation column. Here there was no focus, no network of contacts to tie into. Nor were there any economies of effort. Pyle's every travel column was the result of his effort and his alone, not an elaboration of an item someone had phoned into his desk at the *Daily News*. Six pieces a week—six thousand words—is a lot of copy, the product of hours of labor at the typewriter. Consider, too, the travel and interviewing time, and it's no wonder Pyle was defensive when his friends accused him of being permanently on vacation. Even so, the fruitfulness of Pyle's efforts was at one with the difficulty of getting there, because getting there, wherever that was, always became part of the story. Ernie considered what happened along the way to be worth writing about, and his readers agreed.

Network radio had come into its own by the mid-1930s, and national magazines were abundant, but the mass-market economy, slowed now by the Depression, had yet to work its leveling effect on American regions. America was a teeming patchwork of local variety, its regional distinctions potent. The day of a television set in every home was still decades off, and people in one region were still curious about how people lived elsewhere. To the observant and curious visitor, local color and custom abounded. The continental United States was a big place, three quarters the size of Europe. There was lots of ground for Pyle to cover and lots of people to meet.

Local editors could be counted on for tips, and so could readers, who sent Pyle letters and postcards by the score. He filed reader suggestions by state in a little wooden box he carried in the car. Mostly, though, Pyle found his columns by chance. He rarely took notes, rarely conducted anything approximating a formal interview. Where he went and when were almost always up to him. He would collect material for a week or so, then find a congenial hotel in which to write. There followed a hellish several days of frantic composition, revising and retyping, keeping carbons for his files, and sending the originals to Scripps Howard Newspaper Alliance. With few exceptions, Ernie dispatched his pieces via first-class mail. In seven years, not a single one was lost.

Nostalgia

In 1893, seven years before Pyle's birth, the historian Frederick Jackson Turner had declared the American frontier closed and with it the first period of American history. But in Pyle's fanciful imagination—and to a lesser extent in actual fact—the American West was still frontier country. During his travel years, Pyle returned again and again to Arizona, New Mexico, Texas, Utah, Wyoming, and Colorado, their big skies and vast, thinly populated spaces a delightful contrast to the crowded East, which he had grown to dislike intensely. "Am I glad to get West again!" he wrote a friend from Seattle in the spring of 1937. "The three months in the East damn near killed me (literally)—too many things to do, too many people to see, too much of everything. When I crossed the Mississippi River I felt as though I'd shed a big burden."

It was in the West—the most fabled of American regions, object of our national restlessness and our search for a better, less restricted life—that Pyle felt the freedom he'd hoped for. A child of the midlands, he longed for drama in terrain, nature writ large. The far-reaching horizons of the desert country and the sheer rugged beauty of the mountain country inspired in him a sense of independence and well-being. It also fueled his yearning for a mythic past, the lawless, excessive, hard-driving Old West of the frontier, known to men of his grandfather's generation but alive now mostly in legend and in the romantic imaginations of men like himself.

True, he loved the land and the freedom implicit in its openness. He liked Westerners for their democratic sensibilities, their friendliness and general companionability. In this they were like the rural Midwesterners he had grown up with, not at all like Easterners, for whom class lines were sharply drawn and forever the object of hushed speculation. But the greater part of Pyle's attraction to the West was pure nostalgia. He was a man approaching middle age who believed he'd lived his life one step removed from dramas spectacular beyond imagination. Missing World War I because his parents wanted him to finish high school had been an especially bitter disappointment, all the more so because his closest neighborhood friend had gone to the war.

People for whom the past exerts such a bittersweet tug harbor the sense that time has betrayed them by positioning them in such prosaic circumstances as the present. They reluctantly content themselves with searches for others' imperfect memories and the discovery of a few relics here and there. So it was with Pyle and the West and, to a lesser extent, Alaska. Many times in the following pages occur sentiments much like these from a column on Virginia City, Nevada, atop the Comstock Lode, "the richest vein of ore ever found in America." Virginia City's glory days were past by the time Pyle arrived in November of 1937.

> I wanted to be impressed, and excited, when I came around the bend and saw this sight of my grandfather's day. But I don't even have that privilege. The skeleton is there, but progress has slipped inside the bones and made a mundane stirring. . . .

Why, I wonder, can't an old place really die? Why can't it lie down amid its old drama and wrap its romantic robes about it and pose there, unstirring and ghostlike, for the trembling contemplation of us latecomers?

Pyle's nostalgia found its best expression in the West, but it was by no means limited to that region. Nostalgia, in fact, was endemic to the whole roving-column enterprise. "American roads have always been more about the past and future than about the present," Phil Patton has written. Pyle's avoidance of the big cities and his fondness for small towns and the open countryside was in itself evocative of the recent past, though less obviously so.

As a boy, growing up on a farm a few miles outside Dana, Indiana—population about a thousand—Ernie had been a restless child, anxious for an expanded life. Early on he had decided that most of what interested him was happening elsewhere, and that he wanted badly to be a part of it. Arriving in Washington to work on the *Daily News* in 1923, after a few months of reporting on a newspaper in La Porte, Indiana, Pyle had been pleased not only to have a job in the nation's capital, but to leave the Midwest behind as well. Washington represented all the expanded possibilities he'd hoped for. Now in his mid-thirties, Ernie entertained the notion that what he'd left behind had a validity all its own, though he would never have dreamed of returning to the farm or settling in a small town. In reality, what he had left behind had changed dramatically, and he knew this.

By 1935, America was primarily an urban-industrial nation, but the folk memory of a recent past lived on farms and in small towns was still vivid, all the more so during the Depression. For no matter how elementary was unemployed workers' understanding of economics, they soon learned that their misfortune in these hard times was largely outside their control, the result of their dependence on a system that had gone awry. The temptation to romanticize the past in agrarian America was hard to resist. (Conveniently overlooked in these moments of reverie was the truth that rural America was beset with problems all its own in the Depression years, and had been for well over a decade.) Living in a city often meant surrendering the close personal contact with friends, neighbors, and family that had marked their early years. Thus Ernie's datelines from small, out-of-the-way places were themselves a pastoral look back.

When Pyle wrote about his family on the farm in Indiana, he chronicled the near-term American past, still recognizable but changed forever. And his readers, most of whom lived in cities, responded warmly. One wrote Pyle's mother in 1939, "I hope that you may sometimes think, as is true, that through your son you have a part in bringing interest, entertainment, education, and a greater faith in the goodness of people to so many who read his column. It seems to me you have contributed largely to the world."

In any but its mildest form, nostalgia is at cross purposes with life as it's lived. Ernie was pensive about the changing American countryside, but he was still very much the individualist who as a boy longed to shed the restrictions of country life. Thus many of the people whose stories Pyle told were a bit offbeat, living slightly apart from, if not exactly contrary to, the mainstream. This was no accident. For in Pyle's view, character proceeded from eccentricity. The greater the likelihood of an individual's neighbors considering him to be an oddball, the greater his character quotient. When Pyle wrote about people on the road, he defined their character as the sum total of observable details of personal thought, circumstance, or action, and he piled these on at great length. Some were revealing, some not, but all spoke to Pyle's incomplete understanding of character—an understanding based on externalities. He once wrote a column about the world bowling champion, a man who was "intelligent and friendly and a gentleman, but he is not colorful. He doesn't brag or say odd things that make a man interesting in print." Pyle searched out people sufficiently odd to be interesting in print.

The routineness, the banality, of most people's lives struck Ernie and Jerry as the equivalent of premature death. In a 1935 piece on movies versus real life, Pyle wrote:

Of course, characters on the screen are made to suffer their tragedies, just as we humans do. But their suffering is so dramatic and romantic, while ours here on the globe is the dull, achy kind that embitters and wastes, with so little drama to soften it.

Why in real life, he asked, can't we humans "just go stare out a window and bow our heads and look grave and heartbroken for a few seconds, denoting a long period of grief and yearning, and not have to go through the actual months and years of it?" For Pyle's part, a "flash of happiness" would be preferable to "happiness strung out," because then "there is no dulling." He concluded:

> Yes, just wake me up for the peaks and the valleys, just the tops and the bottoms of them, and please have the anesthetist ready when we come to the plains, and the long bright days when nothing happens.

During his travel years, Pyle went a long way toward acting on these sentiments. Forever on the move, he sought the peaks and valleys, a journalistic outsider who arrived and departed quickly. In New Mexico, an isolated family so enjoyed a visit from the Pyles they begged them to stay. "But we had engagements ahead and we had to run away, as we always have to run away," Ernie wrote.

The traveling life

Although the 1930s were a time of unusually strong community sentiment among the American people, the Pyles shared in this not at all. They had friends from all walks of life, but their rootlessness allowed them to control their interaction with other people to an unhealthy degree. They were without the scrutiny that close friends and family, living nearby, can bring to bear on misguided ideas and actions. Ernie and Jerry created for themselves an insular life on the road, neatly contained and free of obligations other than maintaining the column. "Stability cloaks you with a thousand little personal responsibilities, and we have been able to flee from them," Ernie wrote of their traveling life.

It was a manageable existence—bags systematically packed in the trunk, hotels picked according to a scheme Pyle worked out—and despite its being premised on constant movement, it had a quirky rhythm, broken only by periodic drinking bouts and frequent ailments, the alcohol often contributing to the illness. Ernie and Jerry were aware of what was happening in the country, but their traveling life protected them from most of the details. They were out of touch with the world around them and eventually with each other. On a 1937 trip to Alaska, Pyle wrote his college friend Paige Cavanaugh, "I haven't had any mail for three weeks, and haven't seen a newspaper or heard a radio for a week, so I don't know what's going on in the world and furthermore don't give a shit." Even when he was getting mail, reading newspapers, and listening to the radio, Pyle showed little interest in the big events that shaped his times.

Though their origins were common enough—his in rural Indiana, hers in small-town Minnesota—Ernie and Jerry had consciously distanced themselves from middle-class America for most of their adult lives. When they were married by a justice of the peace in July of 1925, they didn't tell their Washington friends; they simply moved in together and told everyone they were "shacking up"—everyone, that is, except their parents. Jerry even substantiated the fiction by refusing to wear a wedding ring until she was in her early forties.

Even as youthful puckishness goes, this was bold for the times and an indication of the extent to which the Pyles saw themselves as immune to middle-class pieties and expectations. Though they were without the smugness that so often attends success, the very idea of success was something they made fun of. The way they had lived in Washington reflected this. Their priorities had been to pay the rent, send a little money home to their parents, buy food (not much, for neither cared about eating), and spend the balance on liquor and tobacco. Clothes, furniture, having a family—none of it interested them. Their outlook on life, fatalistic and frankly self-indulgent, was primarily a product of Jerry's manic swings and Ernie's emotional pliability, which rendered him all too vulnerable to her moodiness.

Ernie and Jerry were both master dissemblers who, for the most part, had the good sense and good taste to keep their contempt for convention to themselves. Most everyone they met genuinely liked them, particularly Ernie, who, though shy, had an easygoing, democratizing manner. This spilled over into the column and accounted in no small part for its success. "I find that kids, Civil War veterans, capitalists, professional men, and WPA workers all read everything you write," the editor of the *Rocky Mountain News* told Pyle in a letter. And from the editor of the *Oklahoma News* came this: "[Readers] say, 'Ernie talks our language.' That, I think, is the . . . key to the column's success. It's folksy, human and as unsophisticated as nine out of ten readers"—a compliment, apparently.

What the Oklahoma editor mistook for a lack of sophistication in the writing was actually a savvy bit of calculation on Pyle's part. Because the subject matter of the column was in constant flux, Pyle himself was the only link between daily installments.

He understood this. He knew his popularity was based upon his readers' illusion that they knew him personally, and his approach to the column fostered the perception. The voice of the travel columns was a carefully developed product that owed its variety to the demands of the marketplace and to the rigorous nature of the assignment itself. And though it shared much with Pyle, it belied much, too.

Most human-interest columnists today produce three or four pieces a week and draw their material primarily from the local. Pyle operated nationally and published six times a week. Column material was abundant, particularly early on, but six thousand words a week was a tall order. Because he had to allow for travel time and the occasional unproductive segment of a trip, Pyle often resorted to personal essays to keep the column going.

The essay persona was that of a Chaplinesque character forever beguiled by faulty zippers, lingering colds, errant drivers, dreams of glory as a racecar driver, and snake phobia. Here was a likeable reporter with an uncannily good ear for American idiom, an endearingly self-effacing manner, and a good sense of humor (laconic, in the Midwestern way)—a man for whom the American romance was alive and well, the Depression be damned. "We must print [the] bad news—but fortunate is the newspaper publisher who can balance that bad news with your wholesome and cheerful account of your journeyings," the editor of the *Memphis Press-Scimitar* told Ernie.

Pyle was often not so temperate in his private correspondence. Here the column persona gave way to the more acerbic side of his personality. From the Yukon, Pyle wrote Cavanaugh:

> [Alaska is] too damn cold for me, even in June. It's just like Hollywood—warm for about three hours in the middle of the day, and the rest of the time you freeze your balls off. Haven't had a comfortable day since I left Seattle two and a half weeks ago. I'm a hot-country man. . . .

Mostly, Pyle's columns were characterized by a moderate voice, but sometimes he let fly at people he clearly disliked—auto mechanics were frequent targets—or disapproved of. Here he is on Americans living and working in the Panama Canal Zone:

> One of their own, who sees them clearly, has called them "stall-fed." They have surrendered the important quality of egotism—the eter-

nal conviction that you could do it better than the other guy. They have given up all personal ambition, natural instincts of competition, all the lovely mystery of life, for a security that gives them a life of calm and a vague discontent.

That last clause is interesting: *for a security that gives them a life of calm and a vague discontent.* It describes with some disdain the aspirations of the very audience for which Pyle was writing: Depression-bound stay-at-homes who looked to his column for a vicarious lift from their troubled circumstances. For many Americans in the Depression years, security was a much-sought-after commodity in whose name they would have happily endured discontent, vague or otherwise. His bohemian posturing aside, Pyle's restlessness was forever at war with his own deep need for security. Every so often he needed to trumpet his disdain for the latter, as if seeing it in print would confirm his defiance of it.

The curse

For Pyle motion was an end in itself, a trait he shared with millions of his countrymen. Unlike most of them, though, he had the means to realize his restive dream, and increasingly it became a curse. The pressures increased with the column's success; what had begun for him as a flight from encroaching obligations and responsibilities had become a tremendous burden. Editors began to vie for his circulation-building presence in their areas, just as military units would compete for his morale-building attention during the war. Five Scripps Howard editors in Ohio sent a joint telegram to Pyle's superiors in Washington in June of 1938:

> OHIO SERIES BY ERNIE PYLE WOULD BE OF VITAL IMPORTANCE IN DEVELOPING VACATION READING TO HELP HOLD CIRCULATION IN THE OHIO INDUSTRIAL CITIES PARTICULARLY HARD HIT BY THE DEPRESSION. . . . PLEASE GIVE THIS IMMEDIATE URGENT CONSIDERATION BECAUSE ERNIE PYLE IN OHIO WOULD BE A PRACTICAL ASSET WHICH COULD NOT BE EQUALED BY ERNIE PYLE IN NEW ENGLAND, SOUTH AMERICA OR ANY OTHER REMOTE PARTS.

Pyle went, begrudgingly.

Readers, too, applied pressure. They wrote him long, appreciative letters, some pouring out their problems, some enclosing tips for future columns, a few chiding him for his not-always-perfect grammar or his occasional use of mild profanity in the column. Whatever the content of the letter, Pyle believed its author deserved an answer. At first he responded to reader mail himself, but later he hired a secretary in Washington to answer the letters. More problematic were those readers who showed up to meet him in person. "We fled San Diego yesterday," Pyle wrote his friend Paige Cavanaugh in October 1939.

> . . . I am disillusioned with fame. Not disillusioned, for I never had illusions about it, but I'm badly frightened. For in San Diego, Mr. Pyle is not second even to God, and the clamor that was set up down there really got me panicky, and we almost went under for the third time under the tidal wave of dinners and drinks and visitors and people who "just want to shake hands" and you know. . . . The whole thing, Mr. Cavanaugh, is something that I do not want anything of, and why can't a fellow just quietly make an honest living?

Readers in the Southwest reciprocated Pyle's enthusiasm for their region with enthusiasm for him and his column. On stops in Deming, Silver City, and Lordsburg, New Mexico—all within the circulation area of the *El Paso Herald-Post*—Pyle couldn't leave his hotel room or eat in the coffee shop without fans crowding around him, all expressing pleasure in his work. Pyle wrote Lee Miller, his editor:

> I know it must sound awful to you for a guy like me to say this, but we actually know what it is to have to eat in our rooms and sneak out the back way. I'm not trying to overtoot my own horn and I certainly couldn't have the courage to be so immodest to anyone else, but I am just trying to show you that the powers-that-be have no idea what a hold the column really has—and what a basis for selling it if they were interested.

Pyle was alternately pushing for and retreating from syndication outside the Scripps Howard chain, but he was always cranky over whichever way management was leaning at the moment. Already a celebrity, he knew the pressures on him would redouble with increased circulation; on the other hand, as he told Miller, "I'd gaily take a little more money if I could get it, but even that isn't on my mind, for we're able to save some as it is. I guess I'm just like an old screwball I wrote about up at Silver City—all I really want is to be appreciated."

Appreciated by the masses, he might have added, for just as Pyle had learned how intoxicating constant travel is, he was learning how addictive is the attention of strangers. Never mind how "panicky" this made him, or how fame was something he wanted nothing of. Pyle knew perfectly well that a man whose name and picture appeared above a daily newspaper column—especially one that touched as many responsive chords as his did—had no basis for bemoaning his inability to "just quietly make an honest living." He also knew that he had given up any semblance of a normal life for an enterprise that was getting way out of hand.

The parting

When Ernie and Jerry said goodbye to each other at the Toledo railroad station in April of 1937—she bound for Washington to close out their apartment and put their furniture in storage, he to Alaska for three months of hard travel—both were sad, as Pyle said in the column. Though he believed the Alaska trip would be too much of a hardship for Jerry, the prospect of a three-month separation from her was a difficult one for Ernie: Jerry had been a big help to him on the road, just as she had been during their Washington days. She had helped him overcome his melancholy over the column's not being well received one place or another, or over his inability to get a particular piece just right.

Jerry was an extremely literate person, a good critic, and a shrewd judge of character. She was also an ideal traveling companion for Ernie in that she talked very little (thus giving him time to think as he drove), made few demands on his schedule, and could generally be counted on to retype his columns once he'd pencil-edited the drafts. This is not to say she was passive; on the contrary, she exerted a powerful influence over Ernie and his sensibilities. But she had no career aspirations of her own—none that she voiced, anyway. Pyle's readers knew her not as Jerry but as "That Girl who rides with me," which sounds condescending and offhand, but which was actually a bow to Jerry's demand for privacy. She had no desire to be known through the pages of a newspaper.

Jerry wasn't particularly interested in the traveling life, but this didn't alarm Ernie. As he saw it, life anywhere—their old life in Washington included—held very little for her. Jerry was chronically uninterested in anything but reading, writing poetry, working crossword puzzles, and playing the piano. With the exception of the piano, her interests were mobile enough: couldn't she read *The New Yorker* or work crossword puzzles in Garden City, Kansas, every bit as well as she could in Washington? It was all right that she didn't accompany him to interviews—she was forever waiting in a hotel room or in the car—or share in the romance of the open road. The traveling life was still better than sitting alone in an apartment all day, dwelling upon whatever it was she dwelled upon.

As it turned out, Jerry didn't agree. And although they traveled together periodically in subsequent years, their parting in Toledo was the beginning of ten years of being more apart than together, with Pyle either traveling around the United States or reporting from war zones thousands of miles away. It was also the beginning of Jerry's descent into a hellish spiral of depression and drug addiction.

The crack-up

One expects to return home at the end of a journey, but where was home for Jerry? A changing woman, she lacked so much as a permanent address against which to measure the scope and nature of the changes. Her life was without context, anything or anyone to divert her attention outward, away from the churning emotions that so frequently kept her in the darkest of troubled states.

Living with her mother in Minnesota or her sister in Denver, staying with friends in Washington or Albuquerque, Jerry's mental health badly deteriorated. Already an alcoholic, she became addicted to Benzedrine, an amphetamine, which, mixed with alcohol, gave her a short-term synergistic high and unnatural vigor, after which she would be listless and without appetite for days. Add this cross-addiction to her longtime dependence on caffeine and nicotine and her lack of interest in food or exercise, and it takes little imagination to see that Jerry was physically and psychologically headed for disaster. But Ernie missed or ignored a great many signs of what was to come.

After all, it's difficult to comprehend the depth of another's despair when you're forever lighting out for the territory. Out of personal preference and professional necessity, Pyle was long accustomed to ignoring suffering around him. As we have seen, he moved quickly in and out of the lives of the people he encountered on the road, quick to sense where the story lay and quick to move on. Now he moved in and out of Jerry's life, too, seeing her when he could, traveling with her when she was able or willing to ride along, but always, always on the move. Just as he had fled Washington to avoid the debilitating complexities of the managing editor job, now he fled Jerry to escape the seeming hopelessness of her condition and what it implied for both their futures. He had so arranged his life that his personal compulsions took on the force of necessity: there was *always* the column to think about.

A deeply intuitive man capable of expressing what he saw or felt clearly and powerfully, Pyle was nonetheless badly confused about intimacy—its meaning, what it demands of those who share in it—just as he was confused about character and what it comprises. He once wrote, "We have worked up a whole new continent-wide list of intimate friends, and consequently we keep up a personal correspondence with about three hundred people." It's impossible to maintain a personal correspondence with three hundred people, or even half that many, but the statement reveals much about Pyle. Like most of us, he was an uneven sort, operating at some remove from his deeper self. Constant travel only abetted this. A man spread too thinly over too great an area, he was incapable of the depth of understanding, the jumps of creative intuition, that Jerry's situation called for.

Ernie had long worried that Jerry's not having a permanent interest in something that at least marginally involved other people would lead to problems. His sense of all this was vague but nonetheless prescient. For as Ernie's popularity grew, Jerry's feelings were mixed. Much as she believed he deserved the recognition and was glad he was getting it, Jerry clearly resented the extent to which Ernie's readers and the editors who ran his column had taken her place in his life.

He was no longer hers. She no longer exerted a major claim on his attention. "I'm just a pawn in the great newspaper game," she wrote a friend. Sure, his letters were profusely sentimental, yearning for the old days when they were always together, but he chose to live his life away from her. Oh, she understood the reasons, and they made sense enough. Yes, she could rejoin him on the road anytime she wished, and he'd be glad of it; but except for certain spectacular instances when she became too sick to care for herself, it was the road and the column and all those readers who held sway. Though Ernie seemed genuinely delighted at their reunions, he also seemed to have gotten along well enough without her in the interim. She could hardly say the same for herself.

In the best of circumstances, marriage is a complex web of interdependency, hard to sort out; in difficult circumstances, it virtually defies scrutiny—certainly from without and often from within, too. But that complex web becomes a hopeless tangle when asked to accommodate mental illness, multiple addictions, and sexual dysfunction. According to Lee Miller, Pyle's editor, "during some of their years together [Ernie and Jerry's] was a nonphysical union, due to a functional incapacity on Ernie's part...." Pyle was impotent and had been since early in the travel years. When they traveled together, Ernie and Jerry slept in twin beds, except in those rare instances when only a double bed was available—and then both slept poorly.

Ernie's problem further compounded Jerry's troubles, especially when, lonely and depressed, she decided that having a child would answer her emotional needs. She apparently had some doubt about whether her husband's impotence was organic or emotional, a reaction to her, perhaps, or a general fear of intimacy. When Pyle answered her letter about wanting a child, he told Jerry that it would be irresponsible for people their age—forty-one—to have a baby; and further, "I *can't* give you a child, as you know. I haven't been lying when I've told you that the power of sex had gone from me."

Traveling together through New Mexico during the summer of 1940, Ernie and Jerry had to part ways when they received news that Jerry's mother had broken her shoulder and needed Jerry to look after her. Ernie took her to the airport. "We are wandering people," he wrote in the column, "and fate hurls us about to odd destinations. We don't know when we will see each other again. When she got on the plane, we both felt a kind of futility, a small desire to travel again, for a little, in the same direction." They *were* traveling in the same direction, toward mutual disaster, and it came in the early spring of 1941, when Ernie returned from three months in bomb-torn England.

The trip had been a great success for Pyle and the column. It had revived his flagging spirits and had given his writing new energy and increased circulation. There was also the pleasure of returning to a real home: the Pyles had built a house—the first and only one they would ever own—on what was then the outskirts of Albuquerque, and Jerry had seen to its decoration during Ernie's absence. She had looked forward to his homecoming after a long absence on a trip that had horrified her. But there was to be no break from the pressure, no quiet pleasure in their new house with its wonderful view of the mesa. Pyle had to rent a hotel room in which to write by day, so many were the friends stopping by to see him after his long trip. After a short time at Albuquerque, he had to hit the road again to keep the column going: his editors didn't want to lose the new subscribers the column had gained during Ernie's time overseas.

There followed a tortuous year during which Jerry, alone, tried to kill herself by turning on all the gas jets on the stove and closing herself off in the kitchen, and during which, also alone, she almost bled to death in her bed when a stomach ulcer, irritated by alcohol and poor diet, hemorrhaged. On both occasions Ernie dropped the column and stayed at home to care for her. Continuity is the lifeblood of any column, particularly one as personal as Ernie's, but his Scripps Howard superiors were understanding, although many papers outside the chain dropped Pyle for other features during his protracted leaves.

Ernie resumed the column in December 1941, the week after the Japanese attack on Pearl Harbor and the American declaration of war on Japan. Jerry's stomach had healed, and her health continued to improve under the watchful eye of a private nurse Ernie had hired—or so the nurse and Ernie thought. His letters tell the story. "I've talked with Albuquerque every night for the last four nights—one night twice," Pyle wrote to Cavanaugh on March 19, 1942:

> Jerry has been put under opiates for three days. Nurses around the clock again. Just went clear to pot again the last couple of weeks. Fooling everybody in the daytime, and drinking all night apparently. The nurse told me she carried from her room *ten* empty quart [bourbon] bottles at the end of one week!

Pyle felt himself thinning out, the roving-reporter adventure gone pale; his writing lacked the verve of the earlier years and was now a flat recitation of a city or a region's vital statistics or tourist appeal. Increasingly he relied on his column persona to carry the daily installment, but it, too, had thinned, its tone becoming desperately chatty. Pyle had found the traveling life held endless banality, just as the everyday, rooted life did. Now no amount of road noise could diminish the hum between his ears. Alone, he had much time to think about himself and Jerry—their onetime life together and their lives apart, the wreckage of it all.

Ernie had hopefully sought treatment for his impotence from a group of San Diego urologists in the spring of 1942. This, too, was a disaster and left him convinced his sex life was over forever. The treatments were "agonizing and cruel" and yielded no results. Bitter, he wrote Cavanaugh, "The doctors all say, 'Now get lots of intercourse.' Which is like W. C. Fields' sure cure for insomnia—'Get lots of sleep.'"

Jerry was a difficult person, dismissive in her dogmatic way of others' attempts to scrutinize her. And yet, she reached out for help in her own tortured fashion, assuring Ernie that at last she was on the way to recovery, that she had regained some of her earlier resilience and composure and could begin to put herself back together. There was a time when Ernie would have been only too happy to hear this, only too willing to believe it. But now he was beyond ignoring the reality of their lives by pining for the time when Jerry's inner life had been more in check and his limited powers of comprehension less taxed. Now, in March 1942, he voiced to friends his doubts about Jerry's ever recovering.

After a month of exchanging tortured letters and phone calls with Jerry, Ernie was on the verge of collapse himself. He dropped the column—forever, he thought, or at least until the war was over—and returned to Albuquerque. On April 14, Ernie and Jerry were divorced. Both regretted the move, and yet neither could think of any other solution. Ernie hoped the shock of the divorce would force Jerry to right her life. Remarriage was a possibility, assuming she got busy and solved her problems. Meanwhile, they continued to live together in the house in Albuquerque, and Ernie continued to look after her. Her condition worsened. Jerry, Ernie wrote Cavanaugh on May 5,

has been in a Christ-awful shape this week. Nurse and doctor here almost constantly. Part of it is genuine, part of it self-induced. She hasn't had any Benzedrine since January, but yesterday she pleaded with the doctor and cried like a baby for some. It was so pitiful I couldn't even stay in the room. He told her no, that she had to face it this time right out of her own soul. And she is much better this morning, although still very depressed. She just can't accept the fact that we are divorced and that I'm going away again.

Again leaving Jerry in the care of private nurses, Pyle traveled to Washington to discuss his future with Scripps Howard management, which wanted him to start writing again, perhaps take another foreign trip. Shortly, the government would cease to draft men thirty-seven and older, but for now Pyle was eligible for service. He took the Army physical and was declared 1-A. Meanwhile, the Army's having delayed his induction, he prepared to travel to Britain, this time to report on the training of American troops. While the government processed his travel request, Ernie worked on the copy desk of the *Washington Daily News*. He wrote to Jerry on May 8 that his friends and former colleagues in Washington were "under the impression that I've gone all to pieces, and damned if they haven't got me about half convinced of it myself." His letter to Jerry continued:

> I feel that if I could just run back to Albuquerque and start a life of utter simplicity I would be happy. But I guess I can't, and I have determined not to come back until you have won your great fight. I can't tell you the sadness and almost overwhelming frenzy and depression I've been in these three days; and the feeling that I couldn't live unless I came back to you; but I won't, darling, I'm determined that even should I go clear under, I will not come running back until you have had a chance to do your job under these new conditions. I am confident that you can and will do it; otherwise I would be utterly insane with despair.

Nineteen days later, Jerry's sister and brother-in-law, with the support of Ernie and other family members, took her by train to a sanitarium at Pueblo, Colorado. Jerry was sedated to the point of unconsciousness. Ernie's travel plans were firm by mid-June, and he arrived in New York to await a plane to Ireland. From the Hotel Algonquin, he wrote Jerry a farewell note. The date was June 18, 1942.

> Darling—
>
> I am taking off within the hour. I came here because I couldn't stand to go to the Piccadilly without you. I am not excited about going, but do feel a last-minute sense of fatalism or something. I am all alone. Be my old Jerry when I come back. I love you.
>
> Ernie

The steadying point

Pyle's was a generation born to calamity. Many a young man born at the turn of the century had fought in World War I, had difficulty finding employment upon his return, had struggled to raise a family during the Depression, and now, in early middle age, watched as a son or sons left home to fight in yet another global war. Pyle had shared in none of this. His parents had blocked his joining the Army during the first war, and he had been steadily and profitably employed throughout the Depression. Because they had no children, Ernie and Jerry were spared both the expense of raising a family and worry over how sons would fare in what promised to be another long, bloody war.

In his seven years of travel, Pyle had stiffly resisted doing pieces on serious matters. Apart from a series on the Dust Bowl and one on public relief in the small town of North Platte, Nebraska, Pyle's dispatches had been mostly free of any but casual references to the economic disasters visited upon millions of Americans in the 1930s. When his editors suggested the North Platte series, Ernie bristled. "I don't like that idea, it sounds too important!" he complained to Cavanaugh.

In the range of options open to him, in his freedom to indulge his restlessness, and in his disconnectedness from community ties, Pyle shared little with his countrymen. By the time America entered the war he was a man so out of step with the times that he despaired of ever finding a place again. In the American way he had equated movement with growth, and circumstances had proved the fallacy of the notion. "Being on the move is no substitute for feeling," Eudora Welty has written. "Nothing is. And no love or insight can be at work in a shifting and never-defined position, where eye, mind, and heart have never willingly focused on a steadying point." The war was to be Pyle's steadying point, and love and insight the hallmarks of his writing. What would make Pyle's war reportage of enduring value would be his decision—and it would be his alone to make—to stop fleeing unpleasantness. In his years as a war correspondent, Pyle would still be on the move, but now the movement would have meaning: the link between the columns would no longer be Pyle and his restlessness but the war and the changes it worked in the men who fought it.

Much as he was a case of arrested maturation, badly as he needed a moral education, Pyle had nonetheless developed considerable skill as an observer and writer. Soon he would find both personal and professional salvation through service to his countrymen, by plying his skills on behalf of the all-consuming effort in which they were engaged. He would become for the first time in his life morally connected to an undertaking of great moment, and he would enjoy the sensation. The war would strike him as an unqualified disaster, not like the great bombing of London on the night of December 30, 1940, had struck him—as something out of a show. Pyle had watched the bombing from the balcony outside his hotel room, and it had all

> seemed more like something put on just to look at; like some ulti-
> mate Billy Rose extravagance, at last attaining to such proportions
> of Rose giganticism that it passed beyond the realm of human cre-
> dence—but still remained a form of entertainment.

Curious sentiments, those, considering that down below people were burning to death and others were losing everything they owned. It was not the sort of thing he could have written after even a month of living with the infantry in North Africa, so quickly would experience burn away his romantic understanding of war.

Like so many Americans, Pyle had been painfully slow to respond to the gravity of events overseas. The war that was now to claim his attention and eventually his life had for so long been an abstraction, something real enough but remote from his personal experience, just as the Depression had been. The man who had been in Death Valley looking for the castlelike home of a desert recluse the day German troops marched into Austria would soon be with American men as they marched into North Africa—and thence to Sicily, mainland Italy, France, and the Pacific.

And Pyle would be especially good at describing a particular kind of soldier with a particular kind of American past. Throughout the war he would insist that a goodly number of the men he wrote about derived their strength of purpose from an upbringing close to nature or from the ties of a small community. His fondest profiles would be of men fresh from the country or small towns, unsullied by the fractiousness and wise-guy posturing of the big cities. It wouldn't be that these men were necessarily better soldiers than their city counterparts, or even better human beings; but they would strike him as somehow more *American,* or at least closer to what an American ought to be, anyhow.

Such sentiments would hardly be unique to Pyle. The celebration of rural and small-town values and people would be a set theme in much World War II feature writing. But Pyle's affection for such men would be neither a stylistic crutch nor a jaundiced bow to wartime convention. It would be heartfelt, an outgrowth of his own rural past and his years of prewar travel in the United States. Main Street may have been dead, as Bernard De Voto had declared in 1940, but it was to have a bright future in the nation's wartime mythology. And Pyle would have much to do with its resurrection.

A familiar voice

Like millions of men his age and older, my father went abroad during World War II, and my grandparents, still subscribing to the *Indianapolis Times,* continued to read Pyle's column. Now they relied on Pyle for news of a different sort: they wanted to know how young men like George and other boys from the neighborhood were getting along all those thousands of miles away. Sure, George wrote letters home, but the letters were censored. And the frontline news dispatches—with their breathless leads and action-packed headlines—said so little about the men themselves. Pyle bridged the gap, daily telling the folks at home what was happening to their loved ones across the seas. He told them their young men were changed forever, coarsened by what they had seen and done. Pyle's was the sort of copy few censors bothered to hack away at; in their eyes it was pretty benign stuff. But it had a potency all its own, as thirteen million daily readers could attest.

My father's being overseas didn't prevent his reading Ernie Pyle. By arrangement with Scripps Howard's United Features, Pyle's column ran daily in *Stars and Stripes,* the newspaper for service personnel. While stateside readers read about the boys overseas, the boys overseas read about themselves. Almost always they were pleased with what they read: here was a guy willing to share their fate, not because he had to—he was too old for this crap, anyway—but because he wanted to, felt somehow he *had* to.

A fair number of these young men had read Pyle's column before the war. They were happy to still get their daily dose of

Ernie Pyle. It was ironic, though. Pyle's column had inspired in many of them, like my father, a desire to see the country. And what happened? The world went to hell, the Army latched onto them, and their first real taste of travel was to war in Europe or the Pacific. Well, anyway, it was good to read Pyle just the same. His was a familiar voice, sort of like getting a letter from home.

Epilogue

Ernie and Jerry were remarried by proxy in early 1943, while Ernie covered the infantry in North Africa. As she had during their travel years, Jerry continued to move in and out of extended periods of depression. Sometimes she wrote Ernie several long, loving letters over a two-week period; at other times she wouldn't write for months. Her drug abuse and heavy drinking continued.

Ernie made two trips home during the war. And in both cases he met with crushing pressure from friends and strangers alike. When he came home for the last time, in September of 1944, his emotions were "wrung and drained" after covering the Normandy invasions and the liberation of Paris. "My spirit is wobbly and my mind is confused," he wrote before leaving France. "All of a sudden it seemed to me that if I heard one more shot or saw one more dead man, I would go off my nut."

Shortly after he arrived in Albuquerque, he returned from the dentist's office one day to a scene as bloody as many he had seen at war. Jerry had locked herself in the bathroom and had tried to commit suicide by stabbing herself numerous times in the throat with a pair of long-bladed scissors. Ernie broke down the door to discover Jerry standing before the sink, the bathroom awash in blood. He held her as a surgeon cleaned and sutured her many wounds. Surprisingly, given their severity, Jerry's physical wounds healed quickly, though her emotional ones never would.

Still badly shaken by Jerry's suicide attempt, wanting to stay home but drawn back to war to finish the work he had begun, Ernie began his long journey to the Pacific Theater on January 1, 1945. He died instantly when a sniper's machine-gun bullet pierced his left temple the morning of April 18, on the small island of Ie Shima, near Okinawa. He was buried in a shallow grave between the bodies of two soldiers. According to the newspapers, "That Girl" took the news bravely, but in truth she lost all will to live.

Jerry flew to Washington that summer to accept Ernie's post-humous Medal for Merit, jointly awarded by the Army and the Navy, and to see a preview of Lester Cowan's film *The Story of GI Joe,* based on Ernie's dispatches and with Burgess Meredith playing Ernie. Seeing Washington again undoubtedly increased Jerry's pain. There were surely many memories of meeting and falling in love with Ernie half a lifetime ago. The candlelight dinners in their first apartment. Parties with the crazy newspaper gang and the airmail pilots from National Airport and Bolling Field. Fires in the fireplace on a winter's evening as she talked Ernie through another blue period. How hysterically they'd laughed about the uniformed chauffeur's having to deliver the White House Christmas card to their shabby little apartment. And that Christmas Ernie had surprised her with a brand-new piano, a baby grand, with a big red ribbon tied around it—the elaborate ruse he'd concocted to get her out of the apartment so the deliverymen could wrestle the piano into the living room. And then his somewhat sheepish announcement that he'd bought it on time. But the payments weren't too much, he'd said, and the dealer would take it back if they were unable to pay. She'd tried to object, really tried to give him hell for that, but she hadn't been able to conceal her pleasure—a baby grand of her own!

During the fall of 1945, not long after her forty-fifth birthday, Jerry, more emaciated than ever, contracted influenza. A short time later her kidneys stopped working. She died of uremic poisoning the morning of November 23 at St. Joseph's Hospital in Albuquerque, where the good sisters of St. Joseph had befriended her during the lonely years when Ernie was overseas, even allowing her to live for a time in a cottage on the hospital grounds. Perhaps it was from watching them that Jerry had decided she wanted to learn to pray, a notion she had mentioned in a letter to Ernie shortly before he was killed and which he had been at a loss to understand. When the sisters of St. Joseph gathered for chapel the evening of November 23, they likely prayed that their troubled friend had finally come to peace, and that her wish had been granted.

All too often our perception of the Great Depression is one of unmitigated gloom, a notion helped along by those duotone archival photos that appear in magazines and on book covers, the tinge of brown accentuating the period's distance from the

Kodachrome present. What we forget is that amidst the suffering, everyday life went on, though greatly altered in many cases. We forget that these years were also a time of celebration of things and places American.

The Great Depression was the most amply documented period in American history. Writers and photographers, some on their own and others employed by the federal government, took to the road in unprecedented numbers to record in words and pictures the pulse of America during a troubling time. In its subject matter and tone, Pyle's travel work closely parallels some of the entries in the Federal Writers' Project *American Guide* series and the life-history interviews Ann Banks collected in *First Person America;* but with few exceptions the Depression in the pages that follow is a mere backdrop.

For my part, I'm glad Pyle chose not to write directly about the Depression and its victims during these years; I'm glad he wasn't out jamming a thermometer down the throats of the people he came across. We're the richer for that escapist agenda of his, for while part of the America he wrote about has long since passed into memory, we still have a vivid picture of it in his writings.

As I see it, this book amounts to a documentary look at America during an important time in its history. I believe Pyle's dispatches can add to our understanding of the era just prior to America's coming to the fore of world leadership, the time before the war that changed the world forever. During his travel years, Pyle consistently wrote the kinds of stories more conventional journalists ignored. We're left with a richly descriptive record that tells us much about the rhythm and tone of American life in the 1930s, through the attack on Pearl Harbor and America's entrance into World War II. It's a highly selective record, for reasons I've discussed, but a rich one nonetheless. Almost fifty years later his rendition of people and places casually encountered is still exciting.

Many mornings over the years I've worked on this book I've awakened with a vividly familiar picture of a place or a person in my mind. One was a vision of New York City on a freezing winter evening, just as the neon signs were coming on. I was looking out the window of a hotel room, watching the colors explode in the darkness. Another was of lushly forested mountains, their green tops lost in rain clouds. Yet another was the face of an old black man, seated in a restaurant booth, talking about his not having had the chance to meet Franklin Roosevelt.

Sometimes I was momentarily at a loss to distinguish whether the vision was mine or Pyle's. Invariably I concluded that I was dreaming of a scene from a Pyle piece I'd read the evening before, probably for the third or fourth time. But there were times the illusion persisted that I'd been to this or that place, experienced the very thing I saw in the dream, met that exact person and had that conversation with him.

Morning torpor accounts for some of the confusion, but the greater explanation lies in Pyle's considerable narrative gift. The people and places in his word portraits stick with me and have a way of planting themselves in my conscious mind at unlikely moments. It's snowing outside my window as I write, and I'm thinking of Pyle's description of a snowstorm in the Cumberland Mountains. In a way I can't quite explain, I'm curiously animated recalling his lines. And my animation has to do with that American restlessness I spoke of earlier, a vague discontent with here and now that would be nicely eased by lighting out for the territory.

I'm going to do just that. My father and I are going to pick up what was once Route 66 in Illinois and drive to California— the southern route, through Missouri, Oklahoma, Texas, New Mexico, and Arizona. America has been my home for thirty-two years, but what I've seen of the country has been limited to what little you can see from the window of an airliner at thirty thousand feet, or through the windshield of a car on the interstates that so often circumscribe the indigenous.

One of Pyle's biggest gripes was that from what his contemporaries read in the newspapers or heard on the radio, they could easily get the idea that American life centered in New York and Washington and sometimes Los Angeles—that nothing in between mattered. At great cost to himself, Pyle worked hard arguing for the specificity of person and place as an important part of our American past and present. And today that's more important than ever. Meager assumptions are what we get from most media reports about what's going on "out there." I'd be hard pressed to prove it, but I suspect our immersion in this so-called information age has more blunted than enhanced our sense of the country's teeming diversity of geography, local custom, and individual character.

I have a hunch vestiges of the country Pyle described are still out there, and I want to see them. Reading his pieces over and over—sifting, selecting, editing—I came to realize the extent to which I've been affected by those meager assumptions I speak of. I realized, too, how deeply set in me is the American romance of movement—not as a way of life, but as a periodic tonic. It's more than time to get out of town, clear my head, and listen to a few American voices speaking unself-consciously in their American places.

So we're going to take the back roads, my father and I, and eat in small-town diners and maybe sleep in some of the remaining tourist cabins. It will be a leisurely trip. We're going to fixate upon the journey itself, not the destination. I'm going to take a copy of this manuscript along and refer to it as we go. I want to measure the country as it is now against Pyle's rendering of it almost half a century ago. I guess that will make this doubly a book of nostalgia—mine and Pyle's. That's fine with me; my restlessness can always use a little structure.

My father tells me old Route 66 will be hard to find. Interstates have replaced most of the old route, sometimes overlapping the same right-of-way, in other places taking a whole new course. Sections of the old pavement remain, but it will likely take some doing to stay on course. We'll probably have to ask questions of many strangers.

David Nichols
Fort Wayne, Indiana
January 1989

EDITOR'S NOTE

"In five years these columns have stretched out to the horrifying equivalent of twenty full-length books," Ernie Pyle wrote in November of 1940. "Set in seven-point type"—which isn't very big—"they would make a newspaper column three quarters of a mile long."

I read each of Pyle's travel dispatches at least four times over a two-year period. With each reading I sorted out the memorable from the less memorable.

Although this collection comprises what I consider to be the best of the pieces Pyle wrote in seven years of travel, it's only honest to add that, for a couple of reasons, a fair number of very fine ones didn't make the final cut.

For one, Pyle's travels were not confined to the United States and its territories or protectorates. He also spent time in Canada, Mexico, Central and South America, and Great Britain. Delightful as some of this material is, I have not included any of it here. Pyle was at his best on native soil, and my purpose here was to assemble a portrait of the United States based upon his travel dispatches.

For another, my final selection had to strike some balance, albeit an imperfect one, between regions, and to represent as fully as possible the enormous range Pyle exhibited in these years.

Even so, you'll notice that the West and Southwest sections are quite long compared with the Midwest and the East. This is because Pyle spent a lot more time in the West and Southwest than he spent in other regions, and because he often produced exceptional work there. Like any writer, he wrote best about what interested him most.

Overall, the book's organization is chronological, with dated sections—those containing material tied to historical events or Pyle's personal life—assuming their proper places in time, and regional sections interspersed throughout. In the East, the Midwest, the West, the Southwest, and the South, I have arranged the pieces by state in what seems to me a logical sequence, without regard to when they were written.

Some readers may quibble with my regional divisions. Is Oklahoma really part of the Southwest, as I have made it here, or is it in the West South Central area, as the United States Census Bureau has it? Is Virginia a Southern state or a South Atlantic one? My intent is not to propose new regional clusterings, but to divide Pyle's writings into reasonable and readily recognizable sections. My apologies to anyone who finds himself suddenly dislocated by my organizational scheme.

Most of the Pyle columns I've included appear in their entirety, but some I've abbreviated. The former bear headlines, while the latter do not. I have deleted some of Pyle's asides—comments that probably played well at the time but wouldn't almost fifty years later—and smoothed transitions and syntax here and there, made single paragraphs out of what had been two or three short paragraphs, and standardized usage. These changes are not indicated in the text. Any bulk deletions, however, I've marked with points of ellipsis. All textual space breaks are Pyle's.

My source for Pyle's dispatches was the mail copy Scripps Howard Newspaper Alliance sent to papers in the Scripps Howard chain. This copy reflects the edits of Alliance editors in Washington but not those made by local editors. I've used the release dates assigned by Scripps Howard, and these appear at the end of each dispatch. (The mail copy is housed at the Weil Journalism Library at Indiana University, Bloomington.)

Two final notes. Pyle often used the pronoun "we" in his copy. It was a habit he developed early on, when his wife generally traveled with him. Later, when Jerry traveled with him only infrequently, Pyle continued to write "we" when he meant "I." I have not tinkered with his choice of pronouns.

Finally, the Scripps Howard organization has dropped the hyphen from its name. Thus any references to the company in Pyle's dispatches or in his letters retain the hyphen, while mine do not. Hyphens, it seems, are dropping like flies all over the English-speaking world. Personally, I miss them.

D.N.

ERNIE'S AMERICA

I have no home. My home is where my extra luggage is, and where the car is stored, and where I happen to be getting mail this time. My home is America.

—Ernie Pyle

PROLOGUE

A Traveling Man

NEW ORLEANS—If ever I lose my job as a roving reporter, I'll be in fine practice to be a traveling salesman. For I know the back roads, the jerkwater hotels, and the cracker-box vernacular of two-thirds of the states in the Union.

It is my job to travel around over the country for the Scripps-Howard newspapers, covering something specific part of the time—such as TVA, the Dionne Quintuplets, the Florida Canal, or Major Bowes' hour; but most of the time just writing about anything interesting I bump into—such as an engineer who plays tunes on his locomotive whistle, or a tobacco auction, or a Broadway newsboy.

In the past year I have covered some thirty-five thousand miles by auto, train, airplane, and boat, but mostly by auto. I live in hotels (both good and bad) and in private homes, and stop with friends once in a while. When I'm not on a trip, I live in Washington.

There are only a few roving reporters in the world. It is a queer job. My friends think it is an easy job. They think it's just a vacation. They think I'm getting paid just for seeing the world. My poor, simple friends.

They don't know what it is to drive and dig up information all day long, and then work till midnight writing it. One story a day sounds as easy as falling off a log. Try it sometime.

But there are good sides to this job, too. You see a lot of fascinating things. And you learn so much. In the past year I have learned more about American history than sixteen years of schooling ever taught me. Learned it from hearing people talk, and from reading books about the new places I visited.

As a roving reporter I have learned that the mountaineers of eastern Tennessee are the purest Anglo-Saxon strain in America, and tremendously sharp and capable; that in Nova Scotia they say "good night" as a greeting, just as we say "good evening"; that Texas is the only state with the power to divide itself into smaller states if it wants to; that tourists with Illinois license tags are the wildest drivers on the roads; that in New Orleans masking of the face is allowed by law one day a year, on Mardi Gras; that it costs seven hundred and fifty dollars a day to run the average-sized freight ship; that people in shrimp canneries work from four in the morning till six at night; that Natchitoches in Louisiana is pronounced "Nackitosh."

And as a roving reporter I have seen some wonderful things—the long, soft shadows of the Arizona cactus under a desert moonlight; the awful panic in the eyes of people running before a Canadian forest fire; the slow rising of the Southern Cross into the vast tropical sky as you see it from a freighter at sea; the deep preoccupation on the faces of men and women at the gambling tables in Las Vegas; the amazing speed with which a jumble of tin and steel becomes an auto in Detroit; and the amazing speed with which an auto from Detroit becomes a jumble of tin and steel on a slick, snowy road in North Carolina.

*

In twenty-seven thousand miles of driving in one year, I have had only one flat tire. Picked up a nail in Louisiana. Only in one place (on the Gaspé peninsula in eastern Quebec) have I had to go into low gear to get up a hill. I have paid from twelve to thirty-five cents for gasoline. I have run out of gas twice, and both times it had apparently been siphoned out by thieves, and neither time did I have to walk for gas.

Seldom do I go more than fifty miles an hour anymore. I almost never drive at night. Some days I go only twenty-five miles. Other days three hundred. I have never been stopped by a cop. I have driven through a blizzard in southern Mississippi, and a dust storm in Nova Scotia.

I have never left anything in a hotel room, except one toothbrush. I have had good hotel rooms for seventy-five cents, and bad ones for five dollars. In the back country I have seen pigs hitched to little wagons, hauling wood. And men and women hitched to plows. I have eaten papayas, and cactus candy, and enchiladas, and oranges right off the trees. I have seen (but not eaten) canned rattlesnake meat.

Once in Maine I rounded up half a dozen stories in less than two hours. Another time, in Washington, I worked a whole week on one story. Sometimes I can write a story in half an hour. Other times, when I am out of the mood, I start a story and never do get it finished.

Roving has taught me that people in general are good. Once I stopped at a house in a little village in northwest Florida to ask the direction, and they invited me to stay for lunch. Once, standing right on the precipitous bank of the St. Lawrence River, I talked for ten minutes with a native, and he spoke in French and I in English and neither of us knew a word the other said, but we understood. Once I spent two hours at an abandoned gold mine on a mountain in Arizona, talking with the old watchman who lived alone with his dog. In Ottawa I stood on the sidewalk and chatted with the Premier of Canada for fifteen minutes. In Minnesota I picked up the same hitchhiker four times in one day.

How do I find things to write about? Well, some things by design, some by accident. In a strange town, I go to the local newspaper, or the police chief, or a doctor, and they tell me the most interesting people in town. Then I go talk with the people.

Nobody has ever refused to talk with me. Only one man has ever refused to let me write about him, and even he was friendly and we talked for an hour.

There have been many stories I couldn't write. One was the time I went with a doctor far back into the mountains, to an old log cabin, to see a dying old man. He lay there in his bed like a movie mountaineer, with his shotgun standing at his bedside. When I came in, he rose on his deathbed and held out his feeble hand, and in a whisper welcomed me to his home. It made a lump in my throat, but I couldn't write about it.

There are times when the life of a roving reporter is so thankless and bare that you feel you would rather dig potatoes for a living; but at times such as now, when you sit down and start remembering the things you have done, and seen, and especially the things you have felt—then you know you want to keep going on.

March 18, 1936

BOOK ONE

Home Country

"I was a farm boy, and town kids can make you feel awfully backward when you're young and a farm boy."

OF THE SAD WIND AND A BOY FRIGHTENED OF SNAKES
CEDAR RAPIDS, IOWA—It was soon after crossing into Iowa, coming south from Minnesota, that I gradually became conscious of the wind.

I don't know whether you know that long, sad wind that blows so steadily across the hundreds of miles of Midwest flat lands in the summertime. If you don't, it will be hard for you to understand the feeling I have about it. Even if you know it, you may not understand.

To me the summer wind in the Midwest is one of the most melancholy things in all life. It comes from so far, and it blows so gently and yet so relentlessly; it rustles the leaves and the branches of the maple trees in a sort of symphony of sadness, and it doesn't pass on and leave them still. It just keeps coming, like the infinite flow of Old Man River.

You could—and you do—wear out your lifetime on the dusty plains with that wind of futility blowing in your face. And when you are worn out and gone, the wind, still saying nothing, still so gentle and sad and timeless, is still blowing across the prairies, and will blow in the faces of the little men who follow you, forever.

As soon as I became conscious of the wind, I was back in character as an Indiana farm boy again. Like dreams came the memories the wind brought. I lay again on the ground under the shade trees at noon, during my half-hour rest before going back to the fields, and the wind and the sun and the hot rural silence made me sleepy, and yet I couldn't sleep for the wind in the trees. The wind was like the afternoon ahead that would never end, and the days and the summers and even the lifetimes that would flow on forever, tiredly, patiently.

It's just one of those small impressions that will form in a child's mind, and grow and stay with him through a lifetime, even playing its part in his character and his way of thinking, and he can never explain it.

*

There's another impression that has come up with me out of childhood. I have a horror of snakes that verges on the irrational. I'm not afraid of being killed by a snake; it isn't that kind of fear. It's a horrible, unnatural mania for getting away, and it is induced in equal proportion by a six-inch garden snake and a six-foot rattler.

I happened to think of snakes because, in fifteen thousand miles of driving this year, I had not seen a snake until I drove through southern Minnesota. And there, in less than two hours, I counted fourteen snakes along the road.

Ask my mother about snakes. She'll tell you the snake story. In all the years I have been away, she never fails to tell it again when I am home to visit.

I was a little fellow, maybe four or five. My father was plowing at the far end of our farm, a half mile from the house. I was walking along behind the plow, barefooted, in the fresh soft furrow. He had just started the field, and was plowing near a weedy fencerow. Wild red roses were growing there. I asked my father for his pocketknife, so I could cut some of the roses to take back to the house.

He gave it to me, and went on plowing. I sat down in the grass and started cutting off the roses. Then it happened in a flash. A blue racer came looping through the grass at me. I already had my horror of snakes at that tender age. I screamed, threw the knife away, and ran as fast as I could.

Then I remembered my father's knife. I crept back over the plowed ground till I found it. He had heard me scream and had stopped. I gave him the knife, and started back to the house.

I approached the house from the west side. There was an old garden there, and it was all grown up in high weeds. I stopped on the far side, and shouted for my mother. She came out and asked what I wanted. I asked her to come get me. She said for me to come through by myself. I couldn't have done that had it killed me not to.

She ordered me to come through, and I began to cry. She told me that if I didn't stop crying, and didn't come through, she would whip me. I couldn't stop, and I couldn't come through. So she came and got me, and she whipped me—one of the two times, I believe, she ever did.

That evening, when my father came in from the fields, she told him about the crazy boy who wouldn't walk through the weeds and had to whipped. And then my father told her about the roses, and the knife, and the snake. It was the roses, I think, that hurt her so. My mother cried for a long time that night after she went to bed.

It has been more than thirty years since that happened, but to this day when I go home my mother sooner or later will say, "Do you remember the time I whipped you because you wouldn't walk through the weeds?" And then she will tell me the story, just as I have told it here, and along toward the end she always manages to get the hem of her apron up around her eyes, just in case she needs it, which she always does.

September 23, 1935

Pyle's parents still lived on the family farm near Dana—population just under a thousand—fifty miles due west of Indianapolis. Save for the rolling bottomland near the Wabash River, Vermillion County—long, narrow, sharing a border with Illinois—is wide-open grain prairie, a driver's view of the horizon broken only by an occasional stand of trees or a gentle mounding of the earth. The Pyle farm sat astraddle one such mound, said to contain Indian relics, a source of intrigue to Ernie as a boy. Though he considered Dana his hometown, Ernie never lived in the town itself. Home was always the farm a few miles outside of town.

"Dana," he wrote, "is a pretty town. Nearly every street is just a cool, dark tunnel, formed by the great arching maple trees on either side.

"People who have been around say Dana is a medium-good town. I really don't know whether it is or not. I have never felt completely at ease in Dana. I suppose it is an inferiority hangover from childhood. For I was a farm boy, and town kids can make you feel awfully backward when you're young and a farm boy.

"I have never got over it. Even today I feel self-conscious when I walk down the street in Dana, imagining the town boys are making fun of me. I shouldn't, of course, because all that was long ago, and the people I see on the streets are people I've known all my life, and many of them are our farm friends who have moved to town in their declining years. . . ."

WILL PYLE

DANA, INDIANA—Perhaps you have heard of my father. He is the man who put oil on his brakes when they were squeaking, then drove to Dana and ran over the curb and through a plate-glass window and right into a dry-goods store.

My father is also the man who ran with Roosevelt in 1932. He ran for township trustee, was the only Democrat in the county who lost, and was probably the happiest man who listened to election returns that night. He couldn't think of anything worse than being township trustee.

And the reason he lost was that all the people figured that if he was trustee, he wouldn't have time to put roofs on their houses, and paint their barns, and paper their dining rooms and fix their chimneys and do a thousand and one other things for them. I guess when my father is gone this whole neighborhood will just fall down.

My father has never lived anywhere but on a farm, and yet I don't think he ever has liked the farm very well. He has been happiest, I think, since the war. He started renting the farm out then, and ever since he has been carpentering and handymanning all about the neighborhood. He is a wizard with tools, where other people are clumsy. He is a carpenter at heart.

My father did start out to see the world once when he was a young man. He went to Iowa to cut broom corn, but broke a leg and had to come home. He never went anywhere again till he was fifty-five, when he went to California to see his brother. He sat up all the way in a day coach. Since then he has been to New York, so now he has seen both oceans.

My father is a very quiet man. He has never said a great deal to me all his life, and yet I feel we have been very good friends. He never gave me much advice, or told me to do this or that, or not to. But he didn't spare me, either. I worked like a horse from the time I was nine.

My father never shows much emotion. He has never seen a big-league ball game. Yet my mother came home one afternoon during a World Series and caught him sitting in front of the radio, all by himself, clapping and yelling for all he was worth.

My father used to work as a hired hand over on the other side of the Wabash River. When he was courting my mother, every Sunday he would ride a horse six miles to the river, row a boat across, and then ride a bicycle ten miles to my mother's house. At midnight he started the same process going home. Mother figured he either loved her or else was foolish and needed somebody to look after him, so she married him.

My father is getting a little deaf, but Mother says he can always hear what he isn't supposed to hear. If my father doesn't like people, he never says anything about it. If he does like people, he never says much about that, either. He is very even-tempered. If he has an enemy in this whole country, I have yet to hear about it.

He bought me a Ford roadster when I was sixteen, and when I wrecked it a couple of weeks later, he never said a word.

My father doesn't swear or drink or smoke. He is honest, in letter and in spirit. He is a good man, without being at all repulsive about it. He used to smoke cigars, but he quit the Fourth of July that Johnson fought Jeffries in Reno—I think it was 1908. The event didn't have anything to do with it. His holiday cigar simply made him sicker than usual that day, so he quit.

When my father was in Washington, he kept butting his head against those big glass cases that hold exhibits in the Smithsonian. The glass was so highly polished he couldn't see it. We all thought it was awfully funny. He got a splitting headache from it.

We got our first automobile in 1914. We kept it up in the north end of the wagon shed, right behind the wagon. At the south end of the wagon shed there was a big gravel pit.

One day we came home from town, my mother and I got out at the house, and my father went to put the car away. We saw him make the circle in the barnlot, and then drive into the north end of the shed. The next instant, the south end of the shed simply burst open, a wagon came leaping out, and with one great bound was over the cliff and down into the gravel pit. My father said he never did know exactly what happened.

September 24, 1935

MARIA PYLE

DANA, INDIANA—My mother would rather drive a team of horses in the field than cook a dinner. She has done very little of the former and too much of the latter in her lifetime.

My mother is living proof that happiness is within yourself, because she has done nothing for a whole long life but work too hard, and yet I'm convinced she has been happy. She loves the farm; she wouldn't think of moving to town as other "retired" farmers do. She would rather stay home now and milk the cows than go to the state fair.

She is the best chicken-raiser and cake-baker in the neighborhood. She loves to raise chickens and she hates to bake cakes.

She and my father took a trip East, and saw Niagara Falls, after they had been married thirty years. She didn't want to go, and was glad to get home, but did admit she enjoyed the trip. The highlight of the journey—which included Washington and New York City—was a night in a tourist cabin near Wheeling, West Virginia. It was fixed so nicely inside, she said, just like home. She talks about it yet.

My mother probably knows as little about world affairs as any woman in our neighborhood. Yet she is the broadest-minded and most liberal of the lot. I don't remember her ever telling me I couldn't do something. She always told me what she thought was right, and what was wrong, and then it was up to me.

When I was about sixteen, I forgot and left my corncob pipe lying on the windowsill one day when I went to school. When I got home that night, she handed me the pipe and said, "I see you're smoking now." I said yes, and that was that. She thinks it's awful for women to smoke, but I imagine if she had a daughter who smoked, she'd think it was all right.

My mother is a devout Methodist and a prohibitionist. Yet she and my father voted for Al Smith in 1928, because they thought he was a better man than Hoover. Some of the neighbors wouldn't speak to them for months because they voted for a Catholic and a wet. But they didn't care. They are always doing the things they think are right.

My mother has had only three real interests in her whole life—my father, me, and her farm work. Nothing else makes much difference to her. And yet, when I left home seventeen years ago, to be gone forever except for brief visits, she was content to let me go, because she knew I was not happy on the farm.

My mother has quite a temper. I remember once when the liniment man came, and said we hadn't paid him for a bottle of liniment. My mother said we had. The man said we hadn't. So my mother got the money, opened the screen door, and threw it in his face. He never came back again.

She always tells people just what she thinks. A good many of our neighbors have deservedly felt the whip of her tongue, and they pout over it for a while, but whenever they're in trouble, they always thaw out and come asking for help, and of course they get it.

My mother is the one the neighbors always call on when somebody gets sick, or dies, or needs help of any kind. She has practically raised a couple of neighborhood kids and always has been the confidante of the young people around here.

I started driving a team of horses in the fields when I was nine. I remember that first day perfectly. My mother had gone to a club meeting, but she came home in the middle of the afternoon, and brought me a lunch of bread and butter and sugar out to the field. I suppose, too, she wanted to make sure I hadn't been dragged to death under the harrow.

My mother doesn't realize it, but her life has been the life a real prairie pioneer. You could say she is one of the sturdy stock of the ages who have always done the carrying-on when the going was tough.

She isn't so well anymore, but she seems to work harder than ever. We try to get her to rest, but she says, "Oh, the work has to be done." We say, "Yes, but *you* don't have to do it. Suppose you were gone. The work would still be here, but you wouldn't have to do it." But she doesn't understand what we mean.

September 25, 1935

AUNT MARY BALES

DANA, INDIANA—My Aunt Mary was born thirty years too soon. If she were forty instead of seventy, I'm sure she would be in Congress now. She always did want to be in politics, but she was born to the farm instead. She knows all about politics and national affairs, yet she never went beyond the eighth grade.

My Aunt Mary was past forty when she married. I remember when Uncle George first started going with her. She lived at our house then, and he would come to take her riding before breakfast. He drove a fractious sorrel mare, hitched to a two-wheeled racing sulky, with just a little seat on it.

He would stop out in the road and yell till we were all awake, then Aunt Mary would go out and get in with him. She was ashamed to ride up and down the road in a racing sulky on a tiny little seat with a man before breakfast, but she liked Uncle George, so she went.

And I remember the night they were married. There were a lot of people at our house that night. I was a little shaver, but I had sense enough to know that as soon as the knot was tied, the kissing would start. So I hid behind the couch.

Sure enough, as soon as the ceremony was over, Aunt Mary, crying as though she had just buried Uncle George instead of married him, wanted to kiss everybody in the place, especially me. And I couldn't be found. The search finally got so frantic I decided to come out and get kissed and have it over with. Which I did.

*

Uncle George lived on a farm, but he wasn't a farmer; he was a dreamer. He would fuss all day around his garden and his flowers, and play his beautiful big black square piano, and order whole freight-car loads of lime fertilizer he couldn't pay for, and talk by the hour about his prize sweet corn, and spend whole half-days studying the flower and seed catalogues he had sent away for. My Uncle George was a great man, and he worked like a Trojan, but he never got anything done, and Aunt Mary had to make the living.

And she did a nice job of it, too. She raised hundreds of chickens, and she raised her own hogs and cows, and through twenty years she kept the treasury from going flat. She worked from four in the morning till nine at night, and found time to go to a couple of weekly clubs and to run the country church, too.

She even bought an automobile as early as 1915 and learned to drive it, and drive it well, too, when she was fifty years old. Uncle George never would drive the damn thing, so she had to haul him around, too.

*

Then, some ten years ago, Uncle George died. Aunt Mary was sixty years old. She had been born on a farm, had never been off the farm, but she was alert, she had more energy than a buzz saw, and she was tall and straight despite a lifetime of killing work.

And so, at sixty, she went to Indianapolis, all alone, to make her way in the world. And she did make it. She worked at all kinds of jobs. She worked as a supervisor in a girls' reform school. She worked in a restaurant. She took care of a sick woman. She worked as a housekeeper. And today, at seventy, she's still working, not only making her own way, as we say of boys just out of college, but helping keep a lot of other people, just as she always has.

In the city, my Aunt Mary has had time and opportunity to keep up with what's going on in the world even better than she did before. She knows all about the New Deal, and is in favor of it. Most farm people and churchmen are fundamentalists. But my Aunt Mary would need take only a couple of jumps to be a full-fledged socialist. She has pretty advanced social ideas, and if she were forty instead of seventy, I'll bet she'd make the capitalists holler.

But Aunt Mary's main interest in life still lies in the little community where she lived for sixty years. Every letter to her has to tell how Minnie's chickens are doing, and who wasn't at church last Sunday, and when Edith is going to have her baby, and what Grace's new dress looks like.

About twice a year, she goes back for a few days, and those are happy days for her. And people say to her what a shame she has to go back so soon, and she says, philosophically, but spirited-like, too, "Yes, I'd sure like to stay, but I've got my own way to make, you know."

And here she is, at seventy, still hammering away at life and getting the best of it. She makes a lot of us younger ones look cheap.

September 26, 1935

BAREFOOT DAYS

DANA, INDIANA—Bob came past in his dad's car and picked me up. We drove down the road half a mile to the creek in Mr. Webster's pasture where I used to fish. Mr. Webster has been dead more than twenty years, but everybody still calls it Mr. Webster's pasture.

I have fished in that creek hundreds of times, but this was the first time I ever went down there in an auto. I always used to walk, in my bare feet. It had been twenty years, I guess, since I fished there. The creek was never very big, and it hasn't grown any in twenty years. You can jump across it almost anyplace. It is muddy, too, and grass is grown up all along the banks.

We stopped the car at a little cement bridge and got out. Bob said there were fish there. The hole must have been five feet across, and all of a foot deep. Bob had dug the worms, and had them in a tomato can, just as we used to carry them. The last time I fished in that creek, Bob wasn't born yet. "Do you still know how to bait a hook?" he asked.

"Sure," I said, and shoved the worm down over the hook. Bob watched me, as though I were a woman and couldn't bear it. I felt sorry for the worm, but I didn't say anything. I don't remember having any feeling about hurting a worm when I was little. When I was through I spit on the bait, and threw the line in.

"I bet I catch something within a minute," Bob said.

"I'll bet you don't," I said. "You can even make it three minutes."

"How much you bet?" Bob said.

"A nickel," I said.

He threw his line in. The cork never stopped at the surface, just went right on down. Bob gave his pole a jerk. Out came a little sunfish about as long as your finger. It hadn't been three seconds, let alone three minutes. We threw the fish back in. It was too little, but it counted. I forgot to give him the nickel.

*

When I fished down there last, Bob's parents hadn't even heard of him. And now he's bigger than I am. He has bright yellow hair, and finishes high school next year, and he's going to Chicago to be an artist. I wonder if he'll be coming back here to fish twenty years from now. Maybe he'll come back and paint a picture of Mr. Webster's pasture.

We sat there on the bridge, pulling in little sunfish, and talking. Bob said I should have brought my camera and taken a picture of the old fishing hole. I suppose I should have, at that. Except it isn't the same hole. Creeks change, too, like people, and my old fishing hole was a couple of hundred yards over in the pasture. We didn't go over to see if it is still there. I suppose it isn't, because Bob knows all the good holes now. Anyway, there might be snakes.

Bob said sometimes they go swimming in these mud holes. So I told him we used to, also. It wasn't really swimming. We called it mud-crawling. The water wasn't up to your knees, so we'd just lie down and walk along on our hands and kick with our feet. I kept my BVDs on this time I was telling him about, and suddenly I felt something swishing around my stomach. I let out a yell and jumped up and grabbed at my underwear. I had a fish. He had swum inside my underwear and got caught. I don't know what kind of fish it was. It was round and blue, about a foot long—the biggest fish we had ever caught in that creek. I took it home and we had it for supper. That was a long time ago. I don't wear BVDs anymore.

Another time, long ago, I was sitting on the bank half asleep, and with my bare feet dangling over the edge, a foot above the water. I don't know now, so long since, whether I heard something, or just sensed something. But I looked down and there, right under my feet, was a whole nest of little water moccasins. I screamed and dropped my pole and ran out to the safe sandy road, and then ran the whole half mile home. My father went back the next day and got my fish pole. He said he couldn't find any snakes.

*

The fish were biting pretty good, better than I ever remember them biting in the old days. We caught about thirty in an hour, but only eight were big enough to save, and they weren't really big enough, but we had to take something home. I caught the two biggest sunfish, and Bob caught a catfish, but it wasn't as big as my sunfish.

After a while they stopped biting, and we pulled in our lines and got in the car and drove home. The old creek down in Mr. Webster's pasture didn't even know the great fisherman had been away for twenty years, I suppose. And for that matter, I don't suppose it knew he ever came back.

June 22, 1936

NOTHING LEFT TO GIGGLE ABOUT

ORLANDO, FLORIDA—My friend is an overseer of an orange grove at the edge of town here. The oranges don't take much of his time, so he sits in a boat out on the lake, all day long, fishing.

My friend and I were buddies from the time we were six years old. We lived about a mile apart, on farms in Indiana. There was a time when we thought the world would end if we didn't see each other every day. We went through the giggly stage. It got so we couldn't sit down at the table, either at his house or mine, without choking from the giggles. Our mothers would want to know what we were giggling about, and of course we weren't giggling about anything, and our mothers would get provoked and make us leave the table.

I went to see my old friend yesterday. I have seen him only three times now in seventeen years. We talked for about an hour. We didn't get the giggles.

*

When we were little, my friend had a black-and-white Shetland pony. I had a small sorrel Indian horse, and a new saddle from Sears Roebuck. For quite a while we were knights in Sir Arthur's Round Table. We took the lids off our mothers' wash boilers for shields, and made daggers out of pieces of lath, and took long rug poles for spears, and fixed up hoods over our ponies' bridles, and started out.

If we couldn't find any other knights to fight—and we never could, because we were better riders than the other boys—we would fight each other. We graduated from that to become great trappers of the north woods. We sent away for booklets on bait, and on curing and stretching skins. We caught muskrats and skunks, and a few tomcats.

After that we started smoking. At first we smoked corn-silk cigarets, out in the fields or in the attic of the old log house back of his parents' new home. Later, we adopted the corncob pipe, with real tobacco. We smoked on the way home from school, and we had a woodpecker hole in a fence post where we hid our pipes. Sometimes we would hide them in rabbit holes under the grass, along the road.

My friend and I finally got to the girl stage. Neither of us was very crazy about girls, and I think we started just because it was expected of us. He had more nerve than I, so he made dates with a couple of girls for one Sunday night. I worried about it all week, and would have backed out but my mother made me go.

It took me all Sunday afternoon to get dressed. I had on a Charlie Dawes hard collar* and a new brown suit. About dark I went over to his house. It started pouring rain. We went out to the barn and hitched up his little Shetland pony to the only thing available, a huge old phaeton. The pony only came to the

---

*An old-fashioned high, stiff collar of the sort worn by Charles G. Dawes, the Chicago banker who served as Coolidge's Vice President and the head of the Reconstruction Finance Corporation under Hoover in the early years of the Depression.

level of the shafts, and when hitched up was at least five feet from the dashboard. It looked comical even to us.

We drove five miles to the girls' house. They were as scared as we were. We took them rather formally to church, all four of us riding in the phaeton, and got stuck in the mud, and had to get out and lift. When we got back to the girls' house we played Authors for a while. After that the whole thing sort of bogged down. We couldn't think of anything to say, and we wanted to go home, but didn't know how to get started. Our misery was acute.

Finally, along about midnight, we heard a motherly voice from the other room. One of the girls went in, was gone for a minute; we could hear whispers, and then she came out, shyly holding up an alarm clock. She didn't say a word, just sort of giggled. We said something about not knowing it was so late, and rushed out.

*

My friend was almost a year older than I, so he left for the Army in 1918. He sent me postcards from Texas. At commencement exercises that spring, there was an empty, flag-draped chair on the stage for him. I could hardly bear to go to commencement, I was so ashamed that I wasn't in the Army, too.

My friend spent a year in an Army hospital in New Mexico. Later I went away, too, and when we both came back, we went one day to visit our high school. Our former Latin teacher was a little thing who liked both of us, and while my friend and I were visiting her class we got our old-time giggles and couldn't stop. She got the giggles, too, and finally had to dismiss class, and the three of us sat and talked.

That episode was the end of our youth together. We went our separate paths, and the water began to flow swiftly under the bridge.

*

Seventeen years later I pulled up in front of his cottage under the orange trees. He was glad to see me, and I was glad to see him. He wanted me to stay a couple of days and fish, and I was sorry I couldn't.

We don't know each other so well anymore, but we are still friends, and I expect we always will be. As I drove away, I was wondering why there isn't anything anymore for us to giggle about.

March 2, 1936

The East

"I had heard that all New Englanders say 'down east' when they mean 'up north.' They do say it, but the only explanation they can give is that it *is* down east. What do you say to that?"

PENNSYLVANIA

A BOOMING, CRAZY-QUILT CITY

PITTSBURGH—Pittsburgh is undoubtedly the cockeyedest city in the United States. Physically, it is absolutely irrational. It must have been laid out by a mountain goat.

It is the only city in this country in which I can't find my way around, the only one of which I can't get a mental bird's-eye picture. I've flown over it, and driven all around it, and studied maps of it, and still I hardly know one end of Pittsburgh from the other. It's worse than irregular—it's chaotic.

There's just one balm—people who live here can't find their way around, either. One friend of mine who was born and raised here says she could drive to almost anyplace in the city but probably couldn't find the shortest way.

Another friend of mine has lived here six years, and all he has ever figured out is how to get from his house to downtown. Every time he gets off this path he is lost, and although he has asked hundreds of people how to get somewhere, nobody ever knew.

The reason for all this is the topography of Pittsburgh. It's up and down, and around and around, and in betwixt. Pittsburgh is hills, mountains, cliffs, valleys, and rivers. Some streets are narrow; some are wide. None runs more than a few blocks in a straight line.

You may have a friend who lives half a mile away. But to get there you circle three miles around a mountain ridge, cross two bridges, go through a tunnel, follow a valley, skirt the edge of a cliff, and wind up at your friend's back door an hour after dark.

Right downtown, a freight train goes by a fourth-story office window. One side of the city post office is coal-black, because the railroad is right against it. The main passenger line of another railroad runs smack through the center of a steel mill—right under its roof, even. There just wasn't anyplace else to put the railroad. Trolley cars run over the tops of houses one minute and through a tunnel the next.

There are more than two hundred bridges in Pittsburgh, because there are, you might say, three big rivers right in the city. The Allegheny and the Monongahela twist around through town, and then come together within a stone's throw of the business district to form the Ohio.

There are countless tunnels right in the city—tunnels for autos, for trolleys, for trains. The big Liberty Tubes through Mount Washington are a mile long, and when traffic gets jammed the drivers start honking their horns and you think you're in a madhouse.

And there are many inclined railways. I don't mean cable streetcars, such as San Francisco has. I mean the funny little things that run at forty-five degrees right up the side of a mountain on tracks built onto steel trestlework.

And then the steps—oh, Lord, the steps! I was told they actually had a Department of Steps in the city government. That isn't exactly true, although they do have an Inspector of Steps. There are nearly thirteen miles of city-owned steps in Pittsburgh, going up mountainsides.

The well-to-do people drive to work. The medium people go on streetcars and "inclines," which is what they call those cable cars. And the poor people walk up the steps.

*

Pittsburgh has everything you can think of, and yet no one distinctive character. You can't say it's a city of easy liberty, like New Orleans, or a city of high cosmopolitanism, like San Francisco. People here just work, as one fellow put it. Business, rather than people's spirit, dominates Pittsburgh. And steel is the dominant business.

Pittsburgh is booming now. Some of the mills are even turning out a daily production far beyond their theoretical capacity. They say there is work now for every man who wants to work.

Pittsburgh is smoking and roaring into a boom that is likely to go beyond anything of the pre-Depression days. Money is flowing again. And when Pittsburghers have money, they spend it. The mill-town stores are overrun. Steel workers, after years of scrimping, are buying radios, and new rugs, and clothes, and everything else they haven't had for eight years.

There's an old saying in Pittsburgh, dating back to the days when the mills paid off in gold—"No coal dust, no gold dust." Well, there's plenty of coal dust now and gold dust, too. Pittsburgh is a dirty city. It wasn't libeled a bit when it got that reputation. But Pittsburgh people, like people everywhere, love prosperity. And a dirty shirt collar here means prosperity. So people don't seem to mind.

April 16, 1937

"Now You Know What Hell Is Like"
PITTSBURGH—I'd always wanted to go through a steel mill, and now my wish has certainly been gratified. I spent nearly a whole night in the steel mills here.

We walked for miles, we climbed our heads off, we got dirty, we got tired, and we saw strange scenes that took on an exaggerated weirdness at three o'clock in the morning.

In fact, we saw too much. The whole thing became eerie, and new sights crushed out old sights, and things merged into a sleepy-eyed dream, so that I can't remember half that I saw or heard.

But there is one outstandingly bright memory of the night. It was when the superintendent of the Jones & Laughlin plant said, "Now I'll show you something no visitor to a steel mill ever sees." We got into a huge freight elevator. We went up and up and up. A door rose, and we stepped onto a wooden platform. Several men were up there, wearing pith helmets and thick gloves, and doing nothing at the moment. They spoke to us. The superintendent handed me a pair of dark-blue glasses. "Now come over to the railing and look down," he said.

I held on and peeked over. And I was looking right down into the seething insides of a Bessemer furnace. "Now you know what hell is like," the superintendent said.

You would not dare look into that terrific fire without those glasses. But they were so dark they made the eye-shattering glow look mildly purple. You could see every detail.

The molten metal didn't just boil. It leaped, viciously, against the sides of the furnace, like surf beating on a cliff. The temperature in there was around twenty-nine hundred degrees. I could look no more than two seconds at a time. Although we stood fifteen or twenty feet from the furnace mouth, the scorching heat was unbearable. My face felt blistered. The awfulness of the power in that golden maelstrom made me tense, and I held on to the railing as though I might fall, although there was no danger.

*

We went back down to the floor of the furnace room, and then up to another platform on the other side. We were below the seething mouths of the furnaces, but still we had to wear dark glasses to look upon them.

These furnaces, I should explain, are built in the shape of an immense urn, big at the bottom, curving to a smaller neck at the top. The only opening is at the top. They are three or four stories high, and set on huge cradles so they can be tipped over and the molten metal poured out.

We stood in a room of levers and valves. A window opened onto the furnace room. "Here," said the superintendent, "pull on this lever, and then watch the furnace." So I pulled, timidly, and in a second the whole urnlike furnace began to swing slowly over. I shoved the lever back to neutral, and was quick about it. "Go ahead," said the superintendent. "Pull on it hard."

So I pulled again, and watched it move further. It was really a thrill, but I didn't like it much. I could feel the pain of responsibility run up through my arm. If I had kept pulling that lever, and if nobody had knocked my hand away, I could have turned

that whole vat over and dumped tons of molten metal all over
the place, killing men and ruining machinery. But I didn't. . . .

April 17, 1937

PITTSBURGH—Some weird and awful accidents happen in the
steel mills. For example, one night in one plant they opened the
spout from the mixing furnace to pour tons of molten yellow
metal into a vat on a little freight car.

But the engineer got his signals mixed up and didn't have his
car under the spout at the right time. The metal came pouring
out—heated to twenty-nine hundred degrees, bright and liquid—and it cut the locomotive squarely in two, just that quick.
The engineer died instantly. . . .

April 20, 1937

NEW JERSEY

*Complaining about President Franklin Roosevelt's attempts to ease the
suffering of Depression victims was a favorite pastime for Roosevelt-
bashers. Particularly irritating to Roosevelt's critics were public-works
programs, which they charged were nothing but government-backed boon-
doggling. Pyle wrote this column in the summer of 1935, three years into
Roosevelt's first term.*

A JERSEYMAN'S VIEW OF THE NEW DEAL
SPARTA, NEW JERSEY—The man who fixes autos in a little town
near here said if I could find five people in the town who would
vote for President Roosevelt next year, he'd give me five dollars
apiece for them.

"What's the matter?" I asked him.

"Everything's a big mess," he said. "The Three-A* has ruined
the farmers around here. We pay big processing taxes, and the
money all goes to the Midwest. Practically none of it comes back
to the farmers around here.

---

*Agricultural Adjustment Act. Passed in 1933, it sought to restore farmers' badly sag-
ging purchasing power by paying farmers to restrict their crop production and by
imposition of a processing tax on food processors. An amendment provided for lower-
interest farm mortgages.

"And the way they spend the money. See this road along here? From here down to that next telephone pole there used to be a row of nice big trees. Well, sir, they cut them all down, and then they dug a shallow ditch along the side of the road; then they put the dirt back in the ditch, then dug it out again and threw it on the other side. Then they put it back in the ditch again, and you can see for yourself they didn't widen the road an inch, and I'll be damned if it didn't cost two thousand dollars. Such stuff as that!"

I suggested that President Roosevelt personally didn't even know that road existed, so how could you blame him for doing that kind of work? Wasn't it the fault of the local dispensers of work projects? And wasn't even such wasteful work better than just paying the money out in straight relief, which would have had to be done otherwise?

The man didn't know about that. It was just all a big mess. And anyhow, the guys doing that relief work were out-of-towners. His town didn't have anybody at all on federal relief.

Only four people there were unable to scrape along somehow, he said, and the townspeople—not federal or municipal relief money—were taking care of them. The town isn't very big; it doesn't even appear on some maps. My guess would give it a population of five or six hundred.

"And the banks," the man said. "There's another thing. The bank examiners are a lot of kids who don't know what it's all about. Right here in this county the receivers and the examiners have accepted notes from the government that not a banker in New Jersey would have taken, and they threw out notes that within six months would have paid every cent. Such stuff as that!"

"Who are you going to vote for?" I asked.

He grinned for the first time. "Well, I don't know," he said. "There don't seem to be anybody. Maybe I just won't vote at all."

August 10, 1935

POSTSCRIPT: *President Roosevelt won reelection overwhelmingly in 1936.*

VERNE TREAT, RETIRED MAIL PILOT
FREEHOLD, NEW JERSEY—There was a time when Verne Treat rode nightly with death. He was dean of all the mail pilots on what is now the vast system of Eastern Air Lines.

He flew the first load of mail the night the line opened, way back in the twenties, and he cracked up before he got to his destination. That was the start of four-and-a-half spectacular years.

Twice Treat had to jump for his life. Twenty times he wrecked airplanes in forced night landings. That sounds as if he wasn't a good pilot. But it wasn't his fault that engines quit, and it takes superb skill to land just any old place at night and not kill yourself. Treat never had a scratch.

He is a small fellow who had to sit on extra cushions so he could see out of the cockpit. He was quiet and sober, and a cautious and heady flier. He had been flying since the war, and had barnstormed with Ruth Law,* and the other boys looked up to him and asked him for advice.

Four years ago Treat retired. He is the only aviator I ever heard of who just up and voluntarily quit the flying game. He quit partly because he had a chance to go into business, and partly because the strain of flying was getting him in the stomach. He came to Freehold, and went into the auto business.

So I came past Freehold today to see Treat for the first time since he quit. We were old friends and I wanted to say hello. I also wanted to see if a man can really get flying out of his blood. I still don't know.

I asked Treat if he got homesick for the night mail. He said no. I asked him if he ever intended to go back on the airlines. He said, "No. I'm forty-two now, and if I went back I'd only have three or four more years of flying, and then where would I be?"

Treat seldom sees any of the boys anymore. Once in a while one of them drives through Freehold and stops, as I did. But Treat never goes up to Newark to hang around the airport, although it's only an hour away. "You know how it is," he said. "When you're in the business, you're all pals. But when you're out, you're an outsider. I know how we used to talk about the outsiders who hung around the field. So I never go near."

Treat likes the auto business. He has fifteen people working for him, and he sells a lot of cars, and the competition keeps him on his toes. Of course right now his income is small beside the twelve thousand dollars a year he used to pull down on the night

*The first woman pilot to fly at night and the holder of many altitude and cross-country flying records. With her husband she ran a three-plane flying troupe called Ruth Law's Flying Circus.

mail. But the boys aren't making that much anymore. And Treat likes being his own boss, and he's crazy about this east Jersey country. No earthquakes or hurricanes or floods or dust storms, and only twenty miles from the ocean and an hour's drive from New York.

Treat has never ridden in one of the fast new silver planes the lines are using now. In fact, he hasn't had his own private plane off the ground since last summer, and it's for sale now. His pilot's license has lapsed. He hasn't kept any clippings of his long career, except for the pieces I wrote about him years ago.

We talked for quite a while, and it seemed to me that aviation was pretty well gone from Verne Treat. I started to pay for my lunch and head on for New York. And then somehow we got to talking about that awful snowy night that Treat had to jump just north of Washington. It was five years ago. I remember I got up at three A.M. and went out there. "I was lucky to come out alive that night," he said. "I jumped at three hundred feet. If I'd known I was that low I believe I'd have ridden it on down. The chute opened just as I hit the ground."

Aviation started coming back to life in Verne Treat. We remembered other incidents. We rambled on to the night his motor blew to pieces and caught fire over the Potomac. He couldn't jump, or he'd have drowned. He set the burning ship down on a farm along the river, and the only part of it left intact was right where Treat was sitting.

And then on to the night he ran out of gas and had to come down, and dropped a flare and it set the grass afire, and the report was all over the country that he had crashed in flames and burned to death. He didn't even scratch the paint on his plane that night.

And the night he was "pinched off" and couldn't find a beacon or a hole in the fog, and kept floating around until his gas was about gone, and then pulled up to eleven thousand feet and jumped out backward into the night when the motor died.

And we talked about the other boys on the line, the originals, some living, some dead—about their wild scrapes with the weather, and how nobody knew what it was all about back in those days, and how the pilot was supreme then, and Treat said: "If flying was still like it was back in those days I might go back."

We talked for another hour, and Verne said: "I'm sure glad you came past, and I'm not kiddin', either," and he looked younger and gayer than I had ever seen him, but I don't know yet whether that was because he had stopped flying, or because he had started thinking about it again.

June 30, 1936

NEW YORK

Ernie and Jerry had lived in New York from August 1926 through December 1927, during which time Ernie worked on the copy desk of the New York Evening World *and later the* New York Post.

WE SHOULD HAVE KNOWN BETTER

NEW YORK CITY—Number 25 Abingdon Square isn't there anymore, and we knew it wasn't there, and should have had more sense than to go down there at all.

Abingdon Square is in Greenwich Village, or what used to be the Village, at any rate, and is at the corner of Eighth Avenue and Twelfth Street.

We thought we must see the old place, for 25 Abingdon Square was synonymous with the early years of what you might call our maturity, our first years in the big city, our very lean and hard years, the years that now seem to tingle and glow with sentimentality. And if they do, isn't that all right, even if they didn't seem very good years at the time?

Old number 25—the dingy brownstone with the ROOMS FOR LET sign, and Mrs. Remington and all her damn cats all over the front stoop, and the shades torn halfway off the window of our basement room, and the garbage can sitting out front. Old number 25, and all the other brownstones along that side of the square, where we made friends with other people in their young, hard years. And what do you think all those houses look like now, after nearly a decade?

They look very much like a fifteen-story tan-brick apartment house, with red awnings at the windows, and a penthouse on top, and a footman at the door, and a sidewalk runner out at the curb, and a big sign saying ABINGDON ARMS, or something like that.

I suppose there is a big, powerful furnace right where our basement room used to be, the room where the newspaper gang would come after work and listen to the phonograph and talk gravely about things they weren't informed about—the dingy, dark room where the rats used to run across our faces at night and wake us up.

And up about the fourth story, which was the top story of number 25 Abingdon Square, and which held the little room without any windows where we later moved, the room where we used to try to sleep in the daytime because we worked at night then, and where we couldn't sleep because there were no windows and consequently no air, and where the bugs wouldn't let you sleep even if there had been windows—I suppose up there on about the fourth floor some well-to-do businessman is now enjoying every comfort the Abingdon Arms has to offer.

And up on the fifth floor, which would have been the roof of number 25 Abingdon Square, where we used to climb up through the trap door to have parties on top, and almost drive Mrs. Remington crazy because she thought we'd fall off—I wonder who's living up there on the fifth floor now?

*

We stood on the sidewalk and looked at what was once number 25 Abingdon Square until we'd had enough of it, which wasn't very long, so then we tried old Dr. Uhfelder's drugstore up on the corner.

We used to go in there every evening and listen to him talk. He was a Jekyll-and-Hydish man, a pure apothecary, windy and wild with a gleam in his eye, who didn't know half the time what he was doing because he would get carried away in his own tall tales of how he had sat at Heine's feet, and studied under Hegel and Nietzsche, and been around the world in great ships. But he was great if he liked you, and he did like us.

So we went into the drugstore, and where Dr. Uhfelder's hodgepodge mixing table used to be, behind a falling-over screen, there was a new soda fountain, with a nice-looking young man behind it. We asked him if he'd ever heard of Dr. Uhfelder.

"Yes, I've heard of him," he said. "But he's gone away." He waved his hand and the hand said "long time ago, no come back here, ever." The young man looked directly at us. He said, "God, he's seventy or eighty years old now."

"Yes, we know. Thanks."

*

And that was the end of Abingdon Square. We should, of course, have had more sense than to go down there at all.

August 13, 1935

ON BROADWAY YOU CAN FORGET A LOT

NEW YORK CITY—There ought to be a law making it necessary, and possible, for everybody to see a musical show on Broadway at least once a year. It's good for the soul.

For one thing, sitting among all the gorgeous fur coats and white shirtfronts gives you an illusion that you are really somebody. And then you're likely to kill time before the curtain-up by staring rubelike at the faces above the fur coats and stiff shirts, and that makes you feel pretty good, too.

I don't know why so many women in seal coats and twelve-thousand-dollar bracelets look as though their faces are out of joint, but it seems that they do.

And when the lights go down and the curtain goes up, the big-time illusion is on. The music gets into your head, and you imagine you could dance like that, and you know you could get up and sing a song; and the fresh new costumes, so clean and glittering, make you forget how many rags there are in the world; and the beautiful girls are a charm and a blessing, and the comedians—well, you laugh, and forget about the mortgage, and you think Broadway is wonderful.

The show lilts and swings along, and you get lost in it, and further and further away, and your blood seems to pound and keep time with your feet, and everything is so happy and gay, and everybody is laughing and singing and dancing in their hearts, and you think to yourself, "Boy, this is great, this is living—to hell with all the poor people."

It was George White's new *Scandals* that we saw. It was a happy cast, and a happy audience. . . .

The closing scene was an immense climax of enthusiasm, with the chorus dancing and singing in back, and the stars all lined up in front, squatting down in a long row, and everybody laughing and clapping and stomping, and the orchestra booming, and the audience making a great roar.

The riotous spirit was infectious, and Willie Howard pushed the girl next to him, and she pushed Rudy Vallee, and the whole row lost its balance and went toppling over, sprawling on the

floor, and laughing. And they got up in line again, and a girl
shoved that time, and they all fell over and started pushing, and
it was so spontaneous and youthful and happy that you felt like
jumping up and yelling, "This is the life. Nuts to sad people."

*

When we left the theater, the rain had stopped, and a cold
wind cut down Forty-fourth Street. The sidewalks were
jammed with evening clothes, pouring out of the theaters. We
heard a violin moaning. It sounded strange, outdoors like that,
in the wind. A young man was sitting on the sidewalk, playing
it. He was leaning against a lamppost. People had to walk
around his thin, crippled legs, stretched out in front of him. He
made the violin sound as if it were crying.

I didn't look at him when we passed. All the way down the
street, I tried to walk as though I hadn't seen him at all.

January 14, 1936

NEW YORK CITY—There is a young man who has achieved a
fleeting distinction on the world's greatest street—Broadway.
He was standing at Forty-fourth and Broadway the other night,
and a little crowd gathered around him, listening and smiling.

The young man was selling newspapers. They were stacked
on a bench in front of him, on the sidewalk. His voice was soft
and full of melody. He kept calling: "Hitler bought a mazooza.
. . . Hitler bought a mazooza. . . . Read all about the horrible
horror. . . . Hitler bought a mazooza."

I don't know what he meant. I suppose it didn't mean anything. Homeward-bound theatergoers were amused and
stopped to listen. The young man was smiling, and looking as
though he would like to join the crowd and laugh at himself.

A woman in the crowd whispered to her man: "I think he said
Hitler killed Mussolini. Do you suppose it's true?"

The young man called: "Just think of it. Hitler bought a
mazooza."

He was selling lots of papers. He was creating good nature,
and cashing in on it. "Hitler elopes with Sophie Tucker!" That
was his crowning pronouncement. Everybody laughed and the
young man looked pleased with himself. . . .

*

There was a big crowd gathered around a bench on the subway platform under Grand Central Station the other day. I
edged through and took a peek.

A man was lying on the bench, hat off, tie pulled down, collar unbuttoned, eyes shut, mouth open. I don't know whether he was drunk or dead. Nobody else knew, either. Nobody made any attempt to find out. Just came and looked for a minute, and then went on, and new ones came to take their places, and look for a minute. . . .

January 15, 1936

NEW YORK CITY— . . . I wish everyone in the world could have the privilege, sometime in his life, of sailing into New York from the sea. It's indescribable, so there's no use in my trying to describe it. But I can say it is an almost overpowering experience.

We've come into New York several times before. And each time I can't help but wonder what must have been the feeling— and what must be the feeling, even more so these days—of the millions of immigrants, and now refugees, when they get their first glimpse through the fog of that monster forest of uncanny spires that is the fabled Manhattan skyline. . . .

September 16, 1940

NEW YORK CITY— . . . The Billy Minsky burlesque enterprises have five theaters—one each in Manhattan, Brooklyn, Boston, Miami, and Hollywood.

Backstage in every theater is a cat. It has gotten to be a tradition. Nobody knows how it started. Now and then the cat wanders onto the stage during the show. If it doesn't, then somebody throws it out, just for fun.

One day, at the Brooklyn theater, the cat had kittens. And as a hospital bed, Mama Cat picked out a stripteaser's overcoat, which had fallen on the floor. Miss Stripteaser came back to find her overcoat covered with new kittens.

She was overjoyed. "Oh, this is wonderful," she shouted. "This is a good omen. This will bring me good luck."

That night she was fired for being drunk. . . .

April 12, 1937

NEW YORK CITY— . . . The United Airlines bus took us into New York. At Thirty-fourth Street I got into a taxi, driven by none other than one Irving Welednigen.

He saw me get out of the airline bus, and he thought I was in a hurry. For sixteen blocks he whirled that skylighted old cab through traffic like a bank robber getting away. He clipped trunks, brushed an old woman, cussed pushcart men, and fanned the fronts off a whole bunch of corner pedestrians in his way.

And then, enraged almost beyond endurance by this outlandish New York traffic of which he is unconsciously a dominant part, Irving turned full around to me without ever slowing up, and shouted:

"They dare you to hit 'em, by God, they just dare you to hit 'em!"

Righto, Irving. They do. But this is New York, you know. *You* are New York. Irving, we are glad to see you looking so well.

May 22, 1939

NEW YORK'S INHUMAN TEMPO

GOING EAST ON THE BOSTON POST ROAD—So that was New York, was it? The biggest in the world. The city they write about, and sing about, the city where almost every young American dreams of going. Why? Don't ask me. I don't know. I hate New York.

And my dislike for this greatest of all cities is no casual thing, either. I lived there two years and two days. The two years were a decade ago; the two days have just ended. And this short visit brought back all my old repulsion for New York, like a bad dream remembered.

It's hard to analyze fervor against a city; you get all mixed up. I love to ride the subway trains as they roar and sway through the black tunnels. When you stand at Forty-seventh and Broadway at night, and look up and down the brightest street in the world and watch the lights that bind and spell, the breath stops a little as it does at the first sight of the Grand Canyon.

But I hate New York. Ten years away had dulled my memory of its inhuman tempo. I had forgotten what New York does to people's faces, how zoolike they look. I had forgotten the deafening crash of the elevateds, had forgotten that you can't walk a block without getting dust in your eyes, that people rush staringly along all day, bumping and dashing, and for what?

I had forgotten how frightening and unnatural are the piled-up skyscrapers; I had forgotten the squalor of the seven million, the filth of the rivers, the rudeness of the crowds, the pitiful clamor of the fun-seekers, the tawdriness of the beach mobs.

I had forgotten all about the phonies and the freaks, and the distrust and the fear in the hearts of people. I had forgotten all this, but one hour in New York brought it back like a slap in the face.

In my native Indiana town they tell a story about a young fellow who went away to the big city and didn't make good. But he stayed and stayed, years passed, and finally one day, I don't know why, he came back for a visit. And his classic remark to the home folks was that he would rather have a leaning-place against a lamppost in New York than any two-hundred-acre farm they could give him.

Apparently there are some seven million people who can understand that, but I can't. And I'm not crazy about farms, either. No, New York is not for me. Someday, I am sure, the whole business is going to come tumbling down over all those seven million.

August 14, 1935

THE STUNNING VARIETY OF LONG ISLAND

ORIENT POINT, LONG ISLAND—Sitting on the pier at Orient Point, waiting for the ferry to New London. Two hours to wait. Who ever heard of Orient Point? I'll bet not a soul in Florence, Arizona, knows that such a place exists. Or vice versa.

How obscure some places can be, and how contented and peaceful. It's quiet here. Hardly anybody in sight. Two or three kids fishing out at the end of the pier. A breeze blows softly, but the water is silent and flat. A mile or two out you see some islands, and beyond them the Atlantic.

Way out here on the tip of Long Island. Who would have thought five years ago that on a sunny July afternoon I would wind up at Orient Point, sitting on a dock? Who would have thought, or cared?

*

And what brought me to Orient Point? Well, for a long time I have wondered what Long Island was like, wondered what lay beyond Garden City and Mineola—desert, forest, swamp, or long, cold tableland? Now I know. It is all these things. It's a hundred and forty miles from New York City to the tip of Long Island. For the first two hours it is all city, all part of New York. Then there are short open spaces, and then longer spaces, and then small towns.

What towns! I wouldn't be caught dead in one of them. New Yorkers needn't go more than thirty miles from Broadway to find the crossroads of Kansas, only worse. Maybe they make the towns this way just to set off the big estates. For between the towns are the homes of the rich, which are well-shielded from the eyes of vulgar folks like me.

All you get is a beautifully barbered hedge fence, ten feet high and a mile long, that you couldn't see through with an X-ray machine. In the center is a great entrance gate, with a graveled drive curving away behind a grove of high shrubbery and flowers. Just occasionally you get a haunting glimpse of a turret or a roof corner, far back from the road, among the trees.

Long Island really is lovely there on the north shore. I believe there are more trees along the roads in Long Island and Connecticut than anywhere else in America. Trees absolutely arch the roadway. And the roads are winding, up and down, as they should be. This is a garden spot. It is country for people to live in, and not be bothered with work.

The middle of Long Island is not so good. The country changes, becomes flat, and the rich splendor vanishes. Colorless middle-classness sets in. It is a land of small farms. We drove across the center of the island at dusk, from the north shore to the south. I have never been more lonesome in my life. You have a lost feeling. You can't even find a place where you want to eat, or stay all night.

Going east again, two thirds across, you come once more into pleasant territory. Flat, but green and with real trees, and prosperous-looking farms, and, believe it or not, Long Island ducks. Yes, those famous Long Island ducks actually come from Long Island. We saw thousands and thousands of them, sitting in the sun, fields of white ducks, like clover.

And then, on toward the far point, you are in the sand-dune country. The island narrows to a strip. You can see across it. The dunes lift and fall, and they are covered partly with a sort of green sagebrush.

And then finally to Montauk Point, where you stand on the rise by the lighthouse and look at the last tip of America below you, and on out toward Europe. Montauk Point is Carl Fisher's folly. It is a ghost town. The man who built the Indianapolis Speedway and who made Miami Beach had an idea about Montauk Point, but it didn't work.

You see a huge castle of a hotel on a knoll, and a country club, and a fine church, and a big police station—and there's hardly anybody around to go into them. I'm sorry Montauk Point didn't "develop." It's grand out there. I don't know why it didn't go. . . .

*

Back to East Hampton. North to Sag Harbor, a lovely village. Short ferry to Shelter Island. This is the spot for me. It's grassy and full of trees, and the houses are all low, shingled on the sides, covered with vines and flowers. It's all New Englandish, and quiet, like a fishing village without fish. . . .

And from Shelter Island on over, just a few miles, to Orient Point, the northeast tip of Long Island. . . .

July 6, 1936

WALTER'S SOFT AND SOULFUL TONES

ALBANY, NEW YORK—We were sitting in the hotel room last night when all of a sudden the whole town seemed filled with "Home on the Range," coming from nowhere.

We looked under the beds and in the bathroom and out the window, and finally decided it was coming from the top of the City Hall tower. It was "Home on the Range" on bells.

Now I've always hated music that came from bells in tall spires. Because it was always a mournful hymn or something far too classical for my hotcha tastes. But when you hear bells playing "Home on the Range," that's different. So today I tracked down the heretic. His name is Floyd Walter, and I found him at the Elks Club, having a midafternoon loaf. He is a big fellow with a short pompadour, and is as affable as his music.

"What makes you play human on a carillon?" I asked. "Never heard of such a thing."

Two years ago he went to a convention of carillon players. When the players discussed programs, they all talked about Beethoven and hymns. And then Walter jumped up. "I don't know who is paying you fellows," he told them. "But I know who's paying me—the taxpayers. And if the taxpayers of Albany want 'Lazy Bones,' that's what they're going to have."

*

The Albany carillon was installed in 1928. It's the first carillon in America that actually belongs to the people. It cost sixty thousand dollars and was bought entirely by public subscription. The city operates it.

The huge steeple spire on the City Hall was already in place, but they had to reinforce it to hold the huge carillon bells when they arrived from England. There are forty-eight of them, all shaped like cowbells. The biggest weighs seven tons and is taller than I am. The smallest is forty-five pounds, and isn't much bigger than the old school hand bell. Each is hung rigidly from a steel crossbeam in the tower, a hundred and fifty feet above the street. The carillonneur's room is right beneath the bells. You get there by going up circular dungeonlike stone stairs until you're all out of breath. The room is small and very hot in summer.

Carillon-playing is hard work. These hot summer nights, Walter strips down to his underwear and locks the door.

The keyboard is something like an old-fashioned organ, except the keys aren't keys; they're wooden handles on the ends of levers, three or four inches apart. You push down about an inch to ring a bell. Down below are two long rows of foot pedals. These are duplicates of the hand keys, because in a fast piece two hands aren't enough. The apparatus is mechanical, not electrical. When the player hits a key, it pulls a rod that runs up through the ceiling and whacks the clapper against the bell.

It's fun to watch the carillonneur play. He wears leather gloves, with the outsides of the little fingers heavily padded, for when playing fast, he just pounds the sticks with the outside of his fist.

I wish you could see Floyd Walter play. There he sits with a cigar stub gripped in his teeth, his face rigid, sweat rolling out, his hands fighting bees, his feet stomping out fire, his whole body jouncing as though in a fit, and the wooden sticks rattling so you can hardly hear the bells above. It's a funny contrast to the soft and soulful tones you hear half a mile away.

Walter played two pieces, ran a few scales, then told me to give it a few bongs myself, just to see how it felt. It felt powerful, and very soft. People in the street probably thought the carillon had gone crazy. . . .

Walter plays on all holidays and Sundays. Whenever a prominent Albany citizen dies, he plays something sad and full of feeling. Then two evenings a week he gives a forty-five-minute concert of popular music. People sit in the parks and sing with the bells. . . .

August 25, 1938

CONNECTICUT

Time Is the Loser

HARTFORD, CONNECTICUT—You drive slowly along the roads in Connecticut. You drive slowly because you're watching for something. You're looking for black-and-white signs on the fronts of houses. Every house in Connecticut a hundred years old or older is marked. You can drive all over the state, and get further and further back into time with the houses, until you've marched back to 1640, and there you stop.

Connecticut is three hundred years old this year. The houses are marked as part of the tercentenary celebration. The first colony in what is now Connecticut was founded at Wethersfield, on the south side of Hartford, in 1635. No houses of that first group are still standing, but it was only five years later that Lieutenant Walter Fyler built one to stay.

And there it stands today, on the north edge of Hartford, back about fifty feet from the highway, all surrounded by cherry trees and flowers and bushes and a picket fence, looking so old and humble. It is right down to the ground, has just one story, and is a dark, weather-beaten brown, needing paint, but not at all shoddy. People are living in it, and the doors are open, and it looks very inviting.

*

These old houses are not at all infrequent, and they don't look as old as they are. They've been painted, of course, and a lot of them have been remodeled. But the insides are still there, and so is the early-day comfort and roominess, and the character that even a house can acquire from slow and thoughtful and sometimes harsh living.

Go inside, and look at the wide, worn boards in the floor, or the queer low doors, with their long hinges and heavy locks, or the deep fireplaces. Or find yourself one of the secret staircases so many of them had, or go up into the attic and look at the joists and beams, so uneven and ax-marked and old. Then you won't doubt these houses have seen things we have never known.

*

It seems right that they should be in Connecticut, for it is certainly a charming state. I know of no lovelier country than that soft, sweeping woodsy land between Long Island Sound and Hartford.

It is not spectacular country. But it's a little more than gently rolling, so that you get a long view when you top a rise, and it is so green and mapled and shaded and quiet—you get a feeling that the country has character, like a person.

You can think of yourself as having sat down under a tree in Connecticut three hundred years ago and still be sitting there, growing mellow with the land, and you the winner and time the loser, because time had to pass on and you're still there in Connecticut. That's the way it makes you feel, anyhow—sort of ageless.

August 16, 1935

F. E. INGALS AND HIS FIRE DEPARTMENT

GUILFORD, CONNECTICUT—You've read about men who are nuts about going to fires, and even have gong systems in their homes so they won't miss an alarm. Well, those birds are just sissies. They don't even know what a real fire hobby is. Listen to this.

F. E. Ingals owns two fire engines and a chief's car and a station house and the equipment that goes with it. There's no catch to it. He actually owns them privately. His personal fire department is better than Guilford's municipal fire department. There isn't a pumper as big as his within miles and miles of here. He answers all Guilford calls, and he personally attends to a lot of grass fires himself.

*

When Mr. Ingals was about ten, he was in a hotel fire at a lake resort in Wisconsin. His nurse rescued him. That put the fire fever in him. It's been forty-five years now, but that hotel fire today seems to be the most prominent thing in his mind.

Mr. Ingals had an aunt who owned land on the north shore of Long Island Sound. So he came over here from Wisconsin, years ago, to help her with the property. She's dead now, and he owns the property. It's twenty-four acres, right on the waterfront, and at high tide it is surrounded by shallow water. He calls it Chaffinch Island.

It wasn't until 1925, when Mr. Ingals was forty-five, that he really began to indulge his fire-engine hobby. It started in a small enough way. He just rigged up an old Ford truck as a sort of fire wagon. His island was three miles from town and he wanted protection. Since then he has had six or seven trucks, always getting better ones. Finally he came to do nothing but work around his fire trucks. He has never had a fire at home.

He has a station house right beside his home. The two big engines and his chief's car are lined up, just as in a real station, ready to go. He keeps the place heated in winter, so they'll start quickly. His trucks are as modern, as red, and as shiny as any fire engine in a kid's dream. And each one has a hundred and fifty dollars' worth of gold-leaf lettering on it.

Mr. Ingals drives one truck himself, and hires a man to drive the other. He never gets to take his chief's car to a fire, because he has to drive the truck. Over the front of his station he has painted CHAFFINCH ISLAND FIRE DEPARTMENT. He has bells and sirens all over the place. He gets a call as soon as they do in Guilford.

As soon as he gets to a fire, nine men from the city fire department jump on his two trucks and start to work. He is the backbone of the fire force, because his trucks are the biggest and best. The city pays him nothing. He isn't even a member of the department.

*

He goes to about sixty fires a year. He has missed only three in ten years. He has never been hurt fighting a fire. Two people have burned to death in fires he helped fight; both were tramps, sleeping in old houses, probably drunk.

About half the fire alarms come at night. It takes Mr. Ingals about four minutes to get up and under way. He keeps his firefighter's clothes right by the bed, but sometimes the woman who comes in to clean takes the pants out of the boots and mislays things, and he gets tangled up trying to hurry.

Mr. Ingals says he has about fifteen thousand dollars invested in his trucks, but I think he was holding the figure down so as not to seem silly. It looks to me like the figure is nearer thirty thousand dollars. He isn't rich, but he has an income from stocks, and doesn't have to worry about a living. He puts practically all his income into keeping up his fire engines.

"People think I'm either a millionaire or crazy," he said. "But that's my hobby, and I get pleasure out of it, and I can't take any money with me when I die, so why shouldn't I spend it this way? Some men spend their money on fast women, and some on golf, and they don't have a thing to show for it. I've got something to show for mine. But I told the fire-engine people these were my last trucks. They'll last me ten years, and then I'll be sixty-five, and I won't be going to fires anymore. I'll be retired."

*

Mr. Ingals lives alone. He has never married. The cleaning woman comes in twice a week, but he does his own cooking. "It isn't very good," he says, "but I can eat it." He wears dirty overalls and a blue shirt, and has fireman's badges on his galluses. When I drove up I thought he must be the man who worked for Mr. Ingals, but he turned out to be Mr. Ingals himself. He is a 1908 electrical-engineering graduate of the University of Wisconsin.

He has a big tan bulldog named Duke, and Duke is getting old and stiff. Duke is a nut on fires, too. He rides the engines on every alarm. He used to have a special seat, but now he just rides up with the driver. He has his name on a fireman's badge clamped to his harness. Duke won't go to very many more fires.

Mr. Ingals gets quite a bit of mail from people who have heard of his hobby. Once a fellow wrote for his autograph, saying he already had an autograph of President Roosevelt. He got a letter from a fire chief in Germany, and he's had several from California.

I asked him if he knew of anybody else who owned a private fire department. He said yes, a woman up in Rhode Island, called Chief Nancy. He heard about her and wrote to her. She sent back a nice letter. Mr. Ingals says you could tell from her letter she knows her stuff, but she has only one fire engine.

Mr. Ingals goes to state fire conventions once in a while, and down to New Haven, where he knows all the fire captains, but not often. "I don't travel around much," he said. "I can't leave. There might be a call at any time, and I've got to be here."

July 9, 1936

MASSACHUSETTS

WILLIAMSTOWN, MASSACHUSETTS— . . . New England this fall has made an encroachment into our souls. The West still remains first on my list of good places to be, but New England has at least lifted itself out of the category of places I hate.

New England and I have had a long tussle. My first venture

into these parts years ago turned my head elsewhere. I did not like the rock-ribbed Northeast, nor anybody in it. Nor on the second trip was my heart melted from granite into butter.

But this time a softening process *has* taken place—nothing very definite, but I can feel a twinge of appreciation. There may yet be harmony—even love, who knows—between New England and me.

For one thing, I've found that New Englanders aren't all grim and cold. There has not been one instance this fall of anybody being even a shade less friendly than in the West. And the land itself seemed more mellow this time. Among the hills and farms and neat little towns, there is an air of composure that is good for the heart.

Possibly I like it because the abandon of youth has left me, and I am easy prey to the sense of good solid security in the New England scene. Or possibly it is nothing more than my fleeting ardor for a green hillside and white barn.

But whatever, I must come someday and roam New England with greater leisure, and really know the things that now I am only beginning to sense, as you might sense the odor of fresh earth after the thaw, too young yet to know that it portends spring.

*

In no large area of this country do you find as few shabby houses as in New England. In the towns and in the country, homes are a glistening white, set with green shutters.

On a farm, the house and barn and miscellaneous outsheds are all connected. They form one immense sprawling building— rambling, white, and full of character. . . .

October 1, 1938

MORNING OF A CAPE COD FISHERMAN
PROVINCETOWN, MASSACHUSETTS—When Joe Oliver knocked on the door at four o'clock in the morning, there was thunder all around the sky.

The faraway sheet lightning gave an ominous feeling to the Cape Cod night. It would soon rain, and I wondered if we would go. And then I realized that a commercial fisherman always goes, so I stumbled darkly into my sweaters and overalls and picked my way downstairs to the kitchen.

Mrs. Oliver had coffee and rolls ready for us, and then she said good night and went back to bed. "I hate to eat this time of day," Joe said. "Every morning I can hardly get these damn rolls down my throat."

Joe Oliver is Portuguese, as most Cape Cod fishermen are. Joe's grandfather came from the Azores. His father was drowned just off Race Point here, before Joe was born.

Joe is still a young man, but he has been fishing for twenty years. He is the perfect example of how times have changed. He is proof that you can be a fisherman without looking and acting like a Cape Cod cartoon.

Like every fisherman I've known, he says it's a dog's life. But also like every other fisherman, he says it's the best life, because you're independent. You can walk down the street and tell anybody to go to hell.

*

When we walked into the net shed down on the dock, the gloomy light bulb shone on four men in overalls lying on heaps of net, all asleep. They opened their eyes, and said nothing, and shut them again. The place smelled of fish. "You'd better have some boots," Joe said.

We sat for about ten minutes, Joe and I talking low, because the others were asleep. Finally Joe looked at the sky and said, "I guess we'll go now." He hadn't raised his voice, but the others got up and put on their boots. Nobody said anything.

We took four oars and tramped across the sand into the water. A little light was in the sky, but I could hardly see where we were stepping. We rowed about a quarter of a mile, anchored, transferred to a gas-powered boat, and headed out to sea. Lightning was still playing on the gray horizon. Joe steered, and the four men went about stowing canvas, moving booms, laying out line. Nobody said anything at all. They were finished before we got to the traps.

A Cape Cod fish trap is round, and about sixty feet across. It is made by driving long heavy poles into the ocean bottom and then hanging net around the circle. The net forms a wall and a bottom. It lies on the ocean floor, even when it's forty-five feet deep.

Between two of the poles is an opening. The boat eases through, right into the trap. The men grab ropes on pulleys and pull the net gate up behind us, trapping the fish inside.

Now the engine is shut off; all five men line up on one side of the boat and begin pulling the net up. As the last few feet of

net approaches the surface, you see thousands of things swimming and darting under the water. You look sharply, to see if
there's anything big or exciting. It's like opening a surprise
package.

They get the fish aboard with a hooped net, hauled up by a
line over a winch. The fish are dumped into the bottom of the
open hold. One man stands down there sorting out the hideous
goosefish and other unsalable ones. They pile up around his
boots until he is nearly hip-deep in fish. They wiggle for a few
seconds and then lie still.

We were probably twenty minutes emptying each of Joe's
three traps. It rained and it poured. "Goddammit," Joe said. It
was rough, and I had to hold on to the cabin railing to keep from
falling off. The rain went right through my sweaters.

It finally got light, but the sun never came up. Just the rain
and wind. "This is a hell of a morning," Joe said. And then: "I'm
afraid we're not going to get any tuna."

Tuna—those big fighting fish, sometimes weighing a thousand pounds. They have to gaff them with a hook, and then
rassle them aboard. There isn't a fisherman in Provincetown, I
suppose, who hasn't been pulled overboard into the net while
rassling a tuna.

There had been tuna in the traps the day before. "But I knew
damn well there wouldn't be any today when I wanted to show
you," Joe said. He was disgusted. . . .

*

After the last trip we headed back toward Provincetown.
They threw overboard the dogfish and big flounders. The gulls
swarmed and squawked around us till we could hardly hear. At
the dock it took us nearly an hour to unload.

The four fishermen talked to me while they were unloading.
Every one of them was pleasant and polite. Even a fisherman
can't see any sense in talking before daylight. By nine o'clock we
were back home in bed, the day's work done.

September 8, 1938

PROVINCETOWN, MASSACHUSETTS— . . . They still have a town crier
here. The city has never been without one. I may be wrong
about this, but I believe he's the only one left in America. He
cries out a little news, and advertises places that pay him.

The old crier, who died four years ago, always went around

in overalls. But the new one wears sort of a Miles Standish uniform. The locals don't like the idea, but it impresses tourists. . . .

September 9, 1938

BOSTON— . . . Boston is famous for being the easiest city in America to get lost in. The streets are so twisty and cut up that you can make one turn, suddenly find the afternoon sun in the east, and swear that somebody must have pushed you. . . .

I pulled up to a corner to ask the way to Cambridge. (I wasn't lost, just slightly confused.) The policeman said I'd have to turn right. Because I was already halfway across the street, I asked if I could back up, then turn. The policeman was gruff, but no typical cop language came from his lips. What he said was exactly as follows, so help me:

"Reverse promptly. I wish to use the street." . . .

September 16, 1938

MAINE

LINCOLN, MAINE—Just before we got in here there came such a cloudburst over Maine that we couldn't see the road, and had to feel our way over to the side and stop. Only twice before has that happened to me.

This town is just a little place, and its hotel isn't even listed in the big AAA guide. The hotel is sort of old-fashioned, but it's clean as a pin and has an excellent dining room.

When I mentioned casually to one of the clerks that I believed I'd write and ask the AAA to put it in the book, he said the owner didn't like publicity and won't even put up a road sign outside of town. He just likes the old, old customers who have been coming here for years. I think that's wonderful. Also, it's Maine.

September 24, 1938

AT THE CENTER OF A WHIRLWIND
EASTPORT, MAINE—This is the easternmost city in the United States. It is very old, quaint, a sea town that smells rankly of sardines.

Eastport is about to become a boom town. By that I mean boom towns like the West used to have in the wild gold-and-oil days. It seems out of place in rock-ribbed New England, but here it comes, anyway. The great Passamaquoddy dam project is the reason. The project is less than two months old, yet already it is impossible to get a room in Eastport. Restaurants are crowded; so are the aged and narrow streets. The boomers are flocking in on every train. The daily train carries twice as many coaches as it used to. Freight cars have tripled.

Soon new restaurants, new boardinghouses, new stores will spring up. Prices will skyrocket. The slick-tongued city fellows will arrive to take the boys with cash in their pockets for a ride. It's always thus in boom towns. New England has always done a stern and tight-lipped job of repelling its invaders, but I doubt that it can cope with the gentry who follow the gold, and the oil, and, in recent years, the big dams.

Maine is loosening up on gambling. Just a few days ago mutuel betting was started on the sulky races at the Skowhegan fair. Whether Maine will permit Eastport to become another Las Vegas, with forty gambling casinos and forty saloons, I don't know. But if it does, what a shock New England is going to get.

Eastport is small, about four thousand. It has one main street, about three blocks long. The street, wide enough for a sea town, is now a congested *mess*. The sidewalks stand a couple of feet above the old asphalt pavement. On one side of Main Street, the town rises sharply up a hill. On the other side, with one row of buildings between, is Passamaquoddy Bay. The stores that front on this side of the street hang out over the water's edge.

It is in one of these buildings, an old warehouse, that the Army has established administrative headquarters for the Quoddy project. Tied up at the rear of the building is a large ship, the *Sea Hawk*, on which all the Army men are living until Quoddy Village is finished and they can get their families here.

Right out in the Bay of Fundy, just a few hundred yards, is what is said to be the greatest whirlpool in the world, caused by Fundy's swirling tides. Sometimes the core of the whirlpool is thirty feet deep. In 1919 a schooner and all its crew were swallowed up right there, within throwing distance of the wharf.

Eastport itself is starting to doll up for its onrushing prosperity. The day we were there they were painting diagonal white lines on the main street for parking, the first such intrusion that decrepit old asphalt had ever felt.

*

Colonel Philip Fleming, the officer in charge of everything at Passamaquoddy—medium-sized, tanned veteran of a thousand lesser-scale water-building projects, dressed in work uniform—walks proudly through the fresh loam of sprouting Quoddy Village.

He stands by a stake where a house will be, and points out over a neck of water, and beyond that to the spruce-covered hills, and asks if you ever saw such a spot for a home. He gives an order here and there to a foreman he has never seen before, then jumps into his car and hurries back to his desk and papers.

Captain Roy Lord, second in command, youthful, pleasant, serious, wears dark pants and a green sweater, and can do a hundred things at once. His job ranges from picking out colonial lighting fixtures for the village houses to organizing and directing the ten thousand men who will build the Quoddy dams. He is neither fussed nor officious. At Quoddy you get none of the Army's infamous red tape or runaround.

There is pride in both these men's eyes, and although they are merely putting into effect a lifetime of training, they are aglow with the drama of the thing, its bigness, its romance, its challenge. I think they are pleased to hear you gasp when you're told a city will be created in forty-five days, the whole dam project in two-and-a-half years. . . .

August 26, 1935

POSTSCRIPT: *President Roosevelt canceled the Quoddy project eleven months later in the face of Congressional charges of waste and scandal. Eastport-area residents were shocked. "The sudden cutting off of funds leaves them high and dry, in debt and gloomy toward the future," reported the* New York Times. *"They hope the visit of President Roosevelt to his summer home in Campobello Island, N.B., about a mile from the scene of dying construction operations, will mean a revival of 'Quoddy.'" It didn't. Construction work stopped in 1937.*

NEW ENGLAND IS WONDERFUL
CALAIS, MAINE—The Atlantic Coast from New York to Portland is an abomination and a curse. It is neither beautiful nor placid, nor is there any enchantment in it. It is one long, hideous summer resort for four hundred miles, with millions of unhappy-

looking people running in and out of hot-dog stands in their
bathrobes.

This coast is typified by the Boston Post Road. You can drive
a hundred miles east of New York on this road, and never reach
the country. It is continuously town or suburb, or eating places,
or rows of signs and filling stations. It is a nightmare of roaring
trucks and careening cars. It is an incinerator of burned-gasoline
fumes. Driving on the Boston Post Road is, I imagine, like
driving in the Indianapolis 500 with a hangover.

*

But when you get thirty miles inland anywhere from the
coast, or when you can pick an authentic old shipping town out
from among the summer cabins, then New England is wonderful.

One thing that gives me a feeling of harmony with it is its
sleepiness. All the dashing about is done by the "foreigners"
who come in from New York and elsewhere.

Vermont frightens me. The people who live there like it, and
it is beautiful in a colossal sort of way. But in Vermont I can
think only of the bitter winters, and the rocky hillsides, and the
barrenness, and of people forever being beaten by nature, and
of the ominous wind and the hurrying snow clouds on a gray
November afternoon, and of Calvin Coolidge, lying up there so
alone amidst the bleak hills.

*

South-central New Hampshire is the neatest and seemingly
the most prosperous area of New England. The frequent farmhouses literally sparkle in the sun. Just an hour ago they must
have finished painting every one of them a glistening white, and
all with bright green shutters. The fences are new, the lawns are
mowed, flowers are everywhere, and people look happy.

In New Hampshire you see signs all along advertising TONIC
5¢, and after wondering for a long time what it is, you stop and
buy some, and it turns out to be Moxie, something like Coca-
Cola.

In New Hampshire and Maine the houses and barns and all
the tool sheds are built together, all under one roof. In all the
old sea towns up the New England coast, there is always a
Middle Street and a Pleasant Street.

I had heard that all New Englanders say "down east" when
they mean "up north." They do say it, but the only explanation
they can give is that it *is* down east. What do you say to that?

*

And here we are in Calais—pronounced *callous*—Maine, ready to cross the bridge into Canada and more new worlds.

August 27, 1935

ew
eal
Washington
ctober-
ovember 1935

"The New Deal, it is true, has brought a new alertness to Washington, and people with responsibility on their faces do rush about, but they seem to rush sort of slowly, in tune with the character of the city."

WASHINGTON—Six thousand miles behind us, and the white glow in the night of the Capitol dome ahead.

Six thousand miles of Canada and the United States, without getting lost by as much as a block. And here, within eight miles of the White House, we go through a place called Merryfield, Virginia, which we have never heard of before, and have to stop and ask the way.

It is an hour after dark. How I hate to drive at night. All day long I can sit behind the wheel and bat the roads hour after hour, good roads or bad, but when dusk comes I am through. This last hour, coming into Washington in the exasperating half-light of dusk, and then the real darkness, is harrowing. . . .

October 1, 1935

> *Though he had lived in Washington virtually all his adult life, Pyle wasn't exaggerating when he wrote, "Big things are going on here, but I don't know what they are." Much had changed during the three years he had served as managing editor of the* Washington Daily News, *and, deskbound, he had had almost no firsthand experience of New Deal Washington. To keep the column's daily installments up while he took a break after his first journey as a travel columnist, Pyle explored his adopted city as it was three years into the Roosevelt Revolution.*

AN EASY ENCHANTMENT

WASHINGTON—It was in the soft, warm spring of 1923 that I first saw Washington.

My lot was that of a cub reporter, and the editor had compassionately invited me to stay at his hotel until I found a place to live. We were walking to work that first morning, walking with the world ahead of me, walking through McPherson Square, so green and pretty, with people sitting leisurely on the benches even as early as seven o'clock, and the editor said to me:

"You'll probably like Washington. But let me warn you. Don't stay here too long. It's a nice, easygoing city, and people get in a rut, and if you stay till you get to liking it too well, you'll never leave. You'll settle down to a pleasant routine and never amount to anything."

I was too young to ask why it was necessary to amount to something .f you could be happy without it. I didn't think of that, and the editor's words impressed me very much, so much so that I have never forgotten them for a minute.

So for a dozen years I have been heeding the editor's advice and getting out of Washington. But somehow or other I always keep coming back. Maybe it's the city that pulls me back, or maybe it's some stubborn part of me that doesn't want to amount to anything. Anyhow, here I am again.

*

The Washington of today is a very different place from the Washington of that morning a dozen years ago—different in appearance, that is. But the character of the place seems to change hardly at all, and there is still the same easy enchantment in the streets and the trees.

A few weeks ago I wrote a piece about the three North American cities with character—San Francisco, New Orleans, and Quebec. Somehow I forgot about Washington. It has character, too. Washington, as people so truthfully say, is really a big city that has achieved a small-town character. It has running water and electric lights without the sewing-circle gossip. It has the personal liberty of that most cosmopolitan of cities, New York, without its cruelty and lonesomeness.

The business section of many a smaller Midwestern city would put Washington's to shame. And yet you see more handsome men, more beautiful women, better-dressed people in general here than in any other city I know.

I have often wondered how Washington has achieved that ideal—the appearance and niceties of a small town, while retaining the best features, as the ads say, of the big city. My own guess is that Washington, on the edge of the real South, naturally has some of the South's delightful slothfulness. A good percentage of the population came here from somewhere else, many of them from small towns. Physically, Washington is broad and smooth, its parks are big and frequent, its streets wide and its buildings low, and the result is spaciousness. Many of its people live in apartment houses; hence the city doesn't spread all over the Eastern Seaboard. A good part of its population is in comfortable circumstances, so that the pinched look and the anxious stare and the goad of hurry, hurry, hurry settles but seldom on the citizens of Washington. The whole thing, summed up, makes for easy living.

The New Deal, it is true, has brought a new alertness to Washington, and people with responsibility on their faces do rush about, but they seem to rush sort of slowly, in tune with the character of the city. And if they stay they'll slow down even further, and eventually not amount to anything at all. I think it's a rather nice prospect.

October 2, 1935

BIG THINGS ARE GOING ON

WASHINGTON—All day long I have been sightseeing, as it were. No, I didn't go up in the Monument, or to Mount Vernon, or to Arlington Cemetery. I was sightseeing in the new Washington, the new boom-time, good-time, hustle-bustle, rattle-clatter Washington—the New Deal Washington.

Big things are going on here, but I don't know what they are. I have seen a lot of things today—thousands of people bending over reports, great buildings filled with row after row of desks, offices crammed into private homes and theaters and old factories; and men and women working and thinking, working and thinking—and here I am in the evening, very tired, looking out my window at the city, and my head hurts and I don't know what to make of it all.

Out all over the country the people with a little money are complaining because the government is spending so much on the people who have no money. Out over the country the people with no money are complaining because the government doesn't give them more work.

Here in Washington so many people are at work planning projects for the other people to work on that they can't even find room for their desks. And still the people out in the country want more to work on, and the people with money don't want the money spent. My head hurts and I think it's time for another aspirin.

*

Twelve years ago, government here was concentrated in a score or so buildings. Today government is scattered all over Washington, and overflowing into corridors and almost onto streets.

On my walk today, I dropped into the Washington Auditorium. It is a great, ugly barnlike structure, a block square, designed without taste but built amidst beauty in downtown Washington. It has held an awful lot of people at a lot of affairs. You wouldn't know the auditorium now.

Take, for instance, that seat on the right-hand aisle in row six of the orchestra, where I sat and heard Paul Robeson sing; the seat from where I listened to Clarence Darrow and old Senator Stanley of Kentucky debate prohibition, the seat I occupied the night Amelia Earhart told of her flight across the Atlantic, and Trubee Davison of his wild-animal trip to Africa. Do you know where that seat is now? I don't either, but where it stood is the cubbyhole office where Mr. Spinko, a minor executive of WPA [the Works Progress Administration], sits talking into a Dictaphone. And all over that vast sweep of floor, where once stood tier upon tier of seats, there are now little offices, partitioned off with gray wallboarding, and filled with people.

And over there in the left-hand box, second from the front, where I sat one night as a guest at one of Elder Michaux's whoop-'em-up revival meetings, there is a little desk, and a girl sitting at it, staring, tapping her pencil and thinking, apparently.

And up in the balcony, where I sat one night wishing for a pair of field glasses so I could see, as well as hear, the ape men known as "rasslers" do their grunting, even up there they've taken out seats and put in partitions and built offices up the incline.

And down on the stage—that same stage where I sat one noon as part of a reception committee for Wiley Post and Harold Gatty—on that stage where Wiley got up and stammered and stuttered so helplessly into the microphone that the crowd almost tore the house down, they liked him so much—on that stage there are about two dozen desks, and more typewriters and tables and Dictaphones.

And down in the basement, where I used to go yearly to write pieces about the new models in the auto show, down there the people are crammed and packed in like sardines, and mimeographing machines are clanking, and people are running here and there.

And back in the wings among the big light switches, and up in the stars' dressing rooms, and out in the lobby, and even right in the doorway, so that you can hardly get in, are desks, desks, desks, until you wonder how there can be enough problems for all these people to think about.

But there must be enough and more, too, for this is the headquarters of WPA, the organization that directs the spending of most of that almost-five-billion-dollar fund for work relief, and they can't turn out projects fast enough to give work to all the poor people who have no work. But they're sure making the dust fly trying, anyhow.

October 3, 1935

When the Great Depression started in 1929, American farmers had already endured a decade of depressed prices following World War I. Now farmers were beset by new problems—drought and erosion. When the Roosevelt administration came to power in 1932, it immediately sought relief for the nation's farmers. The Resettlement Administration was one such effort. Its head, Rexford Guy Tugwell, was a former Columbia University agricultural expert, one of the original "brain trust" Roosevelt assembled to advise him and help formulate New Deal policy. Tugwell's leading-man good looks once earned him the dubious distinction of being named the handsomest New Dealer by readers of one Washington newspaper.

WARDING OFF A GREAT AMERICAN DESERT

WASHINGTON— . . . The Resettlement Administration is one of the newest, as well as one of the biggest, of the New Deal agencies. It has more than twelve thousand employees, forty-five hundred of them here in Washington. It was started last June and ends next July, unless Congress extends it.

Rex Tugwell is in charge, and is giving his full time to it. The thing is so octopuslike it's hard to understand, and even harder to organize, as the administrators have well learned. But it's all based on a theory, and if you know the theory, you can grasp more easily what the Resettlement Administration is.

The theory is that farmers, ever since we can remember, have simply gone out and farmed their land. In doing so, they wore it out, then moved on to new lands. But in this country there isn't much new land left for them to move to. Their method of crop rotation (or lack of it), coupled with grazing, has exhausted the land, denuded it, and now it is blowing away.

They say that in twenty years our farmland is going to be pretty well shot unless something is done, and that in seventy-five years even a self-respecting cactus wouldn't be seen on most of it.

So, the Resettlement Administration was formed to do something about this land, and, more immediately, something about the people going hungry on it.

The Resettlement Administration has two hundred and sixty-one million dollars to work with for a year. They'll use a hundred and eighty million of this to help half a million farmers right where they are. In other words, it's a form of relief. They keep them on their farms, give them some help, and try to get them back on their feet.

There are a million farm families on relief. Resettlement has already taken over five hundred and fifty thousand of them. The others are to be taken care of on Works Progress projects. In addition, fifty thousand farm families will be moved this year by Resettlement. There isn't any mass movement from one place to another. No covered-wagon caravans or long freight trains full of furniture. Usually they'll just be moved from a poor farm to a better one nearby, and the government will help them get started again, through loans and so on.

Resettlement will spend forty million dollars buying ten million acres of no-good land. Some of this will be made into parks. Some will be reforested. Some of it the farmers will remain on, trying to build it back up. The farmer who sells can either buy a new farm somewhere and move, or he can take his money and go get drunk. That's up to him.

The WPA will spend another forty million in putting this land back in shape, either as farmland or as forested parkland—anything to keep it from blowing away. Most of this land is being bought in the so-called Dust Belt of the far Midwest, and in the cotton-raising South. That's where most of the moving of the fifty thousand is taking place, too. . . .

Resettlement doesn't plan to depopulate any vast areas. It isn't as spectacular as that. But they feel that if the program of shifting from bad land to better could be continued for twenty years, with the proper reforestation and the right kind of farming, and good fertilizing, all the bad land could be built back up again, and the bugaboo of a Great American Desert seventy-five years hence thoroughly scotched.

October 16, 1935

THERE'S PURE BEAUTY UP THERE

WASHINGTON—People in the East are going wild over the Skyline Drive. In its first year, a hundred and fifty thousand cars have been over it. On Sundays this fall, it has been stop-and-go, stop-and-go, while the solid line of traffic jerked up and over the packed highway.

Skyline Drive is America's latest example of what man can do with mountains. Man can't improve on mountains, but he can help us get up there on them for the long look down.

The Skyline Drive is in central Virginia, in Shenandoah National Park. You drive about ninety miles southwest from Washington. You see the mountains coming, and your road wanders up into them. You top a ridge turn to your left, and then for thirty-two miles you sail up and down and through and around the pinnacles, thirty-two miles along the serrated ridge of the Blue Ridge chain, with the great valleys first on one side and then on the other. People will be coming from many thousands of miles away to ride the Skyline, as its fame spreads.

The highway was built by the federal government—the National Park Service and the Bureau of Public Roads. They started it under Hoover, in 1932. It will be ninety miles long when finished. The first thirty-two miles were opened about a year ago. . . .

It was all done under contract, but the CCC* boys helped out with the light work. There are eight or nine CCC camps in Shenandoah Park. Four of them are along the thirty-two miles that now constitute the real Skyline Drive. The boys build stone guardrails, trim ledges, fix overlooks so you can park and see. The camps are neat and clean, their green barracks and little gravel streets as trim as any Army camp you ever saw. The boys at work wave at you as you drive by.

*

It is getting cold up on that ridge now. The wind whines and whips the leaves, and it will be snowing soon. Autumn has touched the hillsides and passed on to use its brush on mountains further south. But there is still magnificence up there, for the brilliance of the leaves has faded ever so slightly into a gentler harmony with the distant blue haze. . . .

There is none of the sheerness on the Skyline Drive that makes the Rockies so appalling, and so harsh. There are no great flat rock walls, with drops of thousands of feet. There is no feeling of awe at mere bulk, or at prodigious upheaval. Rather there is the feeling of pure beauty, with no need for extremes of nature. There is height and depth in the view, with sloping gentleness between them, and sky and fanciful forests of color.

October 30, 1935

WASHINGTON—Although it is only one-third finished there has grown up already, in its twenty-eight years of building, a great deal of legend about the Washington Cathedral.

There is a legend, for instance, that a laborer, having worked on the cathedral for years and become infused with its spirit, sought to have his wife buried there. When he was refused, the story goes, he had her cremated, and then one day he dropped the ashes in a barrow of fresh cement, and his wife was forever entombed in the cathedral he loved.

---

*Civilian Conservation Corps, a widely praised New Deal program that gave two-and-a-half million young, unmarried men jobs planting trees, fighting forest fires, and restoring beaches, rivers, and parks, and, says historian Robert McElvaine, helped its participants "survive the Depression with some degree of self-respect."

Nobody but the man himself, if there is one, knows whether the story is true or not. Bishop James E. Freeman says no such request was ever made of him. But it might have happened before he became bishop. Cathedral officials say it could easily be true, and they think it probably is. . . .

November 8, 1935

The Midwest

"On Saturdays the little boys of North Benton, Ohio, catch snakes and hang them over the infidel Chester Bedell's headstone. On Sundays the tourists see the snakes and kneel and cry, 'Praise the Lord.'"

MICHIGAN

A BIG-TIME TOWN

DETROIT—Detroit is a dreadful city in a way. It's so big, and it's dirty and smoky with all these auto factories pouring out black clouds, and there are so many poor people here, and the streets are jammed and you have to travel so far to get anywhere.

But Detroit has something. It has a personality. You don't sense it at first, but after you're here awhile, you pick it up in people's faces, and the way they talk, and the way they act.

Detroit is a gambler. Detroit is like the old Mississippi riverboat gamblers, hungry one day, eating stuffed partridge the next, happy-go-lucky, take things as they come, often down but never out.

Detroit was one of the first, and one of the hardest-hit, victims of the Depression. The city suffered terribly. But you ought to see it today. Prosperity is definitely back. The auto plants are going full-tilt. The streetcars are crammed with workmen, lunch pails on their laps. The cocktail lounges are overflowing with rich-looking people. Theaters, many of them closed for years, are jammed to the hilt. Detroit is happy again.

*

Detroit is an emotional city, as an up-again-down-again city would have to be. It goes wild over anything. It worships prize-fighters, and symphony orchestras. It does nothing halfway. It is a great follow-the-leader town. If you're a hero out here, you're a big hero. Take Mickey Cochrane and his ball team. Right today, you could stand out in the street and yell "Hurrah for the Cubs" just once, and you'd wind up in the hospital. . . .

Detroit, the auto capital of the world, has an awful time with its autos. Everybody has a car, everybody and his brother. It's as bad as Los Angeles for old cars. And do they drive them! And do they kill people! Yes sir, right and left. The traffic toll here so far this year is two hundred and sixty-one dead.

One day last week the *Detroit News* had a ninety-six-point banner line across the front page, saying NO AUTO DEATHS FOR 48 HOURS. When the auto doesn't hit the man, that's news. . . .

*

Yes, Detroit is a big-time town, but I guess I'll be getting along most any day now. For I can't take my hard times with the good grace that Detroit does; and I can't take smoke up my nose, so much of it that you have to change handkerchiefs twice a day; and I can't take taxis that charge half a day's wages for riding you home; and I can't take these winter blasts that come cutting across Canada and the Lakes; and I don't think I'd ever learn how to make an automobile or knock a home run. So I guess I'll be getting along toward home about this evening.

November 16, 1935

CARS, BODIES, AND BEER

DETROIT—Charlie Yeager says finding people's bodies in the water doesn't give him the creeps at all, because he always figures it's going to make somebody happy.

That sounds a little left-handed somehow, thinking that finding a body would make people happy. But what Charlie means is that when he fishes a suicide out of the Detroit River, it at least eases the family's anxiety.

Charlie Yeager is Detroit's municipal diver. Only a few cities have them, and he is the only one here working for the city. He is underwater from eight forty-five till eleven-thirty, and from one to three forty-five, practically every day. He works right through the winter, too, even when they have to chop holes in the ice. He has Sundays and holidays off, so on those days he takes on private jobs, raising barges, searching for bodies, and so on.

Charlie has been diving for thirty-one years. He is fifty-one now. He says an old friend used to tell him to save his money, for a diver's active life was only about ten years. But he expects to go to sixty-five, and then retire.

Charlie is a short fellow, not fat, but heavy and strong as a bull. He has a happy face, and a gold tooth, and short iron-gray hair. He finds life on the whole pretty good.

Most of his work for the city is along the river shore, in about twenty-five feet of water, drilling in the rock bottom, setting dynamite, and blasting out holes for pier and building foundations.

It's tough work, running an electric drill underwater. Divers get hurt, too, setting off dynamite blasts. In fact, Charlie has only two fingers on his left hand. A little underwater blast off the coast of Carolina did it, many years ago. He thinks nothing of it, though.

*

Charlie spent sixteen years in the Navy as a diver. He has helped pull up submarines, and ships sunk by German U-boats. He was nearly eaten once by a shark while underwater in Panama. He has been diving for Detroit, his hometown, for nine years.

He says the Detroit River is the muddiest thing he ever saw. When he's underwater, he can't even see his hand if he crosses it in front of the glass door in his helmet. He works entirely by feel. He says he's done it so long now he could go right on being just as good a diver if he were suddenly stricken blind. . . .

*

The year before last he fished nineteen bodies out of the Detroit River—suicides and accidental drownings. He just runs onto some of them. Others he is actually down looking for. He gets a hundred dollars for finding a body, if he has taken the job of looking for it. But he says lots of times the relatives are poor people, so he doesn't let them give him anything.

He finds a lot of autos underwater, too—just stumbles onto them. People, it seems, run them off the dock, report them stolen, and collect the insurance. But you can't ever prove that they weren't stolen and driven off by a thief. Charlie found three all at once, right off the end of one pier. Lots of them are brand-new cars, and expensive ones, like Cadillacs and Duesenbergs.

There's a lot of beer on the bottom of the Detroit River. During prohibition the agents would just rip open a case and heave it into the river, without breaking the bottles. Once Charlie found an auto on the bottom, and all around were full bottles of beer. So he took the bottles and stuck them in between the wire spokes of the wheels. The photographers almost died laughing when the car was derricked up out of the water.

*

Charlie Yeager is married, but childless now. He had a fine son, twenty-one years old. He was a grand-looking boy, and quite an athlete, and he was getting to be a crack diver, too. He liked the water, and liked to be under it.

His dad sent him on a vacation trip to England a couple of years ago. On the way back he was turning a handspring on deck. He missed his footing, landed hard, and fractured his skull. They buried him at sea.

November 14, 1935

OHIO

WHERE PERRY MET THE ENEMY

PUT-IN-BAY, OHIO—Put-in-Bay is in Ohio. But it isn't where the rest of Ohio is. It's on an island, in Lake Erie. . . .

The French priest Marquette touched here in the early days of America's settlement. On one of these islands was the biggest

Civil War prison for Confederate officers. It was here that Commodore Oliver Hazard Perry defeated a British fleet in 1813, and it was from Put-in-Bay that Perry sent the message "We have met the enemy and they are ours."

There are about a dozen and a half of these islands. They are at the west end of Lake Erie, about halfway between Cleveland and Toledo. The nearest ones are but a jump from the Ohio shore, and they stretch on across the lake into Canadian waters. In fact the biggest one of all, Pelee (pronounced *Peely*), is on the Canadian side.

The smaller of the islands are mere hunks of rock, uninhabited and covered by a few stubborn trees. The larger ones are eight to ten miles long, and people have been born on them, grown old and died, almost without knowing there was a world outside.

You can stand on top of the Perry Memorial and see every island in the group, and even Canada. This memorial is three hundred and fifty-two feet high. It was built in 1913, on the hundredth anniversary of the Battle of Lake Erie. The elevator trip to the top costs twenty-five cents, and it's worth it. . . .

*

It was during the War of 1812, between the United States and the British. John Bull had six ships in Lake Erie. The United States hastily built nine ships out of green timber at Erie, Pennsylvania, and Perry was put in command. He sailed them over to Put-in-Bay. His ships were smaller than those of the British. They weren't even as big as the ferry that now runs between Put-in-Bay and the mainland.

Perry heard that the British fleet was near. So he sailed out to meet it. The battle started about ten miles north of Put-in-Bay. Perry's flagship was sunk, and he moved over to another one. The battle lasted all afternoon. Finally the British surrendered. That evening Perry sent his famous message to Washington.

A good many men were killed in the battle, including three officers on each side. The men were buried at sea. The six officers were brought ashore, and both sides joined in the funeral services. The officers were buried in what is now the shaded little park in the center of Put-in-Bay town. When the Perry Memorial was being built twenty-five years ago, they decided to dig up these bones and put them in the memorial.

There is a story around here that a couple of townsmen dug

and dug, and kept refreshing their spirits with frequent nips of the plentiful island wine. Finally, toward evening, having found nothing, they threw their shovels down, went to a butcher shop and bought some cow bones, and took them to their new resting place under the memorial.

The guide at the memorial says the story isn't true, and it sounds mighty fishy even to a confirmed liar like me. But regardless, these bones and this memorial mean a lot more than just the commemoration of a victory of a few little wooden ships over a few others.

For, ever since that victory, for a hundred and twenty-five years, there has stretched between these two countries three thousand miles of border, absolutely unfortified and unprotected, and there has never been the slightest hint of war.

July 25, 1938

PUT-IN-BAY, OHIO—Put-in-Bay is the capital, you might say, of the Lake Erie Islands. This is where the stores are; life radiates from here. It takes forty minutes on the ferry from the mainland to Put-in-Bay. You can bring your car along. There are seventeen miles of roads on this island. The harbor is circular, about a quarter of a mile across, and the town stretches all around it. A road circles the little harbor.

Put-in-Bay lives off wine and summer excursionists. It is a town in faded glory. Once it was a place of great exclusive hotels. Now it is bait for thousands of city excursionists who come for the ride and two hours of loud music.

In the morning, things are peaceful and quiet. . . .

But all this is broken by noon. The ferry brings in a few vacationists. So does the airplane. At twelve-fifteen the *Chippewa* is back from Sandusky with her load. Fifteen minutes later comes the steamer from Detroit, with hundreds and sometimes thousands of one-day excursionists. At two-fifteen comes the big *Goodtime* from Cleveland.

And then for about four hours Put-in-Bay becomes the most awful caterwauling place you've ever seen. Hundreds are picnicking from lunchboxes on the park benches. Women sit on the stack of old cannonballs to have their pictures taken. Children ride little merry-go-rounds, and cry.

Gay vacationists fall off tandem bicycles. Top-down taxis drive around and around the square, the drivers calling out their rates and sightseeing spots as they drive along. Other thousands sit in the vast, quick restaurants, eating quick lunches, drinking quick beers or quick cocktails. Orchestras blare away in some. In others, music boxes hooked to loudspeakers disgorge noise clear across the bay. The crowds dance and sing. Women dance together. So do little children. Elderly sports, a little heady with wine, cavort on the dance floor with fat partners. The waiters sing. The chef behind the hot plate sings. The cashier sways to the music.

Everything is "good old days." The songs are "Let Me Call You Sweetheart," "Beautiful Ohio," "I Want a Girl Just Like the Girl," "I'm Forever Blowing Bubbles," "Smiles."

After a couple of hours the crowds grow weary. Some stretch out on benches; some stroll toward the boat landing. The bicycles are put up. Spirits wane. Boat time comes. And suddenly, with the afternoon sun still high, Put-in-Bay slides back into silence. You can sit in the park again, and the few people you see are moving slowly, and there is peace once more.

Put-in-Bay has seen better days. Even before the turn of the century it was a place of magnificent old-fashioned hotels, of flashy teams and millionaires and statesmen. But trends changed, and the hotels went through an orgy of burning down. Today there are only a few comfortable places on the islands to stay overnight. . . .

Two other things—prohibition and the change in the younger generation—helped put the islands on the skids. Prohibition killed the main industry—grape-raising. Vineyards ran down, grew up with weeds, died from lack of attention. Since repeal they have not been fully built back up.

For no longer do the young folks want to stay. It's the same story the world over. The youngsters leave, go to school, yearn for the cities—and leave the peace and old pride of the grape islands for more exciting lives. The old folks shake their heads.

July 26, 1938

PUT-IN-BAY, OHIO—More than a thousand people live permanently on the half-dozen or so Lake Erie islands that are inhabited the year round.

Many consider it paradise. You don't have to worry about getting run over by an auto, they say, or being knocked on the head by a holdup man. Things are peaceful. Yet in this week's local paper I've just read of an auto turning over three times on a Put-in-Bay road, and of a thief who was sent off the island last winter and ordered never to come back.

Life on the Erie Islands isn't what it once was. Isolation has become only relative. The main islands are connected by telephone. They're putting in a dial system this fall. There is a telegraph cable to the mainland. There are lots of autos. Steamers and airplanes run from the mainland in a stream. Speedboats can rush you to the farthest island in less than an hour. There are schools and churches and a jail.

But regardless, there is something different about living on an island. Something that once in a while gets under your skin, like sitting in a room by yourself and brooding.

A friend of mine who loves the islands says that in daytime everything is fine. But sometimes at night, he says, when darkness comes down and all is so quiet, you get an eerie feeling and get the itch, and wish to God it was bedtime. . . .

July 17, 1938

PUT-IN-BAY, OHIO— . . . Put-in-Bay has a funny little weekly newspaper, published by the men who own the Crescent Hotel, Herman's Bar, the bicycle concession, the park benches, and a few other things. The paper is fundamentally to publicize their businesses, but they cover the news, too, and sometimes riotously.

For instance, among the personal items, you'll run onto something like this: "The captain and mate of the yacht *Sea Hag* can usually be located sleeping on Roy Webster's woodpile." Or among the ads: "Bicycles for rent. Special rates to drunks."

Some of the citizens of Put-in-Bay are afflicted with periodic bouts with demon wine. They finally wind up drying out in a mainland sanitarium. The local term for this affliction is "June-bug fever."

So, frequently in the columns of the *Gazette* you will read that "no cases of June-bug fever were reported to the Board of Health this week." Or that "So-and-So"—they actually give his name—"is eating ice-cream cones this week after a protracted case of June-bug fever." . . .

July 28, 1938

CHAMPION ICE-BREAKER OF THE GREAT LAKES
TOLEDO, OHIO—Doc Millard skippered tugboats on the Maumee River for better than thirty years. Up until six years ago he had

probably towed every cargo ship on the Great Lakes, and he knew every captain by name.

But he's a big executive now, and leads a sort of double life. When he's uptown he does civic things, and belongs to the Chamber of Commerce, and I believe he goes to Sunday school. He's an all-around leading citizen.

But get him down on the waterfront and he talks river talk. He can still outcuss any tugboater on the Maumee. He is large and hearty, with a body like a bull and legs like an athlete, and he does a lot of laughing.

He's the Toledo manager for the Great Lakes Towing Company. He thinks they made him manager because he knows so much about tugboats. That's a joke on him. They really made him manager because he knows so much about men. He's a natural-born getter-alonger with people.

Doc Millard was born in Toledo. He has never sailed on anything but tugboats. He started out to be a doctor, and went to medical school for a year. That's why they call him Doc. His real name is Ralph.

But medicine couldn't keep him. The river got him, and he wound up on tugboats. His medical education gave him one thing, though: it made him the first tugboatman on the Lakes who could cuss a man out in scientific terms.

Some say Doc Millard is the champion icebreaker of the Great Lakes. Every spring for more than a quarter of a century he has been out butting and ramming at the Maumee River ice; and every fall he plows out into the lake to pull out some tardy freighter captain who tried to stretch the season too far.

Doc says a tugboat can plow through ice three inches thick and just keep right on going. After that, you have to back off and take runs at it. I always thought that when a tugboat was breaking ice, it just crashed through as far as it could go and then tried again. But that isn't it. The bow of the tug is built so that when it hits the ice the whole tug slides up on top, and then the tug's weight crushes the ice underneath.

The Great Lakes Towing Company practically has tugging sewed up in all the Great Lakes ports. The company owns ninety tugboats, which cost a hundred thousand dollars apiece, and Doc Millard has seven under his tutelage at Toledo.

Doc's main interest in life right now is getting a big ship-mooring basin for Toledo. At present there's room for only ninety ships to be laid up here for the winter. They'd like to make room for a hundred and fifty more. That would mean that the coal stored during the winter could be moved out two weeks earlier when the ice breaks, because enough ships would be right here on hand to carry it. That would mean more business for Toledo—and, of course, more towing for Tugboat Doc.

Doc has a little office under the end of one of the bridges. When I went down to see him I thought they might have a tug going out and I could catch a trip. All the tugs were in for the day, but that didn't make any difference. Doc just trotted one out and we went for a ride anyway, just for the fun of it. The skipper was Captain Frank Wigton, and when Doc introduced us he said, "If you think I'm an old-timer, just look at this withered-up old son of a bitch. He's a hundred and eighty years old if he's a day." They are old cronies.

Captain Frank made some sly uncomplimentary remark to his boss and pulled a cord or two, and we went steaming up the Maumee, riding like millionaires. I don't know of anything that's funnier-looking outside and cozier inside than a tugboat. . . .

The river was so high our tug wouldn't clear some of the bridges, so Captain Frank would blow his whistle and they'd swing the draw up for us. It sure gives a fellow the Napoleon complex to be sitting there in the pilothouse of a little old tugboat and looking up at all the autos lined up on the bridge waiting for us to get past, and all we're doing is just taking a joyride. It's enough to make Communists out of people.

We steamed up the river a few miles, and then we turned around and came back, and they had to open all the bridges for us again. Doc and Captain Frank got to laughing and reminiscing on the way back. But Doc said, "Don't get this old son of a bitch to telling stories or we'll be here all night." Which was what I tried to do, but we got back to the dock and had to get off.

May 11, 1937

ALEXANDER McDOUGALL'S DREAM
TOLEDO, OHIO—A whaleback steamer is a beautiful thing. Most people have never seen one. Most people will never see one, for there are only four left. And it is a pity, for I know of nothing else built by man that is so nearly of the sea as a whaleback.

The story of the whalebacks is a tragic one. A friend of mine, who lives on the misty rain-drenched waterfront of Toledo and knows all the ships that sail the Great Lakes, told it to me.

One night back in the 1880s, a shipbuilder had a dream. His name was Alexander McDougall, he lived in Superior, Wisconsin, and even then he was building big freighters for the Great Lakes. In his dream, Alexander McDougall thought he had built a ship that looked like a whale. In his dream he saw that it was natural to the water, graceful and swift.

When he awoke he said to himself, "Why not?" Before dusk next evening plans were under way in his yards for building a steel ship that looked like a whale. Alexander McDougall's first whaleback hit the water in 1887, just fifty years ago. Wooden ships were on their way out then, and the whaleback was a strike. Within six years there were forty-six of them on the Great Lakes. A whaleback steamer looks just like a whale with his back out of the water, minus the whale's spout of spray, of course.

Some of the whalebacks have superstructures built up, fore and aft, which take away some of the fishlike symmetry of their appearance. But others are superstructured only in the rear, with their round noses sloping right off into the water, and at a distance they resemble nothing so much as a ship just about to sink.

Alexander McDougall, on the strength of his dream, became rich and famous. But it didn't last. The odds were against him. Like the Merritts of the Mesabi Iron Range, like discoverers and pioneers before his time and since, he lost to more clever men—Rockefeller and Carnegie.

I am not straight on the story of just what took place. Neither, as the yarn was told to me, was Alexander McDougall. He never did understand what happened. He thought it was a Wall Street plot. But whether it was or not, long, snaky ships of a different design began coming out of the yards of Buffalo and Cleveland, and before he knew it the whaleback was doomed.

Alexander McDougall spent the rest of his life running to Washington, running to New York, running to capitals of the Great Lakes states—lashing, flailing, crying out against he knew not what. But the industrial sun had set on his beloved whalebacks.

When the World War came, only a few were left. The war brought them excitedly back to life for a brief time. The government needed them on the ocean, for coastwise service. But they were too long to go through the Welland Canal, around Niagara Falls. So the government cut them in half, boxed up the ends, floated them through the canal, welded them back together again, and used them throughout the war.

Since the war, a few have roamed back onto the Lakes, once again being cut in two and welded back together. Today only four of the original forty-six are left afloat.

*

We parked the car and walked through the cold rain over the slips of the C&O coal docks at the mouth of the Maumee. A reddish-colored ship, bare and sleek, lay at the dock. On the bow was painted a name, *Alexander McDougall.* She was a whaleback.

We went aboard, up a homemade stepladder from dock to deck. A man in boots and overcoat shook hands and said he was Captain Gustav Clausson. He didn't look over forty-five, but the boys later said he was nearer seventy.

Captain Clausson isn't sentimental about the whalebacks, but he likes them. "This handles as nice as any ship I've ever been on," he said. "It's one of the nicest ships I've ever been on."

"Then why are they a thing of the past, if they're such fine ships?" I asked.

"Here's why," he said. He pointed down around us at the steel deck. "See how the whole thing is shaped? It's all a curve. Not a straight plate on her. And see how thick the steel is? It's too expensive to curve all those plates. She'd cost half as much again to build now as an ordinary ship. That's why there aren't any more of them."

Captain Clausson's *Alexander McDougall* was the last whaleback ever built. Ironically, she used to be named the *Rockefeller,* but she was renamed recently, to honor her maker.

She came off the ways in 1898. She's nearly forty years old today, and she looks practically new. "She ought to be good for another forty years, oughtn't she?" I asked. Captain Clausson said, "Awww, my, yes."

May 12, 1937

Unionism was on the rise in the thirties, aided by the Wagner-Connery Act, which forced management to deal collectively with labor unions and which created the National Labor Relations Board. Labor history had been made at Akron in early 1936, when members of the United Rubber Workers pioneered the sit-down strike against Goodyear, Goodrich, and Firestone.

By the time Pyle visited Akron in the spring of 1937, other CIO unions were using the successful technique in other industries across the country.

RED-HOT AND RED-APPLES

AKRON, OHIO—Twelve thousand men were on strike in one tire plant here when I wrote this piece. Two new sit-down strikes were started and finished in the twenty-four hours after I arrived in town. The papers carried just a few lines about them.

Akron was smoking, and the odor of burning rubber was everywhere in the air. The streets were full of people. The store windows were handsome. I couldn't get rooms in one hotel. The coffee shop of another hotel sounded like the stock exchange on a busy day. In other words, things looked mighty prosperous.

So I started asking about it. How come, in an industrial city like Akron, there's practically no fuss with almost a fifth of the rubber industry shut down?

"Oh pooh," they said. "You just don't know Akron. We're a year ahead of all other cities in our labor relations. Why, the very first sit-down strike occurred in Akron, more than a year ago. We've had a hundred and fifty small sit-down strikes, and two huge ones, in the past year. We don't any attention to them anymore.

"We laugh at Detroit. They make such a fuss and get in the headlines all over the country when they have a big strike. But we've got twelve thousand men out in one plant here, and there isn't even a story in the paper about it every day. We just know how to take it."

That's what I heard from a man who wasn't a rubber worker and wasn't a capitalist. So then I went out to the picket line, and had lunch in the strikers' soup kitchen. "Yes, I guess Akron is a good bit ahead of other cities in the labor situation," one striking worker said. "The pay has always been pretty good in the rubber plants. And the companies have made a good many concessions to us in the last year.

"This isn't a sit-down strike. We don't have to sit down. They wouldn't try to operate the plant with strikebreakers. There's a picket line out there, but there's nothing to picket. The plant is shut up cold. A year ago there would have been trouble.

"It's true what you've been told about Akron's not paying much attention to these strikes. Why, it's gotten too peaceful.

We have trouble keeping up enough excitement to keep the boys interested. It's just too quiet."

So far, so good. A layman says nobody pays any attention to the strikes. A striker says it's so quiet the men get bored. They agree that Akron goes on about its business, and nobody worries. Now to get one last side of the picture, and clinch the argument.

I went to a prominent businessman. I told him what I'd been told, and said I just wanted his views represented. "Am I being quoted?" he asked. "That will have to be up to you," I said. "All right, then, I'm not. I'll tell you what the businessmen think of the situation in Akron.

"They're all scared to death. They don't know where we're going. They have no assurances whatever that there'll be any business a year from today.

"There isn't a businessman in town who would think of putting any improvements into his property until we see how things are going. I don't think Akron is going to disappear or anything like that. But we have to lay our plans on the premise of a growing city, and with things the way they are, I don't think we have any assurance at all that Akron will continue to grow. Business can't help but be hurt with a fourth of the buying power off a couple of times a year for weeks or months.

"I guess it's true that we don't apparently pay as much attention to strikes as they do in other cities. But I don't think you can say we take them in our stride or don't worry much about them. I think its just that we've become reconciled to them."

I had started out in search of a another kind of column. I wanted to talk with an old man and have him tell me about his years in the mill—just portraying a career that would represent life in the rubber plants. Not capital, not labor, just what it's like to work in the tire plants.

But I talked to half a dozen tire workers, and they said there wasn't any such animal in Akron now. "You can't talk to anybody without getting his story mixed up in the labor situation," they said. "You can't separate his job from his union feeling right now. You won't find an unbiased tire worker in Akron. Everybody will either be a red-hot or a red-apple."

I asked what that meant. They explained that a red-hot was a dyed-in-the-wool union booster, while a red-apple was a worker with strong nonunion views. It's that way with everybody else in Akron—red-hots and red-apples.

May 4, 1937

THAT LETTER-WRITING FARMER

WEST JEFFERSON, OHIO—Arnett Harbage is probably Ohio's best-known farmer. He got that way by taking his nation's affairs as his personal affairs, and writing letters to the newspapers about it.

He tells about a young fellow just out of a military academy who came out to the Harbage farm one day and was standing in front of the mirror, admiring himself in his uniform, and said, "I'm a self-made man." And Harbage looked at him and said, "Well, you did a hell of a poor job of it." So Arnett Harbage says of himself that he isn't a self-made man; he's a "newspaper-made man."

Arnett Harbage is quite a character. He made a quarter of a million dollars by plain dirt-farming, and then lost every penny of it. At one time he had half a dozen big farms in Ohio and a five-thousand-acre rice plantation in Georgia. He lost the last of his farms a couple of years ago. That was the old home place.

It's only a few miles from where he lives now, but he hasn't seen it since they moved him out. He drives out of his way to keep from going past it. Outside of that one little gesture, he doesn't seem to mind. "I owned my money," he says. "It never owned me."

One of the reasons Arnett Harbage has done so well in his recent career of writing to the newspapers is that he looks, talks, and acts like the farmer you see in cartoons. He goes around the house in his stocking feet, and has several days' collection of fried egg on his overall bib. He was a college man once, but that was a long time ago. He says "ain't" and keeps baby chickens in the kitchen. He loves being in the limelight.

His great coup came a few weeks ago when he up and filed a suit against the whole Ohio legislature, charging the legislators with trying to collect mileage pay for traveling they hadn't done. It got big headlines in Ohio, and photographers were out snapping pictures of Arnett in his overalls and gum boots.

Of course it made a lot of the legislators sore. Some people told Arnett it wouldn't be safe for him to go to the statehouse for a while. But he drove into Columbus the next morning and went right over to the capitol. A crowd of state representatives gathered around him—some of them razzing him good-naturedly, some of them sore as wet hens—and one of them said, "All right, Arnett, if you won't let us have our mileage pay, I guess we'll have to come out and live off of you."

That gave Arnett another idea. He went back home and got

a price from a nearby country church to feed a hundred and fifty people for fifty cents a head, and then invited the whole legislature out to dine with him. But they didn't accept.

*

Harbage watches the news closely, both state and national, and if something isn't going to suit him he types off a letter to the papers about it. Some of the papers call him "the watchdog of the Ohio treasury."

I asked him if he did it for a hobby, or because he felt it was his duty, or what. He said he guessed it wasn't either one—he just enjoys doing it. He says he never means to be venomous in his criticisms. He makes it a practice, after criticizing somebody, to get down to Columbus the next morning and try to run into the fellow on the street, and shake hands with him.

Arnett is getting along in years, and he sprained his back last year, so he doesn't do so much hard farm work. He hires it done. "I never was a very good farmer, anyway," he says. "I was too careless." I suppose that's how that quarter of a million got away. He now lives on a small farm about twenty miles out of Columbus. It isn't paid for. When he lost the last of his land he was down to four dollars and seventy cents and an old horse.

He says he never tries to keep any of his affairs private. "The other day I had to have five hundred dollars," he says. "So I just called up the bank on the party line here, and everybody in the country could hear, and I told them I was up against it, and wanted to borrow five hundred dollars."

He says the best investment he ever made was buying some stock in a Colorado gold mine. He got it from a guy he met on a train. The gold mine never did turn out, but Arnett checked up on the fellow and found he had some land in Kansas, so he made him put this land up as security, and it finally fell into Arnett's hands. He sold it at a hundred-percent profit.

His ambition now is to write a newspaper column giving dirt farmers' views on national affairs. Because there are so many farmers in the world, he thinks a daily column of what they think about things ought to be good reading.

May 1, 1937

THE REDEMPTION OF A YOUNG LAWYER

WESTERVILLE, OHIO—One night fifty-five years ago, in Corning, Iowa, a young lawyer was burning the midnight oil preparing a defense in a murder case.

His name was Howard Russell. His father had been an Episcopal minister, but Howard didn't want any preaching in his life. There wasn't enough money in it, and anyhow he didn't feel that way. He wasn't wild, and he wasn't bad. But he professed no formal religion.

Howard Russell had married the daughter of the man who fathered him into the law business. He had had his eye on her for five years, and finally he got her. Her name was Lillian. She by no means shared her husband's apathy toward religion. And her mind was made up. Howard was going to become a Christian.

She had mentioned it to him a number of times. But he had a little saying with which he turned it aside. He knew some conversational German, and his reply to Lillian's excursions into the realm of conversion was always *"Das ist verboten"*— don't talk about that. And she would stop.

But this certain night attorney Russell, after a full evening at his office, came home about eleven o'clock. Lillian was usually in bed by then. But he saw a light in an upstairs bay window. "Lillian is up," he thought to himself. "She is going to talk to me about religion again." He went on up.

Lillian was sitting in the bay window. Her husband greeted her. She came toward him. "Howard, I'm worried about you," she said. He knew what she meant, but he answered, "Why, I've never been in better health in my life."

"It isn't your health I'm worried about," she said. "It's your soul. I'm worried about your spiritual life."

"Das ist verboten," laughed Howard, but his laugh was a little dry, for he was getting annoyed beyond his patience. He had warned her many times that he didn't care to discuss the subject, and such hospital-bed attention to his soul was rubbing him a little too far the wrong way. But he couldn't stop Lillian.

"Howard," she said, "will you kneel down and let me pray for you?"

That was too much. Lawyer Russell didn't say another word. He put on his vest, and his coat, and his hat, and he turned and walked out the door and down the steps, and he went to a hotel and got a room and went to bed. And he slept, too. He never had a better night's sleep in his life.

Next morning he went to his office. He did not go home for breakfast, lunch, or supper. He worked all day, without going home to see his young wife. He was punishing her for her impudence. That night, after his work was done, he went back home.

The light was burning in the upper bay window. She was waiting for him. He began to feel bad, like a brute, in fact. After all, it wouldn't hurt anything to let her pray for him. If she asked again, he'd say go ahead. He went into the house.

Lillian rose from the window seat and came toward him. She was smiling, and happy. She put her arms around him and kissed him. She got their baby from the crib, and snuggled it up to him. She kissed him again. "Howard," she said, "you went away last night. But I knew you were all right. I was awake all night, and till after daylight, praying for you. Howard, will you kneel down now and let me pray for you?"

"Why, yes, I reckon," said Howard, thinking it wouldn't do any harm.

And so they knelt, and Lillian started to pray. She had taken a leaf from her husband's profession, and her prayer was a listed series of indictments against his character. She prayed on and on. ". . . and dear God, Howard drinks . . ." she said. Howard Russell listened. And suddenly he felt chains of heavy thorns around him, binding his arms to his chest, crippling him, stifling him.

He was conscious of the thorny fetters, and then as she prayed on and on, he became conscious that they were breaking. He could feel them give, one by one. And then he was free. Like a great light in the sky it came. He knew he had broken the fetters of selfishness and stubbornness and willfulness that bound him round.

He turned jubilantly to Lillian. "I am giving up," he said. "Giving up what?" she asked. And he shouted back, *"I am giving up sin! I am free!"*

"Will you go in the morning and tell the preacher about it?" she asked.

"I certainly intend to, even before breakfast," he said.

"And will you get up and tell the congregation about it?" she asked.

"You couldn't keep me from it," he said. "I want everybody in the world to be as happy as I am."

*

And that was the scene in a little town in Iowa one night fifty-five years ago, the simple little scene that brought God and man together into a driving force that gave America the Anti-Saloon League, the Eighteenth Amendment, and fourteen years of prohibition.

Today, the Reverend Howard Hyde Russell, LL.D., D.D., L.H.D., founder of the Anti-Saloon League, the dauntless spirit of prohibition, chokes up and his voice breaks when he tells you about that scene, he is so happy.

April 24, 1937

PORTRAIT OF A PROHIBITIONIST

WESTERVILLE, OHIO—Dr. Howard Russell will be eighty-two next October. The specialists tell him that if he shortens his working days and takes care of himself, he may have ten more active years.

And that would make Dr. Russell very happy, for within that time he expects an event that would crown his fading days with a glorious climax. He expects to see national prohibition back in ten years.

Dr. Russell is the founder of the Anti-Saloon League. He organized it on May 24, 1893. The incident related in this column yesterday changed the course of his career—and the course of history. Within six months after his conversion, Howard Russell closed his law practice in Iowa. He went to Oberlin College Seminary, in Ohio, and studied for the ministry. He served parishes in Kansas City and Chicago.

And then, when he felt himself sufficiently trained—ten years after that momentous night in Iowa—he gave up the pulpit for a lifetime war against the demon rum. The Anti-Saloon League, contrary to popular belief, was founded at Oberlin, not at Westerville. This town became its headquarters in 1930. Dr. Russell has lived here ever since.

He lives in a yellow two-story frame house across the street from the shady campus of Otterbein College. His house and its furnishings are old-fashioned—old-time rocking chairs, old upright piano, paintings of Christ.

During his forty-four years of war against liquor, Dr. Russell has personally collected around four million dollars for the League. His salary from the League for many years gave him a good living. But since the Depression the Russells have been on hard times.

Dr. Russell is thin and spry. He hears perfectly, his voice is solid, and he speaks rapidly. His memory for names and details is amazing. He has an almost childish curiosity; he wants to know your middle name. He has a genuine zest for living. He

is neat, and his face is kindly. He wears a little bow tie in a
starched collar, and heavy spats. His clothes are nicely pressed.
He carries a small thermometer around from room to room. He
looks at it once in a while to see if the room is warm enough.
It isn't.

Dr. Russell works hard. His secretary comes in every day for
dictation. And he still makes a great many trips. He has had a
desk in Washington for forty years. He went to Florida this
winter. He speaks frequently in adjoining states. He has been in
every state capital.

He works hard, but he regiments his days. He is always in bed
by nine and awake at five. From five to six A.M. is his hour of
meditation. He's in the silences then. He prays, and recites the
Beatitudes, and receives messages from God.

Dr. Russell is a truly engaging personality. I spent several
hours in his home. He told me of his whole life, and an interesting story it was, too. He was born in Indian territory three years
before it became the state of Minnesota. He told me how he
herded cattle across the Great Plains from Iowa to Colorado in
the 1870s, how he "got" his buffalo, how he educated himself in
the law, how as a youth he made part of his living giving "recita-
tions" at meetings.

He told how he set his cap for a certain girl, and how he finally
got her, and how on their honeymoon—by boat from Duluth to
Chicago—she discovered to her horror that he was a drinking
man. (It seems he went out to Pabst's brewery in Milwaukee and
hoisted a few too many.) This led to the spiritual crisis that
turned young Russell's life around.

Dr. Russell talks enthusiastically, and so naturally that even
I was at ease in his presence, and then suddenly he changed. He
spoke of the "setback" of repeal. He clenched his hand. His arm
stiffened and he shook his fist. His eyes blazed. And he
shouted—just the two of us were sitting there in the little parlor—he shouted oratorically:

"We've had a setback. *But—we'll—have—a—comeback!*"

Dr. Russell is, of course, fanatical when it comes to liquor. He
quotes biblical passages, and uses the pre-prohibition phrases
"liquor traffic," "beverage alcohol," and "total abstinence."

Before I left I asked to meet Mrs. Russell. I wanted to see the
woman who had prayed for her husband that night fifty-five
years ago in Iowa. Dr. Russell had choked up and cried a little
when he finished telling me the story. When he called her in, he
said, with immense pride in his voice, "There is the woman who

is responsible for the Eighteenth Amendment." He said it as though he dared anybody to deny it.

Mrs. Russell said to me, "Are you a total abstainer?" It would have taken a daredevil courage to answer no. And she said, "How long have you been one?"*

Dr. Russell held on to my hand as we walked to the street. He said he was so happy he had made a new friend. I went back to the hotel. A few minutes after I got there the phone rang.

It was Dr. Russell. He and Mrs. Russell had been talking it over. He was calling to make sure that I put the right shade of meaning into the column I wrote about him. He was afraid he had seemed boastful. He wanted it clear that he took no credit for his life's work—that the Divine Creator was the guiding hand through it all, that his life and his wife's life had been God-led.

They wanted to be pictured in a spirit of humility before God, he said.

April 26, 1937

An Infidel with a Flourish

NORTH BENTON, OHIO—A couple of months ago when I visited my parents in Indiana, they related a story told by an evangelist at a revival meeting this spring. The story went like this:

In North Benton, Ohio, a number of years ago, there was an infidel. On his deathbed he challenged God, "if there *is* a God," to prove it by putting snakes in his grave.

According to the evangelist's story, they could hardly get the grave dug for the snakes. The ground was full of them. And even today, the evangelist said, snakes burrow into the grave, and crawl in and out all day long.

My mother, who is a good Christian, said, "I don't believe a word of it. Why don't you go there and write a column about it?"

So here I am in North Benton, looking for snakes. This is a farm town of two hundred people. The snake story, as the evangelists tell it, is not true. Yes, there was a man in North Benton who was an infidel. His name was Chester Bedell. He died just thirty years ago, when he was eighty. He was quite a character. He *did* challenge God to put snakes in his grave. But I've talked with old-timers here who knew Chester Bedell intimately, and

*Pyle was a heavy drinker who once said he didn't trust anyone who didn't drink.

they don't remember any snake incidents connected with his burial.

It *is* true that an occasional snake does crawl into the graveyard. But why not? There are snakes all around here, and a snake doesn't know a graveyard from a briar patch. In fact, there are three graveyards near town, and people say one of the others has more snakes than the infidel's cemetery.

There are no snake holes in Chester Bedell's grave. The lawn around the grave is closely mown. I'll bet there isn't one snake in five years that crawls right over the grave. The best proof of the dearth of snakes is that even old Snake-Phobia Pyle wasn't a bit scared to walk all around here.

*

Bedell had been dead about twenty years before the yarn got to circulating; now it has reached all over the country. The grave has become a sort of sinful charm for the devout. People have come from every state in the Union. One man hitchhiked from California. On a recent Sunday there were three hundred and sixty-five tourists at the grave.

Most of them are intent on proving the story true. When local people say it isn't, the visitors call them liars. Visiting preachers are especially insistent, and have even made scenes. They say to the local people, "Oh sure, the Bedell family pays you to say it isn't true."

One preacher from Pennsylvania, seeing no snakes around the grave, went out in the weeds and found one, put it in a glass jar, took it home, and draped it over his pulpit the next Sunday while he preached his infidel sermon.

Chester Bedell has three children living—two daughters in nearby towns and a son who is a farmer a couple of miles from here. He's seventy now, and they say he is a nonbeliever, too. He gets mighty fed up with these silly people who come to gloat over his father's grave.

Long before he died, Chester Bedell had a life-sized statue of himself put up in the family plot in the graveyard. It is bronze, and stands on a stone pedestal higher than your head. One foot of the statue is crushing a scroll entitled SUPERSTITION, while the right hand holds high a scroll on which is written UNIVERSAL MENTAL LIBERTY.

How ironic it would seem to Chester Bedell that his strong feeling against superstition should merely have fanned further the fires of fanaticism.

For tourists, in their righteous wrath, have shot bullets twice into the statue of Chester Bedell. You can see the bullet holes. Tourists have even tried to pry the statue off its base and upset it. Tourists have trampled the freshly seeded lawn near the grave. Tourists have chipped off part of the wall around the Bedell lot. Tourists prod the grave with sticks. Tourists stand over the grave and hiss. Preachers come and hold services over the grave, damning the infidel Bedell.

On Saturdays the little boys of North Benton catch snakes and hang them over the infidel's headstone. On Sundays the tourists see the snakes and kneel and cry, "Praise the Lord." . . .

July 14, 1938

THE CLOSED-MOUTH WORLD OF SOAP-MAKING

CINCINNATI— . . . You might say Cincinnati is the soap capital of the world. Soap-making is the city's dominant industry.

There are several soap factories here, but I visited the huge plants of Procter & Gamble, who produce about forty percent of all the soap made in America. They employ about four thousand people here, and have other plants all over the world.

The first thing I asked was, "What makes Ivory soap float?" I had to ask three people before I found one who knew. Ivory soap floats because it's whipped and beaten much longer than other soaps. It gets creamy, and full of tiny air cells. Then when it hardens, the air is sealed inside these cells, forming a sort of water-wing effect for the bar of soap.

That means, of course, that Ivory isn't as dense as ordinary toilet soap. As far as I could learn, this extra whipping doesn't do the soap any good or any harm, either. It just makes it float. Other companies have soap that will float, too.

Another surprising thing: because Ivory is almost odorless, I supposed they didn't perfume it at all. But they do. If they didn't, it would smell oily. They put in just a little neutralizing perfume.

*

I spent a couple of hours in the Procter & Gamble factory and didn't see an awful lot. They are fairly cagey, and jittery about spies, like governments. It seems there are lots of secret processes and secret machinery they don't want other companies to find out about. I don't blame them for being wary, for I am just the man who would run and tattle to Colgate's.

There are other reasons for this caution. They say part of the plant is dangerous for visitors to be in. And finally, I gathered, some of it doesn't smell very good. So we began our tour where the soap had finally reached the cooking stage.

There is a double-row battery of giant vats, made of battleship steel—a hundred of them, each three stories high. These vats have hot coils inside, and the soap cooks in them for two days. The vats are covered on top, but you can look down through a little window and see the boiling. The soap cooking in there, which will eventually be a beautiful cake in your bathroom with a come-hither smell, looks exactly like the brown soap my mother used to make out of cracklins and lye in a black kettle over an outside fire.

*

I tried to find out how many cakes of soap Proctor & Gamble make each year. They wouldn't tell. But I did find that until a few years ago, they used twelve thousand whales a year in their soap. But the whale is by way of becoming extinct, so high taxes and stricter laws have been put on the whaling business, and soap-makers have had to cut down on whale oil.

Coconut oil is now the main staple in soap, and Procter & Gamble each year uses somewhere in the neighborhood of three quarters of a million coconuts. Just think how many coconut trees that would be for the soft tropical winds to sigh through while you lie under them on the South Sea beaches drinking in the silent silvery moonlight. . . .

July 2, 1938

CINCINNATI, OHIO—The making of soap is a process of chemical mixing. But what a chemist can do, he can also undo.

For example: recently a group of salesmen was entertained at a banquet in the Procter & Gamble factory. The meal was finished off with ice cream and cake. After the last salesman had wiped his plate and licked his chops, the chemists announced that the cake had been made of Camay soap!

They had ground up soap, disentangled all the elements that originally went into it, used the ones they needed for cooking, and made cake. . . .

*

Of course I had to embarrass the soap people by asking them about dead horses.

"Do you still put dead horses in soap?" I said. The soap people were perfectly honest about it. They said they weren't sure.

They buy all their animal fat from brokers. These brokers have a million sources all over the country—slaughterhouses, butcher shops, disposal plants, and so on. They render the fat, then ship it to Procter & Gamble in the form of tallow. It arrives just as white and pretty as a candle.

So the soap people here don't know the original source of all that tallow. "But," they said, in an orgy of frankness, "we wouldn't be a bit surprised if somewhere along the line an occasional horse does stray into that tallow."

*

One more thing I learned about soap. You've heard the Saturday-night-bath gag all your life. Well, that joke is a bad understatement. Statistics show that the average American does not take even one bath a week. One in two weeks would come nearer to it. But even so, we are the best-washed nation in the world.

Here is the proof: Americans buy, on the average, twenty-five pounds of soap each year per person. Holland is next cleanest, with twenty-four pounds per person. Canada and Denmark tie for third, with twenty-two pounds each. Then Germany, twenty-one pounds; France and England, twenty pounds each; Cuba and Sweden, eighteen pounds each; and then clear down to Italy, with only about ten pounds.

The Chinese are a people after my own heart. They can't be bothered with appearances. They use just two ounces of soap each, per year. That means a cake of ordinary toilet soap would last a Chinese couple a whole year, and would do their laundry, too.

*

It seems the American public is funny about taking baths. That's one question on which Americans have a completely closed mind. They are not open to propaganda about more baths. Fourteen of the biggest soap companies got together and put on a terrific national propaganda campaign designed to make people wash oftener, so the soap companies could sell more soap.

They spent two million dollars, and they might as well have poured that two million down the drain, or given part of it to me. Because when it was all over and the checkup was made, they found they had not increased the national bath-taking average by even so much as the dabble of one toe in the bathtub. It was discouraging. . . .

July 2, 1938

INDIANA

CHAMPION SODA-JERKER

EVANSVILLE, INDIANA— . . . Harold Korb is the champion soda-jerker of the United States. He doesn't take his honor lightly. He is proud and serious about it.

It isn't like being a celebrity to him, or like winning a race; it's more as though he had been given a medal by a scientific society in recognition of years of research.

And the funny part about it is that Harold Korb isn't a soda-jerker at all, and never has been. He's an ice-cream salesman. But he sure knows how to make a chocolate soda.

Only I shouldn't have said it that way. You never make a soda. Or jerk a soda. Or mix a soda. What you do is *build* a soda. I gathered that in my conversation with Harold Korb. He speaks very gravely.

Korb's great distinction came last December in Cincinnati, at a convention of ice-cream salesmen from all over America. There were sixty-five besides himself. These salesmen must be better soda-jerkers (builders) than the jerkers themselves, because it's part of their job to tell the jerkers how to do it.

Well, at this convention, every salesman had to build a soda. The judges didn't sample the sodas; they just looked at them. That's the way to judge a soda, anyway. "Eighty-seven percent of everything that's bought is bought by sight," Harold Korb said. And it was such a beautiful sight to watch Harold Korb build a chocolate soda that they told him even before he was finished that he was the winner.

His prize number he called the Mellow-Cream Chocolate Soda. He put in an ounce and a half of chocolate syrup. He put in two soda spoons of stiffly whipped cream. He shot a very fine stream of carbonated water into the glass until it was three-quarters of an inch from the top. Then he plied (yes, *plied*) two number-twenty-four dips of ice cream, one gently on top of the other, so it would remain sticking out of the soda and the customer would see it. . . .

*

Harold Korb was born about twenty miles north of Evansville. When he was nineteen he started gathering up the neigh-

borhood milk and hauling it to Evansville dairies. The dairy
finally put him to work in town. He drifted into a specialty, ice
cream. He and Eskimo Pies got off to a good start together.

Eskimo Pies slowed up, but Harold Korb didn't. Always he
has gone up—steadily, efficiently, methodically. So many years
as a helper on a delivery wagon, so many years on a route of his
own, so many years delivering and packing ice cream for confectioners.

And always studying, and watching the other fellow's work,
and improving his knowledge of how to serve ice cream most
delightfully. For that was the way to lift yourself—learn, and
tell the client, and the client could sell more, and that meant
more sales and more commission and more success for Harold
Korb.

He isn't a smooth-tongued man. But confectioners must sense
that he's awfully honest, and awfully thorough, and he certainly
knows the psychology of ice-cream eaters. If I were in the soda-
fountain business, and Harold Korb told me to stick a corncob
in every chocolate soda, I'd stick a corncob in every chocolate
soda.

His years of close attention brought their reward. Today Harold Korb is a white-collar man in the dairy's promotion department. He has come a long way from gathering up milk cans in
the country. He has a wife and children. He owns two homes.
He is only thirty-five.

I laughed and said, "Well, you're really a big shot now, aren't
you?"

Korb laughed, too, but he said, "I've never been anything but
a big little shot to Harold Korb. I've never for one minute felt
myself bigger than the other fellow."

Success has not turned the head of the man who built a better
Mellow-Cream Chocolate Soda.

May 20, 1937

*Pyle attended Indiana University from the fall of 1919 through January
of 1923, when he quit college just short of earning his journalism degree
to accept a cub reporter's job on the* La Porte Herald *in La Porte,
Indiana. There was an additional incentive for leaving the campus: his
girlfriend had broken up with him, and Pyle was fractured.*

A SENTIMENTAL RENUNCIATION VIOLATED BY CHANCE
BLOOMINGTON, INDIANA— . . . For more than fourteen years now
I'd been saying it—saying never again would I lay eyes on the

campus of my college days. I felt sort of sentimental about it. I didn't want to see all the changes.

Other people can go back, and think they're young again, and pretend to enjoy it. But not me. I had more sense. Never intended to go back.

And I didn't *intend* to, either. It was really fate that caused it. We were rushing through the long drive from Evansville to Indianapolis, two hundred miles in an afternoon, just my dad and me in the car. We had mapped our route, and it would carry us twenty miles wide of Bloomington. It was after three o'clock when we passed Vincennes, and still a hundred and forty miles to Indianapolis. We'd make it by dark.

At Switz City we stopped for gas. That was the mistake, stopping for gas. We asked the fellow about the roads, and he said the road ahead was terrible, and that everybody was going by way of Boomington. We could go through, he said, but there wasn't any sense to it.

I still think that if I'd been alone, I'd have gone on through. But a fellow's dad would think it pretty silly to drive over bad roads when there was a good road just as near. A fellow can't be silly in front of his own dad. We swung to the right and headed for Bloomington.

*

The hills of southern Indiana roll and sweep and are beautiful beyond speech in the springtime. My dad kept remarking about the "broken" country, and how pretty it was. "But how could anybody make a living farming down here?" he asked. I didn't know, nor care. The hills were but old ghosts of memories to me. Ghosts of people I'd known, and things I'd done, and girls I'd loved—ghosts of another world that is now gone forever. Things piled up on my memory, and I drove in an excited misery of old thoughts.

We stopped in the village of Lyons, and I asked a kid if he knew Joe Benham. The kid said he did, and I drove away fast, full of fear that I might see him. I didn't ask at all after another memory—a girl I knew. I wanted to ask, but somehow I couldn't.

Bloomington finally came. I didn't recognize anything at all as we came into town. If I had followed the highway numbers we'd have gone right on through. But we didn't, and I told my dad I couldn't figure out where we were, and then I told him I knew now. "That's the Phi Gam house right ahead," I said. It sits on the campus. We were back.

We still could have driven right on. But we stopped. I asked a student where Dean Edmondson's office was now. He showed me, in that fancy new building there. There wasn't any building like that in my school. But I went in.

"Dr. Edmondson has gone," the secretary said. "Is it important?"

I said, "Well, sort of, maybe. We're old friends . . . fourteen years . . . first time . . ."

She telephoned three or four places. Finally I heard her say, "Mrs. Edmondson." "Here," I said, "let me talk to her." I took the phone. "Do you remember . . . ? You do? Swell, I'll wait right here."

I waited. In a few minutes Dean Edmondson arrived in a rush, and Mrs. Edmondson came from the other direction in the car. Old friends. Good friends. *How long can you stay?* Only an hour at most. *We'll go out to the house. Come on.*

Mrs. Edmondson took my dad, and the dean rode with me. "That's the new women's dormitory," he said. "And that's the new school of music. Were they here when you were here?"

"No. Nothing was here when I was here."

"How long since you've been back?"

"I've never been back. It's fourteen years now."

"Fourteen years!"

"Yes. I hadn't intended to ever come. Had funny ideas about it. I can't tell you how I feel. For an hour I've hardly been able to keep from crying."

"I understand that, Ernie. I know exactly."

*

The Edmondsons are high spots in my life. They were never deans to me, even in the old days. They were people. We were friends, and I believe they taught me more of what life is about than anybody else in my youth, except my parents.

They were so sane. It was they who told a restless boy to go ahead and quit school and go to China if he wanted to. It was they who signed the note for the borrowed money. It was they who told him to quit school a second time, when the offer of a job came. It was they who sat in understanding and talked in their calm, slow voices the night he thought the world had come to an end for him. They were sane. It was wonderful to see them again.

In the house we talked and laughed and told about things that had happened in fourteen years. "And you still roll your own cigarets," Mrs. Edmondson said. Dean Edmondson used to roll his, too, and it was from him I got the idea. And I'm still rolling them, but he smokes ready-mades now.

We didn't talk about school. We talked about ourselves, and talked fast, for time was short. They gave me their pictures, and went to the car with us, and told my dad I belonged partly to them, and said they didn't know when they'd been so glad to see anybody.

It was dusk when we left. I hadn't looked at the campus or the new buildings as we came in. I didn't look at them as we drove out. I had come back, but I *hadn't* come back—and never could.

I knew my dad and I wouldn't talk much on the way to Indianapolis. The lights shone dimly on the black pavement, and I left the dash lights off. It was dark in the car. The night was chilly, and we turned on the heater. Its fan made a steady drone. The curves kept winding at me out of the rolling hills, and I took them, but hardly saw them.

May 21, 1937

MISSOURI

"I'D HAVE GIVEN HIM A CIGAR"

ST. JOSEPH, MISSOURI—This is the city where Jesse James was killed, where the Pony Express started, where thousands of forty-niners equipped themselves for the awful journey to the California gold fields.

Yet in the bookstores of St. Joseph you cannot buy a book or a pamphlet on the fascinating history of this place. You can't buy a book about Jesse James. You can't buy a book on the Pony Express. You can't buy a book on the forty-niners or the Overland Trail.

You can buy all these books in Denver or New York City, but you can't buy them in St. Joe, where it all happened. The Chamber of Commerce can give you the exact value of manufactured products in St. Joseph for 1937, but it doesn't know whether Jesse James is buried here or not.

St. Joe has lived too long with its own history to be excited about it.

I did meet one man with a Jesse James story, however. The man is vice president of a bank, he is eighty-three years old now, he is as spick-and-span as a diplomat, and a nicer old man you never met.

His name is Max Andriano. He left Germany when he was seventeen and came right to St. Joseph, where he had a cousin, and he says he fell in love with the place instantly and was never homesick for a second. He has been a banker here for more than sixty years.

In 1882 he was a messenger, daily carrying a big sack of money from one bank to another. As we sat at his desk talking, he pointed out the window and said, "Right there on that corner, just across the street, is where it happened."

He came out of the bank one afternoon with his sack of money. A tall stranger was loafing in the bank's doorway. The stranger said: "Young man, you're pretty young to be carrying so much money around alone. Don't you need some help? Better let me go with you."

To which young Mr. Andriano replied: "I may be young, but I'm old enough to mind my own business, and that might be a good idea for you, too." The loafer laughed, and Mr. Andriano says he never saw such a satanic smile on a man's face. Mr. Andriano went on alone, and delivered his money safely.

That night Jesse James was killed. Mr. Andriano went down to the morgue the next morning to look at the corpse. It was the man who had spoken to him. "I wouldn't have talked back so smart if I'd known it was Jesse James," says Mr. Andriano. "I'd have given him a cigar." . . .

May 11, 1938

MINNESOTA

Pyle wrote this in the fall of 1935, during his first trip as a roving reporter.

A TOWN PROSPERING UNDER THE NEW DEAL
MANKATO, MINNESOTA—Here is the end of the rainbow; here is the famous spot just around the corner. For here, ladies and gentlemen, is prosperity.

This city of twenty thousand, center and heart of the fertile Minnesota River Valley farm country, is on the verge of a mild boom. The farmers have money in their pockets. The merchants are remodeling their stores and sprucing up. People are spending. People look happy.

A friend of mine runs a daily newspaper here. I asked him if the people hereabouts were for or against the New Deal. He said, "What can they be but for it? Even the Republicans admit that things are better than they were a year ago. Better than two years ago. And the New Deal has caused it. They'd be fools if they weren't for it."

*

The merchants were opening a three-day contest the night I arrived. About forty of the stores had set up window displays, each one representing some popular song, and the people were to guess which one. They were giving away about a hundred and fifty dollars in prizes to the people who could name the most songs.

The main street was closed to auto traffic for about ten blocks. And that street was so jammed with people it looked like a county fair. My friend who runs the newspaper estimated ten thousand people were on the street.

You might argue, of course, that the people were so poor and desperate that they all came down in the frantic hope of getting a part of the prize money. But that wasn't it.

I pushed along through the mob, looking at people's faces, and their clothes, and listening to their talk. They didn't look or act like the Depression people I have been seeing everywhere the past few years.

A good percentage of them were farmers. They were dressed nicely. There was none of the beaten look you see on Depression faces. They were downtown just to be with people, and have a good time, and look at the things they were going to buy.

*

Two things account for this return to better times in southern Minnesota. One is that the Minnesota River Valley is exceptionally fertile, and that the farmers of southern Minnesota and northern Iowa are and always have been unusually progressive; the other is that the New Deal has definitely raised farm prices, and given the farmers something for their work.

The farmers have started buying again. The stores are doing almost as much business as before the Depression, and it can't be denied that the store business reflects the general financial status of the community.

The farm-implement factories and distributors are running at full steam. After years of getting along with old tools, the farmer has worn out his machinery, and he starts replenishing the minute he has the money.

In the fields you see much new machinery, and on the roads you meet, a dozen times an hour, new tractors or binders or mowing machines, their new paint glistening in the sun, being taken home to the farm. The tractor factory in Waterloo, Iowa, has been running double shifts for almost a year.

*

There are only a few people on relief in and around Mankato this summer. They say there is no excuse for anybody able and willing to work to be without a job here this summer. There will be people on relief this winter, of course, but they don't expect as many as last year.

And prospects for the future are good. The corn crop, while no record-breaker, is good. If the frost will just hold off for a little longer, everything will be all right. They've had a spell of cold weather that scared the farmers, but it has warmed up again now. Another week without frost, and the corn will be mature.

September 21, 1935

THREE PALS

BAUDETTE, MINNESOTA—This village has a trio of great friends, three men who have been pals for thirty years, drawn together by their love of fishing and hunting, and by their native esteem for any genuine sportsman.

They are Jack, John, and Bill. Jack Collins keeps the hardware store. John Kennedy is the United States Customs man at the border here. Bill Noonan is editor of the weekly newspaper. These men are not "characters." They are human, kind, and intelligent men, the same as you might find in any town, except there is something about them that I can't explain, a quality that seems to me to exist only in people who have lived the raw life of the frontier.

Jack and John are getting close to seventy; Bill is younger. These three have their separate lines of work, but what they really live for is to hunt and fish. Each says he would want to be dead if he couldn't hunt and fish anymore. Jack and John are natural outdoor men; they are woodsmen as well as sportsmen.

They are as much at home around a campfire at night as they are with guns at their shoulders in the daytime.

Bill likes to hunt and fish, too, but he is a little different. He goes on all the expeditions into the woods or up to the lake, but the other two get awfully mad at him sometimes. It seems Bill isn't domestic, even in a campfire way, and he couldn't learn to do anything around a camp on a bet. They tell funny stories about him.

Once they had a little portable cookstove with them up in Canada. The first night out they pitched camp, and while Jack and John went out to see what they could scare up, Bill was to get the fire going. They even gathered the wood for him. But when they got back Bill was sitting peacefully in the middle of a great cloud of smoke, reading a book. He had not only kindled up a blaze in the firebox, but he had built a fire in the oven, too, and didn't know the difference.

Another time they camped in a lodge that belonged to a doctor friend. It was a very modern affair, with a gasoline stove that had six burners and a big oven. They had brought a ham with them, so they explained to Bill just how to start the stove, and just how to put the ham in, and everything. Then they went out for a couple of hours' shooting.

It was raw and cold, late fall and late evening, and their blood was like ice and their stomachs were empty when they got back. Their minds were on that beautiful ham Bill would have ready. He was sitting at the jug, reading a book, when they walked in.

"How's the ham, Bill?"

"It ought to be done by now," he said. "I put it in a couple of hours ago."

So John Kennedy went out to see. He was back in a minute. "You blankety-blank so-and-so!" he said. "I'm going to shoot you." Jack Collins took a look, and said, "No, please don't shoot him. *I* want to shoot him."

What was the trouble? Well, Bill had put the ham in, and just turned on the pilot light. He thought the pilot light would cook the ham. It was still sitting there in the oven, cold as a chunk of ice. Jack Collins and John Kennedy were laughing and telling me these stories about Bill Noonan. "But," John said, "he is a wonderful man. He's the wittiest man in this part of the country. And he's so kind and gentle, I don't suppose he ever thought a bad thought about anybody in his life."

*

I wish you could see the office of Bill Noonan's newspaper, the *Baudette Region*. It is a tiny old one-story plank building on a side street. It has never been painted, and it has started to lean over into the adjoining lot. There is no name on it. The inside looks more like a machine shop than a newspaper plant. One corner is partitioned off, and that is the editor's office. He sits there at a typewriter, in the middle of a jumble of papers and scraps that admits no contact with either of the four walls.

At one side is a wood stove for the forty-below days in winter. It is all covered with cigaret butts now. Behind the stove, running from an old ledger lying on a chair, up to the wall, is the biggest and handsomest cobweb between here and Minneapolis.

And out of this jumble comes one of the best country weeklies you ever saw. It is a paper with life in it, and it has all the local news, and all through it runs the spirit of Bill Noonan—the gentleness of his character, his slow, understanding wit, his calm wisdom from thirty years of living in the North. . . .

August 13, 1936

JOHN KENNEDY, RACONTEUR

BAUDETTE, MINNESOTA—John Kennedy gets a lot out of life.

He is Scotch-Irish. He loves the woods. Fishing and hunting are almost a mania with him. He loves people. He talks and talks, and tells wonderful stories. He is always doing nice things for people, and he also plays awful jokes on people. There is nothing so despicable to him as a poor sport. He is nearly seventy now, and a grandfather. He is full of energy, and his legs are nimble, but his eyes are weakening a little. He can't shoot as straight as he once could.

Kennedy was born and raised on the frontier. When he was born, a little west of Minneapolis, all the north was untouched forest. White men didn't live here, only Indians and wild animals. Kennedy was brought up with the Indians. He can speak Chippewa as well as he speaks English. He never got beyond the log schoolhouse, but he has vastly educated himself through an inquisitive mind and a taste for reading and a harmony with nature.

For fifteen years he was a timber cruiser, a man who traveled on foot through the forests, surveying, judging, marking out timber lots to be cut next. The timber cruiser lived as close to nature as any animal. John Kennedy has been in the forests, alone, for as long as fourteen months at a time. He has never been hurt in the woods. But he has been busted up time after time by autos here in Baudette.

In 1901 he entered the United States Customs Service. Baudette was just forming then, and he has lived here ever since. He will retire in a year or two. He has all the money he wants, through savings and timber investments from his cruiser days.

*

John Kennedy has had fun all his life. I'm sure he almost drove everybody crazy in the days when Baudette was a frontier settlement. Just one example, out of hundreds. There was an old man, the town drunk, who finally died of his alcoholism on the floor of the hotel lobby. They carried him down to the little clapboard church, took the door off the hinges, and laid the corpse on the door inside the church.

They set another old man to watch the body. To keep up courage for his grim task, the old fellow had to run back to the hotel about every hour and get a drink. After a few he got to waving his gun around and saying nobody would steal the corpse while he was on guard.

So Kennedy and a friend slipped over to the church, ran some twine through cracks in the wall from each side, and tied the twine around the corpse's wrists. Then they hid outside the church. When the old watchman came back from his tippling, Kennedy and his friend starting pulling the strings back and forth. The corpse's arms started flying. The old man screamed and dropped his lantern and ran. The lantern started to set the church afire, so Kennedy ran in and threw it out the door. That scared the departing watchman even more. Kennedy cut the twine off the corpse's wrists, and beat it.

The old man spread the alarm. In a couple of minutes this whole town, Kennedy among them, came surging down to the church. They decided the old man was having visions. They decided to hang him, but somebody talked them out of it. Maybe it was Kennedy. He didn't dare tell the truth of that story for years afterward. . . .

August 15, 1936

JACK COLLINS, CHAMPION SPORTSMAN

BAUDETTE, MINNESOTA—Jack Collins says it is a lie that he tells lies.

He says he never tells anything but the truth. He says he was hunting deer one fall, and a beauty came out of the woods toward him, four hundred yards away, so he pulled up and let him have it. Just as he shot, he says, the deer made a lightning reverse turn, and started back for the woods, but dropped dead after a step or two.

Well, they went down and started cutting up the deer. They saw that the bullet had hit the deer in the eye. Suddenly one of the fellows said, "Hey, what's this?" He pointed to a small tree nearby that had been freshly splintered, apparently by a bullet. So they looked around, and traced the splinters over the snow about fifteen feet, and there lay the bullet. It came from John Collins' gun all right, and he had fired only one shot.

Then they examined the deer more closely, but found no place where the bullet had come out. So the bullet had gone into the deer, and apparently not come out, and yet there it was on the ground. How would you explain that?

Here's how Jack Collins explains it: "Remember," he says, "that the deer made a fast reverse turn just as I shot. Well, what happened was that the bullet went into the deer's eye but the deer changed ends so fast that the bullet, still traveling in the same direction, came right out of the deer's eye the same place it went in, and then hit the tree and bounced off. It was the damnedest thing I ever saw."

*

Jack Collins is one of the world's great fishermen. He has certificates to prove it. Along one wall of his hardware store hang mounted fish, and the heads of deer, and all kinds of fowl and small game. One of the fish is the biggest muskellunge ever caught. It weighed fifty-six-and-a-half pounds. The other is the biggest trout. It weighed forty-four pounds. The framed certificates from *Field and Stream* attest to the veracity of the catches, in 1931 and 1934. . . .

*

After hunting gold in Alaska (he never found any), and working on the Iron Range around Hibbing, and running a boat service on Rainy River, Jack Collins drifted into hardware in Baudette. His store gives him a place to hang his fish on the wall, and sell sportsman's equipment, and sit in his little office and write funny letters to people.

He got a card from a fellow in Oklahoma, wanting to know all about fishing on Lake of the Woods, and what to bring, and how cold it was in summer, and so on. Collins wrote him a long reply. It went, in part, like this:

"Texas, as well as Oklahoma, sends us some good fishermen, if they are allowed to go at it their own way. They drive the muskies all into a bay, and then start cutting out the big ones with a rope, and oh boy how they do pull them in. You Oklahoma fellows should be handy with a rope and I would advise bringing one along.

"Should you come up during the middle of July you won't need any snowshoes or skis. In fact we have two or three weeks in July that we don't even fire the furnace.

"One thing I feel obligated to warn you of is the snow snakes. During that warm period in July is when they are most vicious. Wear very high boots, and fill your pockets with Limburger. Our snow snakes are furbearing and quite valuable.

"Dress warm and ask your old family doctor to prescribe a good old-fashioned remedy for frostbite. I will have a good fire going in the furnace when you arrive."

Jack Collins never got an answer from this fellow.

*

For twenty years Jack Collins has been having trouble with his legs. He thought it was rheumatism, but they say it is some strange form of arthritis. He has been to many doctors, but gradually he gets worse. He shuffles along with a cane, and in the snowy winter he must tie the cane to his wrist, for if he dropped it he could not get down to pick it up.

But he won't give up to his pain. Each fall he hunts; each summer he fishes. His old friend John Kennedy almost had tears in his eyes when he told me how Jack Collins grits his teeth and goes on hunting anyhow. Last fall they were out together, after grouse. Collins was a little way apart from the rest, on a sort of rise, shuffling alone with his cane and his gun. Some grouse got up in front of him.

Kennedy stood there in the cold and watched his great old pal set himself on his bum legs, and bring his gun up into line, with the cane dangling scarecrowlike from his wrist, and watched the gun swing swiftly along the circle, and heard the *bang, bang, bang,* and saw the grouse drop one by one, like targets in a shooting gallery.

"He shoots by instinct, by intuition," Kennedy said. "He'll be bringing them down just like that when we have to carry him out and set him on a stump."

August 17, 1936

Isolation Is About All There Is

FLAG ISLAND, NORTHWEST ANGLE, MINNESOTA—This afternoon I stood on a rock that is the northernmost foot of land in the

United States. Tonight I am sleeping on an island so isolated you'd have to have a sextant to find it. I am in the Northwest Angle.

The Northwest Angle is that little spot of United States that lies illogically over in Canada, forty miles across Lake of the Woods from the northern Minnesota mainland. It is not connected with any part of the United States except by water. It has Canada on the west side, and water on the three other sides.

There are no roads into Northwest Angle. The only way you get here is by boat in summer, or across the ice in winter. Or, now that we're in the twentieth century, by airplane.

You might say Northwest Angle is in two parts—the mainland, and the islands. The islands are the most attractive. There are about a hundred of them, ranging from mere rocks to one island of thirteen hundred acres. They extend from the mainland eastward into Lake of the Woods for about ten miles, to where the unseen international boundary cuts them off from their fellow islands in Canadian waters.

The Angle mainland is about ten by twelve miles, and it is all muskeg, or swamp, and nobody lives in it except along the shore. The Angle has a total permanent population of fewer than a hundred. About half live on the mainland, half on the islands. There is no town in Northwest Angle. There are two post offices, both on islands, with two or three families living around them. People come by canoe to get their mail.

There are two fishing camps in the Angle, where tourists may come to rest or fish. But it would be stretching a point to call it resort country. The tourists come in dribbles instead of droves, and they are mostly sportsmen.

*

I have never been anyplace where the inhabitants know so little about their own history as the people of Northwest Angle. Not a person I talked with knew why the United States–Canadian boundary was drawn so ludicrously around this isolated spot. The accepted story is that the British surveyors got the Americans drunk, and they drew a line; and then the Americans got the British drunk, and they drew a line.

But from the best information I could gather elsewhere, it was really like this:

A treaty between the United States and Canada was made shortly after the War of 1812. At that time they didn't know the exact location of Lake of the Woods. So, according to the treaty, the boundary was to run east and west along the middle of Rainy

River until it emptied into Lake of the Woods, then across the water to the northwestern corner of the lake, and thence either north or south, whichever it might be, to the forty-fifth parallel.

And when they surveyed it, Lake of the Woods turned out to be farther north than they had thought, and the northwest corner was way up in Canada, so when they drew the line back down to the forty-fifth parallel, that left this strange Northwest Angle as United States territory. And here it is today.

Northwest Angle isn't any bargain, especially. The islands within the American boundary are nice, but they're the poorest in the lake. There are fourteen thousand islands in Lake of the Woods, which means that about thirteen thousand nine hundred of them are in Canada, toward the north and east sides of the lake. It is up there that the scenery is so startlingly beautiful, that the forests are so big, that the fighting muskellunge lie waiting just offshore. The United States got the poorest end of the Lake of the Woods.

*

Northwest Angle was opened to homesteading early in the century. It has had one of the greatest turnovers of any homestead land in the country. People came, and couldn't make it, and left. You can't live in the interior at all. Almost all of the land has gone back to the government.

I had heard that a strange race of people inhabited this isolated spot. That is not exactly correct. They are strange only in that they have an intense lack of ambition. They are satisfied, most of them, to just barely exist. And that's all most of them do. They raise a little hay in the summer for a couple of cows. They do a little commercial fishing. In winter they trap muskrat and mink. Most of them don't get into Warroad, Minnesota, fifty miles away, more than once a year.

August 19, 1936

LIFE IN THE NORTHERNMOST UNITED STATES

OAK ISLAND, NORTHWEST ANGLE, MINNESOTA—If you were to sit down in dusty Kansas on a hot afternoon and think hard, I have no doubt you could think some very romantic thoughts about the Northwest Angle.

Way up in the Lake of the Woods . . . beautiful islands all around . . . pine forests . . . dark cool waters . . . northwest breezes . . . far away from auto horns and binders and politics . . . nights that are silent and full of sleep . . . lots of fish . . . lots of time . . .

But wait. Life here is awfully harsh. You should know about that, too.

For example, there are two schools in Northwest Angle. One is on Oak Island, the other on American Point, also an island. Each one has about six pupils. The kids on Flag Island, for instance, are three miles away from school. They have to get over to Oak Island. In early fall and spring, they go by outboard canoe. But during the two-week freeze-up in November it's too icy for boats. So the children stay on Oak Island those two weeks, and for two weeks during the spring thaw.

All winter they walk the three miles across the ice. A grown-up always goes with them, for there are treacherous air holes in the lake. "The kids never missed a day last winter," says Papa McKeever of Flag Island. "They usually started school about eight. But a few mornings it was fifty-six below zero, and we waited until about ten o'clock. It had warmed up to forty below by that time."

*

Mail comes to Northwest three times a week—by boat in summer, by plane in winter. The plane missed only one trip last winter. There are two post offices in the Angle, on Oak Island and American Point, just like the schools. American Point serves the people on the mainland. That post office is called Penasse, Minnesota. It is the northernmost post office in the United States. The postmaster is George Arnold. He also runs a sawmill and keeps a store. He has lived there for twenty years, and raised a family as modern as you see anywhere.

Arnold gets a lot of mail from philatelists, to be remailed from his farthest-north post office. It used to come in by the shoebox full. But since the China Clipper flight, he doesn't get so much. He guesses philatelists have turned to airmail. Usually just one person comes over from the mainland to get all the mail, and the others pick it up whenever they happen by. Twice last winter the snow was so bad the plane couldn't land, so the mail was dropped by parachute.

*

Both Oak Island and American Point have a general store and a beer parlor. The people who live on the islands "run over to Oak" just as farmers go to town in the evenings. Instead of hopping in the car and driving to town, they hop in the out-board canoe and go whizzing over the water.

The channels among the islands seem just like streets, and after a while you get to know them as well as you know your own block. You're liable to hear the roar of an outboard on a dark night, skimming the water at twenty miles an hour, and it's so black you can't see it till it's ten feet from the dock. They learn to get around in a boat up here.

People "run over to Oak" just to gather and talk in the evening. And on Saturday nights there is a dance, and everybody gets full of beer and goes roaring home through the darkness in their boats.

*

There are two or three autos up here on the Angle. They aren't used at all in the summer, because there's no place to run them. But in winter they drive over the ice, right across the lake, the fifty miles into Warroad. They don't go often, though, for the ice is sometimes very rough. Before the autos, people used to drive into town by horse and sled. It took two days to make the trip. There hasn't been a team of horses into Warroad from the Angle in two years now.

In winter the people trap muskrats, and they get up the whole supply of wood for the next winter, and they cut ice from the lake and store it. Winter is their busiest time.

*

There have been some strange murders on Northwest Angle in the last few years. A young couple came up to homestead. One evening the bride was discovered in the middle of the floor with a knife in her back. They never decided who did it. Some people outside have told me they thought the Angle was pretty much a hideout for fugitives. But George Arnold, the postmaster, says that isn't true.

In the first place, he says, the population is so scant that everybody knows everybody else, and a stranger would be the center of attention. And further, he says, a man not accustomed to the country, or not well-versed in the primitive life, could not exist alone through the terrible winters.

August 20, 1936

SOUTH DAKOTA

Pyle stopped at Mount Rushmore, South Dakota, in the fall of 1936, for a look at the monument the artist Gutzon Borglum was carving there.

*Borglum and fifty helpers had been at work eight years and had spent four
hundred thousand dollars. At the time of Pyle's visit, the sculptor planned
to spend eighteen more months and three hundred thousand more dollars
to finish the project.*

MOUNT RUSHMORE, SOUTH DAKOTA— . . . Do you wonder how an
artist can get a sixty-foot stone face to look like George Washington, or Thomas Jefferson, or Abraham Lincoln, or Teddy Roosevelt?

Borglum makes a big plaster cast of all four figures. Then he
puts a rod into the top of, say, Washington's head, and drops a
plumb line down over the face. Then he measures down the
plumb line, and also from the line in toward the face, all over it.

Now, up on the mountain top is another rod, stuck in the
rock, and another plumb line dropping down over the stone
cliff. So they just multiply the scale figures by twelve, and measure down the face of the rock, write the measurements on with
chalk, and the drillers start gouging.

After they've drilled and blasted, purely by measurement, for
several months, it begins to look like a face—and, strangely
enough, like Washington's face. Then comes the artist's touch.
Borglum is up there every day. He looks at the face close up. He
goes miles away and looks at it. He starts to mold and shape it.
He orders a brow bulged a little more, a hunk taken off the nose.
They may blast off a whole carload of rock just for the shading
effect on a cheek. . . .

September 21, 1936

THE SCULPTOR OF MOUNT RUSHMORE

MOUNT RUSHMORE, SOUTH DAKOTA— . . . Gutzon Borglum doesn't
seem the type of man you'd picture from reading the reports
about him. He doesn't spout, nor blow off, nor seem the least bit
violent. He doesn't use those artistic phrases that befuddle the
layman. He is intensely earnest about Mount Rushmore, and
seems to feel a sort of reverence about it.

Borglum is of Danish descent. His father was a Nebraska
country doctor. There were no artists in the family before.
Gutzon is going on seventy now, but he doesn't look it or act
it; he has amazing courage and vitality. He works hard and long.
He is medium-short and heavy. His head is bald and he wears
a heavy mustache. Around his neck is a scarflike piece of batik,

the ends tied down about his waist, like the sling for a broken arm. That's the only artist's effect.

He hates politicians. He swears when he talks about them. He won't let politicians tell him how to do his sculpturing, or how to spend the money. That's what most of his rows have been about. But he isn't just plain bullheaded. I see his point. And I was surprised to learn that he will compromise a small point to get something big. He's a practical genius. . . .

He feels so deeply about the historical greatness of Mount Rushmore that it seemed to me that anything he does after this would be anticlimactic in his career. But he doesn't feel that way about it. He says it took him quite a while to get the artist's feel for dealing with anything as massive as a sixty-foot face on a mountainside. He says even now, after being away during the winter, it takes him a week or two to get adjusted to it. . . .

Borglum, even at seventy, climbs the high mountain several times every day, or rides up in the chicken-coop cable car, high across the valley. . . .

Just now, the whitish sculptured faces stand out brightly against the dark mountain. Borglum says it will take fifty years for the newness to disappear, and twenty thousand years for the elements to harmonize them completely with the gray rock all around. He says the faces will last as long as the mountains last.

Someday, Borglum would like to do a lone face of an Indian on some nearby mountain—a stoic, almost expressionless Indian head, just carved there in stone, looking out forever over the country the white man stole from him.

September 22, 1936

Much as President Roosevelt used radio to great advantage, conveying a reassuring paternal warmth over the airwaves, he also thrived on traveling about the country, especially during election years. In the fall of 1936, two months before the election, he toured the drought-ravaged Dakotas. Pyle's account of seeing Roosevelt was highly unusual: the President's polio-induced infirmity was rarely mentioned in print. News photographers even went so far as to voluntarily destroy plates that revealed Roosevelt's disability.

A TENDER TRIBUTE TO FDR'S COURAGE
DENVER— . . . In Rapid City, South Dakota, the other day, we happened to run into President Roosevelt's drought party,

weekending there. We were in the same hotel, and our fourth-floor room looked right down upon the hotel entrance—a grandstand seat for the President's arrivals and departures.

It was Sunday, and a large crowd had gathered by eleven o'clock to see the President leave for church. They were held back by ropes, on the opposite sidewalk, and they cheered him as he drove away.

I lay down for a nap and was presently awakened by clapping in the street. It was the President returning from church. The crowd was still there. I watched from my grandstand window.

Out of what I have always felt to be a fine sense of consideration, there have been few mentions in print of the President's partial paralysis. But it seems to me there can be no violation of good taste in relating what happened at Rapid City that day.

The crowd stopped clapping, and stood silently watching, as the car stopped at the hotel. It was a seven-passenger touring car, with the top down. Two of the President's sons and his daughter-in-law got out ahead of him.

Then, while everybody waited, the President reached for the spare seat and pulled it down in front of him. Then he reached to the robe rail, and with his powerful arms slid himself forward onto the spare seat. Then he turned a little, and put his legs out the door, and over the running board, with his feet almost to the curb.

Gus Gennerich, his bodyguard, stood ready to help. But he was not needed. You could almost have heard a pin drop. The President put both hands on one leg, and pushed downward, locking the jointed steel brace at his knee. He slowly did the same with the other leg.

Then he put his hands on the side of the car, and with his arms lifted his body out and up and onto his legs. He straightened up. I have never seen a man so straight.

And at that moment the tenseness broke, and the crowd applauded. The President's back was to the crowd, and he did not look around. It was brief and restrained applause.

I don't know, but I doubt if that has ever happened to the President before. It was the tenderest, most admiring tribute to courage I have ever seen. It was such a poignant thing, so surprising, so spontaneous. It was as though they were saying with their hands, "We know we shouldn't, but we've got to."

When I turned from the window there was a lump in my throat, and there would have been in yours, too.

*

A few days later we were in Cheyenne when the President's train came through. We were at a filling station. The gas boy spoke about it:

"I'd give anything to be down at the station," he said. "But I had to come to work just fifteen minutes before he got in. See that car there with the New York license?" He sort of laughed. "The woman was dying to go see the President. But her husband got mad and bawled her out. He said she wouldn't go while he was around. He said he was for Landon. I spoke right up and said, 'Mister, you're out of place in this country. This is Roosevelt country.'"

September 25, 1936

POSTSCRIPT: *"I swear the reporters and photographers following the President actually make you sick," Pyle wrote his editor in Washington. "With the exception of a few decent ones . . . you'd almost be ashamed to be seen with one of them. And they're all so goddamned smart and know everything—just a bunch of super boys out looking down upon the country hicks. Christ, they haven't even got good manners."*

PORTRAIT OF A DAKOTA SHEEPHERDER

CASTLE ROCK, SOUTH DAKOTA—It's hard to find out exactly what is on a sheepherder's mind. I suspect that a great deal of the time nothing is.

A sheepherder is in solitary. He has hours and days and even weeks with only his dog and his horse and his thousand sheep for company. His actual work is slow and infrequent. He has an abundance of spare time. Should a man with that much time to himself be a smart man or a stupid one?

If he's smart enough, he will have the capacity to endure himself, and pilot his thoughts about like an aviator, and be a truly great man. If he's stupid enough, devoid of imagination, cursed not with the delirium of introspection, then he will become one with the rock and the weed, moving about his shepherding duties with the blank passion of a machine.

In either case, he'll be all right.

But if he should be neither quite stupid enough nor smart enough, then he must eventually flee in terror before so much loneliness, and rage around in his vast valley of thoughts, and become in time what we slangily describe as coo-coo. It would not surprise me to find that a good percentage of the old sheepherders of the world are just a bit touched.

*

A sheepherder has company so seldom that when he does get a chance to talk, he's liable to say almost anything. His conversation sort of flops around, like an old inner tube. For example, sheepherder Allen Bovey said to me, right in the middle of our conversation, and apparently apropos of nothing whatever: "When I was a little baby, my oldest brother ran away from home, and we never heard from him again. That was thirty years ago. He ran away with three Swedes, and we never knew what became of him." That was all there was of it.

I spent about an hour with Allen Bovey, out on the prairie, where it's so flat you can see a man coming for ten miles. He loves his sheep, and his horse Red, and his little dog Tiddy, even though they don't belong to him personally. He has been herding sheep for nine years. Before that he was a cowpuncher for five years. Before that, he was just a youth.

He gets forty-five dollars a month, and grub. He lives on the range, alone. The sheep wagon is his home. It is like the covered wagon of the frontier days. He cooks his meals in it, and sleeps in it. The rancher drives out about once a week with fresh supplies.

*

Every evening at sunset Allen Bovey's sheep come back to the wagon, even if not driven, and lie down and go to sleep. Bovey goes to bed at sundown. He has trained himself to be alert to approaching storms. "If a storm comes up, I have to get out, and right now, too," he said. "Sheep will stampede in a night storm." Every flock has a born leader, and a shepherd controls a herd through that leader. Bovey's leader is a black sheep, the only one in the whole flock. He says it's just a coincidence.

Bovey is up at dawn, which means between three and four A.M.—up with gun handy. Why? Because it's just after dawn that the coyotes come. He has lost three sheep this summer to coyotes. He has killed one coyote, but it's dangerous to shoot when they are among the sheep.

He has to watch for antelope, which get in among his sheep. This country is so empty and so broad—not a tree for as far as you can see—that you couldn't imagine there being any antelope around. But sometimes they come and graze right among the sheep. Once in a while an old buck sheep will start a fight, and then the buck sheep always gets killed.

*

Alley Bovey reads magazines quite a bit, but he says his eyes are going bad from so much reading. His face is leathery brown, and all wrinkled from squinting in the glaring Dakota sun. He doesn't wear dark glasses, although he guesses he should. Two years ago he went to Rapid City, the biggest town for hundreds of miles. He was walking down the main street, and two masked men with guns jumped out and took a hundred and seventy-five dollars from him—his whole summer's work. He has never been back to Rapid City. Nobody ever bothers him on the range.

I asked him what there was about herding sheep that just anybody couldn't do—me, for instance. He said, "You'd go crazy in two days from lonesomeness." I said no I wouldn't. "Yes you would," he said.

NEBRASKA

OMAHA, NEBRASKA— . . . The railroads are doing a land-office business these days. The highway across Nebraska parallels the Union Pacific, and there's just one freight train after another. They go fast, too. I was doing sixty, and a long freight went right past me.

I don't believe there are as many hoboes riding the trains as there used to be. But I did see one delightful sight. It was a flatcar in the middle of a train. It was empty except for a raised platform that apparently had held a threshing machine or something.

And on this platform, speeding along at seventy miles an hour, were four Negro boys just dancing their heads off. As the train passed they waved and laughed and yelled and kept on dancing, as though they were on a stage before a big audience. . . .

August 7, 1941

POCATELLO, IDAHO— . . . [There's an interesting sign] at a fence corner on a back road several miles east of Crawford, Nebraska. It says: NOTICE—HUNT & FISH ALL YOU DAMN PLEASE. WHEN THE BELL RINGS, COME TO DINNER. —B. G. PINNEY.

The Pinneys settled in Nebraska in the 1880s, when it was

open country. By 1900 the homesteaders were getting things pretty well fenced in, and they were full of a great positive feeling, and they put up NO HUNTING and NO TRESPASSING signs all over.

One day B. G. Pinney was in a saloon in Crawford. A rancher said to him, "Pinney, when are you going to put up a sign?" Pinney replied, "Just as soon as I can get one painted." There was a fellow around town whose occupation was drinking liquor, but who painted a few signs in his spare time. Pinney bought this fellow a pint of whiskey, and told him to paint the sign quoted above.

It was put up thirty-five years ago. Quite a few strangers have come to the house and asked if the sign means what it says. They've been told it does, and the Pinneys even tell them where to find the ducks down along the creek. Nobody has ever come to dinner, though, except neighboring ranchers who would have come anyway.

Five or six years ago this sign was in Ripley's "Believe It or Not" column. The Pinneys got letters from all over the world. Most of them were congratulatory. But one preacher wrote in and gave them the devil. He said they apparently were hospitable, but not very religious. He didn't like that "damn" business.

October 9, 1936

KANSAS

ALMOST BERSERK IN WESTERN KANSAS

MANHATTAN, KANSAS—I am a traveler with above-average tolerance. I don't require much, and a little civility spread across my path will be returned tenfold in meekness and pleasant words about the weather.

But something happened when we came out of Colorado into Kansas. I got sore at everything. I'm not sure just what caused it. Nothing big happened. Our crossing of Kansas was simply a crossing filled with little furies.

We drove into swirling dust the minute we crossed the Colorado line. In one town we had to sleep with the windows shut and only the transom open for air. Dust gritted eternally in your teeth, and your nose was like an old flue. On all the horizons lay a yellow haze, and closer to you dust peaks twisted and swirled.

The wind was an almighty one, blowing from a million miles away. It picked at your car, pushed it and rocked it, until you were tense and aching from the strain. Cars swung wildly across the road ahead of you. Bareness lay in the fields. Tumbleweed balls leaped over fences and went jumping fantastically across space.

You could barely talk above the roar of the wind. You kept cranking the car window up, then down, suspended halfway between the alternatives of choking to death or smothering. Gradually the whole thing shrouded you with an immense annoyance.

*

And then people began to get on my nerves. By one o'clock the Sunday drivers were out, and if there could be a National Sunday Driving Contest, Kansas would sweep the board.

People stopped cars in the middle of the highway, to change seats. People stopped cars side by side in the road, to talk. Families drove along at the pace of a terrapin, ogling the magnificent lack of nature in western Kansas, while traffic piled up behind.

I am against high speed. The speedometer needle on my car has never touched sixty. But I say that when a local citizen, all alone, with one elbow on the window and his chin in his hand, takes a half-mile-long blind curve at the infuriating rate of five miles an hour, he should go to jail as quickly as if he'd been doing eighty.

And in the mid-Kansas towns they have never heard of giving signals. In the little city of Beloit they suddenly turn left, turn right, turn clear around—without giving you the slightest hint of any such intentions. And then they glare at you when your brakes squeal.

Twice we stopped for gas, and drove away in a dudgeon because the gas-pump boys were too busy gabbing with the loafers to fill up the tank. We stopped for lunch, and never did get waited on.

By midafternoon I looked like a bundle of wheat sitting at the wheel. The ends of my nerves were sticking out all over. I would delightedly have killed somebody. If you had asked me my favorite state, I would have named all forty-seven of the others.*

*Alaska and Hawaii were still American territories.

It is not pleasant to think of myself going berserk in western Kansas. But in another hundred miles that is what would have happened. Fortunately, things began to change. There came a slight touch of greenness in the fields. Ahead the sky seemed to have clouds in it, instead of mere yellowness. There came small hills, and a bridge across a little creek, and now and then a farmhouse was painted, and there were real trees again.

All this did not come suddenly, but it came during a hundred miles. Lush green crops were on the land finally; it hurt you to see the wind sweep and flatten the little stocks. You could feel a distinct drop in temperature driving between green fields.

At last we had to get gas, or else get out and push. It was in the town of Clay Center, if I remember correctly. The man was at the gas pump before I had the engine shut off. Because there was no drinking water at the station, one of the loafers ran to a nearby house and brought a glass. Another one inquired if we had come through rain, and talked in easy friendliness about the dust and prospects of rain.

Kansas was better after we left Clay Center. Before we got to Manhattan, rolling hills eased the despondency of eternal flatness. And we drove through a springtime freshness. And in Manhattan we found friends of friends, and they put life into us again and brought us back to sanity. For the first time in three hundred miles we felt at home. Kansas at last was good.

*

No doubt a psychologist could get something from all this, but I get only two things.

First, that every time I have to leave the West—you leave it at Denver—a great irritation rolls up inside me. For there is truly something different about the West—the people are different, the whole spirit is different.

And, second, there is definitely something in that three-hundred-mile strip of dust-swept land between the Midwest and the Rockies that gives me the shivers, and I feel a strangeness and an unwelcomeness among the people there that I've never felt anyplace else in the world.

Maybe the feeling is wholly within me, and not in the people at all. And if that should be it, I am sorry. But I do feel it, and I can't help it.

May 7, 1938

A Man People Love to Hate

HIAWATHA, KANSAS—John Milburn Davis is eighty-three years old, has a long white beard and only one hand, and says he's the worst-hated man in Kansas.

People hate him because he spent his money the way he pleased. What he pleased was to put up in the local graveyard a memorial to himself and his late wife. Estimates of its cost run all the way from fifty thousand to a million dollars.

When I asked some people in Hiawatha about the memorial, they said: "Be sure and go see it. It's a monstrosity. There's nothing like it in the United States." So we drove out to Mount Hope Cemetery, and there it was—eleven life-sized stone images sitting and standing around two marble-slabbed graves, one of which is still empty.

Six of the statues are of farmer Davis himself. Five are of Mrs. Davis, who died in 1930, just after their fiftieth wedding anniversary. In one statue Mrs. Davis is an angel, with wings. There is also a big overstuffed sitting-room chair, carved in granite, with the words THE VACANT CHAIR chiseled across the back of the seat.

The statuary represents Mr. and Mrs. Davis at various stages of their fifty years together. All were sculptured from old photographs. They are not exactly grotesque. But they are daguerreotypish, and when you come up to them all sitting and standing around there, big as life and stiff as death, they give you a spooky feeling.

*

After looking all around, we drove back to town. Farmer Davis was sitting on his front porch. He likes to talk about the memorial. Davis was a Kentucky orphan. He landed here in 1880, and got married. Somehow he made a lot of money. He is vague about it. "Always buy what somebody else wants," he says. Mr. Davis doesn't know what put the idea in his head, but when Mrs. Davis died, he decided to put up a statue of each of them, facing each other across her grave. He wanted the best. He went to the local monument dealer. They decided to have the work done in Italy. They sent old photographs, and in due time the statues came back.

"I liked them so well," says Mr. Davis, "that I decided to have two more made. So I sent some different photographs. And when those statues came back I liked them so well I wanted some more. I started it in 1931, and it took three years. It's all through now."

In 1898 Mr. Davis was burning brush after trimming a hedge

fence, and a flame licked up and burned his beard off. Consequently he is clean-shaven in one statue, bearded in the others. Then in 1908 he was cutting hedge fence again, and accidentally cut his left hand off. So four of his six statues show him with only one hand.

I asked Mr. Davis how much it all cost. He laughed and said that's one thing he won't tell. Then I said, "Well, I guess it didn't cost a million dollars, anyway."

Mr. Davis squared around in his chair as though he were mad, and said loudly: "Have you got any real money that says it didn't?" I fished around in my pocket and could find only thirty-eight hundred dollars and some Kansas tax tokens, so we let it stand at a million.

Mr. Davis said: "They hate me in Kansas because they wanted me to build a hospital and swimming pools and parks, and I wouldn't do it. It's my money and I spend it the way *I* please. There's one doctor that won't speak to me because I wouldn't build a hospital. Even the other monument dealers hate the one that got the business."

Around Hiawatha they say Mr. Davis spent all this money on the memorial to keep relatives from getting it after he dies. I asked him about that, and he said: "I didn't do it for that reason any more than you bought that suit you've got on to keep somebody else from having the money. There's all kinds of talk around here about me. About how mean I was to her before she died and things like that. I even get anonymous telephone calls berating me."

I asked him if he'd used up all his money on this memorial. He laughed and looked sort of sly and said, "I'm not going to starve."

Mr. Davis lives all alone in the big house he and his wife came to in 1915. He's pretty vain about the memorial, and every Sunday, when he feels up to it, he goes out to the graveyard and hangs around. Lots of tourists recognize him from his statues. Some compliment him and some abuse him.

One tourist came up with tears in his eyes and said, "You'll be blessed in Heaven for this noble work." And a minute later another tourist came up and said, "You ought to be buried in a hole forty feet deep without even a headstone for this awful thing."

Mr. Davis gets lots of letters, too—some praising, some abusing. He has had letters from all over the world. One came from Holland a couple of years ago, and he's never had it translated.

Most of the letters contain pleas for money. But if you're thinking of writing, you might as well save your stamp. Mr. Davis has never answered a single letter.

I asked him how he felt about all the hatred and criticism of him. He said, "It's just like pouring water off a duck's back to me."

And as I went down the steps he said: "How many copies are you going to send me? Send at least three. And if you ever see me anywhere, be sure and yell. You'd know me, but I might not recognize you. I meet thousands of people."

May 10, 1938

The Dust Bowl

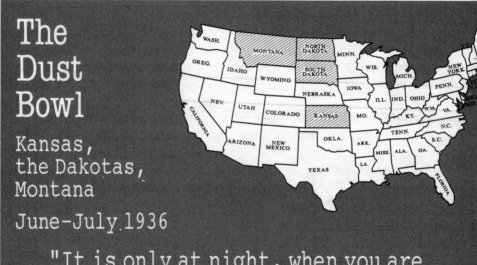

Kansas, the Dakotas, Montana

June–July 1936

"It is only at night, when you are alone in the enveloping heat and cannot sleep, and look into the darkness, and things come back to you like a living dream, that you realize the stupendousness of it."

As if things weren't bad enough, the 1930s also brought drought. The lack of rain and the extreme heat, coupled with years of misguided farming practices, left an area from Texas to the Dakotas a virtual dust bowl. Fallout from blinding dust storms was felt as far east as Washington itself. Pyle's editors in Washington wanted him to cover the calamity. Pyle wasn't in favor of it, but he went anyway and produced a fine series on the calamity that gave rise to the migration John Steinbeck traced in The Grapes of Wrath.

ALL IS CREEPING DESOLATION

GARDEN CITY, KANSAS—If you would like to have your heart broken, just come out here. This is the dust-storm country. It is the saddest land I have ever seen.

Coming in here from Colorado Springs, a one-day drive, you pass through both the sandstorm and the dust-storm regions. Eastern Colorado is a mild form of desert, and hence rather sandy. When the wind blows there, you have a sandstorm. As you get into Kansas, the soil becomes richer and softer, and when it gets dry and powdery, and when the wind blows, you have a dust storm.

*

We were still in Colorado. Far behind, old Pikes Peak lifted its snowy sides into the heavens. Far ahead to the east were faint, hazy clouds of sand. The approach to a sandstorm is a dark and chilling experience.

The yellow sand haze ahead grew heavier and darker, making the atmosphere a queer yellow, the way it is sometimes just before a cyclone. To the right were rolling, foreboding rain clouds, dust mixing with them. And over to the left, over where the wind came from, were pillars of sand—giant yellow columns, miles away, rising from the horizon clear up into the sky, like smoke from a burning town. It was frightening, and sickening.

The wind howled. It came at least forty miles an hour, across the prairie from the north. It was hard to steer the car. The roar of the wind was louder than your voice. The sand film grew steadily thicker around us. It darkened the atmosphere, and a little film settled on the inside rim of the windshield.

The country was slightly rolling. In the valleys it was better. But on the rises, the sand-laden wind cut across the highway like a horizontal waterfall. The sand was not drifting, or floating, or hanging in the air—it was shooting south, in thick veins, like air full of thrown baseballs.

Cars we met had their lights on, and we wondered if it was really that bad ahead. It was. We went into the darkness as an airplane flies into fog. The air was black with sand. You could not see from one telephone pole to the next. There wasn't any sky. The tiny rocks smashed and pounded against the car windows. The wind was vicious, and the car was light on its wheels, and inclined to weave. You couldn't hear the motor at all.

It didn't last long, no more than a mile or two. And then we popped out into rain. The air was washed clear. It was like coming out suddenly into fresh air on the windward side of a forest fire.

*

We came into Kansas. It had been raining for twelve hours. The earth was wet, and we were thus spared the spectacle of a Kansas dust storm. But because the air was clear, we could better see the terrific desolation that is western Kansas. We could not have seen it if the air had been filled with dust.

A few miles from the village of Lakin I stopped, shoved open the door, and stood on the running board, holding on to the car, as the cold wind rushed and roared, and looked around. The land is as flat as a billiard table. The horizon is far, far away. I looked clear around the rim, as you do sometimes from a ship at sea, just following the horizon around. And I saw not a solitary thing but bare earth, and a few lonely, empty farmhouses.

You might truthfully say there is nothing left of western Kansas. As far as the eye could see, there was nothing. There was not a tree, or a blade of grass, or a dog or a cow, or a human being—nothing whatever, nothing at all but gray raw earth and a few far houses and barns, sticking up from the dark gray sea like white cattle skeletons on the desert. There was nobody in the houses. The humans had given up, and gone. It was death, if I have ever seen death.

Today, because of the rain, the ground held firm, and would not give itself up to the wind. But yesterday it did, and tomorrow, after the bright sun, it will again. The air will gradually fill with the earthy powder, and people in its path will scarcely be able to breathe, and houses will be closed. And the soil will blow away from around the roots of things, and pile like snowdrifts against the barns, and fly on the wind south toward Mexico, and leave nothing at all.

As I drove along I thought of all the smart-aleck jokes about President Roosevelt's hundred-mile-wide belt of trees.* I

*Roosevelt personally conceived the idea of the shelter belt, a windbreak. The Forest Service and the WPA planted more than two hundred million trees from the Dakotas through Oklahoma. Roosevelt was proud of his successful innovation, but his critics had a field day with it.

thought of the sneers about the college professors trying to improve the earth. I wonder if any of the criticizers have ever seen a country that has died. A belt of trees, or a belt of soybeans, or a belt of billiard cues stuck in the ground—anything that might faintly halt the march of the destroying wind across the face of our earth—seems to me worth trying.

June 6, 1936

THE DUST SMOTHERS EVERYTHING

GARDEN CITY, KANSAS—The people of western Kansas are hopefully looking for gas to blow the lid off the vacuum the dust storms have made of their lands.

Gas wells have been discovered in the extreme southwest corner of the state. And the people here are hoping the gas field will spread, so they may collect revenues from underground, because revenues from the ground's surface no longer exist. The mere possibility of gas has kept a lot of farmers going through the dust-storm interlude—if it is an interlude. Much of this land is already under option by gas companies, and the small lease fees have helped keep the wolf from the door.

Garden City has suffered much from the dust storms, although this is not the worst of the dust area right here. I spent an evening in the home of a Garden City couple. Their house is a beautiful, modern suburban bungalow. They pulled up the Venetian blinds and showed me the windows. Every window in the house is sealed with surgeon's tape.

The dust storms this year haven't been so bad as last year's, they say. There has been a little more rain, and the wind hasn't blown so hard. Last year, they say, dust half an inch deep would collect on their windowsills, even though the windows were sealed with tape. This year, just a heavy film collects.

Last year, beautiful lawns were smothered out by the settling dust. People even devised big vacuum affairs and went over their lawns, trying to pull up the coat of dust from around the grass roots.

I asked my friend in Garden City to tell me all about the dust storms—what caused them, and what was being done about it, and so on. This is what he told me:

This country has always been cattle-grazing country. There has never been much heavy vegetation; just short grass. But during and after the war, people found they could make more money raising wheat than raising cattle. They started farming. Money came easily. It was nothing for a man to buy a section of land and pay for it with just one wheat crop. It was a utopia. A few months' work, and your year's revenue was in hand. People didn't put much back into the land, or till for the future.

Then, five years ago, came the drought. Most of the farmers were broke. There had been a bumper crop. As far as you could see across these vast prairies, every inch of land was covered with billowing wheat. The market was flooded. The price fell to nothing. The crop that year, even though it was fine, would hardly pay for itself.

With no money in hand, the farmers couldn't afford to let their land lie fallow; they couldn't afford to make the temporary sacrifice that would have insured the future. They couldn't afford to have the doctor now, even though it would have been cheaper in the long run. They continued to plow and plant. There was no rain. The wind blew. The raw ground dried, and started to blow.

My friend told how dust storms are like a disease. They infect other land. The dust settles over an adjoining field, smothers out the vegetation; the blowing dust drills into it, gets a hold, digs in, bares a spot to the wind, and it's all over. Another field has been added to the desolation.

Hundreds of thousands of acres have been completely abandoned. The people have moved to neighboring towns and tried to get day work. Some have found farms to rent outside the dust region.

And what is to become of this country? I don't know. The experts are working on it. They are giving advice, but advice is mighty hard to follow when you're broke. The experts do say this: that if this land were left fallow for a few years, or if it were tilled with method, the country could be restored.

Some people say it is gone forever, that the rich topsoil is all blown away. Others say nonsense, that topsoil extends down thirty feet. Some crops won't grow on this land now, certainly, but others will. The experts say a farmer can terrace land against wind erosion, just as he can against water erosion—you can plow up the ridges, at right angles to the prevailing winds, and these ridges will catch the dust, and form a dam, and keep the soil in place. They have done it in many places.

But the average farmer, even though he may be in accord with the scientific ways of restoring the land, still feels that it is just the plain old farm question of weather, and that as soon as the wind stops blowing and we get back to normal rains, everything will be all right.

June 8, 1936

THE GRASSHOPPER PLAGUE

RAPID CITY, SOUTH DAKOTA—The grasshopper is to the Dakotas about the same thing as a hurricane is to Miami or a tidal wave is to Galveston.

The grasshopper opens and closes every conversation. He holds second place only to the great drought itself. You can't say the grasshoppers destroyed everything the drought left; rather, the two galloped down through the sun-parched summer nose and nose, and it would be hard to say whether the last blade of grass died of thirst or was gnawed by a hopper.

I'd always imagined the aftermath looked like World War pictures of a French woods after a heavy shelling, with only the stumps of the trees still standing. But that's not the case. A cornfield after grasshoppers get through with it looks like a freshly plowed field, just after the soil is turned and is all black and rich-looking, with no vegetation at all.

They not only strip the blades; they eat the stalk, and burrow down into the ground and nibble away the roots. They leave nothing on the surface whatever. They do the same with grain and grass and vegetables.

I wanted to take a picture of a hopper-devastated cornfield, but I didn't want a bare field, because you couldn't prove there had been any corn there. I wanted a field that had leafless cornstalks still standing like sticks, and I drove for a full half day through South Dakota before I could find a field that had even the stumps of cornstalks left. There is only one cornfield in about every hundred and fifty miles that hasn't simply disappeared from the face of the earth.

*

The motorist's first engagement with a grasshopper horde gives him a queer feeling. They don't make a black cloud in the sky. They just sit thickly along the road, and you don't see them until your car stirs them up. And then all of a sudden they are streaking around in all directions, like bullets in a war poster. They jump so fast that each one makes a sort of black streak. They smack and hang all over the car. I was continually dodging and blinking. When you see one coming straight at you, you instinctively duck. And just as you do, he hits the windshield with a pop that sounds as if somebody had thrown a rock.

That first batch lasted for about three miles. I stopped at the first town and bought a grasshopper screen to go over the radiator. Nearly every car out here has one. It costs eighty-five cents, and is made of window screening, cut to fit your radiator. If you don't have one, first thing you know the surface is solid with them, and no air can get through, and your engine gets hot.

The garage man swept the dead ones out with a broom before he put on the screen. I was curious, so I counted them. There were two hundred and eighty-four stuck in my radiator.

Since then, I have been running through grasshoppers at least a third of the time. There are never fewer than half a dozen in the car with me. About three times a day one gets up my pants leg, and I have to stop and fish him out.

You're liable to find them in your hotel room, or in your shirt in the morning, or hopping around the tables in the best restaurants. They can't hurt you, of course, but they get in the way.

The old-timers tell me that grasshopper plagues run in cycles. There was a bad one in 1902, and another in 1922. They usually last three or four years, and they are worse in dry years. This is the third and worst year of the current cycle.

There isn't much you can do about them, apparently. The government has used Paris green. That kills them, all right. But as one farmer says, "For every one that dies, a thousand come to his funeral." It's like trying to bore a hole in water.

The farmers say that when it rains after the poison is spread, the poison washes off and runs down to the water holes, and poisons the cattle and birds. They say that quite a few cattle have been killed, and that you hardly ever see birds anymore.

One farmer said that in 1922, the grasshoppers started dying off like flies, and on every one you would find a little hole just behind his foreleg. Something had stung him to death. This farmer understood it was some kind of parasite the scientists had turned loose against the hoppers. He wishes they would do it again.

July 20, 1936

Of Parched Land and a Hot High Wind
MILES CITY, MONTANA—For a whole day I played host to Roy Meehan, of the South Dakota Meehans.

Young Mr. Meehan is as fine a fellow as I've ever met. He's about twenty-five, nice-looking and very tanned, and he rolls his own cigarets. You could put him on Long Island in flannel pants and a blue coat some evening, and he would be very quiet and everybody would like him.

Roy is a farmer, or rather he *was* a farmer. He's never going to be a farmer again. He has washed his hands of farming in South Dakota.

He was born and raised on the Dakota prairies. He never knew anything about farming. His father died, and left three-quarters of a section to Roy and his mother to handle. They, with the help of the elements and things we can't understand, handed it into the hands of Rural Credit. They don't have a farm anymore.

But this year Roy had a hunch. He rented four hundred acres, and put it in corn and small grain. "I thought I'd make a hit for sure," he said. "I made a hit all right."

We rode along awhile, and young Mr. Meehan said, apropos of nothing, "The cane I planted never even came through the ground." So Roy sold out. He sold his horses, his farm machinery. He has two brothers, not grown yet, and he left them with his mother on the rented farm. And he packed his old black suitcase and started west.

I picked him up early in the morning. He said he had slept in a boxcar the night before. He's going to Fort Peck, Montana, to try to get a job on the big government dam project there. If he doesn't land, he'll keep traveling toward the West Coast.

We saw a lot of things in a day, Roy and I.

*

We saw Mr. Denien, who came to South Dakota five years ago from La Porte, Indiana, to share a farm with a widowed uncle.

Mr. Denien and his wife and children packed everything in their old Cadillac and drove out to the land of opportunity. The Cadillac has not moved an inch since they arrived. It's still parked in the shed, but one of these days, when Mr. Denien gets up his courage, and enough money to buy a license, it may carry them away again.

I have never seen anybody so bewildered and discouraged as Mr. Denien. Here five years. A good crop the first year, but no money for it. No crop at all the last four years. He has five little children. "We came west all right," says Mrs. Denien. "But we didn't come far enough. They say things are good in Idaho."

Mr. Denien was janitor at the La Porte YMCA for many

years. He said he remembered me from when I lived there on my first newspaper job. His eagerness at seeing somebody from "home" was almost pathetic. "Tell everybody in La Porte hello," he said. But I haven't been in La Porte for thirteen years.

*

Young Mr. Meehan and I plunged northward. From Belle-fourche it is one hundred miles to North Dakota. In that whole distance there is just one parched little town, and not more than half a dozen houses you can see from the road. There are no telephone poles, or fences, or trees, or grass.

I had seen range country before—the great rolling spaces—but young Mr. Meehan never had. "Say, this is open country, isn't it?" he would say. We would top a rise and could see for eighteen miles, and the only thing in all that space would be half a dozen canvas-covered chuck wagons stationed around the prairie, miles apart, for the cowboys to sleep in and get a bit to eat from.

We saw a pump behind a house and stopped for a drink. We talked for half an hour with four farmers in overalls and cowboy boots. "You saw that herd at the water hole about twenty miles back?" one said. "That's the last of the cattle in this country. They're driving them to Bellefourche to ship."

The oldest of the group was about forty. He was burned black, and rolled cigarets in the hot high wind that whipped around us. He was, it seemed to me, the smartest of the bunch and the most bitter. He came here in 1909, when he was just a boy.

"We had a bad drought here in 1911, but nothing like this," he said. "Six years now. I don't know any other business. I don't know what we're going to do. We can't leave. We could even get by on this burned grass if we had water. But the springs are drying up. We can't afford to drill deep wells. If next year is like this, with no feed to carry over, there won't be a soul left around here. We'll have to leave. It won't be possible to exist."

*

We stopped in front of a house a few miles west of Rhame, North Dakota, and shouted, "Can we get a drink out of your well?" You have to drink often when it's a hundred and ten degrees. The farmer came out and turned on the windmill, and as we drank the farmer said, "Ain't this the worst godforsaken country you ever saw?"

I said, "This may sound silly to you, but right through here it looks a hundred percent better than it does all across South Dakota."

"That's what people tell me," he said. "We had two big rains. But it's too late. I shipped my cattle just this afternoon. Nineteen head. I'll try to hang on with the milk cows. I don't know what the hell a fellow's going to do. Some people have left, but most of us can't leave. We're just sittin' and waitin'. And this is good country, too, when things are right.

*

We pulled up at a road-grading job a few miles west of Pevna, Montana.

"I've been here twenty-three years," one man said. "I was pretty well off once. But last fall I had just fifty dollars to get through the winter on. I put it in a safe, and every time I took a dollar bill out it was just like pulling a tooth.

"If anybody had told me twenty-three years ago that I'd be working for the state today, I'd have told him he was crazy. But I'm damn glad to get it, let me tell you."

July 21, 1936

Struggling in the Powder River Country

MILES CITY, MONTANA—Denver Williams had been sitting in my room talking for about two hours last night when who should walk in but Dr. Rexford G. Tugwell.

Denver Williams is a cattle man, and he's broke, and he has lots to tell. And Dr. Tugwell is the big works in the Resettlement Administration, and he's out here seeing the drought, and he's a good listener. So for an hour Denver Williams talked and Rex Tugwell listened. This is what he heard.

Fletcher Williams was born in Colorado; that's why they call him Denver. He is forty-six. He has been working and paying his own way in the world since he was eleven. He grew up a cowboy. He looks like a cowboy—tall and lean and brown. He wears a sweeping wide-brimmed hat, and when he's indoors he drops his cigaret ashes in the cuff of his overalls. He talks slowly, and smiles a little all the time he talks.

Denver came to Montana's Powder River country in 1912, working as a cowboy. As the big outfits dwindled and the cowboys started setting up for themselves, Denver did likewise. He got a thousand acres. He raised from forty to a hundred cattle a year. He farmed enough to get winter feed. The years went on and he got himself in pretty good shape.

In 1919—drought. Denver went to the bank for a loan, and the banker said: "Well, the way I figure your assets, you're worth about thirty-five thousand dollars."

In 1920—more drought. When Denver sold his drought cattle and settled up, the banker said: "Well, the way I figure your assets now, you're worth two hundred and fifty dollars."

So Denver left for the Colorado oil fields. He had never seen an oil rig, "but it's good for us to learn new things," he said. He got on as a tool dresser. He sent for his wife. He drew eighteen dollars a day, and they saved thirty-five hundred dollars that year. They came back to Montana and staked themselves to a new start on the ranch.

They got themselves in pretty good shape again. Then, 1924. Rain, rain, rain—it rained him right out of this country of drought. His cows bogged down on the hillsides and died. His steers slid over banks and broke their necks. His little pigs huddled up in the rain and smothered to death.

Denver went to the oil fields again. Three times that has happened. Twice it was drought; once it was rain. Something is about to happen again.

His thousand-acre ranch went in 1934, the year of the big drought. But the bank let him stay on it, just for taxes. There have been six years of drought now. But things looked pretty good this year at the start. Denver had forty head of cattle and some crops. Then one morning about six weeks ago he saw some grasshoppers, and he had a hunch. "I'm letting the cattle go," he said. His wife said, "But maybe it'll rain." And he said, "And maybe it won't."

He saddled the pinto ponies, and he and one of his little girls walked those cattle forty-five miles to a railroad. It took them four days and nights. And then he went with the cattle on the train to Sioux City. He got a good price, because he sold early. But he owed it all to the bank. All he has left is three milk cows, his work horses, and a bunch of pigs.

His horses and cows won't last another two weeks, because the range is burned up and there is no feed. "I finally gave away some pigs," he said. "But I can't give away the rest. Nobody can feed them."

Denver said this country is worse than it was in the drought of 1934. He said the pine trees up in the hills are dying; the cones have fallen off.

Denver saw a man signing up for relief yesterday. Two months ago the man had eight hundred head of cattle. Today he is broke. Denver said it would take a loan of five thousand dollars to get him started again with cattle next spring, and it would take him five years to pay it back. He said he'll have to work some kind of job to see his family through the winter.

"A fellow isn't going to see his kids hungry," he said.

Denver had intended to leave the next day for Idaho to look for harvest work, but now he said he'll wait a little longer. "We're the stayin'est fools I ever saw in Powder River country," he said. "We haven't got sense enough to know when we're licked."

He never preached, never pleaded. He didn't appeal. He just happened to be there, chewing the fat with me, so he just told us how things were. He left after midnight, to drive a friend's car the hundred and twenty miles back to his ranch that isn't his. When he had gone, Rex Tugwell said, "Isn't he a swell fellow? He's the kind that's got to have help, and right now. He's worth helping."

July 22, 1936

RUIN UNDER THE PITILESS SUN

BROADUS, MONTANA—What a magnificent thing this Powder River country of southeastern Montana must have been fifty years ago. "This was the greatest cattle-grazing country that ever lay out of doors," said Ray Wilson. He was born on the range, and he rode it as a cowman and operator until a year ago, when he finally had to close out. He works in a lumberyard now.

"This short, thick grass was the richest in America," Ray said. "You could graze it the year around, except maybe for a month in the hardest winters. You could cut enough wild hay along the river bottoms to carry you through the coldest month.

"The government owned the land then. It was free-range country. The cattle ranged at large, and cowboys rode the way they ride in books. The great herds grazed by the thousands, always moving, always free—no fence lines, no property lines, no water restrictions.

"It was easy to borrow money, and it was always paid back. A cattleman would go to the bank for a loan. The bank might ask how many cattle he owned, but no more questions were asked. It would have been an insult for a bank to send someone out to count his cattle.

"A total stranger could walk into a bank and cash a check, and they wouldn't even look at him twice.

"In those days, any rancher who went away and locked his house was blackballed. You could leave a gold watch and fifty dollars and a jug of whiskey and a sack of tobacco on the table. When you came back home the whiskey and tobacco might be gone, but the fifty dollars and the gold watch would always be there."

And listen to a storekeeper: "In those days your customer came in only about twice a year. But how he bought! It wasn't anything for a cattleman to come in and buy eight hundred or a thousand dollars' worth of groceries in the fall. One man would often buy as much as a store keeps in stock nowadays.

"Maybe a man you'd never seen before would come in. He'd walk along the counter and pick out what he wanted—overalls, shirts, boots, and tobacco. It might total up to sixty or seventy dollars. You'd ask him who he was riding for. He'd say a certain outfit. That's all you needed to know. He'd take the stuff and you wouldn't see him again until fall, and then he'd come in and pay. You never lost anything on those men."

In the old days, the storekeeper told me, "Cattlemen were worth from fifty thousand dollars on up into the millions. They lived in shacks out on the prairie and brought up their families on hard work. But they had money and they shot square."

Today, the storekeeper told me, "Everybody in this Powder River country is broke. Probably nobody has more than fifteen hundred dollars in the bank, free of debt, and those are few. The banks wouldn't lend a dime on your life. The cattleman comes in for one cake of salt at a time, and the farmer takes a sack of potatoes and says he'll pay when he can."

The beautiful rolling green hills are bare, the color of the graveled road. Only now and then do you see a bunch of cattle; the others have prematurely gone to market, lest they wither away. The squat, treeless houses sit in the pitiless sun, far from the road, as always. Around them you see long rows of rusty, motionless machinery. You see the few work horses huddled along a dry creek, swishing the flies. There is no work for them in the fields. The farmers and cattlemen patch fences, or do chores, or just sit and wait.

It started in 1909, when the railroad came through. The gov-

ernment gave the railroad half the land—every other section—
for fifty miles on each side of the right of way. Then came
homesteading. That brought in a new population. It brought the
plow, and the deadly constricting fence that barred off watering
places. It destroyed the freedom of the range. Taxes were applied. Grazing land was cut down. The cattlemen had new
overheads to meet, and less to meet them with. The farmers
plowed up the great rolling plains, and they were scourged by
drought, even in the beginning.

The cattlemen, trying to survive, raised too many cattle in too
little space. Denied the open range, they were forced to do some
farming for winter feed. The country was despoiled. It could
not stand a seven-year drought.

Now the country can never be restored. True, the grass
would come back in a year or two if they stopped farming, and
springs would fill up again in a few years. But, as a mooner over
times gone by told me: "It took character, and free money, and
straight shooting, and we don't have the same things anymore."

All the old freedom, all the old bigness, of the Montana range
is gone. A rancher has to lock his house now when he goes to
town.

July 23, 1936

A DULL, CONTINUOUS FACT

BISMARCK, NORTH DAKOTA—My trip through this withering land
of misery swings to a close, and I am glad. The world of drought
finally becomes an immersion that levels the senses.

You arrive at a point where you no longer look and say, "My
God, this is awful!" You gradually become accustomed to dried
field and burned pasture; it stretches into a dull, continuous fact.

Day upon day of driving through this ruined country gradually becomes a sameness that ceases to admit a perspective. You
come to accept it as a vast land that is dry and bare, and was that
way yesterday and will be tomorrow, and was that way a hundred miles back and will be a hundred miles ahead.

The story is the same everywhere, the farmers say the same
thing, the fields look the same—it becomes like the drone of a
bee, and after a while you hardly notice it at all.

It is that way all day. It is only at night, when you are alone
in the enveloping heat and cannot sleep, and look into the darkness, and things come back to you like a living dream, that you
once more realize the stupendousness of it.

Then you can see something more than field after brown field, or a mere succession of dry water holes, or the matter-of-fact resignation on farm faces.

You can see then the whole backward evolution into oblivion of a great land, and the destruction of a people, and the calamity of long years on end without privilege for those of the soil, and the horror of a life started in emptiness, knowing only struggle, and ending in despair.

I have seen a great deal of this in the last few years. Sometimes at night when I am thinking too hard I feel that there is nothing but leanness everywhere, that nobody has the privilege of a full life, that all existences are things of drudgery that had better be done with. Of course I am wrong about that.

But not only people. I have seen the degradation of great lands, too. The beautiful valleys and hillsides of Tennessee washing away to the ocean, leaving a slashed and useless landscape. The raw windy plains of western Kansas, stripped of all flesh, all life driven away, a onetime paradise turned into a whirlpool of suffocation. And the vast rolling Dakotas where huge herds once grazed with the freedom of the birds, now parched and cramped and mishandled by man and elements into a bed of coals.

July 27, 1936

BOOK TWO

> "Each time, after leaving, I realize that in the West my spirit has been light; I've felt freer and happier."

COLORADO

During a trip to Colorado a few months before he wrote this column, Pyle had regretted being unable to locate and write about an "old-time prospector—one of those dirty old goats with long hair and white beard and a pan and a pick, and a couple of pack burros." Why? Mining men told him the "old boys have died. The new ones—well, you don't prospect that way in Colorado now. You prospect by scientific methods; you go to college and take a course." Pyle was luckier on this trip.

LUCKY JIM MCDONALD

LEADVILLE, COLORADO—Big Jim McDonald is seventy-two now. They say he's worth a hundred thousand dollars. He has never had an ache or pain in his life. He has never been hurt, never been married. He has no regrets. He loves Leadville.

He came to this romantic old silver camp, two miles above sea level, when both he and Leadville were young. They have lived fifty-two years together.

Big Jim came west from Halifax, Nova Scotia. For ten years he worked in the silver mines, for wages. He socked every penny back into leases of his own. Nothing came of them, for ten years. And then he hit. He doesn't have to worry about money anymore. He hasn't had to for forty years. But he still likes to see new mines come in. Mining is his whole life.

Big Jim is a Scotsman. His house is a small but comfortable one on the hill. He wears a cap all the time, even in the house. He lives alone. He keeps a loaded rifle by his bedside, and nobody bothers him. In fact, nobody has ever bothered him. He is too big, a whopper of a man: six foot three. A year ago he weighed three hundred and thirty-five pounds. But he diets now and he's down to two hundred and sixty-five. He eats meat only once a day, and keeps a bag of oranges around to nibble on. He goes to bed at nine-thirty and sleeps like a log until seven the next morning. He says he never worries.

Big Jim's main strength stunt was tug-of-war. He used to pull eight men down as easy as pie. When he was fifty-two they put on a big tug-of-war celebration one night. "It was all I could do to hold five men," he said. "That's the first time I realized I was going down the other side of life. I've never pulled tug-of-war since then."

When he was young, Big Jim used to dance all night in Leadville's Wild West dance halls, and then work in the mine all day without ever going to bed. He could do that until he was fifty. For thirty years Big Jim was in the mines, working as everything from a mucker to superintendent. Then he ran smelters and managed mine properties for eighteen years more. He quit work four years ago.

Now he enjoys doing nothing. He has considerable property to look after, and he sits around town and chats, and reads the papers and the *National Geographic,* and sits in his front door and looks out at the mountains. He is very happy.

Once a year he takes a trip. "I can stick a thousand dollars in my pocket and start out," he says, "and have a thousand dollars' worth of fun." He used to go back to Nova Scotia every seven years, but his mother died, and he hasn't been there for twenty years now. Last year he traveled the West Coast, clear from Tijuana to Seattle. A year ago he took his first airplane ride. He said he'd done everything else; now he wanted to try that. His friends were terrified, and said he'd be killed. "A man born to hang never gets drowned," said Big Jim, and he flew away to Albuquerque.

*

"Maybe I missed a lot by not getting married," he says. "But I was independent. I had to have my own way." But that isn't all the story. He took in two orphan girls when they were five years old. Their parents had worked in the same camp with Big Jim. People said to him, "You don't want to do that. They'll cost so much money."

"What the hell of it?" said Big Jim. "It's my money."

People said, "They'll grow up and sass you."

Says Big Jim today, "They've never spoken a sassy word to me."

The girls worship him. He put them both through college. They're married now. One lives in Seattle, and the other lives next door to Big Jim. He eats his meals over there sometimes. "They were good for me," he says. "They softened me. I'd come home from the mine out of sorts and mad, and they'd crawl all over me and I'd forget about being mad."

*

Big Jim doesn't smoke, he drinks hardly at all, and he swears a lot. "Once in a while, like on Bobby Burns' birthday, I may take a drink, or I may take a dozen," he says. "But I've never let it get the best of me."

He was a Republican until ten years ago. The Republicans took twenty-two thousand dollars away from him in income taxes that he says he didn't owe. He's been a Democrat ever since. Roosevelt will get his vote. He says Roosevelt is the only President who ever did anything for the West.

*

"I've been lucky all my life," he says. "Anybody who works thirty years in the mines without getting hurt is just plain lucky. If I get sick or die tomorrow, I've beat the game. I'm well-fixed and comfortable. I've never been sick a day in my life. I've been lucky all the way through. I've lived my threescore and ten, and two years more, and I've come out ahead. From here on in everything is velvet, no matter what happens."

September 30, 1936

A GREAT AMERICAN EDUCATOR

PINECLIFFE, COLORADO—One of the main things about Denver is Opportunity School. You can ask almost anybody here, and he will tell you that.

Opportunity School is simply a big building downtown

where grown-up people go in a constant stream from eight in the morning until nine-thirty at night, to try to learn something that will better their stations in life.

The school is part of the city school system. Students don't have to pay anything to attend. They come when they can. They are all eager to learn. They range in age from seventeen to seventy. They are not all down-and-outers by any means, but they are all people with hopes for better things.

Opportunity School was started in 1916. Within two months, it had two thousand students. Today it has ten thousand, and a hundred and twenty-five teachers, and needs more. They teach more than forty trades, from beauty-parloring to welding, in addition to reading and writing for grown-ups.

It was, they say, the first adult daytime school in America. And it still is today, after twenty years, the outstanding school of its kind in America, though it has many imitators.

*

Way up here in Coal Creek Canyon, in the mountains forty miles west of Denver, sits a neat three-room cabin. Not seventy-five feet from its back door runs a clear mountain stream. In this cabin lives Miss Emily Griffith. Everywhere this column is published, somebody will read it who knows Emily Griffith, for she is the mother, the soul, the spirit, the everything of Opportunity School. There are a quarter million people, I expect, who know her and love her. She is a most remarkable woman; she is one who really lives for others.

Miss Griffith was a schoolteacher in Denver all her working life. It was what she saw around her when she was teaching in a poor section in 1916 that made her think of such a thing as Opportunity School. She talked the city school superintendent into letting her try it, and from the first day it has been an overwhelming thing. I doubt that you could go into a single block in Denver and not find somebody who has been to Opportunity School.

Opportunity School is practical education mixed with understanding. It is, in reality, the soul of Emily Griffith. Her heart is soft for adversity. Always she wanted to follow the people on the street, the people with empty eyes, and see if she couldn't help.

You could use up pages telling how Emily Griffith started and ran the school. But I don't have pages, so maybe I can give you a clue in just one sentence. She never bowed to a private office.

Her desk always stood in the hall, where everybody passed. More than a hundred thousand students have gone through her hands since 1916.

She knew the names of thousands, the troubles of nearly all. She has been a friend, a teacher, and a mother to most of them. She even loaned students her own money—never saved a penny for herself. Very few of her students, I suppose, have become great men and women. That wasn't her point. Her purpose was to help them along a little, just help them to a little better job, so their lives wouldn't be so meager.

*

Three years ago Emily Griffith bogged down under seventeen years of helping other people. She got so other people's miseries were too much for her. She couldn't bear to look at sadness, or hear of trouble. She was worn out. She had to resign. She came up to this cottage, which she had been building. When she got here, she couldn't sit up longer than half an hour at a time. Now she can walk four miles over the mountains without stopping. She keeps her high leather boots on all day.

Emily Griffith is a pleasant woman—not old, not fanatical, not schoolteacherish. Her eyes sparkle when she talks about Opportunity School. Today she is living solely on the miserable retirement pay of the Denver schools, fifty dollars a month. She and her sister Florence live on fifty dollars a month—a woman who is recognized even by other educators as being one of the greatest in America.

Does she squawk? No. She says it's fun figuring out how to make fifty dollars last a month. And anyway, the good she did over the years sustains her in a way money couldn't.

For example, a few days after she came here to the cabin, a boy working on the section gang saw her. The next day he and six other boys came around with a big box of candy. They were all former students of hers. Every time she goes down to the village post office, there are about forty letters from her boys and girls. Before her breakdown, she made speaking trips to Portland, Oregon, and Portland, Maine, and in each place her hotel room was banked high with flowers from her "children" who had migrated to those cities.

The same thing happens wherever she goes. On Sundays her cabin is full of ex-students from Denver. Emily Griffith may be poor, but she's rich, too.

September 29, 1936

Wafting Along in a Dream

DURANGO, COLORADO—If you drive cater-cornered across Colorado from Denver to Durango, through the Rocky Mountains, you come up over five separate passes, each of them more than eleven thousand feet high.

Mountains are nice, and I approve of them. But after two days of constant hairpin turns, deep chasms, soaring altitudes, gravel roads, and hours of driving in second gear, I can do with a little breathing spell of flat, straight highways.

Loveland Pass, between Denver and Leadville, is the highest. If you were to stop at the summit, and climb up and stand on the hood of your car, your head would be almost exactly twelve thousand feet above sea level.

These high passes give you an eerie feeling. Because you come up out of summer heat and green vegetation and worldliness, and suddenly you're driving along in another world, a world of vast treeless sweeps, and queer roadside marshes that seem out of place, and cold little lakes and pools, and splotches of snow, and there's an indescribable kind of chill in the air, even though it's summer and the sun is hot.

Your breath comes hard, too, and your ears stop up a little so that you can hardly hear your engine, and you seem to be wafting along in a kind of dream. . . .

*

Red Mountain Pass isn't quite as high as Loveland, but its crookeder, grander, more thrilling.

It runs between Ouray and Silverton, in southwestern Colorado. The road across it is called the Ouray Million-Dollar Highway. A toll road was hacked over these mountains in the 1880s. I'm sure glad I wasn't driving stagecoaches in those days. If it's a million-dollar highway now, I'd hate to have been on it when it was a ten-cent trail.

Ouray itself is a fantastic jumping-off place. It's a little town, set in a mountain pocket like a stone in the bottom of a bucket. I've never seen a town even in the Andes that beats it for spectacular setting. The town sits high, around seven thousand feet. You come in through a gorge, and go out the same way, climbing. Mountains rise right up, steeply, all around. Here, too, there is a mysterious chill in the air. The colorings of the gaunt towering rocks almost put a fear into you.

As you climb out of Ouray to the south, the road becomes gravel. And then you're winding and clinging along the edge, with the abyss at your elbow. For miles you climb and twist in second gear. You blow your horn at the sharp turns. The road is so narrow that frequent pull-outs are built for meeting cars to pass.

Near the summit you come to an amazing community of old mines. They stretch up the mountainsides in unbelievably difficult places. You realize that prospectors nosed over every foot of this isolated country decades ago, and it surprises you.

There are local people who drive these roads every day, and who are practically mountain goats on wheels. But I am not one of them. True, I get over these passes all right, but I don't do it without being scared stiff. . . .

June 20, 1939

MONTANA

Pyle liked to write about big dam-building projects. Naturally he was drawn to Fort Peck, in northeastern Montana, where the Army Corps of Engineers was constructing Fort Peck Dam. But much as he had "worked up a sort of mania for big dams under construction," true though it was that to him there was "nothing more thrilling in America" than a big dam project, Pyle found the project's justification lame and its cost excessive. He was intrigued, however, with the town of Wheeler.

A LATTER-DAY WILD WEST TOWN

WHEELER, MONTANA—You have to see the town of Wheeler to believe it. When you drive through, you think somebody must have set up hand-painted store fronts on both sides of the road, as background for a Western movie thriller. But it's real.

Wheeler is today the wildest Wild West town in North America. Except for the autos, it is a genuine throwback to the 1880s, to Tombstone and Dodge City and Goldfield.

Wheeler is a slopover from the government-built city at Fort Peck Dam. It is not on government property and hence is free to go its own way. These boomtowns always mushroom up around a big construction project. There are eighteen of them around Fort Peck. They are shantytowns proper. They have

such names as New Deal and Delano Heights. Their houses are
made of boxes and tin cans and old boards and tar roofing. They
look like Hoover's famous Bonus Army Camp of 1932 on the
Anacostia Flats.*

All except Wheeler. It is the metropolis of the mushroom
villages. It has thirty-five hundred people, and real houses and
stores. It has sixty-five little businesses lining either side of the
main street. Such places as BUCKHORN CLUB, ROOMS—50¢, and,
simply, HOTEL. It has nearly a thousand homes scattered back
behind the main drag. It has half a dozen all-night taverns, and
innumerable beer parlors. The taverns open at eight in the
evening and run until six in the morning.

At night the streets are a melee of drunken men and painted
women, as they are called in books. Gambling and liquor by the
drink are illegal in Montana. But Wheeler pays no attention.
You can sit in a stud game, or keep ordering forty-rod all night.
The taverns don't have floor shows; you just drink and dance.
The music goes until long after daylight. You don't have to pay
to dance with the girls, but they get a nickel a glass for all the
beer and whiskey they induce the boys to buy.

Back behind Wheeler is a separate village where the women
of easy virtue live. This town has an unprintable name. It has
no other name. Everybody calls it by this name. They say a
thousand women have heard the call and drifted in for the easy
reapings among the dam workers.

*

Wheeler is two-and-a-half years old. It started with Fort Peck
Dam, when a man brought in a trailer, built bunks in it, and
rented them to dam workers at four dollars a week. Ruby Smith
was the first real settler. She started an eating place along the
road, and within thirty days the town had sprung up around her
almost to its present size. Ruby now runs the Wheeler Inn, one
of the biggest all-night hot spots. She goes to bed at daylight, and
gets up late in the afternoon. She's coining the money.

Joe Frazier is the entrepreneur of Wheeler. Twenty years ago
he homesteaded a large patch of practically worthless land here
on the bare Montana knobs. It never did pay its way. Joe Frazier

*A group of broke World War I veterans numbering about twenty thousand had settled
in shacks on Washington's Anacostia Flats to demand early payment of bonuses due
veterans in 1945. Federal troops led by General Douglas MacArthur violently evicted
the peaceful though determined veterans and burned their camp, a much-publicized
cruelty.

became a barber in Glasgow, twenty miles away. Then God sent
Ruby Smith and the Army engineers, and it's said that Joe
Frazier will easily come away with a hundred thousand dollars.
He owns all the land Wheeler is built on.

Wheeler won't exist six months after the dam is finished in
1939. So Joe Frazier doesn't try to sell lots. He just rents them.
His income, they say, is twenty-five hundred dollars a month.

*

Wheeler is all wood. There isn't a stone or steel building in
town. It has no water system. They have had sixteen fires since
New Year's. One side of the town has a well. The other side does
not. Fortunately, there has been no epidemic. Prices are typical
boomtown prices. Rents aren't bad, but food is high. There is
one small wooden church, and there are two gospel missions.

Quite a few of the boys indulge in holdups. Motorists on the
road, and cashiers behind the cash registers, have looked many
times down the barrel of a six-shooter. There has been considerable gun-waving, but little pulling of the trigger. The thieves
take their swag and beat it. Wheeler has not developed any
spectacular individual bad man, such as "Curley Bill" of old
Tombstone.

And whereas the cowboys used to get drunk and ride down
the main street yelling and shooting up the town, nowadays the
process is to get drunk and drive down the main highway at
seventy miles an hour. They've killed and maimed as many
people that way around Wheeler as the tough characters used to
with their bullets.

It was the wild criminal driving that finally brought a little
law and order to Wheeler. They have a deputy sheriff and two
constables now. They don't go to extremes, of course, but they
pull in drunken drivers. They say the two justices of the peace
have a very good thing.

Wheeler will be gone in three more years. There may never
be another one. Somebody had better record it for posterity,
before it's too late.

September 17, 1936

BUTTE, MONTANA— . . . This is the greatest copper-producing city
on earth. With loyal spirit, its store windows are packed with
copper souvenirs. They have postcards made of copper.

And the town is so coppery that even the pools in the streets after a rain are copper-laden, and the steering knuckles of the autos are copper-coated from splashing water.

Butte is built on the side of the "richest hill on earth." From this hill has been taken two-and-a-half billion dollars' worth of metal, mostly copper. And there is no end in sight. . . .

Butte is pretty much live-and-let-live. It has a peculiar kind of democracy I haven't seen in any other city. An ordinary miner gets out of his car and argues with a bank president over a parking place. A millionaire gambles side by side with a man in overalls. A miner is just as good as anybody else in Butte. The city has few inhibitions.

Butte never did have prohibition. Of course, other cities didn't either, but I mean Butte never even *pretended* to have prohibition. They are café-bars here today that never once closed their doors during the twenties. And Butte has always had wide-open gambling.

"But so what?" the local people ask. "If there's anybody in this world entitled to a quick and easy drink of whiskey, it's one of those guys who has been down in the ground all day. And if he wants to gamble his hard-earned money, what of it? His bosses gamble on the stock market, don't they?"

Butte wears its badge right on its sleeve. It isn't ashamed. It simply does with intellectual honesty what other cities do sneakingly. I have more respect for the civic morality of Butte, which gambles in the open, than for Washington, D.C., which gambles on the sly and every bit as much. . . .

September 6, 1939

*   *   *

Montana Has the Right Idea

POCATELLO, IDAHO—I wish that every state historical society in America would send a delegation to Montana. They might also invite a few writers of history textbooks along. And if they would then practice what they learned, I'll bet that twenty years from now we Americans would know a lot more about American history.

No one questions that history is fascinating, but it is usually dished up in such indigestible fashion that only a few ever wade through much of it. Montana makes history a thing of joy, instead of a stodgy sermon. Every so often along the highways, maybe twenty miles apart, sometimes fifty miles, you'll see a neat little sign saying HISTORICAL POINT—1000 FEET.

So you coast along, and pull over to a wide graveled area, and there is a handsome signboard. It consists of two logs set upright in the ground, with a third laid across the top, and from this hangs a neat wooden placard, about six feet square. And on this board the historical message is painted in upper- and lowercase print, in black letters a couple of inches high. The message is not only easy to read, but it says something.

For instance, here is one that appears a few miles east of Shelby, Montana:

THE EARLY BOID GETS THE WOIM!

A NARROW-GAUGE RAILROAD TRACK NICKNAMED THE "TURKEY TRACK" USED TO CONNECT GREAT FALLS, MONTANA, AND LETHBRIDGE, ALBERTA. WHEN THE MAIN LINE OF THE GREAT NORTHERN CROSSED IT IN 1891, SHELBY JUNCTION CAME INTO EXISTENCE. THE HILLS AND PLAINS AROUND HERE WERE COW COUNTRY. THE JUNCTION BECAME AN OASIS WHERE PARCHED COWPUNCHERS CAUTERIZED THEIR TONSILS WITH FORTY-ROD AND GREW PLUMB IRRESPONSIBLE AND EXUBERANT.

IN 1910 THE DRY LANDERS BEGAN HOMESTEADING; THEY BUILT FENCES AND PLOWED UNDER THE NATIVE GRASS. THE DAYS OF THE OPEN RANGE WERE GONE. SHELBY QUIT HER SWAGGERING FRONTIER WAYS AND BE-CAME CONCRETE-SIDEWALK AND SEWER-SYSTEM CONSCIOUS.

DRY-LAND FARMING DIDN'T TURN OUT TO BE SUCH A PROFITABLE ENDEAVOR, BUT IN 1922 GEOLOGISTS DISCOVERED THAT THIS COUNTRY HAD AN ACE IN THE HOLE. OIL WAS STRUCK BETWEEN HERE AND THE CANADIAN BORDER, AND THEY ALL LIVED HAPPILY EVER AFTER.

And here is the way other states do it:

THIS MONUMENT MARKS THE SPOT WHERE JOE DOKES FIRST CROSSED THIS PASS IN 1834. ERECTED IN GRATEFUL MEMORY BY THE SONS AND DAUGHTERS OF THE PIONEERS OF IDAHO ON JUNE 10, 1922.

And there you have the difference between history that's read and remembered, and history that isn't even read.

You never see a car in front of these frigid stone monuments with their dull bronze inscriptions. But in Montana you hardly ever pull up to a historical sign without seeing a car or two already there, with people out copying down the inscription, and chuckling.

One grave fellow got up in the Malta Lions Club and introduced a resolution asking the state highway department to tear
the signs down and replace them with something "dignified."
Unfortunately, the Lions didn't string him to a tree, but they
did shout him down. . . .

October 9, 1936

POSTSCRIPT: *Three years later Pyle met the author of Montana's imagi-
native historical markers. He was Bob Fletcher, an engineer with the
state highway department, a "tall, graying, early middle-aged man"
who "talks slowly and tells a good story," a native Iowan who had lived
thirty-one years in Montana and whose affection for his adopted state's
wild past had led to the distinctive prose on the roadside markers.*

*"The state's graybeards have done a little criticizing because of the
saucy language of the inscriptions, but not very much," Pyle wrote. "In
fact, it worked the other way in one case.*

*"The sign for Butte is a jaunty one. It winds up by saying, . . . 'she
was a bold, unashamed, rootin', tootin', hell-roarin' camp in days gone
by, and still drinks her liquor straight.'*

*"Well, if Butte could have a sign, then Anaconda wanted one, too.
Anaconda is the famous smelter town, twenty-five miles west of Butte.
Their histories are intertwined. So Fletcher put up a sign for Anaconda.
It was one of the last. By that time he was a little tired of writing signs
and couldn't think of anything very racy, so he just wrote a straight
historical account.*

*"And Anaconda got sore as a boil. Why? Because the sign didn't make
Anaconda out to be as tough a place as Butte!"*

IDAHO

A VETERAN GAMBLER
POCATELLO, IDAHO—Mizzoo Townsend, even at seventy, claims
he's the champion poker player of Idaho. For years he had a sign
on the front door of his gambling place that said: I'LL PLAY ANY
MAN FROM ANY LAND, ANY GAME HE CAN NAME, FOR ANY AMOUNT HE
CAN COUNT.

Mizzoo said it was more of a joke than anything. Traveling
salesmen used to come through and take him up, and sometimes

they'd win, but usually he would. If somebody had come in with a lot of money, Mizzoo would have had to swallow his words, for he never had any real big money.

Mizzoo Townsend has been a gambler in Pocatello for forty-seven years. They say he's one of the very few of the Old West gamblers still alive. He isn't the kind of old-time gambler you see in the movies, though. He looks more like a gold-prospecting "pocket hunter." He looks as though he should have a burro walking behind him.

He came out about 1885, from Missouri. That's why they call him Mizzoo; his real name is John. He tarried four years on a ranch in Wyoming. The rancher ran a saloon and gambling house for the cowboys and wagon freighters. That's where Mizzoo learned to gamble. He rambled into Pocatello in 1889. It was not a perfect gambling town. It was a railroad town. There was never big boom money here, like in the gold camps.

Mizzoo ran gambling houses here, when gambling was legal in the state, and afterwards, too. He's been arrested and fined several times, but he never went to jail. He ran saloons, and even secondhand shops. Being the house owner, he always came out a little ahead. I'd guess he made about the same financial progress over the years as a grocery-store keeper would.

Mizzoo used to have a blackboard in front of his gambling house. Every morning he'd write something new on it. People would stand around waiting to see what today's sign would be. It would be something like this: FOR RENT—FOUR-ROOM HOUSE. PLENTY OF VENTILATION. WINDOWS ALL OUT. NO EXTRA CHARGE FOR THE BEDBUGS. I STILL THINK I CAN BEAT ANY MAN IN THE STATE PLAYING POKER.

He accumulated a lot of worn-out real estate. He owns houses that nobody lives in, and they're piled full of dust and junk. His own house is a small frame one, east of the tracks, with no grass around it. His son and daughter-in-law live with him.

Mizzoo is running a lottery game now. It doesn't amount to much, he says, but he's trying to build it up so he can leave his son a little business when he dies.

He's sort of a gentle fellow to be a gambler. His eyes puff up and twinkle when he laughs, and you can't imagine him ever getting tough. He says there have been rows in his places, but he never personally had any trouble. He attributes that to the fact that he was a big man and that he never drank.

Mizzoo says he never forgets anything. He can read a name

or a date in the newspaper and it's just as if it were carved in his head. He never had much education, but he has read quite a bit. He doesn't talk about old-men things; he likes to talk about current events. Gambling isn't what it used to be, he says; people spend their money on other things now. There are some little games in Pocatello now, but nothing important, he says.

I asked Mizzoo what was the most interesting thing that ever happened to him. He said it was when he went back through Wyoming a few years ago, past the ranch where he had worked in the 1880s. It's just filthy with oil wells now. He said that was the most interesting thing—seeing all that wealth, and he hadn't had sense enough to know it was there.

*

Mizzoo was puttering around his bedroom, trying to find some pictures to give me. His daughter-in-law was helping him. I kept asking him questions. "What was the biggest amount you ever played for?"

He chuckled and said, "Oh, not very big."

I said, "How long has it been since you played poker?"

He said, "Oh, quite a while."

I said, "What did you do when you found people cheating on you?"

He said, "Oh, just quit playing."

Said his daughter-in-law, "He shoots 'em."

November 8, 1936

WASHINGTON

MAIL BY HORSE AND CHARIOT

SPOKANE, WASHINGTON—Horses, horses, horses—that's what people are always yelling at the Spokane post office. But they don't care; they like their horses.

Spokane, as far as the post-office boys here know, is the only city left in the United States that uses horses in its collection and delivery service.

Spokane is always being razzed about it. People call it a one-horse town. Seattle sends reporters over who write funny pieces about Spokane's horse-and-chariot mail carriers. But Spokane is going right ahead. Tests made downtown have shown that collecting mail in little horse-drawn carts is not only cheaper but faster than by truck.

*

There are six horses in the Spokane postal service, two on downtown collections, and four on suburban delivery routes. The animals are as well-trained as circus performers. Each of the downtown horses has to go over nine routes a day, and there are about fifty mailboxes per route. The horses know every one of these boxes—four hundred and fifty of them.

Each horse will pull over the curb and stop at every box, even though the box may be inside a hotel. He won't move until he sees the carrier coming out the door, and then he starts. The horse knows which corners to turn, and the carrier never has to drive him at all. Once in a while, for some reason, a collector will take a slightly different route, and then he has an awful time getting the horse to turn the right corners.

They say they can put on a substitute postman, who doesn't know the route very well, and he never has any trouble. The horse takes him right over it.

Maggie was the best horse they ever had. She finally wore out, and they put her out to work on a farm. But she had been a city woman so long she didn't know how to take care of herself in the country, and she got sick and died. Katie has been collecting the mail for fourteen years, and is still going strong. That's longer, however, than most horses last pounding the pavements.

The horses work six days a week, eight hours a day, and travel about fourteen miles each day. The carriers used to own their own horses, but for several years now the post office has rented them from a livery stable.

There has been only one horse that absolutely couldn't learn the routes. After three months they gave up and sent this horse back. The others know the routes so well that the collector in some places goes clear through a building and out the back door, and the horse will meet him on the other side of the block.

They are hitched to little two-wheeled carts, built like Roman chariots. None of the horses has ever been hurt in traffic, although autos do graze them once in a while. Only one horse has ever run away. He ran lickety-split clear across town, and smashed his cart and harness. He was dishonorably discharged. Most of the horses aren't afraid of anything. But Helmer Headland, the senior horse-driving collector, has one now named Prince who is afraid of brass bands marching along the street.

Carrier Headland says he certainly hopes they never put auto trucks on the downtown routes. He says he's positive the horses can tell about traffic lights, although he doesn't know whether they distinguish color or just sense when it's time to go.

In the winter, the horses are shod with special nonslip shoes, and during snowstorms they are clad in blankets. It's no fun for the carriers to ride those little open chariots all day in a snowstorm, either. But even so, they say it would be no better getting in and out of an auto.

*

People in Spokane like the horses. They are always feeding them things as they go by—sugar, carrots, corn. One fellow even goes to a bakery every day and gets dry bread to give Prince when he comes by. Another fellow passes the back of the post office at the same hour every day and hands Prince a handful of sugar. It sort of spoils the horses, the carriers say, but they don't want to make people mad, so they don't interfere.

None of the horses has ever bitten or kicked anybody. They do scare people sometimes, though, by reaching their heads clear inside an auto, looking for a handout.

October 13, 1936

TURNING FROM TEDIUM TO THE SEA

SPOKANE, WASHINGTON—Only one in ten thousand of us job-holding mortals would dare do what the Partridge family did.

E. Harve Partridge has always lived in Spokane. He married young and never went to college. By the time he was twenty-five, he had two daughters. At forty-one, he had been a reporter for the *Spokane Chronicle* for eighteen years. His daughters are sixteen and seventeen. The family has a frame house with a small yard; there are millions of houses like it.

Each year the Partridge family would take its little vacation. But early this spring, a bigger vacation dream began to stir in the Partridge breasts. They decided to take a steamer trip to Alaska. Then one evening at supper Harve Partridge said, "Why don't we buy a boat and sail it to Alaska ourselves?"

The kids were wild about the idea. But Mrs. Partridge said, "Don't be foolish. You've never been in anything bigger than a rowboat. We couldn't sail it by ourselves."

But one weekend Harve Partridge took a bus to Seattle, three hundred miles away, and saw a small cabin cruiser for nine hundred dollars. He steered it for an hour around the bay, wrote a check, and took the next bus home. The Partridges were going to sail to Alaska.

The three months of preparation were as much fun as the trip itself. They bought twelve dollars' worth of nautical charts, and a parallel rule, and a two-dollar-and-fifty-cent compass. Every evening the whole family was on the living-room floor. They used a footstool for a boat, with the compass on top of it. They worked out nautical courses, and steered them.

The upshot was that they went to Alaska and back, all by themselves. When they started, Harve Partridge had steered a boat exactly four hours, the others not at all. Not a one of the landlubbers was seasick, although they wallowed through waves ten feet high. Sometimes it was so rough they couldn't cook. They chugged within sixty feet of whales. The girls went out in the little lifeboat and with axes chopped off hunks of floating icebergs for their refrigerator. They drove ahead for hours through thick fog, and hit their destination right on the nose, like Lindbergh.

They were tossed around in terrific tide rips. So innocent were they that they didn't know what a tide rip was until after they'd been through one. They navigated the swirling currents of dangerous, rocky narrows. Partridge learned to fix a broken clutch at sea. Frequently they sailed all night, through rain and darkness. They put their faith in their nautical book-learning and it brought them through.

On the way back the eldest daughter, Jean, was ordered by the skipper to take the wheel at night, lay out her own course, take them through a narrows in pitch darkness, and wake her father when they were safely on the other side. She did.

The Partridges sailed twenty-five hundred miles in three weeks. They spent three hundred dollars. They sold the boat when they returned for as much as they had paid for it.

*

But that isn't all. The up-to-now very normal Partridge family is itching for the spring of 1938. That's when they start around the world, all four of them, by themselves.

Harve Partridge took one step by quitting his job, the one he had held for eighteen years. He got a better job, it's true, but the idea was that it would be easier to quit a new job when sailing day came than one he had held for a good many years. So he did the hardest quitting while the idea was white-hot in him.

They will buy a fifty-foot yawl in San Francisco. They'll fix it up inside just like home, for it will be their home for three years. They'd start right now, except they have to learn celestial navigation, and how to sail a boat. Every night finds the whole family over their navigation books. Three afternoons a week they're out on a nearby lake, sailing a small boat, just getting experience.

During the eighteen years of job-holding the Partridges have lived economically. They have enough savings to make this three-year world trip. If they make any money along the way by writing articles or doing odd jobs, they'll extend the trip by just that much. "It'll be wonderful for the girls," Partridge says. "Certainly better than a college education."

October 14, 1936

Pyle loved Seattle from the time he first visited the city in March of 1922. Ever restless, young Ernie had borrowed money to accompany Indiana University's baseball team to Japan, and Seattle was his port of embarkation. "Seattle is a mighty fine place," he wrote his parents. "It reminds me a little of Duluth, Minn., built on the side of a mountain, with the bay below. The people out here are wonderful. Everywhere we have gone today, the people treated us very cordially and really seemed to take an interest. It is in marked contrast to the treatment one receives on the Eastern coast." He wrote this in Washington, D.C., in a summary of one of his trips, which had included a stay in Seattle:

. . . Seattle has steep streets, like San Francisco. It has the waterfront all around. It has big ships from the East, and hundreds of little pleasure yachts. It has Chinese herb doctors and the University of Washington. It has its beautiful, soft downpour of steady rain, and its gray Saturday afternoons that are so comfortable. It has its ferryboats foghorning through the night, and its feeling of China and Alaska just out through the Sound, and it has Canada next door, and the mountains and skiing only forty miles away, and green thick forests and fish and bear and clear streams and industry and the Navy and the Japan Current and weather that never goes to zero. . . .

February 10, 1937

THE DICTATOR OF HOOVERVILLE

SEATTLE—At no time during the twenty years he spent in North-west logging camps did Jesse Jackson ever conceive of the day when he might become a dictator.

But then it happened, and today he is the ruler of fifteen hundred people. It's a hard job, but he is proud of it. Jesse Jackson is mayor of Hooverville,* a shack city on Seattle's water-front. It is the makeshift home of Depression victims. It looks like the Bonus Army camp of 1932 in Washington, D.C.

Hooverville started about six years ago. Men without homes built huts of boxes and driftwood. The city said they were a menace, and burned them out, just as Hoover did in Washing-ton. They built again. Three times Seattle burned them out. Then a new mayor came in, and he let them stay—if they'd observe certain rules and behave themselves.

A friend of mine who has paid close attention to Hooverville says its main claim to a place in history is the evolution of its government. At first, he says, they tried communism. One for all and all for one. That didn't work. Then they tried democ-racy, with the men electing their rulers and having a continuous voice in their own government. That didn't work, either.

And then they swung into a dictatorship, as the only thing left. Jesse Jackson is the dictator, and everything works fine now. Jesse came up from the Hooverville ranks.

*

Jesse is a thin man. His stomach, instead of sticking out, sinks in. He is in his forties, and he's getting a little bald. He wears overalls and lives in a snug one-room shack, which he built himself and keeps neat as a pin. He cooks his own meals. He was washing the lunch dishes when I walked in. He sat at the kitchen table and I sat in the other chair.

"Some big people have sat there," he said. "Secretary Roper† has sat right in that chair."

"Well?" I said.

"Well, I just thought you'd like to know what big people have sat there. So has Marion Zioncheck, and Senator Lewis Schwel-lenbach."‡

---

*Shantytowns the country over were named in "honor" of Herbert Hoover, whose administration had so spectacularly failed to deal with the Depression's biting human consequences. Hooverville residents slept under "Hoover blankets"—discarded news-papers.
†Daniel Roper, Roosevelt's Secretary of Commerce.
‡Zioncheck was a Democratic congressman from Washington; Schwellenbach was a Democratic senator from Washington.

"What brought Secretary Roper down here?" I asked.

"He was through here on his way to Alaska, and said he'd like to see a town named after a former Secretary of Commerce,* so they brought him down. We had a long talk. Those big men come down here and look around and say, 'Why, you're pioneering. You're living like our forefathers did.' But we say we ain't pioneering: we're jungling."

*

Jesse Jackson has been in the Hooverville saddle five years. His word is absolute law. But his dictatorship sometimes takes on the hue of a wet nurse. He has to settle silly little quarrels between neighbors, and get sick people to the hospital, and quell troublemakers, and look after people's property when they're gone.

In the winter his population runs to fifteen hundred. In the summer it gets down to about three hundred and fifty. The men go "over the ridge" to pick apples and do odd jobs. Most of them are single. No children or young women are allowed to live in the town.

"We're mostly lumberjacks and seamen and fishermen and miners," Jackson said. "We're used to a hard life. We build our own huts here. When you've got a roof over your head, the battle's three-fourths won, you know."

Last winter the inhabitants included practically every nationality under the sun. About a third were Filipinos. They are the best-behaved of all, Jackson said. The Mexicans are the worst. They like to get all jagged up on marijuana. There are several hundred Negroes.

Mayor Jackson's biggest trouble is liquor. He doesn't tolerate rowdies. If a fellow makes too much trouble, Jackson calls the cops and they cart him off to jail. If the fellow offends too many times, Jackson just has him thrown out and burns his house down.

"There isn't a lazy man in Hooverville," Jackson said. "If we get a loafer or a moocher, we run him out. Just look around, and you'll see everybody is busy."

The men gather wood, saw it up, and sell it. They have trash concessions at the hotels and stores. They fish. One fellow builds boats. Some have part-time jobs outside. Even in the winter only a third of the men are on relief.

*Herbert Hoover had been President Calvin Coolidge's Secretary of Commerce.

"There's no excuse for anybody starving in Seattle today," Jackson said. "When we first built here, public opinion was against us. But everything has changed now. There isn't a flour mill in town, or a fish market, or a wholesale grocery, that won't give you a few pounds anytime you go after it. Why, the railroads even switch their old boxcars around here so we can have the wood."

Jackson gets no pay for being mayor. He is, however, honored by having the only electric lights in town. Because he hasn't time to get out and pick up odd jobs, he has about as little money as anybody in town. But the boys are good about handing him a dollar or two whenever they have money. He got about eight dollars from the boys after the bonus was paid.

Jackson doesn't know how long Hooverville will exist. He doesn't see much chance of its passing soon, because it's the only winter home about fifteen hundred men have or can ever hope to have.

October 24, 1936

OREGON

A REVISED VIEW OF PORTLAND

PORTLAND, OREGON—Do you know what Portland is? It's paradise on earth. At least that's what people here say. Personally, I had never thought so, and I'll tell you why.

Ten years ago I came through Portland driving a Model T Ford, wearing overalls, and with a tent and blanket roll tied onto the fender—a young man seeing America.

Well, I stopped at a roadside stand in the suburbs to eat some watermelon, and I was eating along, minding my business, when up came an old codger who right out of a clear sky started bawling me out. He gave me a long lecture, and wound up by yelling that if I didn't stop smoking cigarets and eating watermelon on Sunday I would undoubtedly land in hell. I'd never had any use for Portland since then.

Of course the incident was on my mind as Portland drew near this time. But I said, "No, let's be fair. We'll start all over again with Portland and see what happens this time." About that instant we came around a bend, and there staring us in the face was an expensive signboard, as big as the side of a house, saying in huge letters, ALL HATH SINNED. That's all it said.

Now I don't know whether all hath sinned or not, but supposing all hath, why put up a signboard about it? After that, it took my friends five days to convince me that I was wrong about Portland. . . .

*

Everybody here is crazy about Portland. They rave about it. They don't talk Chamber of Commerce folders; they don't talk about their industries and their schools and their crops. They roar about what a wonderful place Portland is just to live in. People *do* live well here. This whole Northwest country is beautiful, and the climate is pleasant, and existence is gentle.

Portland is a place, they say, where money doesn't get you anywhere socially. I asked what *does* get you somewhere—what, in other words, was the standard for social admittance in Portland? They thought and they thought. They finally decided that the standard was merely an ability to contribute something— usually agreeableness and interest.

Portland has its millionaires and its Depression shantytowns. But people insist it is not a city of great wealth or of great poverty. It is a city of temperateness. It is, on the whole, a conservative place. There is absolutely no public night life here, but there is a great deal of private night life. Portland is a city of homes, a place to raise your children.

It was settled by "down Easters" who came around the Horn. They made the money and became the backbone. They're still the backbone, and the pace-setters of Portland thought. But they have somehow mixed their New England soundness with a capacity for living the freer, milder Northwest way, and it makes a pretty high-class combination. . . .

*

The fascinating part of Portland is that it rises into hills, and they're the most livable hills you ever saw. Thousands of people live up there in magnificent houses, among trees, looking two thousand feet down onto the city.

All about Portland there are small rivers, and green fir trees. Not far away are the mountains themselves. Nature is all around. A friend of mine, searching for the reason he loves the Northwest, finally decided that the sense of having all around

him these clear, cold, tumbling streams had a great deal to do
with it. . . .

October 29, 1936

GOLD BEACH, OREGON—The Rogue River is many things. It is a
treacherous and bounding mountain stream. It cuts through one
of our few remaining frontiers. It is a fisherman's paradise. And
it is the path of one of the oddest mail routes in America.

This route runs from Gold Beach, on the coast, up to Agness,
thirty-two miles inland. People have been living back there in
the mountains for fifty years, and until recently the only way
to get there was by boat.

For many years Indians carried the mail up the river. First it
took as long as three days. Finally they got it cut down to one
long day. They had to pole their boats through the slower riffles,
get out and drag them around the bigger rapids.

But [in 1930] the government called for bids on round-trip
daily service. The Indians' equipment wasn't fast enough. The
contract fell to a man named Roy Carter. He built special boats,
really homemade speedboats—open-topped, wide-bellied, flat-
bottomed. They are rugged like trucks, fast like greyhounds.

Carter sunk big Buick auto engines into their open holds. He
rigged up a rear-end apparatus by which the propeller can be
raised in shallow rapids. Seats are removable; the boats can carry
sixteen people, or a caterpillar tractor, and do twenty-eight
miles an hour. . . .

The boats run all winter, rain or shine. The Rogue almost
never freezes. It did freeze a few years ago, above Agnes, but
that didn't affect the boat schedule. All the Indians thought the
world had come to an end, for they had never seen ice before.

The boats make about twenty RFD* mail stops on the way up.
They just slide along the bank, throw out a sack for somebody
in the woods, and roar on without really stopping.

At one place there is a dog that meets the boat every day and
carries the mail sack in its mouth back to its master. The dog lies
on a high bank each day about ten A.M., waiting for the mail.
Often there will be from two to seven of these red boats, all
alike, going up the river within sight of each other. But the dog
won't pay the slightest attention until the boat actually carrying

*Rural Free Delivery.

the mail comes round the bend. Then he jumps up and runs down to the bank. . . .

October 4, 1939

CALIFORNIA

EUREKA, CALIFORNIA— . . . I don't care how widely traveled you are, nobody has really seen all of America until he has driven through the redwood forests. . . .

. . . [Y]ou have the spookiest feeling there where it's so dark, with those great trunks rising around you so thick and so straight and so big around.

You don't feel they're trees at all. You feel as if they're something half human and half ghost. Everybody I've ever talked to has had that queer feeling about driving through the redwoods. You wouldn't be surprised to see an immense, gnarled wooden hand reach out and snatch you away into nowhere. . . .

October 10, 1939

A VISIT AMONG THE REDWOODS

SCOTIA, CALIFORNIA—The Saxton kids were cousins of mine. There were six of them. They were born in a log house about a mile and a half from our farm in western Indiana. We were poor and they were poorer. I played with them all through my childhood. I always liked them, all six of them.

We used to ride the running gears of an old buggy down the slope and through the creek, making a sputter with our lips and pretending we were race drivers at Indianapolis. And sometimes, after special pleading with home, I could stay all night with them, and we'd sleep in the attic of the log house among the rafters, four or five of us in one bed. We had fun in those days.

But we all grew up, and most of us left home. Some of the Saxton kids I haven't seen for nearly twenty years. Paul is one of them. He's a little younger than I. The last time we rode down the hill on the buggy running gear was probably around 1914.

*

I asked for Paul Saxton at the main office of the Pacific Lumber Company in Scotia. They said he was driving a "cat" down at the Monument Camp. They gave me a pass card, and told me how to go, and said I'd have to leave the car and walk across the railroad trestle to the camp—and to be careful.

A train of flatcars was backed up on a temporary track in a gulch, among tall trees. At the rear, a steam derrick with an ice hook on the end of a cable was lifting immense redwood logs off a pile and laying them on the flatcars. I asked for my cousin. They said he was one of three cat drivers dragging logs down from the woods, and that each driver got down only once an hour. So I waited.

After a while a big yellow caterpillar poked its nose over a hill and started down. Behind it were three of the biggest logs I ever saw. I looked the driver over, and decided it wasn't my man. But just as he came up beside me and stopped, I recognized something. I don't know what it was, for he certainly didn't look like anybody I'd ever seen before. But I recognized something. I started forward to shake hands. And he knew me at the same time. He jumped off the cat with a big grin on his face.

"I wouldn't have known you," he said, "except you look like Uncle Will." That's my father.

*

I made the next trip with him on the cat. It is an immense machine, with a cat trailer behind it, bearing a big derrick that lifts up one end of the logs for dragging. It made so much noise we had to yell at one another.

What a ride that was! We climbed up a worn lane through the forest. We rose more than a thousand feet in half a mile. No auto could ever pull the grades we took. We went so slowly the dust rose around us in a cloud, and my topcoat was ruined from the oil and dirt.

Paul came West eight years ago. He has never been back to Indiana. He seldom hears from home, or writes. He didn't know his oldest brother was married. He likes it out here. He has been in the logging woods all this time. "This is the worst job in the woods," he said, "because it's so dirty. We have to wear masks on account of the dust. But it's about the best-paid job. I high-climbed for three years. That's climbing up and cutting out the top and getting the tree ready to fall. I never got hurt. That's a good job."

Some of these redwoods are more than three hundred feet

high. They're very beautiful, and yet not the most valuable
lumber by any means. It seems a shame to cut them. They're
very brittle; if they don't fall right, they splinter all to pieces.
My cousin said they sometimes worked for a week just preparing a bed for a tree to fall in.

*

It took us an hour to make the round trip. Coming back we
nosed down grades so steep you had to brace yourself and hold
on to keep from falling out. It was like a nosedive in an airplane.
But nothing makes any difference to a cat. Up or down, it's all
the same.

Paul was the one who recalled riding down on the old buggy
running gear. I had forgotten it. He said he bet that hill
wouldn't look like anything to us now. I said I bet it wouldn't,
either.

Finally we came back to the railroad. My cousin hated it that
I couldn't stay all night so we could talk longer. I hated it, too.
Just an hour, after a lifetime, and then goodbye. A couple of
cousins who pass in the dusk of the tall redwood forests.

November 5, 1936

THE HARD LIFE OF A CRAB MAN

SAN FRANCISCO—Two o'clock in the morning, and Fisherman's
Wharf is a bedlam of crab men. Three hundred little boats ready
to go to sea, one man to a boat.

Loud language splits the night air—Italian, profanity, and
English, in the order named. All but five of San Francisco's
three hundred crab fishermen are Italian. Among the five is one
Negro. They say a plain American couldn't stand the life. I
believe it.

I go with Emile Barbara, a young man who was born a fisherman. His tongue is equally at home with Italian and English.
We're on our way by three o'clock. We are in a thick procession,
seaward bound. Everywhere in the darkness you hear *chug, chug,
chug*. Little lights gliding. Voices across the water. Silhouettes
on patches of moonlight.

Out under the Golden Gate bridge, black and mighty against
the moon. Out over "the bar," where the waves leap and twist.
Then into wide-open water, the boats falling into a long string.
Ahead for miles they flow into the darkness, like runners after
the bunched start. Their lights make a skyline of civilization

across the dark Pacific. It is cold out here. The waves leap, and
time passes.

By daylight we are fifteen miles west of the Golden Gate, and
I'm sick at my stomach. The sun is rising very red. "It'll blow
like hell about ten o'clock," says Emile. He stands up and looks
all around, picking an empty spot. We are on the grounds. He
decides, and throttles down. We are ready for the day's work.

Emile puts on boots and a rubber apron. On deck is a pile of
traps. Each consists of a steel hoop, about three feet across, from
which hangs a net a couple of feet deep. In the bottom is a wire
bait cage. Emile takes three sardines from a box—they're big
sardines, six inches long—splits them open with his thumb,
turns them inside out, crams them into the cage, and throws the
trap overboard. A small buoy, fastened to it by a stout line,
marks the spot.

Emile starts the boat going slowly forward. He lays a trap
about every block, in as straight a line as you can make in
wallowing water. There are twenty-four traps.

The traps all laid, we beat it back to the starting end. Emile
grabs the first buoy with a boat hook. He pulls up some line with
his hands, then hooks it over a winch the size of a tomato can,
puts his foot on the pedal, and the winch starts pulling up the
trap. All the time we are moving ahead.

Thrills of a fisherman. The trap comes out of the water. Two
small scrambling crabs inside. Emile swears and throws them
back. He puts in new bait and tosses the trap over again. By now
we are right on the next buoy. The crab fisherman has no rest.
All day it's like that. His boat is never stopped. The fisherman
works fast, and hard.

*

Emile swears—only three crabs from the first "drift," which
is what they call running the line of traps. "We're going to
move," he says. So we take up all the traps. It takes nearly an
hour.

We chug southward. Porpoise leap gracefully around us, some
not twenty feet away. Far to the left we see the mountainous
bare shore, and one tower of the Golden Gate bridge. The sun
is bright now. But it's still chilly. We eat some lunch from a sack.
I feel fine now. The tide is changing. It isn't so rough. We go
south for an hour.

All over again the traps are laid. It is ten o'clock now. We start
our drift. The first trap brings up half a dozen big crabs. Emile

swears. "What's the matter?" I say. "This looks good." That *is* the trouble. "I had a hunch to come over here first," he says, "and I didn't. We've wasted four hours and ten or twelve dollars."

Four times we make our drift on that line. Each one takes more than an hour. I get so I can hardly wait for each trap to come up. It's like seeing what's in a Christmas box. Sometimes we have as many as a dozen crabs in a trap. But you can keep only the ones of seven inches or more. Emile has a ruler to measure the doubtful ones. We throw back four for every one we save, it seems to me. Emile handles them with his big bare hands. A few want to fight.

"That means bad weather's coming, when the crabs are wild," he says.

I count the crabs. We take thirty-one in one drift. On the next drift Emile says, "Could you count the crabs and the traps at the same time?" He has an idea some other fisherman has stolen a trap. They do that. But we still have our twenty-four.

At two o'clock the sea begins to roll heavily again, but I like it now. We start our last drift, stacking the traps on deck as we pull them in. It is hard to control the boat, and it takes us much longer than usual. When we are through, the floor of the crab box is covered solid. They are beautiful with their shells dried— brown and cream-colored. Not a one moves, though they are all alive. We have a hundred and eight, nine dozen. At two dollars and fifty cents a dozen, that's not bad.

We leave the grounds at three o'clock, and it takes two hours to twist and roll our way home. On the way, Emile takes off his boots and lies on the deck, steering with his foot. We have been at sea fourteen hours. Emile does this every day. "How would you like to make your living this way?" he asks.

Not I, I say.

November 7, 1936

SAN FRANCISCO— . . . Many funny things have happened on the [Golden Gate] bridge. Going home from San Francisco late the other night, a man stuck his head out the car window to cough, and lost his false teeth. They hunted around that night and couldn't find them. Next day he came back and hunted some more. And there they were, lying along the curbing. Nothing had run over them.

They have a room where things lost on the bridge are stored. It contains everything from women's twenty-five-dollar hats to old mattresses.

The number of people who show up at the tollgates without any money was astonishing to me. It costs fifty cents to drive across the bridge, and there is an absolute state law against letting anybody across for nothing.

It usually winds up with one of the toll collectors personally lending the money. The sergeant in charge says he has loaned twenty dollars since the bridge opened, and is out only a dollar fifty. All the rest has been repaid. . . .

October 25, 1939

SAN FRANCISCO—You ought to be around San Francisco when they have a heat wave. The local people are a riot.

You see, it practically never gets hot in San Francisco, winter or summer. The wind from the ocean keeps it cool, and the fog keeps it dark, and when a nice, warm day wanders in by accident, San Franciscans think the city is catching fire.

Recently there was a "heat wave" here that lasted a week. It actually did get clear up to ninety-seven degrees. The city practically stopped turning. Schools closed. Local government suspended. People tell me that for the first time ever they saw cops without their coats on.

During that time I never heard a single conversation about any subject but the heat. People actually died from it. And those who lived apparently would have welcomed death. . . .

October 17, 1939

ABOARD A TRANSCONTINENTAL BUS IN CALIFORNIA— . . . When you cross by bus from New York to San Francisco, you do not see any terrifically big mountains. That Wyoming plateau forms a shelf across the Rockies, and you never see a single startling peak. But you see an awful lot of nice empty desert.

The one and only real dash of mountain scenery is when you come down out of Reno into California. There you cross the Sierra Nevadas, and it's as lovely a sight as you want to see.

The mountainsides are steep and violently green; the road is crooked but not frightening; snow still lies in shaded patches level with the highway; you look back down from Donner Pass to a dark blue lake that makes you glad to be alive.

And then the hills fade down into nothing, and the road

gradually swings into a long straight line, and the temperature goes up, and the fruit trees abound, and you are in the lush Valley of Sacramento—and the homestretch. . . .

July 2, 1940

A TOWN SPOILED BY RICH DILETTANTES

CARMEL, CALIFORNIA—Carmel, you know, is the famous West Coast art colony—the Greenwich Village of the Pacific, some have called it.

It is a town of three thousand, some hundred and twenty-five miles south of San Francisco. It is right on the ocean, and it is a charming place. Great writers and artists have lived here, and still do.

Carmel is, at least in dreams, a town friendly to intellectuals and creative instinct and the informality of genius. Anything goes in Carmel—theoretically. But if you were a Carmel storekeeper with inclinations for Roosevelt, you kept your mouth shut this fall. A Carmel businessman dared not say that he liked Roosevelt.

Even worse, liberal thinkers here were amazed when I said there was probably no other town in America where that was true. They had assumed it was true everywhere. Carmel did go Democratic this year, by the skin of its teeth, but only a few will admit their votes.

*

Carmel in most ways is delightful. It is slow and quiet and Mexicanish in atmosphere. There are stray trees in the middle of the streets. Lots of places don't have sidewalks. The streets at night are dark as pitch. The beach is ashy white and smooth; the town rolls up from it. Everything is under pine trees and behind thick manzanita bushes. You never see a whole house, just angles and slices, appealingly through pretty gardens. Snowy stucco is the motif, behind green.

The architecture is a pleasant hodgepodge. Private homes are New England farmhouses, and low English cottages, and beachy places, and jutting Pueblo Indian, and there's the Mexican theme, and even straight Hollywood Spanish. Nearly all are beautiful and livable-looking. I have seen only two or three mansions, and they were grotesque amid the soft quietness of the town. Their owners should be ashamed, but probably aren't.

*

Carmel was started in 1903 by a San Francisco lawyer, one of those poets at heart who was frustrated by being a fine business-man. In the first days, lots were practically given away to artists and writers. If some of those early birds had held on to the real-estate worm, they wouldn't have to worry now.

Fred Bechdolts was one of the early gang. He has lived in Carmel for thirty years, and he isn't old yet. He writes for magazines, and calls himself a hack. He sat all afternoon and talked about the early days.

Carmel's great years, he said, were 1907, 1908, and 1909. You had to come from Monterey by horse and buggy, the road was so terrible. The only nongeniuses in town were the storekeep-ers. The geniuses were sincere ones, not posers—such genuine people of letters as Mary Austin and George Sterling. Sterling's fireplace was the mecca of all the spirits of Carmel, and the fountain of Sterling's own despair.

People thought what they thought, and nobody cared. The artists and writers worked three hours a day, and just lived the rest of the time. There was much social foregathering, in a fresh and simple manner. Jack London came and went, and Upton Sinclair. Harry Leon Wilson came, and is still here. Carmel has been host to great people. Robinson Jeffers, the poet, is its pres-ent celebrity.

Then, just before the war, a different class started coming in from San Francisco—the artistic rich, the men with money who had always wanted to paint. They built nicer homes, and intro-duced the dinner coat into Carmel, and daubed and preened. The war was the end of old Carmel. After the war, the people who retire on permanent incomes got next to Carmel. Living was cheap here, the spot almost idyllically beautiful, the climate nice. In they came, people who never belonged and never will.

Today they have about taken Carmel. It's a shame. And the silly part of it is, they're nice people. I met some of them, and they're grand people, except—they think the way people think who have just enough steady income to ensure them nothing to do from now until death. They're status-quo people. They are Hoover Republicans.

There is still, however, a great deal of liberal thought of the newer school in Carmel. Some tell me the town is now about fifty-fifty, liberal and conservative, with a tiny fringe of out-and-out radical.

Carmel is still a lovely place, outwardly. People go slowly

about their business, or lack of it. People are friendly. They say it's a good place, really, to work, if you want to hole up and do it. It's also a good place to have lots of friends, and cocktail parties every afternoon, and dinner jackets and bridge.

Outside of being pretty, Carmel is now about like any other small town—plus the fact that if you're for Roosevelt the pensioners are liable to buy elsewhere.

November 16, 1936

LIFE AT CAVE SPRINGS

DEATH VALLEY, CALIFORNIA—On your California road maps you will see a place called Cave Springs.

Yet when you get there you find it is not a town. It is not a village. It is not even a country post office. It is just a private home, with two people in it. It's on the map because it's the only house in a stretch of a hundred and forty miles.

Mrs. Ira Sweetman and her cousin Adrian Egbert live there. It is sixty miles to a store in one direction, eighty miles in the other. Either way, it's all desert. There are no telephone poles, no culverts. Sometimes you can hardly tell where the dirt road is.

"Do many travelers use this road?" I asked Mr. Egbert.

"Yes," he said. "There was a car past here just the other day."

*

Mrs. Sweetman and Mr. Egbert live in this bare, out-of-the-way place by choice. They don't have to raise anything, or scratch for a living. They are simply retired.

They are getting along in years—between sixty-five and seventy, I'd say—but they're alive and enthusiastic, they're well-to-do in a modest way, they have every comfort, and they're on the desert because they like it.

They live in a fascinating place. They're in a gap in the mountains thirty-six hundred feet high. From their door you look down into fabulous Death Valley, below sea level. At night you can see a campfire fifty-five miles away on the valley floor.

Their home is perched on the south rim of Death Valley. And on the north rim, a hundred and thirty miles away, is the isolated castle of Death Valley Scotty.

The Sweetman-Egbert ménage has none of the fame of Scotty's castle. And yet it is just as isolated, and just as unusual, too. For while Scotty lives in an incongruously lavish palace, they live mostly in caves!

I know it will be hard for you to think of desert cave dwellers as being sane, intelligent, educated people. But you wouldn't have known Mrs. Sweetman or Mr. Egbert from a couple of good Indiana neighbors.

*

We drew up at Cave Spring just at noon, after the sixty-mile pull from Barstow. I knocked at the door, and asked Mrs. Sweetman if she could furnish us a bite of lunch.

"Why, yes," she said. "Come right on in. This is Mr. Egbert. I look a sight. Sit down and make yourselves at home." So they put on another can of chile con carne, and pretty soon we were all around the kitchen table, eating sausages and yams and chile and coffee and a dish of figs, just like old times.

We stayed three hours, and they showed us all through their amazing place, and got out old letters and pictures, and we talked and talked, and would have been there yet, I suppose, except that Mr. Egbert told Mrs. Sweetman she'd have to stop talking and make us go on, or we wouldn't get to Furnace Creek before dark.

Mrs. Sweetman and Mr. Egbert have both been around. Mrs. Sweetman first saw daylight in Richmond, Virginia. But when she was ten she migrated with her parents to the Black Hills of South Dakota.

A good part of her life was spent there, and she owns stock in the famous Homestake gold mine at Lead, South Dakota. She loves the Black Hills. Occasionally she goes to Los Angeles to attend the banquets of the Black Hills Pioneer Society.

"I never knew I was a pioneer till they started making over me a few years ago," she says. "And now I'm kind of proud of it."

Mrs. Sweetman has been a widow for twenty or thirty years. She likes politics, and has been an active political leader in both South Dakota and Arizona. For several years she was postmistress at Daggett, California, in the Mojave Desert. She and her cousin came to Cave Springs fourteen years ago.

"How did you happen to pick this spot to retire in?" I asked Mr. Egbert.

"Well, sir," he said, "I rode through this gap in '94, looking for a lost mine. There was hardly even a trail here then. Many times after that I came up through here. We always camped here because of the wonderful water in these springs. I liked this spot.

"Well, I had the flu in 1918, and I never really got over it. So in 1924 when the doctor told me I'd better go to the desert for good or I wouldn't live six months, I said, 'Doc, I know exactly where to go.' We bought ten acres here. We hauled lumber and everything for sixty miles in a Model T, and started building. We've been building ever since."

March 21, 1938

A HOME BLASTED OUT OF ROCK

DEATH VALLEY, CALIFORNIA— . . . They live in a three-room cottage and a half-dozen caves. There is nothing nutty about it. The caves are practical and handmade. Mr. Egbert made them himself. He used to be a mining engineer, and he has had construction experience, too. He has scouted mines from the Arctic Circle to Peru. He knew how to construct a little kingdom out of the rocky barrenness of Cave Springs.

Their house is perched on a small bluff, alongside the trail. There is a good-sized living room, with big windows taking in the desert sun, and a kitchen, big like a farm kitchen. And back of the living room is one bedroom, which abuts the solid-rock wall back of it. And now the caves—

One leads straight back from the kitchen door. In it are long shelves, stocked with canned goods. They could live for months on this stock.

The next cave is a house within itself—two bedrooms in the back, and a sort of sitting room in front. Mr. Egbert sleeps here the year round. It never freezes in winter and seldom gets above seventy in summer, even though it goes to a hundred and fifteen outside. A little shaft goes from the back bedrooms up to the surface, for ventilation. The rooms never get damp.

These rooms are furnished just like a house. The walls and ceiling are jagged rock, whitewashed. "What do you think of this for when the Japs come to bomb us?" asks Mr. Egbert.

The next cave is a sort of workshop and office. And the next one contains the most important thing for life on the desert— water.

It seeps through the rock and drips into a tub. Mr. Egbert says it is the most perfect water in the world; he has had it tested. Underfoot, covered with flooring, is a five-barrel tank, in case of emergency, which they have yet to have.

The next cave is a garage, where Mrs. Sweetman keeps her

new golden-brown Dodge coupe. Mr. Egbert's old Model T sits out in the open.

There are still other caves and semicaves. They house little chicken lots, and various machinery, and a little cabin for friends who might come to visit.

*

It took Mr. Egbert years to make these caves. He did it by drilling, and blasting with dynamite, as in a gold mine. The work filled up the cavern of idleness in their first years at Cave Springs. But now they don't need any more caves—and idleness takes care of itself.

Their days have no set schedule. There is an old alarm clock in the kitchen, but the alarm has never been set. They even lose track of the days.

Mrs. Sweetman's gray hair is bobbed and she is smiling and enthusiastic. She drives sixty miles to Barstow about once a week for mail, a hundred and fifty to San Bernardino twice a month for supplies, and occasionally into Los Angeles. She always puts her evening gown and slippers in the back of the car, in case she is invited to a formal party. She's leaving in a few days on a three-month cruise to Central America.

Mr. Egbert hasn't been to town for three years. Just doesn't want to go. And yet he is delighted when anybody drops past. He is a great reader. He uses a pair of glasses that cost sixty cents. He subscribes to about ten magazines. He has a big radio, with two storage batteries to run it. Outside is a little windmill on a tripod, generating power for the batteries.

They burn oil in the cookstove, for there isn't enough wood within fifty miles to start a Boy Scout fire. Mr. Egbert smokes two cigars a day, drinks beer, and lets out a good cussword now and then. He helps with the cooking. They have two cats, and a collie dog.

Mr. Egbert has two cameras, and likes pictures of people's faces. The walls are covered with pictures—the Duke of Windsor in rotogravure, President Roosevelt, a full-page face of a Kansas Dust Bowler out of *Life*, and a large drawing of Hebert J. Grant, president of the Mormon Church. I asked Mr. Egbert if he was a Mormon. He said no; he'd just tacked it up because he thought it was a strong face. . . .

The only thing they raise is a few chickens. But that is hard, too, for the bobcats keep breaking in. Coyotes don't bother them, and there are hardly any rattlesnakes. There are wild mountain sheep in the vicinity.

"But you're not allowed to shoot them, it's against the law," I said.

"Well, I won't let one come up and bite me," Mr. Egbert said. "Three or four have tried!"

Mr. Egbert says they can live on about forty dollars a month. He must mean just groceries, for that couldn't include the new car, and gasoline, and all the magazines. But, anyway, they don't have to worry or scratch. "We made our stake before we ever came up here," said Mr. Egbert.

March 22, 1938

AN ALMOST SPECTRAL BEAUTY
DEATH VALLEY, CALIFORNIA—California's recent floods extended clear back into the barren wastes of the Mojave Desert. And it was the circumstance of the floods that plumped us into one of the most spectacular panoramas I have ever looked upon.

We descended into Death Valley from the south end. I don't suppose one tourist in five thousand ever sees the valley from this angle, or, for that matter, ever gets into the south half of the valley at all.

We didn't make the southern approach through superior wisdom. It was simply that the main paved highways were washed out in the recent floods, and it was a case of come in through the Cave Springs dirt road or not at all.

At Cave Springs, you're on the rim of Death Valley. From there you drop thirty-six hundred feet in a twisty, bumpy, fifteen-mile drive onto the floor of the valley. And every foot of the way down is a grandstand seat for an appalling spectacle of desolation, upheaval, distance, and a silent, almost spectral, beauty.

One thing I had wanted to find out about Death Valley was whether it is actually a place that is limited, circumscribed, measurable—or whether it just spraddles all over everywhere, without any real sides.

Well, it *is* limited. It *is* definite. It *is* like an immense slash in the earth. It has a floor, and high sides. It is a hundred and thirty miles long, and ranges from six to fourteen miles wide. You can't see from one end to the other, because it is too far, and anyway it makes a turn. But there's no place in the valley where you can't look up and see the high, bare mountains hemming you in.

There is nothing consistent about the valley floor. I have driven the whole hundred and thirty miles, and there is hardly a five-mile stretch that is the same. Some places it is sand. Some places very gravelly, with good-sized rocks. Some places actually swampy. Some places hard and black, like old lava. Some places snow-white—salt beds, just as in Utah.

In some places there is no vegetation whatever. But most of the valley has a thin scattering of low shrubs—greasewood, bunchgrass, small mesquite, and even some flowers. There is almost no cactus. In only a few places is the valley floor actually level. Most of it rises and falls in long sweeps.

When we came down into the valley the rough gravel road ran northward for miles and miles, right out into the center of the valley, as straight as a ruler. We had to cross the Amargosa River, which flows (sometimes) down the valley's center. It was rumored in Los Angeles that the bridge over the Amargosa in Death Valley had been washed out. That report was exaggerated, because there isn't any bridge and never has been.

The riverbed is flat, and usually dry. You just drive across it. If there's much water, then the river is wide and you don't cross at all. When we crossed, the river was about twenty feet wide and eight inches deep, and we forded it.

Before you get midway up the valley, the salt marshes set in. Then the road swings away over against the foot of the mountains, and becomes very winding. That famous "lowest point in the United States" is not in the center of the valley but clear over to one side. It's only a few feet from the road, and you could go stand in it if you wanted to wade in the salt marsh. It's two hundred and eighty feet below sea level. If you built a twenty-story building there, its spire would still be lower than a rowboat on San Francisco Bay. . . .

You've heard of Death Valley's terrific summer heat. Well, from what I've been able to pick up, everything is true—and then some. It has been officially recorded as high as a hundred and thirty-four in the shade—and there is no shade, except artificial shade.

I would be afraid to drive down into Death Valley in summer. Every summer, even in this modern day, somebody is lost—a prospector, who should know better, or a tourist who leaves the road against advice and gets stuck in the sand. But even if you

stay on the road—well, pulling up the gradual rise toward the
north end, our radiator boiled, right here at the end of winter.
And our car runs unusually cool. What would it do in summer?

And suppose you broke down? You can walk ten or fifteen
miles in Death Valley in winter. But in summer you and I
would die in fewer than ten miles, even if we had plenty of
water. That's the thing that frightens me. Many bodies have
been found with water jugs beside them. They say that often
you can't see a hundred yards for the heat waves. Walking far
is fatal. Changing a tire is dangerous. Just lifting a jug is exer-
tion. You'll never catch me in Death Valley in summer.

*

As far as I can learn, there is not a single, year-round private
home in Death Valley. There are, however, two spots of lavish
comfort for winter dwellers. One is the Stovepipe Wells Hotel,
on the west side of the valley. The other is Furnace Creek, on
the east side.

At Furnace Creek there is a magnificent desert inn, a dude
ranch, and the headquarters of Death Valley National Monument. Counting guests, employees, and government workers,
you will find several hundred people around there in winter.

But civilization in Death Valley locks its doors on May 1. The
hotels close. Three or four people stay at Furnace Creek, a lone
watchman at Stovepipe Wells. The Indians of the southern end
take to the mountains. If you wander across Death Valley in
July and die, you'll die alone.

March 23, 1938

* * *

YUMA, ARIZONA— . . . We have been many times to California.
You could not count on the fingers of both hands the number
of our trips out here. But always I have refused to come right
out and admit that I liked California.

We would say yes, it might be all right if you could get back
East once a year. Or we would make fun of their sunshine
claims, for we have seen California in flood. Or we would join
the intellectuals and hoot at all the Iowa farmers in Los Angeles.

But maybe as we grow older we grow more honest with
ourselves. Or maybe we just reach a stage where we aren't
ashamed of agreeing with the majority. Whatever it is, I am at
last ready and willing to admit that I think California is wonderful.

Sure, it has spots I don't like. You couldn't hire me to live in agricultural Bakersfield, nor in far-north Eureka, nor in the sham of Hollywood. But you don't have to live in those places.

There are hundreds of miles of startling seacoast, aching to be lived upon. There are thousands of magnificent little valleys, placidly waiting for man to come and despoil them with his enjoyment.

There are deserts where those with a flair for sand and wind could find peace. And there are mountains for the virile, and forests for the woodsy people, and fog for those who hate the sun.

Yes, in full honesty, California does have everything. And we are sad at leaving because, in the way of all things, no man knows but that this backward glance over the shoulder may be his last glance forever. . . .

November 17, 1939

NEVADA

A Desert Tugboat Annie

WINNEMUCCA, NEVADA—Josie Pearl lived thirty-five miles from town. Lived all alone in a little tar-paper cabin, surrounded by nothing but absolute desert.

From a mile away you can hardly see the cabin amidst the knee-high sagebrush. But when you get there it seems almost like a community, such a contrast it is to a world filled only with white sun and empty distance. There really isn't any road to Josie Pearl's cabin. It's merely a trail across space. Your creeping car is the center of an appalling cloud of dust, and the sage scratches long streaks on the fenders.

Josie Pearl comes out to meet you, for she is friendly, a woman of the West. She is robust, medium-sized, happy-looking, and much younger than her years, which are sixty-some. There is no gray in her hair. Her dress is calico, with an apron over it. On her head is a farmer's straw hat, on her feet a mismated pair of men's shoes, and on her left hand and wrist—six thousand dollars' worth of diamonds!

Her whole character is just that kind of contradiction. She is a sort of Tugboat Annie of the desert. Her whole life has been spent in that weirdest of all professions—hunting for gold in the ground. She has been at it since she was nine. She has played a man's part in a man's game. She is a prospector.

She is what I like to think of as the Old West. She has been worth a hundred thousand dollars one day, and the next day flat broke cooking in a mining camp at thirty dollars a month. She has packed grub on her back through twenty-below Nevada blizzards, and has spent years as the only woman among men in mining camps; yet there is nothing rough about her, she doesn't drink, smoke, or swear, and her personality is that of a Midwestern farm woman.

She has been broke as often as she's been rich; but she can walk into any bank in this part of the country and borrow five thousand dollars on five minutes' notice. She has run mining-camp boardinghouses all over the West. She has made as much as thirty-five thousand dollars in the boardinghouse business and put every cent of it into some hole in the ground. She has been married twice, but both husbands are dead now. She never depended on men, anyhow.

She has lived as long as nine years at a stretch at one of her lonely mines. She found her first mine when she was thirteen, and sold it for five thousand dollars. She has just sold her last mine and is well off again, but she stays on in the desert.

Her cabin is the wildest hodgepodge of riches and rubbish I've ever seen. The walls are thick with pinned-up letters from friends, assay receipts on ore, receipts from Montgomery Ward. Letters and boxes and clothing and pans are just thrown—everywhere. And in the middle of it all sits an expensive wardrobe trunk, with a seven-hundred-dollar sealskin coat inside. She sleeps with a .30-30 rifle beside her bed, and she knows how to use it. In the next room are a pump gun, a double-barreled shotgun, and a dog.

But Josie Pearl is not a desert hermit. And she is not an eccentric. Far from it. She has a Ford pickup, and when she gets lonesome she goes and sees somebody. She has a big Buick in town, but doesn't drive it much because it makes her look rich. She puts on her good clothes and takes frequent trips to Reno and San Francisco. She knows the big cities well, and is no rube when she gets there.

She talks constantly, and likes for people to like her. Her favorite word is "elegant." She says, "I have elegant friends all over the West." And "I may tear down this cabin and build an elegant house here."

Nobody can deny that Josie Pearl is elegant to the human race. She has educated three girls, and grubstaked scores of boys and found them jobs. She has nursed half the sick people in northern Nevada. She's known all over the Western mining country.

She says gold brings you nothing but trouble, and yet you can't stop looking for it. The minute you have gold, somebody starts cheating you, or suing you, or cutting your throat. She can't even count the lawsuits she's been in.

She has lost fifteen thousand dollars, and sixty thousand dollars, and eight thousand dollars, and ten thousand dollars, and I don't know how much more. "But what's eight thousand dollars?" she says scornfully. "Why, eight thousand dollars doesn't amount to a hill of beans. What's eight thousand dollars?"

People have been doing her dirt for forty years. But here's a strange thing: every person who has ever done Josie Pearl dirt has died within a couple of years. She isn't dramatic or spooky about it when she tells you, but she thinks she puts the hex on them.

She has been trimmed out of fortune after fortune by crooked lawyers, greedy partners, and drunken helpers. Yet she still trusts everybody, and loves the human race and the whole wide world. And anybody is her friend, till proved otherwise.

On one hour's acquaintance she said to me, "You get your girlfriend and come out and stay with me two days, and I'll take you to a place where you can pick nuggets up in your hand, and I'll make you rich."

Which I considered exceedingly elegant of Josie Pearl. But if I got rich I'd have lawsuits, and even one lawsuit would put me in my grave, so I started back to town—goldless and untroubled. But on the way, a stinging little flame of yellow-metal fever started burning in my head. Me? Rich? Maybe just one little old lawsuit wouldn't kill anybody.

November 19, 1937

A Town for Setting Asunder

RENO, NEVADA—The first time you visit Hollywood you think everybody you see on the streets is in the movies. . . .

It's just like that in Reno. Everybody you see on the street is obviously out here getting a divorce. You can tell by the look in their eyes that they're merely sojourning here for the big decree. You feel like stopping each one and asking, "Why couldn't you get along with him?"

And yet, when you check up, you find that the divorce business is only a small part of Reno's life. Only one person out of a hundred in Reno is getting a divorce. There is a fairly constant year-round population of around three hundred people putting in their six weeks' residence here. But many of them stay at dude ranches outside of town. So we'll say there are actually two hundred living in Reno at a given time.

Reno's population is twenty thousand. That would make one divorce-seeker in every hundred inhabitants.

*

The local newspapers pay almost no attention to the divorce hubbub. They do run the names of all people given decrees, but these are in the vital-statistics column along with births and deaths. They don't even tell where the people are from. But each paper has in its library the social register of every city in America, and if anybody important shows up they carry a story and send it over the wires.

Divorces have been running about three thousand a year in Reno. The number seems to follow almost exactly the nation's business trend. You could draw a chart, with one line showing business activity and the other Reno divorces, and they'd be almost parallel lines. In 1931, before the Depression got up full steam (it was also the first year of the six-weeks law), four thousand seven hundred forty-five divorces were issued in Reno.

In 1933 they dropped to a record low of two thousand four hundred and thirty-eight. But 1935 they were up to three thousand and eighty-eight. Last year they were three thousand and one. Up to November 1 of this year there have been two thousand two hundred and thirty-eight. Figured on a twelve-month basis, that would be only two thousand six hundred and eighty-five for 1937. What's the matter? Things aren't looking so good.

*

Most of us think of all Nevada divorces as being obtained in Reno. Actually, only about three-fourths are. Many people go to smaller towns over the state. But if they do this with the idea of escaping publicity they go in vain, for the press associations have correspondents watching the court records in even the smallest towns.

If you actually lived in Nevada, you could decide at breakfast you wanted a divorce and by noon you could have it. Yet the local people hardly ever get divorces. Only about five percent of the divorces involve actual Nevada residents. The bulk are from New York and other Eastern states, and from California. . . .

Ever since Nevada became a state, during the Civil War, it has had a six months' residence requirement to become a citizen. In most states it's a year. For that reason, Nevada years ago became a sort of divorce haven, and hundreds were getting split here every year. Then in the middle twenties Nevada's legislature put through a three-months divorce law, and in 1931 the six-weeks law. That disgusted many old Nevadans. They said it was a raw and commercial bid for the divorce business, which it was. There was much criticism of the legislature. But the law stuck.

Today, the businessmen of Reno are not keen about the six-weeks law. They say they made more money under the six-months law. For then people had to be here so long they usually rented a house, sometimes bought a car, and had to stay through changes of the season, which required new clothes.

Now, they just come and camp for a short time in anything from a hotel room to a tourist cabin, do little buying, just wait it out. There's a saying out here that the six-weeks law is merely a law for the lawyers and hotelkeepers.

November 20, 1937

RENO, NEVADA— . . . Of course all states have prostitution, but the forty-seven others pretend they don't. Most people think it's better to deny there's any such thing, and consequently let it run wild, than to tell the truth, admit there is such a thing, and attempt to control it.

Prostitution in Nevada has been legalized by the legislature, on a local-option basis. But every big town in the state has adopted it, so far as I can find out. The district is always segregated at the edge of town. In conversation it is referred to as "the line," and in print as the "restricted area."

Nowhere in the state are the individuals licensed. In some towns the houses are licensed and pay a fee, while in other towns they don't. In Reno they pay no license fee but are segregated and under police control.

Winnemucca, a town of about two thousand, is a good example of how legalized prostitution works. There the houses pay for a license and the women are required to have weekly examinations. There are forty women in the restricted area.

They are allowed to go downtown in the daytime to shop, but must be behind the wall by eight P.M. I thought the fellow who told me that was speaking figuratively about the wall. But he wasn't.

We drove out. And there, sure enough, was a high board wall, just like the wall around a ball park. There was just one entrance. You can drive in. Six or eight houses—some big, some little—are grouped around a square, making a sort of plaza in the center.

Almost every house has a bar and dance floor. They have names such as Lucille's Place or Ethel's Place. It looks awfully dead in the daytime. The only person we saw was a girl sweeping off a front porch.

The state, as a whole, doesn't have a very good setup yet for its control of legalized prostitution. But the State Board of Health is working out a system of inspection that will soon go into effect.

Under it, women in all the restricted areas will be given examinations at regular intervals. Those with diseases will be quarantined. Also, clinics will be set up for the public. Those who can pay must pay. Those who can't will be treated free. . . .

And now for legalized gambling.

Downtown Reno is a sight to behold on a Saturday night. It is a genuine cross between Hollywood and Broadway, with a touch of the West thrown in. The streets are jammed. You can hardly bear the leap and flash and glare of the great colored neon signs. There are autos by the hundreds, most of them with California licenses.

You see common people without neckties, and women in thousand-dollar fur coats, and men in evening dress, and cowboys in overalls.

But this potpourri of the streets readjusts itself somewhat into social strata when it starts to drink and gamble. There are clubs for the high, and clubs for the low.

There is a bar or gambling casino practically every other door. The Bank Club, the Inferno, the Fortune Club, and the Silver Dollar are just a few of the dozens. And hundreds of people lay it on the line in every one.

But every night isn't Saturday night in Reno. And I can't see how so many casinos keep going. Of course, we know the percentage is in their favor. There are tables, like life-insurance tables, showing just what any gambling house can expect in the way of profit on the money turned over.

But how about this? One of the swankier clubs here obviously costs scores of thousands to build. Its employees must run to half a hundred. It pays thousands a year in licenses. The overhead is tremendous. And yet I've been there on a week night when the roulette dealers were sadly spinning their wheels in the exciting game of collection from or paying off to one sole gambler, and this gambler was the guy paid by the house merely to attract other customers.

And I've seen them give away one six-dollar pot right after another to the winner in keno, when they weren't taking in a dollar-and-a-half a game from the handful of players.

So how can a place like that keep up? Here's how: they depend on the filthy-rich spender who invariably drops in now and then from New York or Los Angeles or even from a big Nevada cattle ranch.

Then the limit posted above each table goes out the window. If the ultra-moneyed guy wants to bet a thousand dollars a hand on twenty-one he's covered. They're liable to take him for ten or fifteen thousand dollars before the night's over. That's how they keep going.

Of course there's always a chance the guy might get hot and clean the house. That's why they call it gambling. The "bank has been broken" more than once in Reno. When that happens they close their doors, and they stay closed till the owner can promote another roll.

November 22, 1937

A MUNDANE STIRRING

VIRGINIA CITY, NEVADA— . . . Virginia City sits right on top of the famous Comstock Lode, the richest vein of ore ever found in America. It has produced more than seven hundred million dollars in silver and gold.

The Comstock was so rich it was ridiculous. It had ore running as high as five thousand dollars a ton, while all over the West today they're mining five-dollar ore at a profit.

The Comstock was discovered in 1859. For months nobody knew what they had found. They were looking for gold, and were annoyed by the sticky blue stuff that clogged their rocker boxes. Finally someone was smart enough to realize it was silver in gargantuan quantities, and then the rush was on.

In 1859, Nevada was merely a territory, and there were no more than a few dozen people in it. But within a couple of eye-winks Virginia City had a population of twenty thousand. It went wild. It splattered money in its Civil War sort of splendor. The great actors of the world came here to perform. There was a man for breakfast every morning, as the saying goes. In the first seventy-two murders there were but two convictions. It was in Virginia City that Samuel Clemens started reporting on a newspaper, and assumed the pen name Mark Twain.

For nearly twenty years Virginia City was the hottest thing between Chicago and San Francisco. And then exhaustion came to the Comstock Lode. It had given its all and could give no more, they thought. The tycoons moved out in 1878. Old age set in on Virginia City. It has been alternately dying and coming faintly to life again ever since. By 1930 you could count only an auto or two on the main street, and houses stood empty, and leaning.

*

But this is 1937. Every afternoon I drive over here from Reno. It is only twenty miles away, and the mountain road, once a death trail, is wide and excellent.

Virginia City doesn't show until you come round the last bend and look straight upon it. And there it clings, six thousand feet high, plastered to the side of a steep hill—a little old town surrounded and impregnated with countless old shaft houses and long gray piles of dirt and rocks from the tunnel depths—an old town set amid rolling hills and desert.

The main street is mostly still here, in skeleton—the famous C Street. We of this generation never heard of it, but fifty years ago you could have asked almost anybody west of the Mississippi where C Street was, and he would have known.

The big brick building which housed the *Enterprise,* the paper Mark Twain started on, is still here. A plaque on the front tells about Mark Twain, but the building itself is empty. The famous Crystal Bar is now a soda-fountain bar. The Sawdust Corner saloon still stands, with SAWDUST CORNER still worked in frosted glass on its great doors.

Some of the sidewalks are board, some are concrete. There are many vacant lots, and many empty stores. You can see the old Wells Fargo Express office, through which hundreds of millions in silver bullion passed. Second-story porches, twenty feet high, still jut out over the sidewalks.

*

I wanted to be impressed, and excited, when I came round the bend and saw this sight of my grandfather's day. But I couldn't even have that privilege. The skeleton is there, but progress has slipped inside the bones and made a mundane stirring.

There is life in Virginia City, not the old riotous life of bonanza times, but 1937 life, flowing just as it flows in countless hundreds of other American towns. Virginia City cannot truthfully be called a ghost town. True, it has withered and dwindled. Where it used to sprawl for blocks up the mountainside, and spill over the divide for more blocks and blocks into Gold Hill, today the slope is bare, and the houses stretch a mere two blocks from C Street.

But the houses are full. You can't rent a house in Virginia City today. The mines are working again. Since Roosevelt raised the price of gold, Virginia City has oozed back to life once more. It didn't spring. It just oozed.

New shaft houses have gone up and new mills costing a hundred and fifty thousand dollars each. Old shafts have been reopened. Surveyors work the hillsides, laying out property lines. The population has come from a mere three hundred back up to twelve hundred or so. Four hundred men are digging in a dozen mines. Precious metal is coming out of the Comstock again at the rate of two million dollars a year. Autos line C Street.

Why, I wonder, can't an old place really die? Why can't it lie down amid its old drama and wrap its romantic robes about it and pose there, unstirring and ghostlike, for the trembling contemplation of us latecomers?

November 24, 1937

MEMORIES OF A ROUGH TOWN

VIRGINIA CITY, NEVADA—There's an old whitish house on a sort of ledge in the hillside on the upper edge of Virginia City. There is a white fence around it, and a gate with an old-fashioned latch. An oldish man in overalls comes out and shakes your hand. He is small and a little stooped.

He is Jimmy Stoddard. He is the Comstock's only living bridge between the far past and the present. He has been on the

Comstock for seventy-five years. "I guess you go back further than anybody else in Virginia City, don't you?" I asked.

"I think you called the turn on that one, son," he said. "I think you called that one right. I guess I'm the oldest, all right."

Jimmy Stoddard arrived here with his parents from New York in 1864. He was nine then. His parents lie buried over on the hill. You can see the graveyard from his house.

He went to work in the bowels of the Comstock when he was thirteen, and there he worked until he was seventy-one. Fifty-eight years in the mines, right beneath Virginia City. Jimmy Stoddard is eighty-four now, but he still goes out in the hills and prospects around.

He is a truthful man, and admits he doesn't remember awfully much about the early days. He doesn't recall that he ever saw Mark Twain; he does remember seeing many a man hanging from the beams of the shaft houses in the old days. He says he ran the cage that brought General Ulysses S. Grant up from the mines on his visit here in 1878. In the boom days, he says, miners on their way to work would slip an order for stock under the bank door, and when they came out of the earth that evening they'd be five hundred dollars richer, just by speculation, and then they'd go to San Francisco and spend it all. He was one of them.

His memory is clear but not spectacular. Seventy-five years is a long time to recall details and keep things straight in your head. But not all the old-timers remember as unspectacularly as Jimmy Stoddard. The most remarkable remembering is done by those who tell you all about Mark Twain. It's truly amazing how sharp their recollections are.

One old fellow told me that although Twain is known as a humorist nobody around Virginia City ever saw him smile. This old man remembers him well, even refers to him as Sam. He says Twain used to stand all the time in the doorway of the *Enterprise* building and spit tobacco juice onto the steps of the adjoining doctor's office, which happened to belong to this old man's uncle.

So this old man—just a boy then, of course—called his uncle's attention to it, and the uncle put up a sign saying not to spit there. So after that Twain stood in the doorway and instead of spitting on the steps he spit on the new sign.

I thought that was a grand little story, and it was a thrill talking with a man who had actually known Mark Twain in those far days when they called him Sam. Before parting, I asked the old man his age, and he told me. When I got home I figured back on the dates—and discovered that this old man wasn't even born till a year after Mark Twain had left Virginia City forever. That's the kind of memory I admire.

*

Today not a single descendant of the Comstock's great bonanza kings has any financial holdings in the remnants of the Comstock. They have taken other courses. They tell you around here that the first-generation descendants are still interested in Virginia City, sentimentally. Some of them come here occasionally, to talk, and look over old spots.

Clarence Mackay, of Postal Telegraph, whose father was the king of kings of the Comstock, comes back every few years. He always goes into the Catholic church and says a prayer in memory of his parents. But the second generation, they say, has no interest in Virginia City. In fact, some of them are quite ashamed of the roughness of their grandfathers.

I was told of one incident that happened not long ago. The grandson of one of the bonanza kings showed up with his bride. A pleased old-timer volunteered to show them around. So he steered the couple out past the edge of town, up a little gulch a hundred yards or so, and then he stopped and said, with an emotion that was filling him: "Right there is the spot where your grandfather staked his first claim." And the rich grandson said, "Isn't the view gorgeous from here?"

The old-timer thought the young man hadn't heard. So he said again: "There, right in front of you, is the very ground where your grandfather made his great strike." And the rich grandson said, "Aren't the clouds over there magnificent?"

And the old-timer replied, with what seems to me exactly the proper answer, "Well, you can go straight to hell." And he turned and went back down the gulch, leaving them there.

November 27, 1937

LAS VEGAS, NEVADA— . . . Las Vegas is quite a place. It calls itself the "last of the Old West," or something like that. It's an exaggeration, but Las Vegas *is* a rather fascinating mixture of the old desert West and of everything modern.

The population is about five thousand. Being in Nevada, it is wide open. When we were here three years ago, there were more than forty gambling casinos and saloons. That was when Boulder Dam, thirty miles away, was going full blast, with thousands of workers. But now the dam is finished, the workers have moved on, and Las Vegas has suffered. You see casinos closed, doors padlocked, windows gray and empty.

But Las Vegas is no ghost town just because the dam is finished. It is a little metropolis, and always will be. It's the only town of any size for at least two hundred miles in any direction. Tourists, business travelers, ranchers, miners, and just plain desert rats keep its streets always colorful and fairly crowded.

The gambling casinos that are still open don't do the business they used to. There aren't as many people gambling on Saturday nights now as there were on weeknights three years ago. But they're still the same type of people—mostly poor. It is depressing to watch them sitting around the keno tables—poor faces, poor clothes, deadly grave anticipation.

No plungers here. You can play from a nickel up to a quarter per card, and the amount of the pot runs from about five dollars to forty dollars, on crowded nights. Most everybody plays only a nickel. We saw one bedraggled old man, very needy-looking, win the pot, pocket his money, and walk out. These people aren't playing for fun; they're playing because they need to win. . . .

March 30, 1938

* * *

Pyle filed the last report on his Nevada trip from California.

SAN FRANCISCO— . . . We came past Lake Tahoe on the way down here. Tahoe is only an hour's drive from Reno. You come up from forty-five hundred feet at Reno to nine thousand at the pass, and then drop back to six thousand, which is the level of the lake.

Tahoe is one of America's beauty spots—and famous as the resort where the movie people build their summer cottage-castles, although it's a long way from Hollywood.

The lake is big and blue and deep. It is oval-shaped, fifteen miles long, and ringed with mountains and trees. It is two thousand feet deep, and one of the darkest blues you ever saw.

It was cold when we were there, and most of the resorts and private homes were boarded up. In summer it must be wonderful. But, still, I'll take Lake Louise in the Canadian Rockies, which I contend is the most beautiful sight in America. . . .

You can read that Nevada is the most sparsely settled state in the Union. But it takes an example to make you really feel it. Here is one:

There is just one telephone book for the whole state! Every phone in Nevada is listed in it, plus four counties of adjoining California. And the whole thing makes a thin little volume that you could stick in your topcoat pocket. . . .

We beat the first heavy snows through the Sierras. But the road commission is all prepared. For miles there are slender orange-colored poles, about twelve feet high, planted about every two hundred feet along each side of the winding highway. They're put there so you and the snowplows can find the road after the big snows come. . . .

November 29, 1937

UTAH

AN INFINITE BRIGHT BARENESS

WENDOVER, UTAH—It has always been a puzzle to me why the salt beds of Utah should provide the world's most perfect raceway for automobiles. All recent world speed records have been set on the Bonneville Salt Flats. . . .

But I never could quite picture a salt flat, or understand why it would be so good for driving. So we drove on the salt ourselves, and now I know.

*

For a hundred miles west of Salt Lake City the country is common desert, dry, brown, full of sagebrush. Then gradually you come into the salt flats. You aren't taken by surprise. But little by little a feeling comes over you—a weird feeling of unworldliness.

On either side, and ahead and behind, for miles and miles in every direction, the flat salt stretches to the very foot of the far-lying brown hills. The feeling is that of being in the center of a vast frozen lake. The salt resembles ice, and it's as level as a billiard table. Though the sun is shining, the sight makes you feel cold.

And you see mirages. Far out on the bluish "ice" you see black boats, apparently floating a few feet above the surface. As you come along even with them, they become sticks of wood lying on the salt.

Along either side of the oiled highway is a deep ditch. It is blue in the center and white along the edges. It appears to be clear water, running between snow-encrusted banks. You don't know whether it's a mirage or not. You stop to have a look.

You kneel down and stick your finger into the ditch. Yes, it's water all right. Then you taste it. What a taste! Salt such as you never tasted before. The "snow" along the banks is salt crystals. Some of them are perfect crystals, big as dominoes. . . .

*

. . . The surface was a bluish-white—so white that even with dark glasses you could hardly see to drive. It was hard to drive in a straight line, for there was no perspective. Nothing to judge your direction by, except the faraway race camp. There was no road, of course. You could drive anywhere. I understand the speed drivers have to follow a black line painted on the salt; otherwise they'd probably wind up in Idaho.

The whole expanse appeared so much like ice that I couldn't believe a car could have much traction on it. My car is very fond of skidding. So I tried it out. I stepped up to sixty miles an hour, turned the wheel a little, and hit the brakes. I thought we would spin at least three times—and, of course, it wouldn't have hurt anything if we had, for there's nothing within miles to hit. But we didn't spin at all, or even skid. The tires just crunched, and we stopped. . . .

We drove miles and miles around over the flats, and almost got lost. I tried to picture it as it once was—stripped bare once more, stripped of highway and railroad and telephone poles and sticks of wood. And I believe that then it would become an expanse so unbroken, so directionless, so devoid of all things, that to be on it would be like floating in the stratosphere, out of sight of earth or clouds, sailing along in nothing but blue. I believe a man would go crazy on it from the confusion of an infinite bright bareness.

November 17, 1937

CISCO, UTAH— . . . No state ever presented its visitor with a more desolate front yard than does Utah at the point where you come into it from the east over the southern highway. It is desert— complete, unabridged desert. Just a little sage, and all the rest

is long brown emptiness, with ragged buttes rising to the horizon far away. . . .

November 1, 1936

BRYCE CANYON PARK, UTAH— . . . Bryce Canyon is a sort of Carlsbad Cavern outdoors. You stand on the rim of a precipice. You
look down into a valley. And in this valley is a regular forest of
tall and erratically carved stone spires, rising as high as five
hundred feet.

En masse, they look like a huge forest of gigantic stone tree
trunks, without limbs. Or they look like a solar pipe organ. Or
they look like ten thousand pink flagpoles. Or they look like
what you see if somebody hits you on the head with a mallet.

All these poles have weird knots and projections and top
pieces on them. It is probably the best spot in the world for
picking out images. You can find a camel, or William Jennings
Bryan. It is better than seeing faces in clouds or in fireplaces. . . .

The overall color is pink. But there are white spots, and dark
spots, and colors change as the day wears on. The finest time for
looking is just before sundown. Then the dark shadows of these
thousands of spires reach across each other, and they make a
scene of such chaotic fantasy that you just have to stand there
and look till the light is gone. You wouldn't be surprised to hear
flutes.

*

I don't know why they call it a canyon, for it isn't really a
canyon. It's just a high mesa, and then a sudden drop off into a
valley, and then the valley opens out and falls away on the far
side to a vast rich plain. . . .

*

Bryce Canyon is named after Ebenezer Bryce, a Mormon
cattleman who settled down in the valley, at the edge of the
spired tanglework, in 1875. The rest of his life was spent here.

Just before cattleman Bryce died, he was approached to give
a description of the canyon. They felt that his close association
with it over so many years should bring forth a descriptive
phrase that would live with the park for many years. They were
right. Ebenezer thought a long time, and then he said:

"Well, it's a hell of a place to lose a cow."

August 17, 1939

BLUFF, UTAH— . . . Once Bluff was alive. There were cattle here,
and people were rich. But that was long ago.

Bluff is dead, and well it knows it. The immense square stone houses, reeking of past wealth, stand now like ghosts, only one or two to a block. All else is vacant. Sand is deep in the streets. The sun beats down. People move slowly, for there is no competition. Nobody new ever comes to Bluff.

The mail comes in three times a week, by truck. It had just arrived when we came into town. Indians were crowded around the post office, which is in a private home.

After chatting around awhile we got in the car, and sat there rolling a cigaret before starting on. We noticed a man going across the road. He was raising a foot and putting it down once every fifteen minutes.

"Wonder what's his hurry," I said.

"Oh, the mail just got in a couple of hours ago," said my friend, "and he's rushing across to get it." . . .

July 27, 1939

WYOMING

CHEYENNE, WYOMING— . . . Cheyenne is a place that disappoints me. The name of it has always represented the spirit of the West—cowboys, cattle, six-shooters, the open range, the great rodeo.

True, Cheyenne is still cattle country. But it doesn't appear so. You hardly ever see a cowboy on the street. I don't suppose there are any more horses here than in Canton, Ohio.

The town is filled with modern cocktail lounges and curly neon signs. In spirit it is almost indistinguishable from any Midwestern city of twenty thousand. . . .

November 4, 1937

*   *   *

GRAND ISLAND, NEBRASKA—I'm just stopping here for gas, and taking a last, forlorn look back toward the West.

I think it is not necessarily derogatory to the rest of the country for me to say that I leave the West regretfully. I always have left it regretfully, and on each leaving the regret seems to be harder to bear.

I like New England—once I'm there. The Deep South has a charm and a sentiment that captivates me—once I'm in the midst of it. There's nothing wrong with an Ohio crossroads town of five hundred—if that's where you live. I usually like wherever I happen to be.

But what I mean is that I would not voluntarily quit the West for any of these places. For I know deep down that the West is my country. Each time, after leaving, I realize that in the West my spirit has been light; I've felt freer and happier.

You are more conscious of it after leaving than when you are in the midst of it. The spirit of the West seems to affect you just as the altitude does.

When I'm in the mountains I'm never especially conscious of feeling better than at other times. Yet just let me leave the mountains, and drop down to the lower altitudes and the thick, hot atmosphere of the prairies, and I feel so terrible that I suddenly realize how wonderful I felt in the mountains. . . .

August 4, 1941

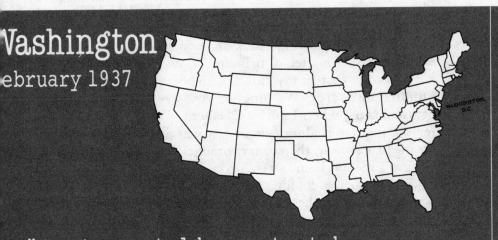

Washington

February 1937

WASHINGTON, D.C.

"I got a mental home-stretch complex. I couldn't bear to stop to dig up stories, couldn't stand the idea of talking to people, couldn't loiter in the countryside and in the little towns, as I usually do."

WHAT DOES IT MEAN WHEN YOU'RE AFRAID OF YOUR FRIENDS?
WASHINGTON—I hope some psychologist will read this column
and tell me what was the matter with me, for I have just been
through some very weird emotions. I not only can't fathom
them, I'm not even sure I can describe them.

To begin with, Washington is my home. More than half my
adult life has been spent here. The greatest number of my
friends are here, my working associates are here, my bosses and
my trunkful of old letters and all my worldly possessions are
here. I know Washington better than any city in the world. And
I have always loved it.

But for two years I have been away most of the time—wandering over the North American continent as a roving reporter. On
the trip just finished I have been gone seven months and traveled
seventeen thousand five hundred miles.

Two months ago I left the Pacific Coast and headed wander-
ingly east—and I definitely knew I was on my way home. But
the truth is, I did not want to come home. There was no special
objection to coming home—it was just that I had no special
enthusiasm for it. I would rather have kept on going, aimlessly.
But a fellow has to come back and touch home base once in a
while, just as a matter of principle. So we headed home.

Here's the first funny thing. Oklahoma City is some fifteen
hundred miles from Washington. And yet, after seven months
of wandering, when I got to Oklahoma City I had the definite
feeling that I was almost home.* It was just a jaunt from there
on in. Just around the corner, practically.

I got a mental home-stretch complex. I couldn't bear to stop
to dig up stories, couldn't stand the idea of talking to people,
couldn't loiter in the countryside and in the little towns, as I
usually do.

So I just "overnighted" in the big cities, and kept beating it
on each morning toward home—and this despite the fact that I
didn't want to come. There was constantly in my mind a picture
of the day of my arrival—not anticipation, not revulsion—I was
just thinking about it all the time, that's all.

And then—this is the part that puzzles me most—when we
were only about two days out, I began to get afraid. Why I

*Pyle had written from Tulsa: "Oklahoma City is an especially friendly town. People
there have a pride about their town—not a silly civic pride, but that same feeling that
exists in San Francisco and New Orleans. They just wouldn't live anywhere else, that's
all."

should have been afraid, or what exactly I was afraid of, I don't know. But I worked up in myself the belief that none of my old friends around the office would speak to me. I got it into my head that everybody despised me. I could picture them giving me the frozen-face when I walked in, and I could see the new reporters, who had been told about me, standing in little groups and staring contemptuously.

And I was afraid of the city, too. I was afraid that it had changed so that not a soul in town would remember me, that none of the old buildings I had known would be there, that everything would be strange and different.

We arrived at four o'clock in the afternoon. During the last hundred miles hardly a word passed between me and the girl who rides with me. We had discussed the thing, and it turned out she was obsessed with the same strange fears that had me down. We both just mentally drew back from the moment of our return.

At last the moment arrived. We swung around the circle in Clarendon, and up over Key Bridge, and there was Washington in front of us. The city that was our home. I said, "There it is. Take a good look at it." I said it sarcastically, and I don't know why I said it at all, for there wasn't any point to it.

It took us a long time to get downtown. Traffic was heavy. I got sore at the way motorists drove. The streets seemed dirty, where before they had always been clean. Buildings were darker and dirtier than I had remembered them.

I watched the people on the streets and hated them. They looked so smug. I didn't see any faces I recognized, and yet I knew that all these people had been there when I left, and that they hadn't been away during that time, and hadn't been in the slightest way aware of Bismarck or Vancouver or San Diego or Albuquerque during the past seven months. It wasn't that I felt superior to these people because I had been around and they hadn't. I don't know what it was. I just didn't want to come back, I guess. And I was excited.

We went to a downtown hotel. The clerk was the first person in Washington I spoke to. I think I must have shouted, and I know I talked faster than usual. And when I went to sign the register, then I realized I was shaking all over. My hand was trembling so badly I could barely write my name. . . .

I was afraid to go to my newspaper office, and yet I couldn't wait till I got there. When I walked through the door of the editorial room I felt as though I were going to burst—not with pride or joy, but with fear and the realization that the awful moment of return was all around me, and that people were looking at me.

The rest of the story is short. Everybody was just swell. People got up from their desks and came over to shake hands, and they laughed and wisecracked, and there was a great deal of talking to do, and when I started back to the hotel two hours later Washington was a grand place, just as it always was, and the people in it were fine, and my spirits were high. I continued to be very excited all evening, and could hardly think or talk sensibly. But I wasn't afraid of my friends anymore. The homecoming was over.

February 4, 1937

Home Report

Dana, Indiana
March 1937

"Indiana farmers know what a 'good neighbor policy' is. It's born in them."

THE GOOD NEIGHBOR POLICY OF WESTERN INDIANA

DANA, INDIANA—In the last few years we've heard a lot about the Good Neighbor Policy among nations.* But to me, and I suspect

*Roosevelt's Latin American foreign policy of nonintervention and trade reciprocity.

to most of us, the phrase "good neighbor" has become a mere academic term.

We who live in cities have almost forgotten what a good neighbor is. But the country people know. It's the same thing it was thirty years ago, and maybe even a hundred years ago. Let me tell you.

My mother was stricken with paralysis on a Thursday night. By Friday morning the whole countryside knew about it. I am sure at least a thousand people, in town and on farms for miles around, had got the news. Word travels fast among the neighbors of western Indiana.

The help began to roll in instantly. The strongest men in the neighborhood came, without being asked, to help lift my mother into her bed. The women came, to help my Aunt Mary with the washing and housework. Others came, and others called, to see what they could do.

Mrs. Goforth baked two butterscotch pies and sent them over. Lou Webster sent up an angel-food cake, and she came twice to help us with the work. Hattie Brown cooked a roast, with dressing and everything, and sent it up steaming hot for our Sunday dinner.

Cousin Jediah Frist, who will be eighty his next birthday, drove down from town in a sleet storm to see if he could do anything. Nellie Potts, who is Lou Webster's sister, brought flowers clear down from Newport.

Mrs. Bird Malone brought a beautiful hyacinth. When my mother had her first stroke a year ago, Bird and Mrs. Malone started over to see her. On the way, the car door came open and Mrs. Malone fell out and broke her arm, at the shoulder. She was in a cast for three months. She still can't close her hand. I told her she was pretty brave to start the same trip over this time.

Oll Potter's mother sent a whole basketful of fresh sausage, and pork tenderloin, and a peck of apples. When I was a little boy, the Potters were the poorest people in all our neighborhood. They were just up from the Kentucky hills, and we thought they talked funny, and never smiled. Dan Potter worked out by the day for farmers.

But the Potters toiled, and saved their money, and all their boys grew up to be workers. Now they live in a nice house and have a fleet of cattle trucks, and the whole country admires them for the way they've raised themselves up by the bootstraps. It was Mrs. Potter who sent the whole basketful of stuff.

Mrs. Frank Davis, the new neighbor just up the road, brought over freshly butchered pork ribs. My Aunt Mary said it was good of her, her not knowing us very well. Mrs. Davis said that once when she was sick over in Parke County people were mighty good to her, and she told them she didn't know how she could ever repay them, but they told her she didn't need to repay them personally, just so she did good things for other folks when they needed it. And that's what she was doing.

My Uncle Oat Saxton brought over a freshly butchered side of hog. My Uncle Oat is the laughingest man in Vermillion County. He laughs at everything, and especially himself, and when he laughs it is like the clear, melodious peal of a cathedral bell. It helped ease the strain to have him come and sit in our kitchen, and take off the lid and spit in the stove, and tell stories and laugh at them.

On Sunday there were thirty-eight people at our house. We couldn't let them in the front room, and at one time the kitchen and dining room were so full half of them had to stand up.

Anna Kerns was one of the thirty-eight, and when she left she didn't say, "Now if there's anything at all I can do . . ." She said, "Mary, I'll be here at seven-thirty in the morning to do the washing for you." And she was, too, and stayed all day, and got down on her knees and oiled the linoleum, and then sat all afternoon with Mother while we rested.

Bertha and Iva Jordan came twice for half a day each. They brought two pies the first time and a cake the second time, and they did the washing and ironing.

Iva Jordan was my first schoolteacher. She is gray-haired now, but she is still pleasant and soft-spoken. She wore an apron and a dust cap while she did the ironing in our kitchen. We talked about my first year in school, and we both hated to realize it was more than thirty years ago.

Jennie Hooker came and stayed all day. She is the mother of my close childhood chum.* Bill and Beatrice Bales came and sat up all night, and ran innumerable errands for us in their car. Rema Myers, the doctor's wife, came one afternoon and did the ironing. When we were high-school age, Rema and I never dared go anywhere together, we always got the giggles so bad. Rema still gets them. She is the prettiest girl in our town.

*Thad Hooker, the World War veteran Pyle visited in Orlando, Florida, where Hooker was overseer of an orange grove. See page 19.

Uncle John Taylor, my mother's brother, came and sat up two nights, and would have stayed every night if we had let him. Claude Lockeridge got out his truck and drove nearly twenty miles on a snowy day to get a hospital bed from Earl White's, north of town. Other people did things, and brought things, and called up, but I can't remember them all now.

For nearly forty years my mother was the one who went to all these people when they needed help. They haven't forgotten, and now they're coming to her in droves. Indiana farmers know what a "good neighbor policy" is. It's born in them.

March 16, 1937

ar
orth
ountry

aska
d the
eutians

ly-
ptember 1937

ALASKA

ALEUTIAN ISLANDS

"Everybody in Alaska knows about Nimrod and the bear's teeth."

AN AGING KLONDIKE KATE

STEAMBOATING DOWN THE YUKON—This evening, coming down the Yukon into Dawson, I sat on the deck of this little river steamboat and heard the story of Klondike Kate from her own lips.

Klondike Kate came to the North in 1900 to perform in the

dance halls of the new Eldorado. She came down through White Horse rapids dressed as a boy. She is a genuine sourdough.

But Klondike Kate is no crude nugget—isn't today and never was, despite her nickname. She is tall and straight and stately. Her table steward told me she has the finest manners and is the most considerate of any person at his table. He says her manners are like that of a queen, even when she's rolling a cigaret.

In 1900 her name was Kate Rothrock. She was young and beautiful and good. It isn't true that every Klondike dance-hall girl was a prostitute. Kate had her man all right, and lived with him. She was a one-woman man. She was in love with him.

Everybody in the Klondike, even today, knows the story of Klondike Kate and her man. They lived in Dawson for three years during the boom days—Kate dancing, her man tending bar, working in stores, finally going into a little business of his own.

You would know the name of the man if I told it. He became rich and famous, known throughout the United States. And it was Klondike Kate who staked him. It was Kate who shelled out her money for him, because she loved him, to give him his big chance "outside." And he took it, and made good, and then he threw her down.

But she didn't cry about it; she went to work like a man. She stayed in show business until a knee injury put her out of professional dancing for good. And then she took in washing. And finally she homesteaded a place back in Oregon, and proved up on it. She traded that for a house in Bend. And that one for another. She built herself a beautiful garden, and a fireplace with rocks of all different kinds.

Somehow she could never learn to hate him. Even in later years, when she went to him appealingly and was turned away, even that didn't teach her how to hate him. She stayed in love, and years passed to ten, and to twenty, and to thirty—and still she couldn't hate him.

During all that time she never went back to Dawson. The Klondike was far, far behind her. And then a funny thing happened. She got a letter. It was from a prospector, somewhere up on one of the Yukon tributaries. He had seen her name in the paper. He said he remembered her from the dance-hall days of 1900, and he wanted to correspond with her.

So they corresponded. And finally the prospector went all the way from the Yukon frontier down into Oregon to see Kate Rothrock. And they were married.

It was one of those unbelievable things. Johnny Matson had fallen in love with Kate Rothrock when she was a Dawson dance-hall girl. But he was a rough, backward man, and she was taken anyhow, so he had said nothing. And then she disappeared; to where, he didn't know. He stayed on in the hills, panning a little gold. Not much, just a little. Through all those years he lived out on the creek, alone. And then he found her. That happened just under five years ago.

*

Kate Rothrock still lives in Bend most of the year. But every summer, on the first Yukon boat, she comes north all the way to Dawson to see her Johnny. They see each other only twice a year. He comes in from the creek for a few days after she gets here, and then again for a few days just before she leaves in the fall, on the last boat out.

She would gladly go out to live with him, but he won't let her. "No, he says he waited thirty years for me, and now he's not going to have me living in a cabin up some creek," she said. "This is what he wants me to do, and I want to do it for him."

All summer she stays in Dawson, living in a room in the home of a friend, strolling the dead boardwalks of the town that once roared and fumed to the touch of gold.

I asked her if it didn't make her sad to be in Dawson again, after all that happened to her there. And to see Dawson so quiet and still now, remembering how it used to be.

"No," she said, "I love it. I've learned long, long ago to live within myself. I had to. Memories of the old Dawson are still here, but they don't hurt me. It's beautiful to be back."

*

"I saw you talking to Klondike Kate," said my friend Albert Moss, a little later. "I don't expect she told you the real lowdown on her life."

"No, I expect not," I said. "What was the real lowdown?"

And then Mr. Moss told me, from his own memory, slowly and thoughtfully as though it were a great epic, the very same story that Klondike Kate had told me. So it was all true. And more so. . . .

"I haven't talked to her on the boat," Mr. Moss said, "but I knew her well in the old days in Dawson. She was a wonderful woman. The man she lived with was a skunk. But I guess she was in love with him. She staked him to everything she had. She gave him a start that made him famous. She gave him forty thousand dollars, and then he absolutely repudiated her."

*

So Klondike Kate Rothrock, who couldn't learn to hate, and her Johnny, who waited thirty years, go at last with each other into the sunset. It is too late now, far too late for either of them, but they did find each other in time to snatch something—a quality of unusual tenderness, and a beauty, surely, the beauty of brown autumn leaves along the north rivers—leaves the frosts can't hurt, because the frosts have already touched them.

July 10, 1937

POSTSCRIPT: *Pyle's portrait of Klondike Kate is at odds with other accounts of her. Kate Rockwell sued her former lover Alexander Pantages—a Greek immigrant who went on to become a famous theater magnate—for breach of promise in 1905.*

Pierre Berton wrote in The Klondike Fever: *"In 1900, [Pantages] became enamored of Kitty Rockwell, a teen-aged dancer who wore a fifteen-hundred-dollar Parisian gown, a belt of twenty-dollar gold pieces, and a headdress of lighted candles, and who claimed to be the convent-educated daughter of a prominent jurist. In her court testimony, Miss Rockwell swore that she bought seventy-five-cent cigars and fifteen-dollar silk shirts for Pantages, and that when they left Dawson together the following year she paid all the traveling expenses. She asked for twenty-five thousand dollars, but [Pantages] settled out of court for less than five thousand."*

Kitty Rockwell died in 1957.

MAKING HIS WAY IN WILD COUNTRY

EAGLE, ALASKA—Adolph Biederman is the sort of man we in the States think of when we think of Alaska.

He's a small man, brown as leather, and wiry, and he walks with a *thump-thump.* He speaks with an accent, and with that jumpy, hard-to-follow narrative style you frequently hear in the speech of transplanted foreigners.

Biederman is the winter mailman between Circle and Eagle. For thirty-five years he has driven the dog-team mail routes of bitter central Alaska. He's sixty-eight and tough as nails. He was born in Bohemia, and came to this country when he was thirteen. He wound up in Alaska at the turn of the century, and has never been out since. He never intends to leave.

He married an Indian woman and has eight children. Some are grown, and others are tiny kids. He lives in a log cabin, stays up all night when the boat is in. He has a summer camp downriver where he catches fish for his dogs.

Biederman loves Alaska. He says he loves it because you're so free. That's what they all say, and I ask them, "Free from *what*, free to do *what*?" I've yet to get a good answer.

The things Biederman has been through would fill a book. I suppose no man knows more about sled dogs, or winter weather, or making his way alone in wild country. He walks with that *thump-thump* because the front half of each foot is gone. It happened twelve years ago. He let himself get caught, after twenty-five years of knowing better.

It happened because he lost his regular dogs. Captain McCann, the skipper of our boat, accuses himself of causing Biederman to lose his feet. Biederman's dogs were coming upriver on a barge that Captain McCann's boat was pushing. They hit a rock and the barge upset and drowned all the dogs.

So Biederman had to borrow a team and start the winter mail run with green dogs. His sled got stuck in an overflow spot. His regular dogs would have circled it. The new ones didn't. Biederman's feet got wet. It was forty-two below zero, and his moccasins were frozen on him before he could cut them off.

He knew he was in for it. He had frozen his feet before, but this time he knew it was for good. He got to an empty cabin not far away. He built a fire, and got his boots and moccasins off. And then he went outside, at forty-two below, and walked around in the snow in his bare feet. But it was too late. He couldn't feel anything. He sat down and pulled his big toe way over to one side, and it stayed there. Then blisters came on his feet, and the flesh was all black.

He was in the cabin four days. When they found him, they sledded him back to Eagle and later to Circle, where a doctor amputated the fore parts of his feet, a little at a time. He was running the mail again the next winter.

Biederman wears regular shoes in summer, and has phonograph springs in them to keep the toes from flying up. In winter he wears three pairs of socks, and stuffs the toes full of rabbit fur. And over these he wears moccasins.

*

It is a hundred and sixty-two miles from Eagle to Circle. The winter mail makes the round trip every two weeks—thirteen round trips during the winter—forty-two hundred miles of mushing behind huskies every winter. Biederman has cabins strung along the route, twenty-five to twenty-eight miles apart. Sometimes he makes it from one cabin to another in four hours; sometimes it takes as long as eighteen hours, depending on the weather.

When it gets under forty below it's almost impossible to go on, because dogs perspire through their tongues, and if a dog sticks its tongue out at fifty or sixty below, the tongue freezes. And, too, the sled's runners stick at that temperature, and it's like trying to pull a sled over bare ground.

I went out to see Biederman's sled dogs. They were corralled in a nearby woods, each chained to a separate tree, and you never heard such a din as they set up. But you never saw twenty-eight such beautiful dogs—each one an individual face, all part wolf.

Biederman's sons have grown up now, and they run the mail most of the time. Horace brings it halfway, and Charlie sleds it on in. They are steely, brown, half-breed boys, wiry and bashful and strong.

I asked Biederman if he rode the sleds, or mushed behind all the way. He laughed and said, "Well, I never ride the slide, but I'll have to say my boys do. I don't know whether they're lazier or smarter than I am, but they ride the runners most of the time."

Biederman knows everybody in eastern Alaska, and everybody knows him. He has a great deal of humor, and talks a lot, although there's a northern grimness about him, too. He cusses mightily, but doesn't drink or smoke. He quit drinking twenty-eight years ago, because he got drunk and missed collecting a hundred and ninety dollars somebody owed him. He quit smoking because it was hurting his wind.

He used to wear a mustache to cover up his bad teeth. Now that he has false teeth he still wears it. He says it frosts over in winter and protects his mouth.

July 14, 1937

NIMROD'S TEETH

EAGLE, ALASKA—All the way from Seattle to Eagle I've been hearing about Nimrod. Everybody in Alaska knows about Nimrod and the bear's teeth.

As the story goes, Nimrod was an Alaskan woodsman who lost his teeth. So he killed a bear, took the bear's teeth and fashioned a crude plate for himself, then ate the bear with its own teeth.

I went to sit at the feet of the great Nimrod and to hear the epic yarn from his own storied lips. I found the story true in its larger elements, but its purveyors had neglected a number of small things.

They neglected, for instance, to say that Nimrod, instead of being an uncouth creature of the wilds, is a cultured gentleman from Maine who still speaks with a Boston drawing-room accent after thirty-nine years in northern isolation. And they didn't mention that Nimrod is an experienced artisan who can do any sort of mechanical work with his hands. Making a set of false teeth was no great task for him.

*

Nimrod was living way up the creek out of Eagle, he and his partner, working at a little gold and cutting some wood. The year was 1905. That winter the wolves got in and destroyed their cache of meat, leaving them with nothing but vegetables and canned foods. Nimrod got scurvy.

Within a few months there wasn't a tooth left in his head. So he decided to make himself some teeth. He knew how.

For the front ones he used mountain-sheep teeth. He says they are almost like human teeth, except longer, so he just filed them down. Back of these, four on each side, he used caribou teeth. And for the grinding molars he used bear's teeth. Just one on each side—a bear's back tooth is so large it takes the place of two human teeth.

He made the plate of aluminum, drilled out holes for the teeth, set them in, and then worked the warm aluminum back over to hold them tight. It took him a month. He made two sets, uppers and lowers. And he wore them for nearly twenty-five years.

About seven years ago, a Seattle dentist offered to make him a set of real teeth in exchange for these homemade ones. So Nimrod sent in his specifications, and back came the store teeth. He's still wearing them today, and the teeth he made are on display in a Seattle dental shop.

As the story is told outside, Nimrod ate the bear with the bear's own teeth. He says he ate a lot of bear meat with them, but not the bear the teeth came from.

*

Nimrod's real name is Ervin Robertson. He was nicknamed Nimrod when he was a boy in New England because he was such a good fisherman. He was a jeweler by trade for fifteen years in the East before he made the break for Alaska in the '98 days.

For more than a third of a century he lived "up the crick" from here, in a cabin. He hunted and fished and cut wood and played at gold. Nothing much ever came from anything. Today he lives in a tiny old log cabin in this streetless riverbank village of eighty-five people, not more than a dozen of them whites.

Nimrod is one of those perplexing human question marks you find now and then in far spots of isolation—buried by choice. Why he came here, and why he stayed for nearly forty years, is something that Nimrod himself probably doesn't understand.

He is a man of acutely fine instincts, and a genius for craftsmanship. He has never let himself slip into shoddy ways, as most self-exiles do. His speech is professorially precise. He wears a neatly laundered gray shirt, with long collar points, and blue trousers with belt and suspenders. He is freshly shaved, and meticulously clean. He apologizes for his appearance, says he hasn't cleaned up today, and stands while he talks.

His ancestral tree goes back to Scotland, and he still has the family crest between tissue in a cardboard folder. He has scads of relatives in New England, and corresponds with them regularly.

I asked him why he came here in the first place, and he said he joined the gold stampede in the hope of making a thousand dollars. He needed that much to develop his ideas for an airplane. "If I had had a thousand dollars I'd have flown long before the other fellows," he says. "But I'm not much nearer to my accomplishment than I was forty years ago." He laughs as he says it, but the culture in his voice of failure makes it a poignant thing.

Nimrod makes his living now by creating small things. He fashions beautiful hunting knives, and fine gold-wire puzzle rings, and he repairs watches. He is a crack rifle shot, and an ardent hunter. He says he hasn't hunted much in the last year because he has been so busy in the shop. The truth is, he hasn't been able. Constantly he makes these little excuses. It's perfectly obvious to you as he makes them, but you wouldn't let on for anything.

Nimrod has been outside Alaska only once in forty years. He probably will never go again. But forty years of isolation have not corroded him. He is still just as polite, just as gay, just as neat, just as gentle, as he was the day he arrived hoping to make a thousand dollars.

And so he sits in his little shop—the man with the dreams to do fine things, but who achieved his fame by putting bear's teeth in his mouth—he sits, still telling you of what he is going to do someday.

July 15, 1937

DAMNED GLAD NOT TO BE IN CHICAGO

SHEEP CREEK, ALASKA—The Yukon very nearly killed Heinie Miller this spring, and yet you couldn't get him out of this spot in the wilderness, where Sheep Creek runs into the Yukon. He has lived here alone in a cabin for thirty-seven years, with nothing around but trees and Indians and wild animals and the big outdoors. And him originally a city fellow, too, born and raised in Chicago.

Heinie has never been outside since the day he came. "Hell, no, and I ain't goin' out," he said. "I didn't lose nothin' down in the States I have to go back after."

Our boat stopped at Heinie's woodpile along the riverbank early in the morning. We had heard about his catastrophe before we got there. The ice breakup had played havoc with his home and his woodpile. They were still a mess, just as the surging waters had left them.

Heinie and the Indians who work for him cut about seven hundred cords of wood each winter. They stack it on the riverbank, to feed the fireboxes of the Yukon steamers during the summer. By spring their year's work is done—piled in beautiful rows along the riverbank.

But this year nature took a hand. The breaking ice was pushed far up the bank, and then floodwaters came rushing out on top of it, and crushed everything before them. Heinie saw the flood break, and started running. He got less than a hundred yards before it was up to his waist, so he climbed a tree.

He stayed in the tree two hours. Then the tree started to go. Heinie got down and waded in water up to his shoulders, toward the woodpile. "It was *cold!*" he said. He made the top of the woodpile, and there he was marooned for sixteen hours. It was just above freezing, and pouring rain. Ten feet of water all around him, and the wood liable to go floating down the river any minute.

The water suddenly went down, though, as fast as it had risen, and Heinie got off the woodpile at four A.M. He started walking to a trapper's cabin, two-and-a-half miles away. He was so tired it took him six hours. He thought sure he'd catch pneumonia and die. He dried out and stayed with the trapper two days. "And damned if I even got a cough out of it," he said.

But even so, nature served Heinie pretty badly. He lost a hundred cords of wood—at eight dollars a cord—and his new log house, which he had just finished last year, was swept off its foundation and tipped over. His radio was ruined, and his icebox and stove and all his tools. He says he never will find lots of his belongings. It will take all summer to rebuild his cabin.

One of the pilots on our boat said, "You'd better move out and go to California to live." And Heinie said, with a dose of his backwoods profanity, "By —— —— no, I love this country and I'm gonna stay right here and die right here."

He says getting washed out is all in a day's work, and he loves it up here because you're so free. "This country's so damn big and there's so few people in it," he says. "That's what makes it so free."

*

Heinie is getting along in years. His clothes are old and not too clean, which could be said of almost everybody who lives in the woods. He needs a shave, and a large brown string of tobacco juice trickles down each side of his whiskery chin. His eyes are as blue as the sky, as I've noticed about so many of these men up here. But Heinie's eyes are going bad. He said he couldn't see our boat until it got right up close to shore. He has a cataract, and he's scared he'll have to go to Seattle for an operation.

One morning a couple of years ago Heinie dreamed he was back in Chicago. He woke up and sat up in bed, still thinking he was in Chicago, and wondered, "What the hell am I doing here?" And then he realized he wasn't in Chicago at all. "Damn, but I was glad," he says. And yet Heinie subscribes to the *Chicago Tribune*. He was a newsboy for the paper when he was a kid, and he has had it sent up here for over thirty years. He says he can't read it anymore, but he still takes it.

There are trappers and Indians scattered through this country, and they get around a lot, by snowshoe and boat. Whenever anybody shows up, it's food and drink time. "The Indians eat me out of house and home," Heinie says. "They always show up at mealtime, and I can't say no. I've been trying to say no for twenty years, but I can't do it."

An Indian named Willie drives Heinie's caterpillar tractor, dragging the logs down from the hills. Apparently it's quite something for an Indian to be driving a cat. "Hell, them Indians come all the way from Dawson, a hundred miles, to watch Willie drive the cat," Heinie says, "and I have to feed 'em."

Every couple of years Heinie takes the boat up to Dawson, and three days later he has shed about nine hundred dollars and is weak and weary from too much celebrating, and ready to go back to his cabin on the riverbank among the trees and the mosquitoes.

July 17, 1937

TRAPPER WOMEN

FORT YUKON, ALASKA—This is probably the strangest story I will find in Alaska. No matter how far you might wander the earth, looking for examples of great strength of character, I doubt that you would find a more remarkable specimen than this one.

*

Nine years ago the world had come to an end for a woman in this mosquito-infested village. She had had more than she could take. She led her four children down to the riverbank. "Come on, let's go for a little ride in the canoe," she said. It would be easy. Over the side with them, and herself over last. You live only a minute in the Yukon River. The cold water stops your heart.

Two of her boys had just been buried—mysteriously drowned in the Yukon. The husband had quit cold on the family. Everything was on her shoulders. And they had grown too weary, from fifteen years of half-living and scraping and scratching in the Arctic woods and villages. It was time to quit. Nobody cared anyhow.

They were at the riverbank, ready to step into the canoe. An old man with long whiskers came and tapped the woman on the shoulder. "Come walk up to my cabin," he said. "I want to talk to you." She barely knew the man.

But she walked. And the man said, "I know you don't want to go onto charity. You can make a living on the trap line. It won't be easy, but it will be an opportunity for you to support yourself and the children."

So she turned trapper. She bundled her four children into a gas-powered boat. The old man went with them. For two weeks they chugged up the Porcupine and its tributaries. The baby boy died on the way. They buried him, and went on. They chugged up the Black River, and up a river that runs into the Black.

Now, Fort Yukon itself is north of the Arctic Circle and about three quarters of a mile beyond the end of the earth. But they didn't stop until they were two hundred and eighty miles beyond Fort Yukon. And then they camped on the bank of a river, under a mountain slope. They built a log house, and fixed it up with stuff they had brought—on two thousand borrowed dollars.

*

That was nine years ago. The three little girls are now young women. The two thousand dollars has been paid back. There is a little in the bank. And they go on trapping.

Only nine times in nine years have Mrs. Maud Berglund and her three daughters been back to Fort Yukon. Eleven months of the year they do not see another living soul. They live alone, among snow and wolves and moose and mountains. Just after the spring ice-break they get into their two gasoline boats and come downriver with their pelts, on a combined vacation and business trip. They sell their furs at auction, and they load their boats with a year's supply of staples.

The round trip takes them two weeks. They tarry in Fort Yukon a couple of weeks. They are gone from home just a month. I was lucky enough to catch the Berglunds on their annual trip here. I spent an evening in their log cabin, and a forenoon with them. I shot their guns at targets and rubbed their homemade salve on my mosquito bites. And they told me about themselves. . . .

*

Mrs. Berglund is a handsome, gray-haired woman—fine of feature, refined in speech, easy and gentle in her manner. I don't know her early story, but I do know she came to Alaska twenty-five years ago from Oregon. The rough life seems not to have touched her personality at all.

But her three daughters are children of nature. They are brownly tanned, their hands show hard work, and their shoulders and legs are strong like a man's. They are Marion Hazel, Evelyn Maud, and Elsie May. They range in age from fourteen to twenty-one.

These girls grew up in the woods. Elsie May was carried over the trap line by dogsled for two years before she was big enough to make it herself. All their education has been given them by their mother. They know no life but the life of the trapper.

They have never been south of Fort Yukon, never seen a village with real streets or brick buildings. They have no conception of what a city is like. They don't know much about men. They have never drunk or smoked, or danced or played cards. They wear men's clothes eleven months of the year. But they only have to shoot once at a running moose, and they can freeze their feet without crying.

Their hobby, their amusement, their recreation, their joy is all in one thing: their dog teams. Each girl has her own team, her own sled, her own rifles. They'll talk dog to you until you're black in the face. They love their dogs above all else.

The girls, although they do not know our world, are smart. They are zestful and eager. Their conversation flows like a torrent, and their eyes shine. They accept new acquaintances at face value; after the first few minutes of bashfulness, they speak forward in a flood of enthusiastic recountings. Out come guns and wolf skins to show you, and moose antlers, and little incidents in excited snatches. These three girls are the freshest in spirit of any women I have ever seen.

July 21, 1937

FORT YUKON, ALASKA— . . . For nearly a decade, the years have gone like this for Mrs. Berglund and her three daughters:

As soon as they return from Fort Yukon to their cabin, they start a busy season of picking and canning berries and wild fruit. They catch salmon with a fish wheel, and dry it and store it for winter feed for the dogs. They repair their dogsleds, and the harnesses, and get the traps in order, and store and pack the four tons of supplies they purchased in Fort Yukon.

When the fall freeze-up comes, they cut ice from the river and store it in the ice well. They kill a moose apiece, and fry steaks, and then freeze the steaks. And then in the late fall, when the snow is on and the season opens, they'll start their winter's work—five months of lonely running of trap lines.

They have more than two hundred miles of trap lines, along

which are scattered some four hundred traps. They run the line with five dog teams, hitched to five sleds. Each sled carries traps, bait, guns, dog feed, tents and sleeping bags, and frozen food.

John Roberts and one girl travel together. Mr. Roberts is the long-whiskered old man who tapped Mrs. Berglund on the shoulder and gave her the opportunity to do something besides drowning her children and herself in the Yukon River. He has trapped with them for nine years, and although he is now aged and shaky, he can shoot as straight as a G-man and tramp behind the dogs all day.

Mrs. Berglund and the two other girls go in the opposite direction. They set traps as they go. Only a trapper could tell you why they set them where they do, but they can tell, by tracks and trails and gnawed bark and other little things, where to put them each year.

Every fifteen miles or so they have a log cabin. It is only about ten feet square, and the door is so low you have to crawl in. They try to reach a cabin each night, but sometimes they don't. Every cabin has a stove, and a couple of bunks. They use candles for light.

Frequently a branch line of traps is laid, at right angles to the main line. When doing this, mother and girls separate, so a good part of their winter is spent traveling absolutely alone. They are away from home four to ten days each trip. And on the return visits at home they stay only a day or two. The majority of their winter nights are spent in tiny candle-lit cabins, alone, scores of miles from home, hundreds of miles from other humans. . . .

And what do the four women trappers make from all this work? Here is last winter's catch: twelve mink, fifteen lynx, eleven wolves, two ermine, thirty-one marten, and one wolverine. These brought about sixteen hundred dollars. Their supplies for the coming year ran them about six hundred dollars. They made a profit of a thousand dollars. Some years they do a little better; other years they barely make "grubstake," as they call it. But on the whole, they're keeping well ahead of the game. . . .

July 22, 1937

FORT YUKON, ALASKA—What will eventually happen to four white women, living alone eleven months of the year in the cold Far North, trapping wild animals?

I asked Mrs. Berglund if she supposed her three girls would

ever marry. "That's something that will have to take care of itself when the time comes," she said. "They don't know anything about the other life. I don't expect they will ever go outside. It would be a mistake to try to make them live in a city."

I asked the girls, "Do you ever look at pictures of people or scenes in the cities?" One of them said, "Yes, we've seen pictures of New York and places like that. But we don't know anything about what it's like, and I don't think we'd ever want to go there. We've got too much freedom up here."

"Are you so busy that you don't have time to get lonesome?" I asked Mrs. Berglund.

"Well, we're busy all right. And we don't get lonesome much anymore. But when we first went up, I would get in these black sloughs, and I couldn't see daylight for days. The girls are a reflection of my mood, and when I got down we'd all get down. But the radio has helped that a lot. We've got two radios now, and when we get low we turn on the radio, and we're soon out of it."

In their home cabin they have gasoline lamps, which make good reading lights. They pick up books and magazines on their annual visits to town. But the girls don't care much for reading; they turn on the radio instead. They have a camera, and on this trip out they brought four rolls of film to be developed. . . .

I said to Mrs. Berglund, "You speak so often of the cabin up there as being your real home. Do you expect to stay there forever?"

"No," she said, "we'll stay till the price of furs or the run of pelts drops so that we can't break even. Then we'll come out. I expect we'll live on the south coast somewhere. But we'll never leave Alaska. We've been here too long.

"Sometimes I like it up there, and sometimes I feel I can't bear it another minute. My health hasn't been good for the last two years. We've eaten too much meat. I've lost thirty pounds in two years. We all have too much meat in our diet. And I've got so I suffer so from the cold." . . .

*

Just before our boat left, Mrs. Berglund told me a secret. It's not a secret by now, so it's all right to tell it. "Mr. Roberts and I are going to be married," she said. "He'll just be in his overalls and me in a calico dress. There won't be any fuss. And in a couple of weeks we'll be on our way back in again. Nobody will ever know how big his heart is, or what he's done for us. He was the only one who sensed what I had come to that day nine years ago down by the riverbank." . . .

You don't burn up with this thing called love, I guess, when you're knocking at the gates of threescore and more. But there is a deep thing called gratitude, and there is another thing known as human companionship, and the two put together sometimes do just as well as love, I guess, or maybe even a little better.

July 24, 1937

THE ALEUTIANS

The Old Man Smiles and Welcomes Me

GAMBELL, ST. LAWRENCE ISLAND, BERING SEA—It was ten-thirty at night when we dropped anchor. The sun had just set, but there was still some daylight, and a faint ribbon of red lay low on the western horizon.

The wind was blowing, and the lonely sea rolled in long, deep swells, and the cold twilight was thick with an acute sense of great remoteness. Davits swung, and pulleys creaked, and down into the water went one of the *Northland*'s surfboats. They lowered a bag of mail, and the doctor's black kit, and then down the ladder went the nine of us.

Every man was in hip boots and heavy-weather clothing. Some of us wore sheepskins and wool stocking caps. Some wore parkas, with hoods drawn tightly over heads. Every man was covered from head to foot with the dress of the Bering Sea. Nine white men, and it was a strange sight.

To our left lay St. Lawrence Island, rising barren and flattish out of the cold black sea. It was a mile or so away, and we could see the white surf breaking on the beach, and we knew there were Eskimos there watching us, but we couldn't see them.

And over to the right—a long silhouette ascending darkly into the purple of the western sky—was Siberia. It wasn't far away. We could have run over there in a couple of hours. It was just a rolling skyline—but it seemed somehow terribly silent and austere.

Our little boat rose high, and fell deep, and a cold spray filled the twilight and whipped our faces as we tossed across the mile of Bering Sea to St. Lawrence Island.

*

I have an Eskimo friend on St. Lawrence, dressed in a reindeer parka, whose name is John Apangalook. I know he is my friend because as we were walking along together I heard an Eskimo voice apparently ask him who I was, and I heard him answer, in English, "My friend."

John took me about the village of Gambell, through the late dusk. He took me into his house, and the houses of his friends. "There are only two of the old-time Siberian-type houses left," he said. "Nowadays we buy lumber and windowpanes and build our houses like you do. Maybe you'd like to see inside one of the old houses."

We stepped high, through a hole about two feet square, doubling up as we skinned through. We were in sort of a shed. It was darkish in there. The smell of walrus was strong. Old gasoline barrels, full of mukluks in brine, stood on the graveled floor. There were pieces of walrus and seal meat hanging around, and walrus hides that hadn't been dried, and reindeer blankets rolled up, and rafter poles loaded down with furry winter clothes.

The back end of the shed was a doorless wall. John went to the wall, knelt down, said something in Eskimo. An answer came from beyond. John reached to the bottom of the wall, and pulled up until he had made a small V-shaped hole. And then I realized the wall was made of hide—reindeer hide. It fell from the ceiling like a stage curtain, making a separate room behind.

On hands and knees we crawled under, into the room beyond. The young Eskimo dropped the curtain behind us, enclosing us. We were enfolded, encompassed tightly, by windowless walls of thick hide, above and below and all around.

The light from a small flame was very dim, and for a couple of seconds I could not see. Then there grew slowly before my eyes the scene. A thin old man sat cross-legged, Gandhi-like, on the foor. He was naked to the waist. A reindeer blanket lay spread across his lap. He was just sitting there, alone.

I said, "Good evening. I'm sorry we woke you up." He smiled and said something in Eskimo. His face was very friendly. "He wasn't asleep," my friend John said. "He is just resting. He is very old."

The ceiling was too low for me, so I squatted in front of the old man, and John squatted, too. The whole floor was bare, like a dance hall. There was no furniture—no beds, no chairs, no stools. Only along the walls, a thin line like surf on the beach, were stacked the few trappings of an Eskimo's household life.

The floor was of walrus hide, dark and smooth like linoleum, and slightly oily. But the walrus smell was only faint in here, and after a minute or two you were conscious of only a vague oiliness in the air.

The dim light came from a small flame on top of an empty tin can. It was a seal-oil stove. The flame wasn't much bigger than that from a kitchen match. This flame was cook stove, lamp, heating plant. The old man sat close to it. He stuck some paper in the little flame, and lighted his pipe with it. I asked how old he was. He smiled and said, through John the interpreter, that he didn't know; they didn't keep records back when he was born.

John and I talked a little, but not much. We just sat and said nothing for quite a while, but there was friendliness, and a feeling of welcome, in the room. And I thought to myself: How far this is from my world, which I always thought was the whole world. How strange, my sitting here at midnight, in the dimness, within these walrus walls. It is a vast world, and I don't understand it.

And I thought: If we could all come and sit in each other's houses for a minute, maybe it would be better. No, I don't know what it's all about. But the old man smiles, and welcomes me— and he doesn't even know my name, but he smiles, the brown old man who has lived out his days and is soon to die in this little world of his, here in the faraway Bering Sea.

September 15, 1937

THE MOST UTTER POVERTY

ABOARD CUTTER NORTHLAND— . . . While our surfboat was still some hundreds of yards from shore, the fine fragrant odor of deceased fish came out to greet us. As we drew nearer, the aroma grew in tone and volume, and finally rose up all around us, like an anesthetic. This odor has prongs on it, like a devil's tail; and it's so strong you sort of walk sideways, edging into it.

The village of Nash Harbor sits not far from water, on a grassy slope. From a distance it doesn't look bad at all. You see only the little frame schoolhouse, and half a dozen board outsheds, and a few small skin boats resting upside down on high poles.

You don't see the people's houses from a distance, because they are half underground and covered with grass, and look merely like knolls on the hillside. There aren't more than a dozen houses in the place, anyway. These houses resemble nothing so much as those half-underground potato cellars farmers sometimes build in the Midwest. You dig a square hole in the hillside, put a few rafters over the top, and cover the whole thing with sod.

The door doesn't lead right into the house. The door is a square boxlike well about two feet across, set into the ground on the downslope side of the house. You step into this, and then crawl back through a narrow passageway for about ten feet, and finally emerge into the small underground room.

We wanted to see the inside of a house so we asked a fellow, lolling on the grass, if we could go into his house. He said, through a schoolboy interpreter, these exact words: "You can go if you want to, but it's too stinky." That man was one hundred percent right. We didn't stay long.

There is no store in Nash Harbor, and no white man. The schoolteacher is half-breed. The sled-dog puppies are beautiful and want to play, but they smell so bad you can hardly touch them. Almost nobody, except the children, speaks English. The citizens walk around in the grass or loll on top of their houses. They are poor and bedraggled-looking. The men's fur parkas are bare in spots, where the fur has rubbed off. They are torn and patched. Most of the women wore parkas covered with calico and lined with fur.

These people are stricken with the most utter poverty. They have nothing. Nature treats them badly. Nature seems to make an eddy, and flow all around them, leaving them barren. They get no walrus. Their only catches this year were dead ones that floated to shore. They get only a few fish, and very few seals. The reindeer belong to Lomen Brothers,* and the Eskimos have to pay twenty dollars when they kill one, and they've nothing to pay with.

They say there is a village about forty miles around the point

---

*Five brothers of Norwegian descent involved in a wide variety of enterprises, including reindeer herding, butchering, and packing. In 1939 the federal government bought the assets of the Lomens' Northwestern Livestock Corporation and made the reindeer herds available to native peoples—a move toward capitalist self-sufficiency.

where nature is more abundant with her sea life. We asked why, then, didn't they all move around there? They said because there is no schoolhouse, so they stay here for the children's sake.

So we asked why the school wasn't built at the other village in the first place. They said that had been the intention, but the day the boat came with the lumber, a high sea was running over there, so the boat just brought it around here and dumped it. And by just such considerate management on somebody's part was created a village—a village so gaunt and poor that it will wake me in my dreams. . . .

And so we said goodbye to Nash Harbor, feeling very sad, and sorry. And yet despite their poverty the people were friendly, and although not gay, they didn't seem especially grim. Outside of the fish smell, their houses weren't any worse than the shanties of thousands of our own forgotten white men who live on the garbage dumps of big cities.

And if I had to be that poor, I guess I'd rather be that poor up here, where you can at least go and lie in clean grass and not have a policeman yelling at you all the time.

September 20, 1937

ABOARD CUTTER NORTHLAND— . . . Except for a few strays, Alaska's Eskimos live only along the west and north coasts, and on the islands of the Bering Sea. They do not live inland.

Eskimos live in everything from grass-covered cellars to shacks built of Standard Oil gasoline cans, but they do not live in ice houses in Alaska. . . .

Eskimos love to imitate whites. They like to dress like whites, and drink like whites. And they are pushovers for gadgets. They are mail-order-house fiends. They get some of the weirdest things. They'll buy elecric irons, when there isn't any electricity within two hundred miles. And so far as I can see, an Eskimo needs nothing in the world less than he needs an alarm clock. But almost any Eskimo hut you go into has from one to four alarm clocks. . . .

*

But it is all a sad business. You are looking at death. Doom has its finger on the Eskimo. In a hundred years, maybe less, they say there will no full-blooded Eskimos in America. Death and the mixture of white blood takes them. They say the average Eskimo family has fewer than three children, and the population in all the villages except one or two is dwindling.

It is sickening to see the degeneration and elimination of a race of people, especially when they are a nice people, as the Eskimos are. . . .

September 21, 1937

he
outhwest

"Here in the Southwest, where the sun beats down, and the desert is long and empty, and cowboys still ride the ridges and high brush country, a piece of history is as exciting to me as a Christmas package."

OKLAHOMA

ONE OF THE MOST THRILLING SIGHTS IN INDUSTRIAL AMERICA OKLAHOMA CITY, OKLAHOMA—It is late at night. You are coming into Oklahoma City for the first time in your life. You know by your map and your speedometer that you're not far away now. You're tired and bleary after a long day pounding the roads.

You see the reflection of light in the dark sky ahead. That's it. That's Oklahoma City. It looks good. The road comes down out of complete flatness, and begins to wind a little. The glare in the sky vanishes around a bend, and reappears again at the next curve.

You top a little rise, and the fog of lights divides slowly into individualities. You see tall buildings all lighted up, still far away. You think what a big place Oklahoma City is, with lots of big office buildings—and lots of people working this late at night, too. Why, it looks like the New York skyline at night, only the buildings all seem about the same height. The tops make a ledge of light across the sky.

You think along like that, with the frogs croaking alongside the road and the motor purring through the night, and you getting closer and closer all the time. And then suddenly it hits you, right between the eyes. Those aren't buildings all lighted up. They're oil derricks! Oil derricks right in the city!

I recommend that moment of realization, and the next ten minutes of amazed staring, as one of the most thrilling sights in industrial America. You just come here and see it for the first time at night, and if it doesn't enchant and bewilder and captivate you, then I'll sit on the statehouse steps and drink every barrel of oil produced in Oklahoma City in the next twenty-four hours. That would be a hundred and twenty-five thousand barrels.

*

You drive on in among the oil derricks. They engulf you. They're all around. There are hundreds of them. They're as thick as trees. Some aren't twenty paces apart. Some are right on the highway, like a filling station. A string of bright lights goes to the top of each one. And down below, on the ground, everything is brightly lighted.

First the sight, and then the sound. In among them, there is a steady, heavy din. The whole field is alive with work. You hear deep, regular poundings; and a throbbing, rumbling circular sound, like a grinding; and the clank of steel tubes and the whirr of great pulleys, and the shooting off of steam. You see muddy autos dashing about, and men at work, and white plumes of steam, and the glare of flame in boilers. Immense activity, and it is nearly midnight. The fiendish boring for oil never stops with the sun.

You drive on and on. People's houses are all around the derricks—or, rather, the derricks are wedged in between houses, on open lots, on filling-station aprons.

You're in the suburbs of Oklahoma City, and pretty soon you see a sign that says CITY LIMITS, OKLAHOMA CITY. You keep driving on, and still you're amidst the oil wells. And you stay amidst them clear into town. They're all over the golf course. There is one on the side lawn of the state capitol. There's one up against the governor's mansion. The bases of some derricks are set flush against the sides of beautiful homes.

*

Three months ago, there were only two oil wells in the northern part of Oklahoma City. Today there are at least three hundred, and new derricks are going up almost by the hour. Residential sections are being gutted. People are wild for oil. It's one of the big oil booms of petroleum history.

Many people are shocked by this glaring display of commercialism. Rearing an oil field right in the heart of a city, ruining homes and fine residential sections—where is the sanctity of the home? Putting oil wells on the capitol grounds—where is the dignity of the state? Greedy, greedy Oklahoma. Is nothing sacred?

Personally, I get a big wallop out of it. My vote is yes. Put up a thousand more derricks. What if it does waste irrecoverable reserves of oil? Grind a thousand more holes in the ground. Who cares for the heartbreaks and the empty tomorrows? Tear down the statehouse. Throw up more silvery steel shafts. Fire up the black boilers. Drill in the gushers, boys. Cheat the poor folks. Ruin the homes. Squander gas. Throw away fortunes. Who cares? It's fun. Everybody's having fun, even the losers. It's a fever. Spread out your hands and catch the sparkling spray. Let oil reign unrefined. Let's all get rich. Boy, hand me that lease, before it's too late. God, it's exciting. It's a boom. It's a mania. It's great. . . .

June 9, 1936

OKLAHOMA CITY, OKLAHOMA— . . . The oil fields have always been full of doodle-buggers. They still are. Doodle-buggers are the guys who say they know how to find oil. Their methods range all the way from the old peach-tree limb up to electrical currents and X-rays.

I have a friend, a drilling contractor, who gets four or five letters a day from doodle-buggers. He showed me three that had just come in. One of them told him he wasn't going to get any oil in the well he's drilling up in the north end of town. Went on to tell him why—how all the drills in the other wells were slanting east, which showed the oil was in that direction, and here my friend's well is on the west side of the field.

My friend sadly threw the letter away in the wastebasket. He says it isn't true that all the drills are slanting in the other direction. But even so, maybe the guy is right about there not being any oil in his well.

It's enough to make a fellow gray-haired, which my friend is.

June 11, 1936

"In the seventeen years between 1889 and 1906, there were eleven land openings in Oklahoma," Pyle wrote. "Half of what is now the state of Oklahoma was colonized by these openings of territory to white homesteaders."

They were hardly sedate events. "Each was full of panic, thievery, cheating, heartbreaks, unbelievable hardships"—in short, the sort of Wild West tale Pyle couldn't resist. The following is the story of the first run, in 1889.

A GREEDY, PANICKY AFTERNOON

OKLAHOMA CITY, OKLAHOMA—Suppose we are sitting by the railroad track at Guthrie, Oklahoma, a little before noon on April 22, 1889.

There isn't much doing. You could hardly call Guthrie a town. It consists of a water tank, a station house, a Wells Fargo shack, and a shed called the Land Office.

Government men ahead of us have surveyed the eight acres that will soon become the town of Guthrie. You can see marker posts spread out over the country. We men already here are officials—Land Office men, railroaders, soldiers, and deputy sheriffs. We look at our watches. It is almost noon.

We know that twenty miles to the north, spread over an unbelievably long line, are thousands and thousands of men and horses, standing there tense and straining, waiting for a pistol shot that will start the first mad rush for land into this new Oklahoma.

It hits high noon. The race starts up north, and many of us deputy marshals hand in our resignations and dash out over the townsite, staking the lots we want. We who do that are "sooners." We have taken advantage of our official positions to get inside the new territory before the opening gun. Many of us will pay with our lives for this smart business before another dawn comes.

*

We sit now and wait, watching the railroad track. We have heard that fifteen trains were lined up at the border, to rush lot-seekers into Guthrie and Oklahoma City, farther south. An hour passes. Then over the horizon comes the first puff of smoke. The first train is long, and resembles a limb on which bees have swarmed.

Thousands are packed into the coaches and boxcars. The roofs are solid with humans. Men ride the rods, hang on to handrails. They are on the cowcatcher, and even atop the cab.

The train comes racing in without slowing up at the edge of the townsite. Greed gets the best of many people. They tumble off the train at full speed. There are not enough lots for all. To the quickest and strongest will go the rewards.

Pack sacks fly out the train windows. Hurtling humans follow them. Half a dozen dash for a lot they've just spied. And instead of driving stakes, they drive their fists into each other's faces. A late-thinker jumps off and stakes the very lot they're fighting for.

We won't forget the woman for a long time. She stands on the roof of a boxcar running at full speed, and throws over her rolled-up tent and haversack. And then in one wild plunge she projects herself into thin air, bent for a Guthrie lot or hell won't have it. She turns five somersaults in the air with her Mother Hubbard flying, five more after she hits the ground, and winds up against the fence with only one broken leg.

As the train finally stops, the massed thousands pile off in a choking melee. Every man for himself, and no quarter asked. One great fat man tries to crawl through the window. He's so big he gets stuck. Another man comes past, openly lifts his wallet, and goes on. Dozens see it, and no one cares.

Men are held up at gunpoint and robbed without a sound or word, so crushing is the mob. As quickly as the throng breaks loose from itself, it spreads out over the eighty acres in a bewildered chasing of itself. A blind man's buff, hunting for lots. You don't know how far to run, where to stop, whether to turn right or left. A greedy and panicky afternoon.

Fifteen long trains come in from the north before sundown.

In five hours the population of Guthrie leaps from two hundred
to fifteen thousand.

*

Counting those who went to other townsites, and those racing
over the prairies, no fewer than a hundred thousand people
entered the "unassigned lands" that afternoon of April 22, 1889.
Long before dark Guthrie was taken, and a tent city had
sprung up. There was yelling and shooting that night, but little
harm was done. The newcomers were too busy. Even before
nightfall, frame houses had arisen. Trains bore in more lumber
and brick and hardware. The transformation of Guthrie was
remarkable. You can hardly believe what you read about it.

In one month there was hardly a tent left in Guthrie. Within
three-and-a-half months Guthrie had streets, parks, a water-
works, an electric-light plant, and brick buildings by the score.
Lots that cost nothing on April 22 were selling for five thousand
dollars only sixty days later.

At the end of those one hundred days there were in Guthrie
five banks, fifteen hotels, ninety-seven restaurants and boardinghouses, four gun stores, twenty-three laundries, forty-seven
lumberyards, four brickyards, seventeen hardware stores, thirteen bakeries, forty dry-goods stores, twenty-seven drugstores,
fifty groceries, three daily newspapers, and two churches—all in
a town of fifteen thousand.

What happened in Guthrie happened in Oklahoma City, on
a smaller scale. For years the two cities were to fight for suprem-
acy. Guthrie lost the last stand in 1913, when the state capital was
moved to Oklahoma City.

Today Guthrie has fewer people than it had on that first night
in 1889. And Oklahoma City has grown to two hundred thousand. Which proves you never know when to jump off a train.

April 24, 1939

"[Y]ear by year, as the government claimed more land from the Indians,
there were other openings. Altogether there were four runs where people
lined up, and at the shot of a gun dashed out to seek home and security,"
Pyle wrote.

"The last one was the opening of the Cherokee Outlet. So spectacularly
mismanaged, mob-spirited, and ruthless was this one that it put an end
to Oklahoma land runs, and other methods were found thereafter to
distribute the new land to settlers.

"The Cherokee Outlet was two hundred miles long and fifty miles wide. It formed the northern slab of Oklahoma. Its north border was the Kansas line. It contained six million acres."

A RUN INTO THE CHEROKEE OUTLET

OKLAHOMA CITY, OKLAHOMA— . . . The day was September 16, 1893. There were homesteads for thirty thousand people. Yet more than a hundred and twenty-five thousand were there to fight it out! For weeks land-seekers had been converging on southern Kansas. They came from every state and territory in the Union. Some had been months on the way. They were hardy men, most of them past middle years—men desperate for a new start and a simple home and livelihood.

Again, Arkansas City, Kansas, just above the line, was the provisioning place for these thousands. Prairie schooners were stocked with grub, horses traded and bought. Broncs had been shipped in from Texas, Colorado, and Oregon. They brought from twenty dollars to fifty dollars apiece, and it was claimed they could run fifteen miles in forty to fifty minutes. The race was to the fleet, and many a man spent his last penny for a fast bronc.

On the night before the opening, the thousands moved down to the very line and camped. All around that two-hundred-by-fifty-mile rectangle there were camps, and trains stood waiting at half a dozen stations to steam into the Outlet at noon next day. But the bulk of the home-seekers were bunched in the vicinity of Arkansas City. The night before, it had been like a vast Civil War encampment, with campfires and coal-oil lanterns and singing and talking.

As dawn broke, this main congregation stretched in a solid line for nearly fifty miles along the Cherokee border. There were cowboys on fast broncs, and men driving swift racing sulkies, and the ordinary wagons and prairie schooners. There were men who unhitched their plow teams and rode the horses bareback into the territory.

All morning, the fifty-mile line was busy and hustling. Horses were rubbed down, axles greased, loose wagon wheels wedged tighter. Water jugs were filled, broncs unsaddled and saddled again, instruction given to families that were to wait behind.

Every few feet a United States Cavalryman sat on his horse facing the line, rifle across his lap.

As noon drew near, last farewells were said, and drivers
mounted their seats. Ponies were resaddled, and riders stood
ready. A terrific tenseness took hold of the line. And then, on
opposite sides of the wide Cherokee Outlet, two tragic incidents
occurred.

On the north side a man past middle age, almost totally deaf,
was astride a fractious bronc. The horse reared, jumped, and
dashed forward. It was eleven minutes till twelve. Thinking he
was deliberately jumping the gun, a soldier fired to halt him.
The shot was too good. It brought the poor deaf man tumbling
from his saddle, dead. His race was over. But that shot broke the
dam and the thousands, taking the signal, surged across the line.
There was no calling them back.

About the same time, a woman on foot jumped the line far
away on the opposite side of the Outlet, near Orlando. A deputy
ordered her back, and she went. But she jumped again, about ten
minutes before noon. The deputy yelled at her. She stopped,
turned around, pulled two six-shooters, and started firing at
him. The deputy shot her in the leg. And that shot, like the
others, was the signal. The two immense hordes of home-seekers, fifty miles apart, rushed toward each other.

*

The start of that wild race across the prairies must have been
one of the greatest spectacles in American history. One who saw
it said there rose from that line a roar like a mighty torrent—a
roar of voices fifty miles long. He said it was a roar so far-
reaching and prolonged that his very sense of hearing was
stunned and his capacity for thought paralyzed. He said he had
heard the roar of sixty batteries of artillery in the Civil War, and
experienced the sound of the Federal yell and rah coming up
from fifty thousand soldiers' throats, had listened to the fiercest
thunder as it rattled among the lonely pines of the Black Hills—
but never had he heard a cry so peculiar, a roar of such subdued
fierceness as that which rose from the prairies to the skies on
that fateful September 16.

In one fraction of a second the line became chaos. Riders were
thrown instantly as horses leaped. Hub caught hub, and wagons
were overturned. Harnessed teams broke loose and ran wildly
away. Men and women were screaming and cursing and fighting to break loose.

In this chaos the whole vast long line seemed to pause, and in
that few seconds' pause all sight was obscured by a dense and

horrid cloud of dust that rose up around them. And then as the red sand began to settle, the thousands of infuriated, unreasoning, half-mad humans broke loose and like an awful flood rolled out across the prairie.

April 25, 1939

OKLAHOMA CITY, OKLAHOMA— . . . The mad racers-after-land scattered swiftly in a fan-shaped pattern far out over the prairie. You could count in minutes the time it took the fastest riders to pass over the horizon.

Prairie schooners rocked across the plains with their teams in a dead run. Light sulkies bounced and jolted. There were cowboys riding steers. Men in striped shirts pumped and heaved ludicrously on bicycles. Slow-moving oxen plugged their tedious way under the hot September sun.

The cowboys on broncs quickly took the lead. And then, far out ahead, they stopped and set fire to the grass, to throw up a wall of fire against those behind. But the grim home-hunters plunged on through. Many horses were so badly burned they had to be destroyed. Others fell into ravines, wrecking wagons, hurting men and horses alike.

One man rode his horse to death, and when it dropped he sat on its side, rifle across his knee, claiming the land his beloved horse had fallen on. Another man had toughened his mustang by riding it full-speed eighteen miles a day for two weeks beforehand. He led the race toward the town of Enid, twenty miles northward. But he, too, fell victim to the grass fires and gullies, and his willing mount came to its broken finish a mile from Enid. He had to shoot the mustang, but he ran the last mile on foot, and was the first one into town.

It was a race for the strong and the long-winded. The *Woodward Jeffersonian,* which began publishing a week after that town was founded, reported the first to arrive there was David Jones, from the Texas Panhandle, "whose horse had more wind than the average newspaperman."

Grimmest of all, it seems to me, were the men on foot. They had left their families back home. They were too poor to buy horses or even bicycles. They ran their own desperate legs against swift mustangs and puffing locomotives. You could see them running out there across the prairie—running till the sweat dropped down and blinded them, running with their shirts torn open, running till their eyes bulged and their faces

were the same with the red dust that choked them, and their
chests heaved with breathless pain. Strong, desperate pioneer
men—running pitifully for a chance in life.

There were lighter incidents, too. One woman rode in black
tights and skullcap. Another, on a fine horse, and wearing a
beautiful blue dress, kept up with the train for miles. And in
that fifty-mile line of racers awaiting the gun was one woman
in a sunbonnet and carrying an umbrella. The others made
wisecracks about her outrunning the mustangs.

But when the signal was fired, she ran pell-mell for a hundred
feet, sat down on the ground, planted her stake, snatched off her
sunbonnet, raised her umbrella, and just sat there. That was her
homestead, and it was just as good as any twenty miles away,
too.

*

Now the thousands streaming over the prairies weren't the
only ones in the Cherokee Run. Other thousands were riding
trains. The Santa Fe railroad that day sold eighty thousand
tickets from Arkansas City to Kildare, twenty miles south in the
Outlet.

Thousands of them were sightseers, drawn by the fame of the
previous runs. Almost every town in Oklahoma that day was
depopulated. Barely a soul walked the streets of Kingfisher.
Stillwater was like a ghost town. Guthrie, too.

People even came from New York to take in the spectacle, and
then unwittingly became a part of it themselves. So dramatic
was the run that plain sightseers were swept into the madness,
and jumped from the trains and ran foolishly across the prairies,
not after land, but just trying to keep up with the racers.

So befuddled were the racers themselves that scores would
stake the same quarter section, all in sight of each other, then sit
on their pack sacks, glaring at each other, well knowing that
only one of them would finally get the land.

Although the Army had burned the grass over much of the
territory the day before to drive out "sooners," the racers found
the country full of them. Men who had slipped across at nighttime had already staked their favorite claims, and now sat
smugly on their wagons selling water to the overheated racers
at a dollar a pint. Some of them were shot in their tracks by more
honest men. There were hangings in the Outlet. Darkness and
distance of that first night veiled the murder of many a claim
jumper, many a disputant over who got there first.

And then, to climax the violent and heartless day, came the

prairie wind. Most of us imagine that dust storms are recent. There are some people who actually believe the New Deal created them. But the storms are not new. They had them before Oklahoma was born.

For three days the biting dust lashed the thousands of new homesteaders. Those who had tents went inside and fastened the flaps. You couldn't see a hundred feet on the prairie. In the new towns, carpenters just had to hit at where their fingers were, unable to see the nail. Many of the homesteaders gave up right at the start, and returned in disgust to their old homes. The winning of the West was hardy business.

But it was wonderful while it lasted. What a pity the movie camera was not there to record the dramatic madness of that historic afternoon. It can never happen again in this country, or probably any other.

April 26, 1939

How the Indian Country Finally Became a State

OKLAHOMA CITY, OKLAHOMA— . . . The last of the famous openings was in 1901. There were four million acres to be homesteaded— the old reservations of the Kiowa, Comanche, Wichita, and Caddo Indians. It was the country around Lawton, about which I've been writing in recent days.

This opening was not a run. The homesteads were drawn by number, in lottery fashion. In fact, the opening is known as the El Reno Lottery. In its way, it was as terrific as the runs.

More than a hundred and sixty-five thousand people came into the town of El Reno in the month preceding the lottery, and left their names in sealed and numbered envelopes. Most of them went back home to wait. Only twenty-five thousand were there the day the big drawing started.

Of these hundred and sixty-five thousand, only thirteen thousand could get lucky numbers and homesteads. The envelopes were put in big wooden boxes, turned by cranks on the end. Every so often an official would reach in and pull out an envelope. It took more than a week to get thirteen thousand names out of the mass. It turned out much more satisfactorily than the runs.

*

Now, when the first run was made in 1889, all of what is now Oklahoma was then called Western Territory or Indian Country or even Oklahoma. But it actually had no legal or official name. Then one year later, in 1890, the government decided to divide definitely this new land that was being homesteaded from the country still reserved for the Five Civilized Tribes brought over from the deep South in the 1830s.

So the west and north part became officially Oklahoma Territory, with the legal status that Hawaii and Alaska have now,* and the south and east part became the Indian Territory. They were about the same size.

What happened to the Indian Territory after 1890? Why did it cease to exist, and what became of the Indians?

Even before the land openings, thousands of white men had gone in and settled on Indian land. Sometimes they were welcomed and even made members of the Indian tribes. Often they married Indian women. This encroachment grew and grew. In 1893, there were seventy-five thousand Indians in their own Territory and a hundred and fifty thousand "intruders," as they were called. By 1900 there were four hundred thousand intruders.

The whites built towns, farmed the land, set up as merchants, spent millions on improvements, and actually became a solid part of the Indians' life. What happened was inevitable.

A commission made a study. The Indians were given homesteads as individuals. And, in addition, considerable areas that had mineral and oil resources were set aside for the Indians as tribes, so they would receive the underground riches. The whites stayed where they already were. Steadily, after 1900, the cry arose for Oklahoma statehood. The two territories—Indian and Oklahoma—sought separately, and it seemed there would be two states, if any.

But gradually the demand grew into a program for one state, combining the two. And that is finally what happened. The Indians and the early white settlers of the runs and the thousands of intruders all came into the Union as the one state of Oklahoma, on November 16, 1907.

*

There are plenty of people left in Oklahoma who took part in the runs of fifty years ago. Many still farm the land they staked out in those wild, greedy dashes for homesteads. Many have never seen a day's decent living in that half century. Others have

*Both were territories of the United States. Both became states in 1959.

come into immense wealth from the new land and what lay under it.

But rich or poor, those people are all past middle age; most of them are living on memories, and their memories are vague. The leaders of Oklahoma today are their sons and grandsons.

Today there is only one Indian reservation in all of Oklahoma—that of the Osages, who declined to take individual allotments, as the other tribes did. There are about sixty thousand Indians in Oklahoma now, more than in any other state in the Union. Fewer than half are full-blooded. The white mixture is great—the Negro, too. I believe it is generally conceded that the Indians got a squarer deal in Oklahoma than in any other place. And that wasn't much.

Oklahoma today is neither wild and bleak, as some people think, nor dull and prosaic, as others imagine. It is a little bit of all these, of course, and a million other things, too.

It has cowboys and farmers and Indians and oil drillers. It has dust bowls and modern skyscrapers and the craziest weather in the Union. It has fundamentalist preachers and anti-liquor laws and excellent universities. It gave us Will Rogers and Wiley Post and the Barrow gang. It is one of America's richest and most interesting states.

April 27, 1939

From Boomer to Ditch-Digger

LAWTON, OKLAHOMA— . . . Charles E. Miller is five feet two, and they call him Shorty. He is sixty-six years old. His clothes are thin. He is on relief. He lives with his wife in a jacked-up Model T Ford truck, which hasn't had its engine started in four years.

Shorty Miller is a "boomer," which means he came to Oklahoma before the wild land opening of fifty years ago. He was in every Oklahoma land opening but one. But Shorty Miller never bothered much with the land. Grubbing a living with plow and hoe was not for him. He stayed in town and thought up ways to get the boomers' money.

"I always kinda thought I'd let the other fellows do the work," he said.

He is a born country showman, and can't be anything else. He started out with a dog-and-pony show, and went down the line to carting a gigantic turtle around the prairies at ten cents a look.

He is a "spieler" by nature. Probably his silver tongue was his undoing. He could make a dollar too easily. He never had to work for it. No matter what he was showing, Shorty Miller could always get a crowd. The oldsters of Oklahoma, Kansas, Missouri, Arkansas, and north Texas remember him when and how.

Sometimes he exhibited animals or trumped-up freaks. Sometimes he bought slow-selling soap from a grocer, cut it in threes, and sold each piece for a quarter, whereas the grocer couldn't get a nickel for the whole bar. He'd buy cheap neckties by the hundred dozen, and spiel them off to the public at five-hundred-percent profit. Once he paid five dollars for a spot-remover formula and it kept him for years. Patent medicine, ventriloquism, ancient "mummies," souvenir dishes—Shorty played them all. He was the prairie counterpart of the long-coated Mississippi River spellbinder.

Shorty always gave the customers something for their money. He says he never worked pea-shell games or any kind of gambling. He has never been drunk in his life. He just loved the open road and the freedom of town-to-town and the witty quest of an easy dollar.

Shorty has been married for thirty-nine years, and he and his wife are still together. "I told her when we got married I'd give her a forty-year trial," he said. "She's just got a year to go now." But I guess Shorty will keep her, for she's sewing at the relief room now, because Shorty hurt his hip and can't work on WPA anymore.

*

One of Shorty's prizes was Congo, a "giant black savage" captured on the banks of the Congo River in darkest Africa. *Step inside and see this astounding barbarian, ladies and gentlemen! Only a dime, two nickels, the tenth part of a dollar!*

"I captured him in a cornfield behind a plow down in southwest Oklahoma," Shorty said. "His name was John Montgomery. He was eight foot two. We painted up his face and put rings in his nose. I paid him twenty-five dollars a month, but he got to wanting so much money I had to let him go."

Shorty's greatest find was Mr. Itt, a strange black-and-white monkeylike animal that a farm woman had captured over in the Panhandle. Shorty paid the woman fifty dollars for it, and before the weird little creature died it made him twenty-one thousand five hundred dollars. He had Mr. Itt stuffed, and still grieves over him, because he loved him.

The Depression put an end to Shorty's show business. "The Depression didn't *hurt* me," he said. "It just *killed* me outright. There wasn't any pain at all. I thought for a while I was gonna starve to death." He tried one more foray with a traveling freak, but it wasn't much good. He finally got on relief work here, and they put him to digging ditches. "I didn't know how to dig a ditch," Shorty said, "but I had to learn. And I guess I did all right. I never heard any complaints."

Mrs. Miller works at the sewing room every day. She was frying potatoes on a portable oil stove when I went out to see them. She is a nice woman. She has followed Shorty for nearly forty years, and would like to start out again right now if it were possible.

The Millers own a small lot on the edge of town. Their two old show trucks are placed side by side, and they live in them. They've lived in a house only once in forty years. Always in a wagon or a truck. They like it better that way.

"What was the most money you ever had at once?" I asked.

"About twenty thousand dollars," Shorty said.

"What became of it?"

"Oh, it just slipped away. I thought a railroad was going through a certain strip of country, so I bought lots in every town along the way. The road didn't go through."

But there is no despair in Shorty's life. "I'm flat broke and getting old," he said, "but if I had my life to live over I'd do it exactly the same way. I've got something the rest of 'em haven't got. All those forty years of memories. I'm a showman. There's something fascinating about making your living with your wits. I had a good time."

April 15, 1939

Will Rogers was a beloved cowboy humorist, actor, and newspaper columnist whose barbs were directed at either himself or whatever political party was on top—never at the underdog. He was killed August 15, 1935, in an airplane crash near Point Barrow, Alaska, with his pilot friend and fellow Oklahoman Wiley Post. Rogers was fifty-six.

WILL ROGERS' HOME

CLAREMORE, OKLAHOMA—This town is practically all Will Rogers.

Here stands Oklahoma's beautiful memorial to him. The hotel
here is named Will Rogers. The restaurants have Will Rogers
sandwiches. In the post office is a Will Rogers mural. The new
city library is named after Will Rogers. On the side of the depot
is advertised one of the Frisco's crack trains, the *Will Rogers.*

You can buy little bronze busts of Will Rogers, see his portrait
hanging on public and private walls, sit in lobbies done up in
semi-cowboy style to cater to his memory.

And Will Rogers never lived here. But Claremore is authentic
just the same, because Will chose to put it on the map. He
bought land years ago at the edge of town, to live on when he
retired. He always spoke of Claremore as his home, but he was
actually raised near Chelsea, about twenty miles north of here.
When he came to visit in later years, he'd always send his daily
newspaper telegram under a Claremore dateline. His relatives
would say, "Will, why don't you give Chelsea a little publicity?"
But he'd just grin and say, "Aw, you mind your own business."

The land Will bought is on top of a knoll, just at the edge of
Claremore. After his death, Mrs. Rogers deeded it to the Memorial Commission. And it is on this land—Will's own hilltop—
that the memorial to him now stands.

*

There are Will Rogers memorials scattered all over the country. Some are pretty phony. But the one here is the real memorial to Will Rogers. It is in the form of a ranch house, built of
stone. It is large—four immense rooms, and some smaller ones.

In the lobby, facing you as you go in, is a bigger-than-life
bronze statue of Will, sculptured by his friend Jo Davidson.* On
the pedestal is inscribed one of Will's quotations: "I never met
a man I didn't like." Two of the big rooms are still bare, and the
other two are formal and museumlike. Eventually, one room
will be given over to a diorama—a biography of Will Rogers in
little scenes, clear around a room, showing the high spots of his
career.

Right now, about the only things here that Will actually used
are a couple of saddles and a stuffed calf, on which he practiced
roping at his California ranch house. In glass cases are foreign
saddles given him on his many trips about the world.

The main room is a semireplica of Will's own living room in
his California ranch house, but it resembles Will's own room

*Davidson later sculpted a bust of Pyle.

in little but the dimensions. It, too, is formalized with saddles in glass cases.

But gradually, year by year, this will become the real Will Rogers room. His family will send on many things—manuscripts, photographs, even the suit he wore when he died. But naturally there are things they don't want to give up yet—any more than you or I would want to break up our own homes.

The question of making the memorial a warm, human thing—expressive of Will Rogers' own personality—is one continuously before the commission. They know that the best memorial would be an informal one, with all the little trays, books, cushions, and doodads that make up a room that Will actually lived in.

That's what visitors want to see in the memorial, and that is what they never can see—simply because of themselves. If an actual family room full of Will Rogers' things were to be created, and the public turned in, they'd clean it out in a week, even under the eyes of guards. So everything will have to be fastened down, or put in locked glass cases. Already the tourists have pulled so much wool out of a Mexican serape on the wall that it had to be put under glass. . . .

April 28, 1939

TEXAS

EL PASO, TEXAS— . . . On the back roads in the desert, where it's scores of miles between ranch houses, you now and then pass a wooden box alongside the trail. Rocks are piled around the box to hold it, and painted on the box is WATER—DON'T WASTE. Inside the box is a jug.

I never could find out who fills these jugs. In fact, there wasn't any water in any of those we saw, but I suppose it isn't necessary to keep them full in wintertime.

The boxes certainly don't look official. Desert dwellers back over the hills, near a spring, must do it just out of the goodness of their hearts. A lot of desert people have hearts like that. And a lot don't. . . .

April 2, 1938

A Negro Teacher Full of Years and Honors

HUNTSVILLE, TEXAS—Sam Houston gave me his best chair, but he stood all the time we were talking. His voice was soft and low. He said he felt honored that I had come to see him.

There is a gentleness of character in Sam Houston that soothes like soft music. It would be to anybody's advantage to spend a day with him, or a week—listening to him talk, assimilating some of his calm philosophy.

The Sam Houston I am talking about is a Negro. He was named for the great liberator of Texas. His father was General Sam Houston's slave—his closest slave, his bodyguard, his personal servant. Slaves took on their masters' names. Joshua Houston was this slave's name.

*

I came to Huntsville because so much of General Sam Houston's career was spent here. The local editor told me where to find Houston's grave, and the house he lived in for many years, and the old Steamboat House where he died. He told me that no Houston descendants are left around here, and that the last three men who had known Houston died a year or so ago. He said the only man in Huntsville with any Houston lore about him was Sam Houston, principal of the Negro school.

*

Sam Houston, the Negro, is a medium-sized man with short, white hair. He is as neat as a pin. You would take him to be not past forty, but he has been teaching school here for forty years.

After General Houston died, his slave Josh set up in Huntsville as a blacksmith. He was thrifty, and had money to educate his children. His son Sam was sent off to Atlanta to school, and then to Washington, to Howard University. After that he got a clerical job with the government in Washington. In 1895, at the age of twenty-four, he came back to Huntsville on a visit. He didn't intend to stay.

"I was looked upon as being important because I had been living in 'the President's city,'" Sam Houston says. "People wanted me to stay here and teach school. But I wanted to go back. I had got used to living in big cities. There was prestige in working for the government, and my job was nice.

"But I got to thinking along this line: 'They don't really need you in Washington. Anybody could do your work. You're just one of thousands. Maybe they do need you here.'"

So he took the teaching job. He got thirty dollars a month.

The log school was so bad he wouldn't use it; he rented a church, paid for it out of his salary, and taught school in it. That was forty years ago. Today the Negro school in Huntsville is a large, modern place, with six hundred students. It is called the Sam Houston School. It is not named for the general, but to honor its Negro principal.

*

Sam Houston doesn't remember a great deal of General Houston from his father. He wasn't so conscious of the Houston heritage when he was a boy. For one thing, Houston wasn't thought so much of then. People didn't know how great he would become in time.

But Sam Houston is conscious of his heritage now. He says that the family slaves, who were closest to their masters, acquired from the white family a learning and a breadth that made them the leaders of their race. His father acquired that from the Houston family, and it has helped make Sam Houston, the Negro, what he is today.

Sam Houston has never written anything about his father, who died in 1903. He's sorry now that he didn't gather material when his father was alive; it would have made a book. He remembers that in his childhood there was an oil painting of General Houston around the house. The last he remembers, though, one of the children had thrown a stick right through the face. The painting has disappeared now.

But Sam Houston, though he remembers little, has learned much of General Houston and of Texas. He is an authority on Texas history, and the life of Houston, too. While I was talking with him at the school, the wife of the town's leading banker dropped in to congratulate him on his speech at the Houston birthday ceremonies here a few days before. Thousands of people were here. All the leading officials spoke, and three governors, too.

"You made the best speech of the whole program," the banker's wife told him.

March 20, 1936

FORT WORTH, TEXAS—Thank heaven, since we were here last, Fort Worth has done away with the bells that rang every time the traffic lights changed.

There is a street here with the simple name of Boulevard. When Vernon Castle, the great dancer and war hero, was killed

in a plane crash here in 1918, a movement was started to call the
nameless street Vernon Castle Boulevard. But no. Castle was a
dancer. Dancing was evil. Some residents of the street filed
objections. The proposal was voted down. The street is still just
Boulevard.

I wish they'd bring it up again. Blue-nosing has lost considerable favor in the past twenty years. . . .

Montgomery Ward & Co. has an immense store in Fort
Worth. When it was opened seven or eight years ago the Chicago headquarters sent down half a carload of skis. The local
manager sent the skis back. The Chicago office was sore, and
wanted to know why. The answer was: "First, no mountains
here; second, no snow." . . .

April 13, 1939

HISTORY DOESN'T PAY

SAN ANTONIO, TEXAS—Noah H. Rose was born in Texas, and he
has never been out of Texas, except across the border into Mexico a few times. He's sixty-two now.

"I did sit on the bank of the Red River once and look across
into Oklahoma," he says. "But I never got over there. I'm just
an old hillbilly. Don't know nothin'. Never saw nothin'."

He was born poor and he's still poor. He went to work in a
print shop when he was thirteen, at two dollars a month. He can
still set type. "I wanted to take fiddle lessons so bad I was crazy,"
he says, "but we couldn't afford it. When I grew up I did take
lessons for four months, and now I play in the church choir."

When Noah Rose was seventeen he won a box camera by
selling the *Youth's Companion*. He still has the first negative he
ever snapped—a shot of his sister, taken forty-five years ago.
From then until today he has been a photographer.

He married young. It lasted three months, and he has never
tried it again. His two sisters and a brother-in-law live with him
now.

For fifteen years he ran a studio at Del Rio, down on the Rio
Grande. Without really being conscious that he was making a
collection, he began gathering old prints and negatives of Southwest lore—Indians, outlaws, peace officers, hangings, buildings,
graves, statesmen, battle scenes. Today Noah Rose has the greatest collection of historic Southwest photographs in the world.
There is hardly a name or a place you can think of that he

doesn't have. His collection is recognized as supreme by museums, libraries, and universities.

It ought to be worth a million dollars. He can hardly pay the rent with it.

*

Fifteen years ago Rose came into San Antonio. He didn't have a studio anymore. He was hard up. So at last he decided to commercialize his collection. He has been living off it, after a fashion, for ten years now. Last year was his best year so far. He took in six hundred dollars. He has no other income.

He rents a little unpainted house in the west end of San Antonio, way out where the streets aren't paved or even graded. Two rooms he has fixed up as a darkroom and workshop. He sleeps in one of them. A few pictures are tacked up.

He has fifteen hundred negatives in all. His most valuable picture, he believes, is of John Wesley Hardin,* taken in life, the only one known to exist. People in the East don't hear much of Hardin, but he really was tops. Billy the Kid was a sissy compared with him.

Through all these years of collecting historical pictures, Rose has picked up an immense knowledge of the Southwest. He knows the history—and usually the descendants, too—of every famous bad man from here to California. He has all the books on the Southwest outlaws. He has places underlined where the authors made mistakes.

Rose is a great talker. He talks all the time. If you had a couple of days with him, you wouldn't need to read any books on Southwest lore.

*

Most of Rose's business, what little there is, comes from individuals making Southwestern collections. He sells some to libraries, too, and book publishers. He has a nice letter from Zane Grey, who used some of his photos. His favorite customer is a Major Sanford of Washington. The major dropped in one Christmas a couple of years ago. Rose was sick in bed. The rent was due. Taxes were due. His last money had gone for medicine. There wasn't a cent in the house.

This sounds like something out of a movie, but it wasn't. The major ordered a hundred and eighty-six dollars' worth of pic-

*A Texas gunfighter who killed at least a score of challengers, retired briefly, and was killed in 1895, at the age of forty-two.

tures, and left a fifty-dollar Christmas present besides. And Rose had never seen him before.

Pictures of bad men are the best sellers, and Indians next. In the last few months, because of the Texas Centennial, there has been a demand for Texas Ranger pictures. He has plenty of rare ones, most of which he took himself.

With all these pictures around, Rose has none of himself. He's a pretty good-looking man, too—bald with a rim of grayish hair fluffing out like a ledge all around his head. He wears tortoise-shell glasses.

He won't let strangers come to the house if he can help it. He doesn't want them to see how poor he is. I just hunted him up in the city directory and walked in. Once there, you're welcome. He never gives his address to anybody. He rents a post-office box, so nobody will know where he lives.

He gets terribly discouraged. People who can afford to pay try to chisel him down on his prices—and him making six hundred dollars a year.

March 28, 1936

SHY GLANCES IN THE PLAZA

LAREDO, TEXAS—In Laredo, you stand on the threshold of all Mexico. From a little height you can look south across the slim Rio Grande, onto the lights of Nuevo Laredo and into the darkness beyond. There lies the vast and ancient land of Mexico.

It is Sunday night in Laredo. The air is soft. The thermometer at the corner of the plaza says eighty-two, and it is a quarter till nine. A light breeze washes past. Stars twinkle, a brittle blue in the dark sky.

All Laredo is bathed in a sweet odor of orange blossoms, and it fades and reappears as you walk along. The trees are green, and occasional palms rise and sweep out in tropical grace. The block-square plaza is covered with trees, and a circular lighted bandstand is in the middle. Loungers, two by two, lie or sit on the grass.

The sidewalks are crowded with walkers. You wander among them. All skin is dark. You hear no English spoken. Laredo is eighty percent Mexican, or Spanish-American, as the transplanted Mexicans prefer to be called. Laredo is run by Spanish-Americans.

Boys and girls, coatless and hatless, are everywhere. They

stroll, and talk, and take their time. But they seem to be more than strolling, here around the plaza. There is something different here. What is it? Gradually it comes to you. There is something deliberate in the way they are walking. There is purpose to it. Now you see. All the girls are walking around the square in one direction. And the boys are walking in the opposite direction.

The girls are in twos, and sometimes threes. Row after row, walking along rather rapidly, like an army on a broken-step march. They never stop, never pause. They just keep going, around and around the square.

And now you notice something else. The outer edge of the sidewalk, clear around the plaza, is lined with young men, standing in a solid row, like a picket fence. They stand mostly in silence, watching the girls as they pass.

I began to ask questions, and I found out what it was. It's a custom as old as Mexico, a Sunday- and Thursday-night custom that the Mexicans brought over into the United States with them. They call it the promenade.

Every town and city in Mexico has its open, block-square plaza, with a bandstand in the middle, and cement or gravel walks leading inward from the four corners. Every Sunday night, and in some places every Thursday night, too, the young people of the town turn out for the promenade around the plaza. All over Mexico tonight girls are walking around the plazas in one direction, and boys in the other, looking at each other.

In the old days, the girls were always chaperoned. If a boy liked a girl's looks, he would turn and fall into step with her, and walk along talking, properly chaperoned, of course. But now the girls parade without chaperons.

The purpose of the promenade is to let the young men see what likely-looking girls there are in town. Many a marriage has come out of the first shy glances in the plaza. But things are different now. I noticed only a few boys joining the girls. After a few Sunday nights, I guess, you know all the feminine faces in town, and there is no possibility of a delightful surprise. The promenade has become more an excuse just to come downtown and stand around.

I stood for a long time watching the girls' faces. But I never saw a face that would launch a rowboat, much less a battleship. They were nice faces, but not what we consider in our country beautiful. The girls were all in light summer dresses. Some were quite small, still in short skirts. Some ranged up close to their thirties. Most of them were slim, although now and then you would see a fat one. There must have been five hundred girls parading, and as many boys walking, or standing along the walk.

Pretty soon a truck pulled up to the curb. It had loudspeakers on top, and it tuned in a Mexican radio station, very loudly. The strollers strolled on, to the music, and the crowds stood, or sat in the grass, and talked and listened. The parading went on for nearly two hours. Gradually the crowd thinned out. At ten o'clock the music stopped. By ten-fifteen the plaza was empty and dark.

The boys had seen the girls, and the girls had seen the boys, and they'd both had their walks, and it was all over for another week.

March 30, 1936

REMEMBERING JUDGE ROY BEAN
LANGTRY, TEXAS—In southwest Texas, tradition revolves around Judge Roy Bean, who was the self-styled "Law West of the Pecos" back in the frontier days when horse-stealing was worse than murder.

Judge Bean held court on the porch of his saloon. He always had two things on the bench in front of him—a law book, which he didn't know how to use, and a six-shooter, which he did.

Books have been written about Judge Bean, and the Southwest is full of stories about his caprices. He died in 1903, but his saloon is still standing in Langtry, empty now, and the big sign LAW WEST OF THE PECOS is still up in front.

I drove through Langtry, and took a picture of the saloon, and asked a couple of loafers if anybody was still around who remembered Judge Bean. They said one fellow was left, and that was Ike Billings, who lived on a ranch four miles out, and maybe I'd find him there and maybe I wouldn't. So I drove out over the desert, across big washes and over rocks and through mesquite bushes raking the fenders, until I got to Ike Billings' place.

He was there. He'd just come in from pointing up lambs, which means cutting their tails off and snipping their ears. He washed up, and then we sat down and talked. Ike Billings didn't look old enough to remember Judge Bean, but he remembers him all right.

Billings is one of those hardworking, well-preserved desert

men. He was fifty-nine last week and has a daughter thirty-seven years old, but he doesn't look more than forty-five. He has a jovial, round, tanned face, and beautiful teeth, and white whiskers when he's needing a shave. He was born in mid-Texas, near San Antonio, and came to the Pecos country in 1893. He settled in Langtry, and he knew Judge Bean well from then until the judge died.

"Sure, I used to play poker with him a couple of nights a week," Billings said. "He was a queer character, but people around here liked him. I think he was a Spaniard or something. He was a slick one.

"I remember once a cowboy fell or jumped off the railroad bridge up here a piece and was killed. They found forty dollars and a six-shooter on him. The judge convened court over the body, and took the six-shooter, and fined the fellow forty dollars for committing suicide, and then had the county bury him because he was a pauper.

"There was a pile of rocks outside Bean's saloon, and he kept a sign there saying ICE-COLD BEER. In those days the railroad ran right through town, and in the summer tourists would get off here for a cold drink. They'd ask for beer, and it'd be hot when they got it, and they'd say 'How about that sign?' and old Bean would roar and yell, 'Who in hell ever heard of ice in this country in the summertime?' But he never took the sign down.

"He had another stunt. These tourists would get some beer and give him a ten- or a twenty-dollar bill, and then he'd monkey around very busy and let on like he was having trouble making change, and the first thing you knew the train was pulling out and the tourists would have to run and jump on without their change."

*

Billings himself was the law here for six years after Bean died. Old man Dodd was justice of the peace and Billings was constable. His territory covered all the country west of the Pecos, and he had to do a lot of horseback riding. Everybody in those days carried a six-shooter.

"But I never did have any trouble," Billings said. "I never was shot at, and never shot at anybody but once, and then I missed him. It was a dark, rainy night, and I was chasing a Mexican who had killed a fellow on the railroad. I shot at him when he ran around a building. We got him the next morning, though."

Billings moved out to the ranch in 1911. He has twenty-five

hundred head of sheep, and some goats and a few cattle. He has twelve thousand acres of desert land, and thirty-five miles of fence around it. "Most people wouldn't give a cent an acre for it," he said, "but we like it here. We don't have things very fancy, but we get along. My wife wouldn't leave here for anything. I guess it's true I'm the only old-timer left around here. The others have died or moved away."

Ike Billings, like every person I ever met on the desert, was friendly and hospitable. "I sure wish you had been here last Wednesday," he said. "We had a big goat-fry down the crick here, celebrating my birthday, and people from all over this part of the country were here. You sure would have enjoyed it."

May 12, 1936

Last of the Frontier Circuit Riders
EL PASO, TEXAS—The Reverend L. R. Millican will be eighty-three in August. He has been a preacher for sixty-two years. He is a relic of the wild-and-woolly West.

He calls himself a missionary, but in the Midwest I guess he would be called a circuit rider. He believes he is the only old-time, frontier-day circuit rider left.

I went out and had a long talk with the Reverend Mr. Millican. He hasn't been feeling well lately, and he's a little deaf. But he gets around. He has long hair and a goatee and looks like Buffalo Bill. "No, I never had any trouble with anybody," he says benignly. "Everybody always treated me fine. I never had any trouble with bad men, or Indians, or wild animals. I never had any trouble at all."

L. R. Millican is a Texan. He was born on the frontier, grew up as a cowboy, has never lived anywhere but Texas. His grandfather came with Austin in 1821. His father killed Indians, and was himself gravely wounded by Indian arrows. Millican was converted at a Methodist camp meeting before he was twenty-one. He heard the call, and jumped on his horse and started riding the great open spaces, not after cattle now but after souls.

He stopped carrying a gun the day he was converted. He has never carried once since, except for a few times when he went with the officers into the hills after a bad man. He has never taken part in a hanging. He has never smoked, or tasted liquor. Next to God and his wife, he loves horses more than anything else. He converted a saloonkeeper once because of their mutual love of horses.

In frontier days he rode constantly, establishing churches, holding meetings. Indians stole his horses, but he never found the Indians. He slept in the open. He always carried a hair rope that he circled around him at night, to keep snakes away. He wore out many horses and many saddlebags. His saddlebags were always full of Bibles and religious tracts to give away. Twice he was nearly drowned fording swollen rivers.

When autos came, he got an auto, for he felt that the more distance he could cover the greater was his work for God. He has worn out six automobiles. He quit driving just a few years ago, because he couldn't hear cars coming from behind, and that scared him.

There is a long scar on his right cheek. A wild horse, rearing and striking in the corral, did that. Another wild horse crushed his chest and broke his ribs.

He's the only preacher who ever personally visited every saloon and gambling hall in El Paso. He went around one day, inviting the boozers and gamblers to come to church. Nobody was nasty to him, he said. And that night such a crowd came to meeting they had to hold it in the opera house.

He doesn't know how many thousands of people he has converted. He had it down in his records, but he lost them several years ago. He never tried to convert Indians. . . .

I asked him if the world is more religious now than it used to be. He doesn't think so. He says the good people are better than they used to be, and the bad people are worse, so that about squares off.

May 5, 1936

A POWER IN THE PANHANDLE
AMARILLO, TEXAS—Gene Howe is the son of Ed Howe, the famous Kansas country editor, the "Sage of Potato Hill." Ed Howe is eighty-three now and spends his winters in Florida. He has always sought to impress upon his children the folly of drinking.

Gene got a letter from his dad yesterday on the subject. It said: "A man is a fool who drinks before he is fifty. A man is a fool who doesn't drink after he is fifty. After you're fifty, one drink just before you go to bed makes you sleep better."

So now his boy Gene can put on his pajamas every night, take a big swig, and topple into bed. For he is fifty-one.

*

Gene Howe couldn't very well have been anything but a newspaperman. When the wires carry all over the country something he has said in his column in Amarillo, you think, "Well, the youngster's following in his father's footsteps, isn't he?" You don't think of him as mature. But the youngster has been a newspaperman for thirty-five years now. In five more years he will be as old as Ed Howe was when he retired.

Gene is owner and editor of Amarillo's two papers—the *Globe* and the *News*. He owns half a dozen smaller but prosperous papers in Texas and the old family paper, the *Atchison* (Kansas) *Globe*. He owns a big ranch, and a home. I don't see how he can possibly be worth less than a million dollars. He's doing all right.

I was surprised when I saw him. I had seen his father's pictures—a thin, wise face, aloof, almost heavenly-looking, very calm and a little sad. He may not be like that at all, but that's the way his pictures impressed me. I had supposed Gene would look like that, too. But he doesn't.

He is medium heavy, is getting bald, wears fine clothes, talks easily and affably, has a business head, knows more people in the Panhandle than anybody else does, and is always out and about. His papers are a personality throughout the Panhandle. He runs them on that old Howe notion that if you put out a paper for the readers, you can let the ads fall where they may.

His papers are metropolitan, in a way; there's nothing hick about them. They have the world news, and the same features you get in the big cities. But you'll also find in them the thing that makes a country paper—lots of news of the people at home.

Howe is a force in the Panhandle. His papers have influence. Before an election, readers by the hundreds call up and ask whom to vote for, and Gene tells them. His papers have never lost a local election. He believes in making his papers known. In winter he hires a troupe that can give a whole evening's entertainment, and he sends it all over the Panhandle, giving free shows every night in the little towns, in the name of the *News* and the *Globe*.

Howe had never made a speech till he came here fourteen years ago, but now he has spoken in every town and nearly every schoolhouse within three hundred miles of Amarillo. It's good for the papers. One man on his staff does nothing but fill requests for speeches. Often the Howe papers have three or four men out speaking the same night, sometimes five hundred miles apart.

*

Gene Howe is a liberal but very critical of the Roosevelt administration's spending. He is a friend of H. L. Mencken, but in print calls him the biggest fool in the United States. Howe says nobody can be elected President nowadays who isn't a good radio speaker. That's the reason he knew Roosevelt would whip Landon. He won thirty-six hundred dollars in bets on the election. His father thought Landon* was a cinch, and wanted to bet on it, but Gene wouldn't take his money. . . .

January 20, 1937

"The Tactless Texan"

AMARILLO, TEXAS—The most important thing in the Texas Panhandle is the hope for rain. They haven't had any to speak of for five years.

The second-most-important thing is Gene Howe's daily newspaper column. It is unsigned, headed merely THE TACTLESS TEXAN, and has a picture of a cross-eyed Ben Turpin at the top. But everybody knows who writes it.

The column is read and talked about over an area six hundred miles wide, all through the vast, flat Panhandle and in adjoining states. Its hold on the people is one of the most thrilling things I have ever encountered in journalism.

A number of times Howe's columns have brought him national attention, for he doesn't mince words. His greatest notice came from bawling out Mary Garden for not giving Amarillo a good opera performance. He and Mary have made up since. He has an autographed photo of her, and gets a Christmas card from her every year.

(Incidentally, Howe knows his opera. He has heard more than a hundred. One year, long ago, he spent a whole summer in Europe with his father, just going to operas.)

He bawled out Lindbergh for standing up a huge crowd that had turned out to see him after his Atlantic flight. Hundreds of

*Alfred M. Landon, the Republican Kansas governor who ran against Roosevelt in the 1936 election and was soundly beaten.

people came in and congratulated Howe, but the civic bodies passed resolutions denouncing him for "besmirching the fair name of Southern hospitality." He says that if Lindbergh would treat newspapermen like human beings, he wouldn't be bothered the way he is.

Howe is the culprit who started Mother-in-Law Day. He didn't realize what he was doing. He just threw the suggestion into his column lightly, to pacify a mother-in-law who had been hurt by something he had said. But the next day a hundred mothers-in-law were in the office, keen for the idea, and women started forming mother-in-law clubs.

The first thing Howe knew Amarillo had a Mother-in-Law Day, with thousands of people and parades and forty bands and a hundred mother-in-law clubs from all over the Southwest. He took one look and went home.

Howe is prolific. His daily column frequently runs three and four full-length columns. I can testify that when you get anybody to read four columns of solid type you've got to be good. Howe's column is simplicity itself. He doesn't go in for dramatic writing, or for the philosophizing of his famous father. He writes plain, ordinary street talk.

He starts the column every day with the weather. He has set himself up as a sort of jovial Panhandle weather prophet. In the winter he gives the probability of snow, in the summer for rain. That's what the farmers want, so they eat it up. He talks about the local football teams, and sings a little song for the people who have died, and asks why the taxi drivers aren't paid a living wage, and boosts a concert, or quotes a visitor from Lubbock, or scoops his own staff on a coming wedding, and even comments on local murder suspects.

Then he'll run Walter Winchell's entire syndicated column within his own column—with credit, of course—and he usually winds up with half a column of shorts he calls "interesting facts." These, too, he buys from a syndicate.

Howe has a way of repeating his words in print. He'll say, "Please, please, please return this little girl's cat to the *News-Globe* office," or "Mr. and Mrs. Greenhill, who just celebrated their fortieth anniversary, are fine, fine, fine folks."

He prints anything in his column. He prints letters from people who want to get married. His column has been responsible for more than three hundred marriages in the Panhandle. He prints letters from women denouncing their neighbors by name, and then prints the neighbors' answers. He says it makes wonderful reading.

Almost every day he asks his readers to go out and help find a lost dog or cat. He has given away hundreds of dollars in rewards for children's lost pets. Once a week he publishes a couple of columns of letters from people wanting jobs. He has placed hundreds.

Howe's column gets around two thousand letters a month. He doesn't try to answer them all. He has turned down offers to go to New York and write a syndicated column. He'd rather live in Amarillo.

January 21, 1937

NEW MEXICO

A BLOODY PRIVATE WAR

LINCOLN, NEW MEXICO—There is a queer streak in me that makes me allergic, as they say nowadays, to early New England history.

If you talk about the *Mayflower* or the cold blue blood of the Bostonians, I wish to be immediately elsewhere. And at night, instead of counting sheep, I can say "Plymouth Rock" over a few times and I'm dead to the world.

But here in the Southwest, where the sun beats down, and the desert is long and empty, and cowboys still ride the ridges and high brush country, a piece of history is as exciting to me as a Christmas package.

The Lincoln County war is like that. I had never heard of it until today, yet it was probably the bloodiest private war in the whole history of the frontier Southwest. Most of my information comes from an excellent book, *The Saga of Billy the Kid*, by Walter Noble Burns.

*

L. G. Murphy studied for the priesthood, but took to the Army instead. He came across to New Mexico in Civil War days. He was finally mustered out as a major at Fort Stanton, only nine miles from Lincoln. He opened a store here, which was a thriving cattle town in those days. He prospered, and not always by legitimate means. His wealth grew into a cattle ranch, a hotel, and a saloon. He was the number-one man around Lincoln.

Then in 1875 another man came across the prairies to Lincoln. His name was Alexander McSween. He, too, had been educated for the pulpit, and he, too, had abandoned it, for a career in the law. But he remained a devout Christian. The same could not be said for Murphy.

It was known in eastern New Mexico that Murphy was paying rustlers to steal thousands of cattle for him. By his financial power he kept his thieves out of trouble. But finally it got so bad some of them had to stand trial. Murphy had retained McSween as his lawyer, and now he ordered him to defend the thieves. But McSween, knowing they were guilty, refused. He went over to the other side, prosecuted the thieves, and sent them to the penitentiary.

Now McSween and another man started a store in Lincoln. They took all of Murphy's business. Murphy was being pushed aginst the wall, and something had to happen. And so, one forenoon in 1878, a score of Murphy men rode out of Lincoln and met McSween's partner on the road. As he stopped his horse and waved to them, they shot him dead.

There was no peace in Lincoln County after that for more than two years. Honest men, cattle thieves, sincere men, highwaymen, plain cold-blooded killers—they all lined up, some with Murphy, some with McSween. The whole thing was ruthless, excuseless, and lawless. It ruined both leaders, and before it was over both were dead. It cost dozens of lives. And it created a national figure in the form of the Southwest's most infamous killer—Billy the Kid—who fought with McSween.

McSween through it all remained the purest of Christians. He fought his side of the war in self-defense only. He never fired a gun. For more than two years the war went on, with good men and bad men almost daily biting the eternal dust. Practically everything ceased, except the stalking and killing of men. Cattle weren't tended; farms weren't plowed. Everybody lost, as in most wars.

Murphy died a natural death in Santa Fe while the war was still going on, but his henchmen carried it to a horrid climax shortly afterward.

The two sides sensed that the zero hour was near. They rounded up Mexicans, cowboys, and highwaymen until there were nearly sixty on each side. On the night of the third day of fighting, Murphy men slipped up and set fire to the McSween home. The fighters stayed inside till the last room was crumbling. Finally they had to leave. The Murphy killers lay behind an adobe wall, their rifles cocked.

Billy the Kid tried to get McSween to take a gun and make a dash for it. But McSween walked out with only a Bible in his hand, stood upright in the glare, and said: "I am McSween. Here I am." Six bullets cut him down in a second. Most of the McSween fighters were slain as they came out. But the preposterous Billy the Kid came out shooting, and was unscratched by the more than fifty bullets fired at him from not thirty feet away. As he ran, he killed one man and gravely wounded two others.

The Kid figured in one more escape in Lincoln. He was captured and sentenced to hang, and a constant guard was kept over him on the second floor of the courthouse. About a week before he was to hang, Billy, although shackled both hand and foot, took a gun away from his guard, killed him, shot the other deputy from the courthouse window, and rode out of town, whistling.

At this point the village of Lincoln died. It is still dead today. . . .

April 15, 1938

A Town That Dreams of Billy the Kid

LINCOLN, NEW MEXICO—At half past noon you find only Señor Miranda, the postmaster, stirring in the village. It is siesta hour.

And Señor Miranda isn't really stirring. He's just sitting in his post-office window looking out the door. But he comes out from behind his mailboxes and stands on the porch.

No, says Señor Miranda, there isn't anyplace in town to eat lunch. There was a café, but it closed. Well, how about the grocery store? Yes, that's it, the grocery store. So from Señor Romero, who is back from lunch now, we buy bologna, cheese, and crackers.

We walk up the gravel street, for there are no sidewalks, to where it says BAR. The door is locked, but from a nearby house a man comes running. He is smiling and gracious, and unlocks the door and invites us in.

He fixes us chairs and a bench. With a pocketknife I carve the bologna and the cheese. We sit and eat, and Señor Román

Maes—proprietor, bartender, and, as his sign says, EXPERT MIX-
EROLOGIST—stands and talks with us the whole lunch through.

Señor Maes owns the only bar in Lincoln. It is right across the
road from the Lincoln County courthouse, from which Billy
the Kid escaped and killed two men.

Is your bar very old, Señor Maes? Oh, very old, as old as the
town. Billy the Kid has stood here. And Sheriff Pat Garrett. All
the bad men have stood here. Douglas Fairbanks was here once
and bought the bar for a hundred and fifty dollars. Of course,
he couldn't wrap it up and take it with him, so he left a twenty-
five-dollar deposit. He never came back for it. Señor Maes still
has the twenty-five dollars, and the bar, too. He wouldn't take
several times a hundred and fifty for it now.

*

The people of Lincoln don't go very far away, or do very
much. Señor Maes has never been past Roswell, sixty miles east.
There are grown men here who have been only a few miles
down the road. Lincoln has been delightfully asleep for sixty
years, ever since Billy the Kid's guns stopped barking. Time
means nothing in Lincoln. The bartender will lock up his saloon
and show you around town. The grocer will come and stand in
the middle of the road to talk.

Lincoln was founded by Mexicans. The white man came and
had his bloody day, but Lincoln ebbed back into its gentle ways.
Nearly all the people are Spanish-American now. As in deep
Mexico, the people are friendly, quietly hospitable, and eager to
tell you anything you want to know.

You sense that it is not decay but peace that has settled over
the old village. Maybe it's just the quietness, and the welcome
heat of the sun. Or maybe it's the contrast with those days when
a man, walking these same streets, never knew whether or not
he would live to walk them tomorrow.

Billy the Kid lore is in every building and in nearly every
mind. He was a hero around Lincoln. Most of the people here
are descendants of the deadly Lincoln County war of 1878–1880.
McSween's store—with sheets of steel in the doors to stop bullets—is still a general store. People live in Juan Patrón's old
saloon, where McSween's killers used to gather. Francisco Maes
owns the house where Billy the Kid carved his name, the only
personal remnant of his career left behind in Lincoln. The carving is on the outer door casing, and simply says KID. It has been
whitewashed over, but you can still see it.

You see where the McSween home stood before it burned. In the backyard, somewhere, lie McSween and other heroes of that awful last night in the Lincoln County war. The graves are unmarked, and nobody knows exactly where they are. They say you can dig up a skeleton in almost anybody's yard.

The adobe walls of the old LaFonda hotel stand surprisingly sturdy. It was from here that Deputy Bob Ollinger, hearing shots, ran out to the road and was shot down by his bitter enemy, the Kid. The hotel burned a few years ago, but it could be restored.

The old courthouse is the outstanding spot. You can see the hole in the wall where the Kid's bullet struck after passing through the heart of Deputy Bell. You can sit in the second-story window where the Kid sat when he killed Deputy Ollinger.

There are still many people in New Mexico who remember Billy the Kid, but only one of them is left around Lincoln. This is Francisco Gomez, eighty-four years old, short and bowlegged and spry as a cricket. He speaks no English. He has a little farm just out of town, and was sprinting down the road carrying a sack of beans when I saw him. We talked, through an interpreter, for quite awhile. Señor Gomez lived at McSween's when the Kid lived there, and he remembers him as a good guy.

Lincoln had its day, and now it has gone back to sleep. It is remarkably preserved. Most of the houses are of adobe, and as old as the town itself. You see women drawing water from old-fashioned box wells. There are hitching posts in front of the stores. Lincoln just dreams nowadays, and it dreams mostly about its hero—Billy the Kid. The place enchants me. . . .

April 16, 1938

A Dream World Beneath the Desert

CARLSBAD, NEW MEXICO—At two-thirty P.M. you are getting close to the end of your pilgrimage through the Carlsbad Caverns.

For hours you have wandered in a world of half-light, amidst millions of shadowed fantasies. You have lost all feeling of reality. You have stepped away from life, become a part of fairyland. Your sense of appreciation aches, and your body feels a cool weariness.

The trail rounds a big rock, and ahead of you lies a white slope, roofed far overhead by solid rock that makes a dark sky.

The light is dim, like the northern moonlight on snow. The dark world widens as you climb the slope, and finally you reach a height, and stop there with your fellow travelers to rest on the dusty white rocks.

A large man in green uniform steps forward and stands at the foot of an immense "candle-dripped" stone column. He is Colonel Thomas Boles, superintendent of the caverns. All day he has kept in the background, one of the crowd. But now he takes charge. He asks for silence, and complete attention. He gets it, even from the children.

Colonel Boles makes a little informal speech. He tells us the number in our party, which has been computed on the surface and phoned down. He tells what states and foreign countries are represented. Then he speaks of the unbelievable things we have seen. He dwells upon the great column behind him. He says that when the Pyramids of Egypt were being built this column was already millions of years old.

He dwells upon the magnificently slow processes of nature— this great shaft has been built at the rate of only one cubic inch per century. Here it stands, tall as a house, big around as a room, hundreds of tons in weight, beautiful as heaven—yet formed so slowly that between the time of the building of the Pyramids and today it has grown not much more than the bulk of your folded fist.

Sixty million years old, they say it is. They have named it the Rock of Ages, for that is what it is. And all of it accomplished down here in total darkness, unknown to man or animal. You feel a new awe as you realize the ponderous patience of nature.

And now, says Colonel Boles, we will see what it was like while all this was going on, in the past millions of years. We will see what it was like before man came and made it visible. We will step back into time, and do a little honor to the Rock of Ages.

He asks that cigarettes be doused, that no one talk or whisper. He waits until the crowd and the cavern are as silent as death. And then the lights go out.

You have never known darkness until you have sat in it eight hundred feet below the surface. You look around for a faint glow somewhere, a shadow, a movement. There is nothing. You are in a complete solid of blackness. And the silence is as thick as the darkness. Your soul creeps, and you sit there in mental obeisance.

And then softly come the notes of a song. Four Rangers, unnoticed, have dropped back down the trail, and somewhere off there they are softly singing "Rock of Ages." It is beautiful coming so weirdly and gently out of the darkness of that cave.

Then, in the far distance, suddenly come dim reflections of light. A Ranger has turned on the lights half a mile away, at the far end of the vast cave room. A few more notes go by, and then comes a new, nearer light. Another thousand-foot section has been switched on. And then at last, as the Rangers' voices sink almost to a whisper, the lights come on all around us. . . .

Now you rise, fall again into line, walk another short way through fairyland, and then rise swiftly through eighty-four stories of solid rock, out into the hot, blinding sunshine of the New Mexico desert.

Life suddenly is real again, and it is impossible that this gray, rolling plain can conceal another world so near. But you will dream about it for a long time.

April 12, 1938

CARLSBAD, NEW MEXICO—Jim White, a cowboy who never finished the third grade, discovered the Carlsbad Caverns in 1901.

He not only discovered them, he fully explored them. He realized the magnificence that was inside. Convincing the world became a mania with him.

But the world is so smart, and knows so much, that Jim White talked and argued and begged for more than twenty years before he could get another white man to go into the caverns with him and see for himself. In 1922 a party of thirteen Carlsbad businessmen finally consented to go down. When they came out, the world found out that Jim White wasn't a liar.

The government took charge in 1923, and the cowboy's dream began to be realized. For it had apparently been Jim White's simple, unselfish ambition that others should be able to see the wonderful things he had seen. Since 1923 more than a million people have been through the caverns. They are coming now at the rate of two hundred thousand a year.

It isn't always that the discoverer gets credit in his lifetime, or reaps any gain. But the government has been good to Jim White. He is fifty-seven now, still looks like a cowboy, and every visitor to the caverns sees him. He has a little stand down where the tourists eat lunch. There he sells the booklet that tells his own fascinating story—his discovery, his exploration, and his long, long fight to make somebody believe him.

He charges seventy-five cents, and deals them out so fast he resembles a chef in a Los Angeles hamburger stand. He must make a fine living. And furthermore, the government doesn't try to belittle his explorations. It gives him full credit. . . .

April 13, 1938

AN OCEAN OF UTTER WHITE

ALAMAGORDO, NEW MEXICO—The White Sands of Alamagordo shine with a dazzling light. You must wear dark glasses or the tears will come to your squinty eyes and there will be nothing in your vision but glare.

There is nothing like the White Sands anywhere in the world. They are an albino Sahara. They are miles of drifted sugar. They are an ocean of utter white. They astound you and they give you the creeps.

Out on the sands there is no sound, no perspective, no single thing to break the vast whiteness. The dunes rise and fall in graceful mounds, some as high as ten-story buildings. There are shadows that make a camera jump. There are dreams and mirages and food for the sober. And for the little people—the sands look so good that children eat them.

These White Sands cover a strip about thirty miles long and fifteen miles wide. What they are, really, is crystallized gypsum. They were made into a national monument in 1933. . . .

*

The White Sands are phenomenal in a dozen ways. They are a desert, yet not a desert. For anywhere you can dig down a few inches with your hands and find water.

There are no snakes in the sands, thank goodness. There are some skunks, however, and ants and various harmless insects. And there are mice that have gradually turned white over the centuries, through the mysterious process of nature called protective coloring.

No janitor is needed for White Sands. Each morning the dunes are white and rippled and clean. All refuse is covered up. The wind does it. . . .

Only in winter, when the snow comes, is the vast uncanny whiteness broken by a little disillusionment. For then contrast

is there, and to your surprise you see that the sands are not really
as white as the driven snow.

Only a little of the sand, right on top, dries out and blows.
Consequently the dunes shift very slowly. The whole area is
moving toward Alamagordo—twenty miles away—at the rate of
eight inches a year. Alamagordo won't have to blow its evacua-
tion siren very soon.

Always the sands are cold. Just under the surface it is fifty-six
degrees. In summer people come out by the hundreds, with
blankets, and sleep away the sweltering nights. . . .

December 7, 1939

How Pablo Abeyta "Kidnapped" Teddy Roosevelt

ISLETA, NEW MEXICO—We sat out in front of Pablo Abeyta's adobe
house in this ancient Pueblo village one afternoon while Pablo
told me about Teddy Roosevelt.

Pablo has long hair, which keeps blowing into his mouth, and
he has two long braids behind, and wears a white lace shirt, like
a woman's blouse, and it's all Indian. Pablo is about sixty-five
and he speaks better English than I do, and because he is smart
and can talk he's always being sent to Washington as an interpreter for Indian delegations.

He has made eighteen trips to Washington, and it was on one
of these trips that the Teddy Roosevelt story began. "We went
into the White House," Pablo said, "and somebody introduced
us one at a time, and the President shook hands and said a few
words. Then we left and were outside when a fellow pulled my
sleeve and said the President wanted to see me alone. So I went
back and the President said, 'Pablo, sit down,' and he said,
'Pablo, I want to know all about your village and what the
Indians need.'

"So we sat there talking and I knew he was busy and I kept
rushing through so I could leave. But he kept telling me to go
on. After a while some Cabinet men came in and sat down, and
finally they got to fidgeting, and one of them took out his watch
and pointed at it, and the President turned around and said,
'Gentlemen, I'm fully aware of the time we are spending here.
Go on, Pablo.'

"Well, sir, I talked to him for two hours and twenty minutes,
and when I left he said, 'Pablo, someday I'm coming to Isleta and
I want to visit you in your own home.' So I came back and didn't

think much more about it, until several months later I got a message that the President was at the main hotel in Albuquerque and wanted me to come right up.

"So I hitched up my horses and drove to Albuquerque and tied my horses outside the hotel. There were two men standing outside the door and they said, 'What do you want?' and I said, 'The President wants to see me.' They said, 'What's your name?' And I said, 'I haven't got any name. Tell the President an Indian wants to see him.'

"So they started an argument and we made so much noise the President heard us, and he recognized my voice and came and opened the door and pulled me in. 'Pablo, you didn't think I'd really come, did you?' the President said. And then he said, 'Pablo, how'll we get out to Isleta without all this crowd following us?'

"So I said, 'Mr. President, give me your hat and coat.' He handed them over without a word, and I put them under my blanket and went down and put them in my buggy, and got another blanket and went back up. When I got in the room I put the blanket around the President, clear up over his head, and then we pulled the blankets up around us and stooped over and shuffled down through the lobby and out across the street and got in my buggy, and everybody thought we were just a couple of old Indians.

"I galloped my horses all the way to Isleta, and we went into my house and the President said, 'Pablo, you didn't think I'd ever come, did you? Now I've filled my promise.' So we had a bite to eat, and sat and talked a few minutes, and then we got in the buggy and drove back to Albuquerque. When we walked into the hotel, the lobby was full of people and the Secret Service men were running around excited because they couldn't find the President. So I gave a big war whoop and jerked the blanket off the President's head, and you should have seen the people stare.

"The guards came running up and they were sore because the President had got away from them, but he turned and said, 'Boys, I was just as safe in Pablo's hands as I am with anybody in the world.'

"And you know, he kept that blanket. I saw him again at the White House in 1915 and he showed me the blanket and said . . ."

"But, Pablo," I interrupted, "Theodore Roosevelt wasn't President in 1915."

"Well, anyway," said Pablo, "he showed me the blanket and said . . ."

So that's Pablo's story. It doesn't make any difference to me whether you believe it. And it probably doesn't make any difference to Pablo, either.

May 29, 1936

ALBUQUERQUE'S FAVORITE SPORT
ALBUQUERQUE, NEW MEXICO—One of the things people do here is go down to see the trains come in. Albuquerque is a city of about forty thousand, but just the same its main attraction, day in and day out, is the arrival of the trains.

There are people here, with nothing else to do, who are as much a part of the arriving train as the engine itself. . . . There is a real fascination about seeing the trains arrive. They come in out of the desert from so far away, to the oasis that is Albuquerque. The platform is brick, and very long and wide, and running along it are the depot and Indian curio shops and the long, low Harvey Hotel, built in Southwestern style.

There are lots of tracks, and I know of no prettier spectacle than to see an immensely long train, sitting there in the evening, the locomotive gone, the Pullmans empty, men in overalls tapping the wheels and loading packages off trucks, the whole thing just sitting there resting, waiting out its twenty-five minutes before it takes on its cargo of humans again and speeds away into the desert toward far California.

There are five transcontinental trains each way, daily, through Albuquerque. In the West, you know, most people get off the trains to eat at the "eating stops." The big trains disgorge from forty to two hundred people, who leap off, stretch, and hurry into the restaurant for a quick meal.

*

There is hardly a day but what there's a celebrity on at least one of the trains going through Albuquerque. A newspaper friend here was telling me how, several years ago, he went to the station to interview Charlie Dawes* when he came through. He finally found him, sulking in his compartment, so mad he could hardly talk. It seemed there was a huge crowd at the station, and

*Charles G. Dawes, Vice President under Coolidge and head of the Reconstruction Finance Corporation in Hoover's administration.

Dawes got off and walked up and down, and nobody paid the slightest attention to him. They were there to get autographs from a minor movie star.

The autograph hounds are a serious problem. If a really big celebrity is coming through, the crowd gets so big that station master Sinclair has to use all six of his railroad policemen, and call in city cops, too. The movie stars got to complaining, and said they'd quit using the railroad if something wasn't done about the autograph hunters at Albuquerque. So now if people get too insistent, they are arrested. A lot of them have been fined.

Charlie Chaplin used to be the biggest drawing card, but he hardly comes through anymore. Mr. Sinclair doesn't know who the big attraction is now; he doesn't want anything to do with them. All he's interested in is keeping people away from the trains. . . .

May 30, 1936

This is an excerpt from a series of columns Pyle wrote about a trip he took with two over-the-road truck drivers from Denver to Los Angeles.

ALBUQUERQUE, NEW MEXICO—When we stopped for coffee at Raton, New Mexico, it was pitch dark. One sleepy man in a white jacket was behind the counter. The town was dead.

But when we drove out of Raton, there was a sense of dawn already there. I've never seen it quite the same. You could sense it, yet you couldn't see it. The hour was four A.M.

Gradually the faint light of day did become real, and it was indeed a moving sight. In the half-light the mesas over to the east stood against the lighter sky like battleships at rest.

The driver said, "There's Venus, the morning star." And when the sun rose, it came up behind a cone-shaped mountain, with a groove right in the top. Our first sight of it was just a fiery pinpoint, rising into this groove. It was like a glowing target in a gun sight.

Frost covered the ground. The rolling, treeless desert stretched as far as we could see. Once again we were in that peculiarly moving vastness of New Mexico, and I was so glad I wanted to shout. I hope I never know the Southwest so well that it disillusions me. . . .

May 8, 1939

A Place for Long Looks at God's Handiwork

SANTA FE, NEW MEXICO—Santa Fe is almost as high above sea level as Mexico City is. It's seven thousand feet high, and a newcomer has to gasp for breath the first few days he's here.

It gets very cold in winter, and there is snow. But in summer it's cool, and people pay two hundred dollars a month for a house that goes for forty dollars a month in winter. The climate is fine for tuberculars. Lots of people you meet looking robust and full of vim came out on stretchers. Yet you don't sense a sanitarium-town atmosphere.

Santa Fe is the second-oldest city in the United States, coming next to St. Augustine, Florida. Coronado came from Mexico and roamed all around here in 1540. This whole Rio Grande Valley drips with history and with ancient Spanish and Indian culture.

Santa Fe is the capital of New Mexico, and it is worse than Indianapolis for politics. It has shops that are the finest between Dallas and Los Angeles. It has some that are the worst. But there's one thing you can't argue about in Santa Fe—and that is the view. I don't know of a town in America that has such astoundingly long unfoldings of nature as you see from just outside Santa Fe.

The town lies in a wide valley. Close by to the east are mountains. Far off to the west are mountains. They are not like the tall, sinister mountains of the northern Rockies. They seem more like neighbors than mountains—but sometimes you can stand in the bright sunshine in Santa Fe and see not five miles away an ominous blackish-gray snowstorm swirling down upon the mountain ridge.

Or if you visit a friend who lives but four miles out of town you can sit in his library and look northwest through the big window and see a vastness of valley and mesa and far-off mountain chain that almost drives you crazy with its immensity.

At various times I have spent a good many days in Santa Fe, and I have yet to see the surrounding country or sky look alike on any two days, and I have yet to see it when it was not fascinating. Boston for Beans, Seattle for rain, San Francisco for bridges, and Santa Fe for long, far looks at what God made.

*

There isn't a city in America that looks like Santa Fe. The business section will disappoint you, in case you've heard too much about the beauties of Santa Fe. For it has a lot of old 1890-type brick buildings, oozing tastelessness.

But scattered throughout are the soft lines of gray stuccoed adobe in the new Santa Fe architecture, and the streets are narrow and twisty as of old, and you hear as much Spanish on the street as you do English, and when you get out toward the edge of town among the poorer people the houses are a solid gray wall, flush with the dirt sidewalk, and you're right down in old Mexico.

Some of the bigger buildings are in this perfectly blended Santa Fe style—the art museum, the post office, the LaFonda Hotel. But others are hideously out of place—the red Scottish Rite temple, the state capitol, the Federal Building. . . .

This new style, which is known only as "Santa Fe architecture," is simply a modernization and a softening of the age-old Pueblo Indian style of building. Outer walls slant slightly inward as they go up, second stories (if any) are always set back, you don't see any roofs, corners are rounded, and poles stick out of the adobe at the ends of the buildings. The houses are made of adobe bricks and covered with smooth, mud-colored stucco.

Fireplaces are in corners, and are the shape of one-fourth of an orange cut off at the bottom. Wood is set on end to burn, not laid flat. Inner walls are plain white. Ceilings aren't quite level, all main rooms have beams carved in old wood, hallways and stairways twist a little—nothing is square, nothing is sharp.

This architecture would look hideous in New York or Memphis or on an Iowa farm. It has to be in the Southwestern desert, under bright sun and amid bare distances, blending with the earth and harmonizing with the mountainside, speaking in silent good manners with the personality of the Southwest.

January 12, 1937

SANTA FE, NEW MEXICO— . . . Santa Fe has fifteen thousand people. About half are Mexicans. But you must never, never, never call a Mexican a Mexican. He is a Spanish-American. Of the seventy-five hundred other inhabitants, about a hundred and fifty are artists and writers. . . .

*

Life among the upper crust of Santa Fe centers by daytime on the LaFonda Hotel, right in the center of town, built in the Santa Fe style. You can go there any time of day and see a few artists in the bar, or see an Indian that some white woman loves, or see a goateed nobleman from Austria, or a maharajah from

India, or a New York broker, or an archaeologist, or some local light in overalls and cowboy boots.

You never meet anybody except at the LaFonda. You never take anybody to lunch anywhere else. I don't see how some of the struggling geniuses afford it. I stayed at the De Vargas.

There is no classifying the art circle. They aren't all alike by any means. They don't fraternize exclusively with each other. Some don't fraternize at all. Others do nothing else. There are lots of cocktail parties, but some of the artists never go. They don't live in a group. Their houses are scattered all over one side of town and far out onto the mountainside. Some are rich and have big homes; others live in shacks. A few live on their art, but many have other incomes.

Most of the artists are genuine people, living normal lives. But there are many freaks and pretenders—people who are artists because they like to sit on the floor and talk about composition, and dress up like Indians and stare into fireplaces.

Many people who come out here stay sane. Some go to pot. Some of them go what you might call *native*, and don't take baths anymore, and ride to cocktail parties on spotted ponies, and dress like Spaniards, and collect pink mice, and live in tents as the Indians used to.

There is one man who insults every stranger at a party. And there is one woman who goes to parties, gets bored, ties a string around her dress, and then stands on her head in a corner the rest of the evening. . . .

The other night we were at the home of some friends here, and just for my edification they got to figuring up how many people in Santa Fe you could actually call interesting. I suspect they made the entrance requirements pretty stiff. As it wound up, they could think of only twenty people who were downright interesting—which, at that, is probably more than you'd find with such a strict yardstick in any other American town of fifteen thousand. . . .

January 13, 1937

COSTILLA, NEW MEXICO— . . . This state has a couple of odd laws affecting travelers.

In New Mexico it is lawful to carry a six-shooter while traveling. But you must have it put safely away within half an hour after reaching your destination.

Why a half hour? I have no idea, unless it's to give you legal time to dispose of any citizens who might be personally obnoxious to you.

The other law has to do with liquor. This law says it is illegal for a traveler to carry more than one quart of liquor. The funny part is that this law was passed during national prohibition, when it was illegal to carry liquor anywhere in the United States.

So you see, if you put these two laws together, it is obvious that the State of New Mexico considers a six-shooter and a quart of liquor necessary to the comfort and well-being of a traveler.

Who said the spirit of the Old West had disappeared? . . .

April 30, 1938

FOUR CORNERS, U.S.A.— . . . This is the only place in America where four states come together. . . .

Way off here in the mountainous desert, at a tiny little mathematical pinpoint, the states of Colorado, Utah, Arizona, and New Mexico all touch each other. There's nothing out here except a concrete post, and two swallows that keep flying around. . . .

You get here by driving thirty miles west from Shiprock, New Mexico, on a dirt road. At thirty miles you turn right, onto a couple of tracks. You follow these tracks another eight miles. It takes you three-quarters of an hour to go the last eight miles. It's uphill, and full of rocks and drifted sand. . . .

*

Very few people ever get to Four Corners. At Shiprock, they say that one car a week would be stretching it.

For one thing, most people never heard of it. For another, those last eight miles are just an old Navajo wagon trail, and aren't even on the road maps.

It is not especially nice right here at Four Corners. The monument is set in the center of a little plateau, a block or so square. From there the land falls away, or rises, into the vast, rolling, desolate, windy country that is this part of the world. The sight is majestic in all directions. But it is not gentle.

Not a hundred yards from the marker post are the crude stone walls of a crumbling building. There is no floor, no roof, no doors. We were told that somebody tried to start a tourist hotel here. But we learned later it was merely a trading post, which went broke.

Inside it now is nothing but a pile of rocks and an old shoe. There is evidence that the wandering flocks of Navajo sheep take refuge in it occasionally. . . .

July 21, 1939

* * *

MUSKOGEE, OKLAHOMA— . . . Two drunks were in a restaurant in the tiny prairie town of Santa Rosa, New Mexico. They were nice-looking young men, obviously town boys rather than ranchers. They were nice drunks, and kept saying "Sshhhhhhh!" at each other. They didn't say anything out of the way. The waitress was enjoying their talk. Finally one of them looked at her and said, very seriously: "Are you an old cowgirl?"

She laughed and said yes.

"I'm a cowboy," he said, and went on eating.

His partner said, "Sshhhhh!"

January 26, 1937

ARIZONA

Worn down after a long bout with influenza, Ernie and Jerry traveled through the Southwest and West during December 1934 and January 1935. The trip was hardly restful, but it did get Ernie animated about the roving-column idea. Back in Washington, he wrote a series of eleven articles about his vacation for the Washington Daily News, *of which he was managing editor, and the pieces were "an instant hit" with management. The following is one of the eleven. It centers on a former desert neighbor of Pyle's friend Paige Cavanaugh, with whom Pyle had gone to school at Indiana University and whose restlessness and craving for adventure rivaled Pyle's. After a succession of sales jobs that interested him not at all, Cavanaugh had built a house in the Arizona desert, where he got to know Lawrence Cruce, who lived about a mile away. "He had a true artist's conception of leisure," Cavanaugh has said of Cruce. "He despised work of any kind." Cavanaugh and his wife, Edna, had left their desert house and had moved back to California by the time the Pyles visited Cruce, but the mere mention of the affable Cavanaugh's name endeared Pyle to him.*

WHERE TIME IS PLENTY

My friend's ranch is about halfway between Antelope Peak on the east and the Barkerville Federal Building on the west, five miles in each direction.

In that part of southern Arizona the Federal Building is always mentioned with a smile, because it is nothing but a board shack, about six feet square, sitting beside a cactus in the desert. It used to be a post office for four hours one day each week, when the mail carrier came forty miles out from the nearest town. But he doesn't come anymore, and the pack rats have undermined the Federal Building until it is about to topple over. And nobody cares especially.

That's what makes southern Arizona so nice; nobody seems to care very much one way or the other about anything. My friend who owns the ranch doesn't worry much about anything, either; in fact, he is the kind of a guy you read about in books. He sits all day rolling cigarets and smoking them, and as far as I was able to observe after considerable study, he does absolutely nothing at all.

Southern Arizona is a land of little rain. Water, being scarce, becomes the source of all prosperity down there. That's where my friend on the ranch has the situation sewed up. He has a deep well.

His well is the only one for miles around. So he sells water. And because there are thousands of thirsty cattle roaming the range thereabouts, he sells a lot of water.

*

I have just recently spent some time with my friend on his ranch. His part of Arizona is all desert, and very beautiful. The average Easterner thinks the desert is barren, but that isn't exactly true. It is rolling, sandy country, with small mountain peaks sticking up here and there, and the ground is covered with cactus (in most of its seventy-five varieties), with mesquite and cat's-claw trees, with many kinds of small grassy shrubs, and, after rains, with a small spreading grass called filaree.

It is cattle country, mostly still unfenced. My friend's own ranch is small (a mere mile square). He homesteaded it seven years ago, he and his wife, and although they say it's just a haven during the Depression years, I've an idea they'll be there a long, long time. Their life is a far cry from the bubble and trouble of our Eastern cities.

They have a two-room frame house, set on the side of a little hill. Their furnishings are comfortable. Their kitchen has running water. They don't need any heat, other than the kitchen stove, which burns mesquite wood.

They have a grass-roofed porch on the west side of the house. Here they have a swinging davenport that came from the mail-order house, and a canvas-wrapped water keg that the sun, by evaporation, keeps cool. On the side of the house is a thermometer three feet high. The highest it has ever gone is a hundred and seven. The country is five thousand feet high, and the heat isn't as ghastly in the summer as you would imagine.

*

On top of the hill above the house is a big steel water tank, and near it is a cement basin which, in the summertime, is a combination storage basin for water for the cattle and swimming pool.

Down below the house, at the foot of the hill, is the well, the cement water tanks, a corral, a small barn, and the cowboy's bunk house. A barbed-wire fence encloses the whole assemblage.

My friend arranged things very nicely for my visit. He arranged for the sun to go down just as he had written me it would, casting for a few minutes an almost purple haze down the little valley to the east; he arranged for a full moon to come shooting up over Antelope Peak like a ball of gold, coming up so fast you could count one, two, three and actually see that the moon had gained altitude in those few seconds; he arranged the combination of a full moon and desert cactus into soft, weird shadows the likes of which you cannot see east of the Pecos; he arranged for the coyotes to come and yell their ghostly yodel just at bedtime, and not a hundred yards from the bunkhouse; he arranged just the proper amount of loose cactus needles on the bunkhouse floor for me to put my bare feet on and make me feel very, very Wild West, sleeping with saddles hung on the foot of the bed and owls hooting in the rafters.

My friend really has only three things to do—cut and carry in enough mesquite wood for the cook stove, feed the chickens, and start the gasoline engine to pump water every other day.

*

Having so much time, he is an expert on many things. He takes *Time* magazine, the *New York Times*, and *National Geographic*. He knows more about the Washington situation than most of us here in Washington. He has very definite theories on what should be done to get us out of the depression; he thinks the NRA* hurts the little man, and he doesn't like so many foreigners in this country.

He is a connoisseur of guns. He owns two six-shooters, a French high-powered rifle, and a shotgun. He always carries a six-shooter with him, for snakes or jackrabbits, or something bigger. They don't shoot very many men down here like they used to.

One of his six-shooters has a solid-copper handle. My friend made it, fashioned it with file and sandpaper out of a hunk of Arizona copper. The gun with the original handle was worth thirty-five dollars. Now, with the copper handle, it is worth about sixty dollars. It took him nearly six months to make it.

My friend is under forty. He is tall and good-looking, his face is the color of his copper six-gun handle, he wears a ten-gallon hat and cowboy boots. He has learned to take his time. When his wife needs wood for the cook stove he smokes three cigarets before he goes and gets it. He is always smiling.

He hates to go to town; not especially because it's so far (forty miles), or because the town isn't much when you get there, but because it's so much nicer just to sit and smoke.

*

He doesn't have many neighbors. Adjoining him on the west is a ranch of a hundred thousand acres, extending eighty miles to the south. My friend waters their cattle for them, for a fee that gives him a comfortable living. Once, during a drought several years ago, he really had to work. His gasoline engine ran steadily for forty-eight hours, and for forty-eight hours without stop they were handling cattle in and out of the corral, past the watering troughs.

My friend likes to have company, for he likes to talk. He has some very funny stores about the cowboys and the Mexicans. My favorite is the egg story.

It seems there is a cowboy living a few miles from him, a cowboy who has grown to middle age on the Arizona range, who has been to Tucson only a couple of times in his life, and who is a very fine man, but a very primitive one, indeed.

*National Recovery Administration, an unpopular New Deal agency that was supposed to oversee business' regulation of itself by means of fair-competition codes. It was partially successful, but the legislation that created the agency, the National Industrial Recovery Act, was declared unconstitutional by the Supreme Court in May 1936.

One morning this cowboy rode up to my friend's ranch. It being the custom to invite any visitor to stay for the next meal, this cowboy was invited to breakfast, and accepted.

As he was washing up, my friend's wife said to the cowboy: "Jim, how do you like your eggs?"

"Oh, I like 'em fine," was Jim's answer.

"But," she said, "how do you like them cooked?"

"Oh," replied Jim, "I like 'em better that way than any other way."

April 2, 1935

This is from the fall of 1935.

LAST NIGHT AT ANTELOPE PEAK

WASHINGTON—The news of their leaving has just come to me in a letter. They mailed it at Tucson, on their way out of the hills.

Their last night must have been sad for them. There wasn't much packing to do, for they had sold out lock, stock, and barrel, and practically everything they had went with the ranch. It was getting on toward nine o'clock. Twilight had come and gone, and the little valley below the house was full of the dark desert stillness. There is no silence anywhere like the silence of an Arizona night.

They had finished supper, and sat in the swing placed on the bare ground out under the thatched porch, as they always did. You couldn't see Antelope Peak from where they sat, for it was on the other side of the house, and it was dark. But in an hour or so the moon would be coming up, and then if you walked around the house you could see the mountain silhouetted big and sharp in the sky.

Everything around them was just as it had been for years—everything except a few things: the car down by the pigeon house was packed full of stuff, for they were leaving at daylight . . . and you couldn't hear the pigeons cooing down there, for they had eaten the last two for supper . . . and old Nap, the great, kind German police dog who was stone deaf but who could smell a coyote for a mile and who was slow and old and lovable, old Nap wasn't rousing up from his sleep every now and then to come and put his head in their laps, for he had gone to live with a cowboy over the hill. Nap wouldn't have known what to do in the city.

*

The man lit a lantern, and hung it on the side of the house, on the hook up by the big thermometer. He went back in the house and got his two six-shooters, the .38 on the .45 frame, the one with the copper handle he had made himself, and the other .38 with the bone handle, and he wrapped them in soft cloth and put them in a bag.

That was about all there was left to do. The swing they were sitting on, and what little furniture there was, and the saddles on the foot of the iron bed down in the bunkhouse, they all went with the ranch. And the two horses he could never find when he wanted them—they were out there on the range somewhere, and the new owner knew their brand, so that was enough. They went with the deal, too. And so did the calves, and the few steers.

They sat in the swing, and he rolled brown-paper cigarets and lit them with big matches and smoked them one after another. Finally she said, "We'd better go to bed." He smoked a couple more cigarets and they went in. She blew out the light and lay down. He went out onto the little earthen ledge they had built on the other side of the house for a porch. There was Antelope Peak, standing up so still in front of the moon. He had climbed up there so many times, and once he had dug in a place that was supposed to be an Indian chieftain's grave, but hadn't found anything. The rattlesnakes were worming around up there now, finding a warm hole for the winter.

Seven years. A long time for a man and woman to live on the desert. Homesteaders who had stuck it out. Cactus and cat's-claw and sand. Miles of it, as far as you could see. And cattle. He had built his house there, a board house, right down on the ground. You could walk around it in thirty steps. One room and a kitchen, but it was nice inside, and they had their easy chairs, and their Aladdin lamp, and nice dishes, and books, and it was always clean and warm. And he had drilled a well, and built cement water tanks, and got a gasoline engine. Water is life on the desert. Water had been life to them. They had watered cattle for the ranchers, and made a living at it.

Sometimes it had been lonesome, with only Mexicans and cowpeople within riding distance, and not many of them. And town forty miles away, and not much of a town when you got there. But they had been happy, too. You liked the easy life, and you never had to do anything at any certain time, and you could sit and smoke and sandpaper a copper gun handle all day long if you wanted to. And nobody to bother you, and the country was pretty, in a desert way. Not flat, but hilly and interesting, and in the spring the cactus were a glory.

Seven years. It's a good country to live in, but it's a hard country, too. Only the cactus survive, eventually. There was much rain this summer. The country was flooded. Cattle didn't need much water out of a well. Just couldn't make it any longer. They got a fair price for their square mile. . . .

Tomorrow at daylight. Little mesquite shadows on the gray sand. Antelope Peak and cattle. Open spaces and solitude. Jack rabbits and rattlesnakes. The little wash they called Happy Valley. Seven years. . . .

He went back into his house and went to bed. The watchful shadows down by the water tanks moved, and spoke. Tonight and forever, the song of the desert. Coyotes. They'll be hearing them in their dreams for a long time in the city.

October 28, 1935

POSTSCRIPT: *Cavanaugh lived in the desert only eighteen months, but he considers those months a highlight of his long life. Now ninety years old, he has a black-and-white photograph of his desert house hanging in the den of his Southern California home. Fifty-four years after he and Edna left Arizona, Cavanaugh periodically removes the picture from the wall and studies it. "What a hell of a time that was," he'll say.*

THE STRANGE CAREER OF IKE PROEBSTAL

TACNA, ARIZONA—Thirty miles south of here, almost to the Mexican border, is a place called Tinajas Altas, which means "high tanks." It is a series of natural basins, one above the other, on a desert hillside. They catch and hold rainwater. Tinajas Altas was a favorite desert watering place in the early days.

On the slope above the basins are countless graves. You can identify only a few now, but when Ike Proebstal first came here thirty-three years ago, he and his brother counted a hundred and sixty graves one day. Every one was of a man who had died of thirst, men who had groped across the deathly hot desert, hoped their last hope of finding water at Tinajas Altas, and, not finding it, died.

Proebstal says the tale is that a Mexican bandit named Blanco operated there in the '49 gold-rush days. He would sneak across the border and drain the water tanks. Then when the thirsting gold seekers, California-bound, had died their choking deaths, he would rob them.

*

Ike Proebstal knows about men who die of thirst. For thirty-three years he has been a prospector and a mining man among these snaky sands and bare mountains, and he has saved many a man from death.

A fellow down the road said to me, "When Ike Proebstal tells you anything about this country you can bank on it being true." Proebstal is an unusual man. He is one of the handsomest humans you've ever seen. He carries his sixty-odd years like a lord. He has a little continental goatee, and I'll bet there isn't a man in Berlin who could so grace a silk hat and opera coat.

He was born in Oregon, studied mining engineering, and then lit out. He was in the South African mines for years, spent a year on the Australian desert, four years in Hawaii, a year in China and Japan. What strange careers these desert spaces gather into their folds! Ike Proebstal has been rich and he has been poor. Today he lives in a one-room shack, but he's no desert rat.

"I wish my brother were still alive to talk with you," he said. "He had a real reputation for finding missing men. But I've saved quite a few, too. The first fifteen years we were here, my brother and I rescued at least two people a year, I guess.

"There isn't much of it anymore. The auto has changed it. People drive right out across the desert, and they can take plenty of water with them. But even so, there's somebody lost from around here about once a year.

"You know, a man dying from thirst always takes off all his clothes. I don't know why, but they do it every time. I remember one fellow I rescued years ago. A man rode into my prospecting camp late in the afternoon. He was more dead than alive, and his horse was, too. He said he'd left his partner under a bush about five miles away.

"I started right out. I ran almost all the way; I knew I could just barely make it by sundown. I knew that if I didn't get there before dark, I'd never find him. He'd get up at dusk and start traveling. They always do it.

"Well, I found him. He was lying there on the sand, naked as a baby. A few feet away was a tripod made of short steel tubing about two feet long, with a kettle hanging on it. I kicked the tripod down and stood there and called to the fellow.

"I said, 'I've got some water for you, come and get it.' The fellow raised up. His face was black as coal, and his tongue was swollen and sticking out of his mouth two inches. He jumped up and ran at me and tried to take the water away from me.

"But I handled him all right. I'd brought a canteen of water, and a whiskey glass. I gave him just one small glass of water. Then I made him put on his clothes and told him if he'd follow me I'd give him a drink every hundred and fifty yards.

"The boys back at the camp had built bonfires so I could find my way back. When we got about halfway there I asked the fellow how he was feeling, and he said fine, that he was sweating. So I said, 'All right, then, you can drink all you want now.'

"He told me later that he was crazy and yet he wasn't crazy. He said he saw me standing over those steel bars, and he knew why I was doing it. He said if it hadn't been for those bars he would have killed me to get at the water quicker."

*

On a blistering hot summer day in the Arizona desert a man lives only three or four hours after the thirst craze hits him. Ike Proebstal himself almost got it once. He tried too long a hike between water holes, and the thirst craze set in. If he hadn't known the ways of the desert he would have died.

"But there isn't much sense in dying of thirst nowadays," he said. "For instance, my wife and I are going on a little prospecting trip tomorrow. We'll take plenty of water in the car, and we'll leave word here where we're going, and if we're not back by ten o'clock tomorrow night they'll start looking for us.

"I don't know what it is about the desert. It's a godforsaken place. But it gets in your blood. I've lived all over the world, but I haven't been away from here now for thirty-three years. I couldn't live anywhere else."

January 4, 1937

PLYING THE SNAKE TRADE

IN ARIZONA—Rudy Hale and his wife catch live rattlesnakes for a living. To me that would be ten thousand times worse than death. But they enjoy it.

These Arizona sands are filthy with rattlers. Rudy and his wife work the desert for snakes as a farmer works his land for crops. Rattlers have built them a place to live, rattlers have kept them in food and clothing for eight years, rattlers provided the start for their little gas-and-grocery business on the desert road fifty miles east of Yuma. They love rattlers.

Rudy Hale was born in Illinois, of German parentage; he still has an accent. He was brought up to be a surgeon. A relative sent him to school abroad. He studied medicine in Austria for four years. Then the relative died and the schooling stopped. His life turned.

He wound up in California. For twenty years he worked as a master mechanic. Then carbon monoxide laid him out and he came to the desert for his health. It was after two years on the desert that the Hales, facing hard times, had to turn to snakes for a living.

They started by advertising in a San Diego newspaper. Before they knew it, they were swamped with orders. They have sold snakes to zoos all over the country, to private collectors, to medical centers for serum, to state reptile farms, to the Mayo brothers.*

"They say there aren't any snakes in Ireland," said Mrs. Hale. "But I know there are, because we've shipped snakes to Ireland."

Today the Hales have their little store and gas station along the road. They live back of the store, alone, and there is no one else for miles. Three steps from their door and you are ankle-deep in bare sand.

*

There are twelve species of rattler in this part of Arizona. The sidewinder is the most deadly. The Hales specialize in sidewinders. They don't even use forked sticks to catch snakes. They just pick them up with their bare hands and put them in a box. They usually hunt for an hour after dawn and an hour before dark. They've caught about twenty thousand rattlers in eight years. Rudy has caught as many as fifty sidewinders in one hour's hunting. They have the desert cleaned almost bare of snakes for twenty miles around.

They used to get fifty cents apiece for sidewinders. "I just wish I could get fifty cents again," Rudy said. "They're down to twenty cents now." The most he ever got for a single snake was seven dollars. That was a rare Black Mountain rattler. He

*Charles and William Mayo, sons of a pioneer physician and surgeon and founders of Mayo Clinic at Rochester, Minnesota.

says the huge snakes don't bring as much as the medium-sized
ones. They're harder to keep in captivity, and zoos don't want
them.

Hale has caught rattlers as big around as his leg. He's caught
them so big he couldn't handle them—they'd overpower him
and pull his arms together—and he'd have to throw them away
from him, and then go pick them up and try again. "I'm careful
not to hurt a snake," he said. "Any snake I ship is a good healthy
snake."

The Hales have never been bitten. Both let rattlers crawl all
over them. Mrs. Hale carries rattlers around in her pockets. But
her brother has been bitten, five times, quick as a flash, by a nest
of sidewinders. He didn't say a word. He just lay down in the
sand, flat on his back, stretched out his arms, shut his eyes, and
lay there still as death for half an hour. Then he got up and went
back to work. Nothing ever happened. The Hales said most
people who die of snakebite really die of fright.

There's really no danger, they say, if you watch your business.
You must not be thinking about anything else when you're
picking up a sidewinder. The hand is quicker than a snake's
strike, and if you miss him the first grab you can jerk back in
time. Lots of times when they see a rattler coiled they'll just ease
up and slide a hand through the sand under him, and lift him
up right in the palm of the hand, still coiled.

Mrs. Hale's brother sat down on a rattler once. And Rudy
himself stepped right into the middle of a huge coiled rattler,
and his foot slipped and he fell down among the coils, but for
some reason he wasn't bitten.

*

It was Rudy who noticed—when I stopped to ask directions—
that all the oil had run out of my engine. So we spent two hours
there while he soldered my oil filter back together. That's how
I happened to find out about this snake business.

He had only one sidewinder on hand. It was in a roofless
concrete tank behind the house. Rudy took me out for a look.
It was after dark. He turned on a dim little electric light.

Then he got a stick with a nail in it, and got the sidewinder
hooked over the nail, and had it lifted almost to the top of the
tank. Just then his little red dog stuck its cold nose up my pants
leg, and I let out a yell and landed way over the side of Gila Bend
somewhere, and never did go back after the car.

January 5, 1937

POSTSCRIPT: *Pyle again stopped to see the Hales in November 1939. They remembered him, even remembered his car and what was wrong with it when they first met him. "The Hales haven't caught a snake since July," Pyle reported. "For some reason the market has completely disappeared."*

Now the Hales were raising hogs and testing the curative power of herbs. "They say they've cured neighbors who were long ill with internal diseases. They've healed up rashes and sores. They've banished kidney stones."

Pyle attempted to visit the Hales again in April 1942, but they were gone. "Their house and filling station were boarded up," he reported, "and a big sign said CLOSED—KEEP OUT. I couldn't find what had happened to them, for the desert is mighty empty out there, and there was nobody to ask."

Ed Shaffer, editor of Scripps Howard's Albuquerque Tribune, *was Pyle's traveling companion on a two-week trip through the mostly uninhabited desert country near the point where the states of New Mexico, Arizona, Utah, and Colorado join—the so-called Four Corners area. Shaffer later wrote that "not once did we leave a place where someone wasn't hanging on the car door, talking to Ernie and hating to see him go."* Teec Nos Pas *was an obvious exception.*

THEY STOOD AND STARED
TEEC NOS PAS, ARIZONA—This column is an account of fifteen minutes at Teec Nos Pas.

Teec Nos Pas is an Indian trading post. There are scores of them scattered about the vast Navajo reservation. Most of them are exorbitantly isolated.

This country is full of vast desolation. You drive, and you look, and you say, "Lord, what wastes! This is utter emptiness. How does anybody make a living?"

The road becomes a mere trail. You jounce over solid sheets of outcropping rock. Thousands of acres of flat, solid rock, like fields of concrete. The end of nowhere. You come around a rough little hill, and there in the valley is Teec Nos Pas. Just the store and a few outbuildings, that's all. A store in the desert.

*

Loafing Indians lay on the porch, lounged against store walls. Indian ponies, saddled and blanketed, were tied here and there. The Indians wore red bands around their heads.

We stopped and walked toward the store. One of two white men lounging on the porch got up and went in ahead of us. All the loafing Indian eyes drilled us coldly.

In the West, there is a friendly greeting between strangers. But not here. The unfriendly stare, the sinister eye, is the greeting at Teec Nos Pas.

The store was old and dirty inside. Lying on the floor, flat on his back, was an old Indian. Just lying there, doing nothing, talking to nobody, looking at nothing. Nobody anywhere doing anything, except staring.

We wanted to buy something, to break the ice. "I'll have a Coca-Cola," said my friend.

"No cold drinks here," said the white trader.

There was no friendliness in that store. Only a belligerent waiting to see who you were and what the hell brought you here. My friend bought a sack of Bull Durham.

"Can you tell me anything about that old building up at Four Corners?" I asked.

The trader leaned one elbow against the high candy case. He pulled at his cigaret, held his head back, blew high. And then he said, with utter finality: "Don't know anything about it."

I knew better. So I waited awhile, and then said, "Never even heard of it, huh?"

The trader waited awhile and then said, again closing the subject, "Yes, I've heard of it."

Then I waited awhile and said, "You been out here long?"

And after a while the trader said, "Yes, quite a while." And then he said, "I thought you were tourists. I hoped you were tourists and gonna look at a rug."

We kind of laughed to ease the tension, and I said, "Well, how can you tell we're not tourists? Do we look too poor to buy a rug?"

The trader said no, that wasn't it.

One by one the porch-sitting Indians were drifting in, and standing around. Not an expression of any kind was on their faces. They stood and stared, like so many animal eyes around a campfire.

There was no conversation except that between the trader and me, and it was toilsome and unwelcome conversation to us both. I tried again.

"I hear somebody tried to start a hotel. That old building up there."

The trader said, "No, it wasn't a hotel. It was a trading post."
"I'd heard it was a hotel," I said.
"That's the Indian agent out there on the porch. He can tell you what you want to know."

*

After a bit the agent drifted in. He did not speak. He sat on the high counter across the store, and studied the old Army shoes my friend wore. Waiting us out. Our move.

"How long has it been since you sold a rug to a tourist?" I asked the trader.

He blew a disdainful answer of smoke through his nose. "God, I don't know. Tourists never come here. Nobody ever comes here."

The Indian agent continued his study. The Indians watched to see if my friend could actually roll a cigaret. He could. Their expression did not change.

The old Indian on the floor never moved. The heat was oppressive, and the needles in the air grew sharper. My friend and I sensed each other's wishes without looking.

"Well, I reckon we better shove along," I said.

"I reckon we better," my friend replied.

Stares propelled us out the door. The rocky road away from Teec Nos Pas felt like a ribbon of velvet. The desert felt clean and safe and pure.

July 22, 1939

POSTSCRIPT: *Before the preceding was published, Pyle sent a carbon copy of the manuscript to Ed Shaffer with a note. "The Teec Nos Pas column will of course make them sore," he wrote, "and we will be shot if we should ever venture back there (which we won't) but I don't see any libel in it."*

TOMBSTONE, ARIZONA—This is the place where they used to kill a man before breakfast every morning, and where the newspaper was (and still is) so aptly named *The Epitaph.*

It is the silver-mining town that blossomed and roared in the eighties. It is the home of the Bird Cage Theatre and Boothill Graveyard. From the reading I have done, I don't believe there was ever a tougher Western town than Tombstone.

. . . Tombstone today is fairly poor copy. It is small and busy and prosaic, and all the drama must come from memories. But memory is kept well alive in Boothill Graveyard. It is on a knoll, just past the edge of town. The earth is hard, and only thorny little cactus growths are in the ground. From among the graves you can stand and look for countless miles. The wind blows hard, and the air is cool, for it is high and spaceless up there.

Many of Tombstone's notorious dead are buried there—five highwaymen who were lynched, a few who were legally hanged, some who were shot to death by Wyatt Earp and his deputies. Nobody has been buried there for more than thirty years. Except . . .

There is one new grave. A shoulder-high fence of yucca sticks surrounds it. The headstone is a lovely piece of petrified wood, set on a large rock. And on it is inscribed:

QUONG KEE
1851–1938
A Friend to All
Rest in Peace

Quong Kee was an old Chinaman. He had lived in Tombstone almost since there was a Tombstone. He knew both the quick and the dead of those early days. He saw everything that ever happened to make Tombstone famous. And he just carried on, being good to people.

He died last year. There was one man who felt it more than the others. He had been an orphan long ago in Tombstone, and Quong Kee had fed him and helped him along. The man today is a well-to-do Arizona newspaper publisher, and he asked that Quong Kee be buried in Boothill. It was he who put up the tasteful monument. . . .

November 27, 1939

*   *   *

LOS ANGELES— . . . All over the country I've been measuring for years the longest stretch of road that you could actually see strung out ahead of you as you came over the top of a hill.

There's one just west of Albuquerque that's nearly thirteen miles. There's one in the San Joaquin Valley, here in California, that's awfully long. There's a terrific one in eastern Oregon.

But we've now found the record stretch, at least for us. It is just east of Kingman, Arizona. You come over a rise, and there it is, straight as an arrow and growing narrower in the distance until it finally becomes a mere hairline as it disappears over the far horizon.

And from the top of that rise to where the road finally disappears, it is exactly seventeen miles! . . .

May 6, 1941

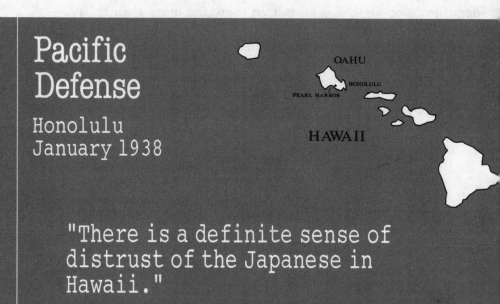

Pacific Defense

Honolulu
January 1938

OAHU

HONOLULU

PEARL HARBOR

HAWAII

"There is a definite sense of distrust of the Japanese in Hawaii."

Like Germany and Italy, Japan had aggressively expanded its sphere of influence during the 1930s. Japanese troops had invaded Manchuria in 1931 and China itself in 1937. When Japanese planes deliberately sank the American gunboat USS Panay *in the Yangtze River in China on December 12, 1937, killing two American sailors and wounding fourteen others, Japan was quick to offer apologies and reparations. It was intent on not provoking the United States, whose isolationist outlook benefited it and other aggressors. When Pyle wrote the following pieces, American military strategists considered a Japanese attack on Hawaii, a United States territory, only a remote possibility.*

DEFENDING AMERICA'S FRONT PORCH
HONOLULU—The war in the Orient has given a new significance to our fortifications in the Hawaiian Islands.

The island of Oahu is fortified like a Gibraltar. What the French would call a "ring of steel" surrounds Honolulu. Most of it is not visible to the passerby. You are hardly aware of it at all.

I don't know why, but Honolulu doesn't seem like a military or naval city, in the sense that San Diego is a Navy city. Soldiers and sailors are all about, yet the military doesn't seem to dominate. I guess maybe it's just lost in the constantly passing scene of strange races, big businesses, steamships, sugar, beauty, vacationists, and Hawaiian lore that make up the personality of Honolulu.

*

Most everyone knows that the government considers Hawaii important in case of war in the Pacific. We all know that a lot of money has been spent over here. But few people on the mainland have any conception of just what these fortifications are like.

First of all, you have to realize the primary theory of defense over here, which was a surprise to me. The Army and Navy are not here, fundamentally, to protect the islands as commercial investments, or to keep people from getting killed. The Navy is here because Hawaii gives it an operating base nearly halfway across the Pacific, gives it a big running start in case anything bad happens in the Orient. It also gives the United States sort of a naval barbed-wire fence twenty-five hundred miles from our front porch of California.

The Army is here for the sole purpose of protecting the Navy's base. Even the Army men have to admit they play second fiddle here. But they hold their heads up by having six times as many men here as the Navy.

The Navy is number one out here because a Pacific war would have to be largely a naval war. Pearl Harbor—the Navy's base—is the very heart in the body of Pacific war planning. Pearl Harbor is where the fleet would refuel, and strike from, in case of war. If Pearl Harbor were captured, or damaged beyond use, the Navy would have to operate from California, a week's round trip from here. A week might be too late. . . .

*

Military theory in the Pacific seems to be swinging more and more to the airplane. Long-range planes could spot an enemy fleet days before it reached Hawaii. It might even be possible for our planes to destroy a fleet before it got within a thousand miles. On the other hand, enemy planes might do the same thing in reverse. There has to be full preparation for fighting off an aerial attack here, and they have it.

*

Honolulu is well organized for war. Many of the prominent businessmen are commissioned in the reserves, Army or Navy. If war comes, the island would go instantly under military law, and these reserve officers would put on uniforms and help run the city as officers, rather than civilians. That would leave the regular Army free to do nothing but fight.

One thing that mystifies me is that, despite the great importance of the whole island group, there are no fortifications whatever except on this one island of Oahu. Some of the other islands are bigger and, except for the presence of Honolulu, even commercially more important. And they're important, too, for an enemy to establish bases on. Yet they are left wide open. Molokai has one soldier—a sergeant stationed at the airport. The big island of Hawaii has a mere vacation camp, holding about two hundred and fifty officers and men on leave.

One civilian explained to me that because the whole point here is to keep open a naval operating base, the War and Navy Departments feel it the best policy to set up just one "Gibraltar," and concentrate on that.

But Army officers say that in war theory, it would be desirable to have fortifications on the other islands. And even now they are seeing that the commercial airports are being improved sufficiently to serve as possible military fields. But further fortification would take a lot of money—and they haven't got it.

January 27, 1938

Nobody's Excited at Pearl Harbor

honolulu—Pearl Harbor is about ten miles west of downtown Honolulu. It is the only large and really decent harbor in the whole Hawaiian group. They say it could accommodate the entire American Navy all at once.

The harbor is shaped like a hand. The wrist is the entrance, and is very narrow. Inside the entrance are the five fingers, some of them running nearly five miles back into the island. The Navy has some kind of equipment in every one of them.

The Navy yard is the main physical part of the Pearl Harbor base. It's hard to make it look like anything in print. This one is like all the rest, only bigger and better.

They are equipped to do anything here that can be done in any other navy yard. There is an immense dry dock, capable of handling battleships and even the big aircraft carriers.

There are great hangarlike machine shops, and derricks you can see for miles, for lifting heavy machinery out of ships. There is a marine railway, such as you see around yacht clubs for hauling little boats onto shore for the winter. But this marine railway can and does haul out a whole submarine or destroyer onto the bank.

Although there's only one coal-burning ship left in these waters they still maintain the coaling docks and a huge store of coal. In case of war, they'd conscript many coal-burning merchant ships.

And circling the harbor are those scores of famous Teapot Dome oil tanks, full of millions of gallons of fuel oil. While driving among them you merely have to whisper "bomb" to make a Navy man fall out of the car and writhe in the street. They hope to have the tanks underground before a war comes along. . . .

Comparing Pearl Harbor again to a hand, in the center of the palm lies a good-sized island called Ford Island. This is an air base. The Navy uses one side of it, the Army the other side. When the Army's great eighteen-million-dollar Hickam Field is finished, the Army will likely move off and leave Ford Island to the Navy. On Ford Island are quartered all those immense flying boats they've been ferrying out here from California in uncannily perfect mass flights.

The most amazing thing about Pearl Harbor to me is the small number of ships stationed here. There are only a dozen or so submarines, a few destroyers, and some minelayers, small gunboats, and so on. Not a single battleship is stationed here, not a single cruiser. Lately there has been a policy of sending one cruiser at a time over here for overhaul, and occasionally other cruisers do drop in. But as for permanent station here, there's nothing bigger than a destroyer.

The subs and destroyers practice all the time. Every morning the officers and crew come flocking by auto from Honolulu, just like clerks going to work. They hop on their ships, cast loose, and get out into the ocean. The subs take a few minutes' start, and when they get outside they submerge. Then the destroyers nose around and try to find them with their electrical instruments. When they've spotted a sub, they drop a theoretical depth bomb on it.

After the day's play they come back and tie up about three o'clock, and everybody leaps off and goes bounding home to Honolulu in his car, to live just like a civilian the rest of his day and night. It hardly seems like the Navy at all.

Very few people live at Pearl Harbor, for there is a housing shortage. There are, in fact, homes for only a few of the higher officers, and barracks for the submarine men. All the others, even enlisted men from the ships, have to rent places in Honolulu.

The Navy has been trying to get the businessmen of Honolulu interested in a cheap-housing program, since most residences in Honolulu are a little hard on a sailor's pocketbook. I don't know why the Navy doesn't build enough houses and barracks right in the Navy yard.

But in spite of no houses and the war scare, nobody around the Pearl Harbor base seems very excited about anything.

January 28, 1938

HONOLULU— . . . Almost any day you drive around the island you can see, somewhere, a portable antiaircraft outfit banging away at a white target towed behind an airplane offshore. They tell me there is almost no hour of the day or night when an Army unit of some kind is not moving somewhere on the island, practicing or working.

The powerful fixed guns in the waterfront forts are fired only about once a year. But when they are, people who have been through it say it's just like an earthquake. Nearby residents are warned several days ahead of time to get their dishes off the racks and leave their windows open, so the concussion won't break them. . . .

The whole population of Honolulu had a fright last spring during maneuvers. People knew the fleet was soon due in, and that Pacific war games were being held. But there had been no notice in the papers that anything was coming off right at home.

And then suddenly one night the big guns started booming, airplanes by the score roared over the city, searchlights in the crater of Diamond Head streaked their beams far into the sky, soldiers and Army trucks and wheeled guns went dashing all over town like fire departments—and the surprised and shocked people of Honolulu thought for a while that real war had broken out, right in their laps.

*

Civilians don't know what new things are taking place in island fortification. The Army is extremely hush-hush in the last few months. It even refuses to discuss fortification spots that every Japanese farmer on the island knows about.

It is true that nobody on the island knows just what the Japanese people here, as a mass, are thinking. There is a definite sense of distrust of the Japanese in Hawaii.

Civilians say the Army intelligence service has every Japanese agitator spotted and catalogued. It has been written that out at Schofield there is a great bullpen already built, into which Japanese sympathizers will be herded if war ever comes.

But I haven't seen the bullpen. And neither has any of my civilian friends who have lived here many years. Probably there isn't any such thing. But the Army has everything else.

January 31, 1938

THE "RACE PROBLEM"

HONOLULU— . . . The white people in Hawaii hate and fear the Japanese. They mean the Japanese when they speak of the "race problem."

They say no man can tell what the Japanese here are thinking. They say the Japanese aren't becoming Americanized, not even the second generation. They say that in case of war these Japanese would unquestionably be loyal to the Son of Heaven. I've heard a thousand stories:

Of the schoolboy who drew two battleships on the blackboard—one a great big one, which he labeled Japan, and the other a tiny one, labeled United States.

Of the schoolboy who, when asked by his teacher what he wanted to do when he grew up, told her: "Join the Japanese army and fight the United States."

Of the Navy officer's wife who asked her Japanese maid—who had been happily and affectionately with her for several years— what she would do in case of war between us and Japan, and got this reply quick as a wink: "I kill you!"

Of the Japanese yard man who wouldn't do anything his employer told him to, and if scolded for it would always say, "How you expect me understand you? You no speak Japanese!"

And at New Year's holiday time you see the waterfront lined with hundreds of little fishing sampans, and the hundreds of flags flying from their masts are the flag of Japan.

*

Nearly every Japanese-hater has some Japanese among his good friends. But as a general feeling, the white Americans in Hawaii consider the Japanese here insolent, arrogant, mysterious, disloyal, and an increasingly grave problem in the mid-Pacific melting pot. Now for the other side.

A young friend of mine, about fourteen, says his Japanese schoolmates are just as American as he is. He says they think like Occidentals, insist on dressing as we do, and want to eat and dance and play as we do. He says he doesn't even think of them as Orientals.

And you'll hear stories of how rice consumption has dropped off in Hawaii because the Japanese kids don't like the nickname "rice eaters" and refuse to eat the dish of their ancestors.

As for personal experience, I've dealt with dozens of Japanese over here, and I have not seen an instance of discourtesy or insolence. I did, however, see a bunch of Japanese fishermen "hog a patch" from two Hawaiian net fishermen who had discovered a school of fish running near the beach.

February 1, 1938

Home Report

Dana, Indiana
May 1938

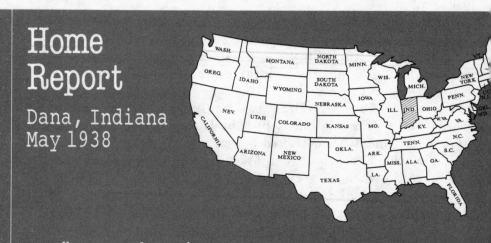

"My mother is not a pampered individual. She doesn't always get what she wants. But she has a way about her."

NO PLACIDITY OF DULLNESS
DANA, INDIANA—Stories about my mother have appeared in this column before. I'm afraid I've made a publicity hound out of her.

For she said last night, and it sounded just like a Washington politician, "I don't want you to write anything about me, but there *are* a lot of people who would like to know how I am."

Of course, I'm joking about my mother's being a publicity hound, but I know what put the thought into her head. At Christmas and Easter she received "Get Well Soon" cards from readers of this column in far distant cities. And once last summer a young couple from the East, touring in this part of the country, dropped in to see her.

Those things touched her, and so she feels that some people who don't even know her are interested in her. Because she's probably right, I'll tell you how she is.

She is up every morning at six. She has her little breakfast, and at six-fifteen she is sitting by the library table, listening to the radio. She sits there till ten-fifteen, when the programs she likes are over. Her favorite is *Mrs. Wiggs' Cabbage Patch.*

I don't know what she does the rest of the day. I guess she just sits on the davenport, or in a chair. Her eyes aren't good enough for reading, and she never read much, anyway. In the afternoon she takes a nap on the sofa. She is usually in bed by eight P.M.

She has had two strokes of apoplexy. For weeks she could not speak. For months she could not move herself in bed. But now she can talk again, slowly, and she can walk short distances if my father or Aunt Mary supports her. Her right arm is useless.

About once a week she spans the hundred yards between the house and the chicken lot to see the little chickens. She takes a ride in the car whenever there's an opportunity. She likes to ride the three miles to Dana and just sit in the parked car, because people stop and talk to her. She went to town on primary day, but they wouldn't let her vote because she couldn't go into the booth alone.

She still likes Roosevelt, and although I didn't ask her, I doubt that she knows there's a war in Spain.* Even if she did, she wouldn't care. Spain is very far away.

My mother comes to the table for meals. She eats only a little, and doesn't care much for that. Her weight is good. All her life she has been a hearty eater, but the disappearance of her appetite is a fortunate thing, for light eating is important now.

*The Spanish Civil War.

Every day when the paper comes, my father or Aunt Mary reads my column to her. I don't think she's much interested in it, but my Aunt Mary thinks it's wonderful, and clips out every one. . . .

*

The finest thing about my mother's partial recovery is her state of mind. She seems to have come to an almost complete placidity—and not a placidity of dullness, either.

At first, she was bitter about being stricken. In the half-delirium after her second stroke, she begged to die. And in months that followed, a lack of interest in life came over her. She would sit all afternoon among visitors and hardly say a word. Her emotions were gone. But now interest and feeling have come to her again. Despondency has left her. She has her sense of humor back. She often gets enormously tickled at something. But with it has come a calmness she didn't have before. She doesn't get excited or upset. She says she doesn't worry, because she can't keep her mind on it long enough.

She is extremely interested in the doings of the neighborhood. She keeps up especially with the younger people, who she has always liked better than older people. The antics of the younger generation never shocked my mother; in fact she considerably approved. She has never grown old or narrow.

It annoys her when old people, with their aches and infirmities, come and complain to her. She makes fun of them, and says she has a right to criticize because she's in the same boat they're in.

My mother doesn't complain of being lonesome. But there must be long hours in her weekdays when Father and Aunt Mary are busy and there's nothing to do but just sit. She wants a little dog to hold on her lap. She speaks of it often, and I believe she wants it as much as any little boy ever wanted a dog.

But there seems to be a division of household opinion on the efficacy of a dog. One side holds that a dog would be too much trouble, and that it might get under Mother's feet and trip her. She disagrees.

A little terrier is available. What the outcome will be I don't know. Personally I am in favor of the dog. But I don't live here, so it's up to the dog-versus-no-dog factions to settle it themselves. My mother is not a pampered individual. She doesn't always get what she wants. But she has a way about her.

May 14, 1938

ERNIE'S FATHER AND PULLMAN "BOOTHS"

DANA, INDIANA—My father has gotten to be quite a man-about-the-country. In fact, you could almost class him as a gadabout.

Last fall he rode clear to the Pacific Coast when my cousin brought my car out to Oregon. They came back on the train by way of the Canadian Rockies. And they still tell a lot of jokes on themselves about the trip.

Neither had been in a Pullman berth before, and their stories about not knowing what to do are good for several years of telling. My father calls them "booths," and I guess they had quite a time with their undressing in such cramped quarters.

Neither of them had ever had a pair of pajamas. Farmers just sleep in their shirts, you know. They saw other people in pajamas and bathrobes, and they didn't know what kind of faux pas they might be committing by sleeping in their shirts.

But my father is now prepared for travel anywhere in the world, by plane, train, or boat. He has bought a pair of pajamas and a little brown zipper bag to carry them in. He has used them once already. He is the Worthy Patron of the local Eastern Star lodge, and recently he was a delegate to the annual convention in Indianapolis. He drove his car, full of women, the seventy-five miles to Indianapolis. He took his pajamas with him, had a nice hotel room for a dollar fifty, and sneaked off and saw two movies. . . .

In a few weeks my father and another man will drive to Bloomington, Illinois, to see the famous American Passion Play. They have their tickets already. They plan to come home the same night, but I see no reason why my father shouldn't take the pajamas along anyway, just in case something turns up.

*

We are disappointed in my father and my cousin as tourists. Last fall we urged them to come back by way of Canada so they could see Lake Louise, which I consider the most beautiful sight I have ever seen. I noticed that he never said much about it in his letters, so when we reached home on this trip I asked him about Lake Louise.

Had they seen it? Yes, they even walked clear to the other end and back. And weren't they impressed by it, by that first breath-taking sight of the blue water and great towering mountain and the white glacier at the far end? No, not expecially. Well, what was the reason? No reason, just weren't impressed. The best thing they saw in the Canadian Rockies was when they got to Banff and went to a movie.

*

My father now has the farm arranged so that he doesn't have to work so hard. He has gotten rid of all the hogs and sheep and most of the cows. In fact, the only fauna on the place are two cows, two hundred and forty-six little chickens, and a few wild-eyed cats. My father is very proud of his poultry. He bought two hundred and fifty-one incubator chicks the day they were hatched, and only six have died.

All the farmland is rented out. The field next to the house is in clover, and it's knee-high now and very lush and beautiful, and I went out and walked around in it. Clover is much nicer to walk in when you know you're not the one who has to stack it in the haymow this summer.

My father has built a new white board fence around the barnlot, and has put gravel and ashes in the driveway that slopes up to the garage. For the first time in twenty years on my periodic trips home, I found the brakes on the car working all right.

We have driven around to see many of our old neighbors here, and on Sunday we all went to Dana and had dinner in Frank Kuhn's new restaurant. My mother wanted to sit in the car and eat, because she was ashamed to have to be helped, but we finally persuaded her to go in.

Frank and Leila Kuhns were our closest farm neighbors, and just a few weeks ago they moved into town and started this restaurant. While we were eating they sat around the table with us, and when we were through Leila said she couldn't bear to charge us anything, but we said that would be a fine way to run a restaurant, wouldn't it? And she finally let us pay. The big chicken dinners, just like we have on the farm, cost thirty-five cents apiece.

May 16, 1938

Washington
une 1938

WASHINGTON,
D.C.

> "Our travel is an escape. In the end
> it sums up to the cowardly fact that
> we don't have to stay and face
> anything out."

WASHINGTON— . . . The last time we came in from a year's trip,
we were afraid. We had somehow got it into our heads that
people hated us. It turned out that they didn't; at least they said
they didn't. But it was a strange and frightening reaction, and
it left its mark on us.

Hence, as we drove into Washington this time, we studied our
emotions like a couple of psychology professors. And imagine
our surprise to discover that we had no emotions. We weren't
afraid this time. Neither were we elated, excited, or anticipa-
tory. We might almost as well have been driving into Bingham-
ton.

That was the entrance. Then things began to change swiftly.
It suddenly dawned on us that we were back home, among the
people we had lived and slaved and played with for a dozen
years. Within two minutes I was on the telephone.

We found our friends, in the main, doing the same things they
were doing when we saw them last. And it seemed to us now
that they were leading a sort of unnatural life, a narrow life,
encompassed and constricted—full of furious sticking to habit,
dashing day after day to the same places, serious about the same

old things, gay in the same old way, wrapped in the same beguiling fiction that Washington is the whole world.

But then, as we grew accustomed to our homecoming, the little strangenesses wore off, and we ourselves slipped back into their ways, and lived through the days without realizing we were doing just as we used to do, and we decided that the Washington way of life was pretty good after all. . . .

. . . Seriousness has set in upon our old friends. Not the seriousness of self-importance. Not that at all. But the seriousness that steps in as the lightness of youth steps out.

Little worries. New and unthrowable responsibilities. Disappointments. Hopes left behind. Sucesses that turn to gall. Little physical aches and sad little pains of the emotions. It is the days and the days marching across them.

And I do not say that of them critically. Because I hold the world's championship in their weight and class. Footloose and fancy free I am. And yet, I can worry more and age faster in any given half hour than the whole bunch of them put together.

June 25, 1938

AVOIDING THE ASHES OF BOREDOM

NORFOLK, VIRGINIA—Once more we have come and gone from our home city—all in a flurry. Our visits to Washington seem almost like dreams.

When people over the country ask us where we live, we say Washington, D.C. We carry District of Columbia tags on our car. We put down Washington on hotel registers. Yet we really have no home at all.

We have friends all over the map. They're in Denver and San Francisco and New Orleans and St. Paul. But it is in Washington that our friends are massed.

And our visits to Washington are so infrequent and so brief that each one is like a daze that we swim through, and we always leave with a feeling of frustration.

For out of the hurry and tenseness and excitement, our visits can't be what we want them to be. We realize at the end that we have talked to lots of friends, yet individually we have talked to nobody. It isn't our fault, nor our friends' fault.

We are prodigal sons, home for a brief moment, and if we are to see our friends at all we have to see them all at once. It isn't successful. There is no time just to sit down with one alone and say, "All right, now let's talk about old times."

We feel the hurt in ourselves. But we also feel that our friends will gradually come to think we aren't worth bothering with—we are too hectic and ill-composed; we do not conduct ourselves placidly because of haste and many little duties; we are not ourselves.

Always, after we leave Washington, we have a little talk with ourselves, and we visualize the day when disappointment in us will have wearied all our old friends, and we see ourselves eventually returning to Washington with nobody at all to speak to us. . . .

*

The question most frequently asked of us is, "Aren't you getting awfully sick of traveling by now?" The answer is an honest no. And I don't say that braggingly, for it isn't impossible that one of these days we might come to hate the impermanency of constant travel.

But so far, we like it. I've tried to figure out myself why we haven't tired of it. And my conclusion is that our travel is an escape. In the end it sums up to the cowardly fact that we don't have to stay and face anything out.

If we don't like a place, we can move on. If something happens that isn't pleasant, we can leave, and settle it later by letter, or just let it go forever. Stability cloaks you with a thousand little personal responsibilities, and we have been able to flee from them.

But just as important with us, I suspect, is the fact that we can't stay long even in the places we love. As it is, there is no opportunity for lingering disillusionment, no space for intimacy to breed ashes of boredom.

I remember once, years ago, that we loved Arizona so much that when we crossed the Colorado River for the last time, we could hardly talk for the lumps in our throats. We left Hawaii with broken hearts. We can hardly speak of the people of Sun Valley, Idaho, without bubbling over. We hardly dare go to Albuquerque, we hate so badly to leave.

And we still love all those places because, you see, we always had to leave before the sweet taste turns to vinegar. . . .

October 11, 1938

BOOK THREE

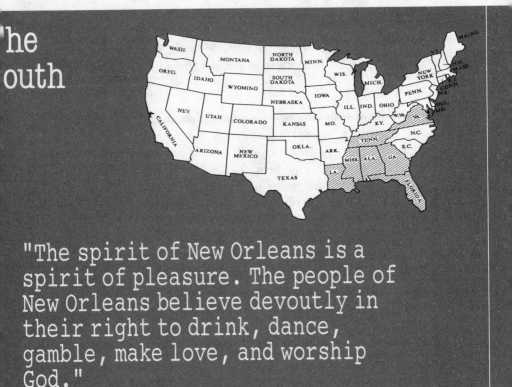

"The spirit of New Orleans is a
spirit of pleasure. The people of
New Orleans believe devoutly in
their right to drink, dance,
gamble, make love, and worship
God."

VIRGINIA

THE MUSICIAN ENGINEER

NEWPORT NEWS, VIRGINIA—The trouble with Ellis Edmunds is
that he doesn't get the same locomotive every night. If he had
his own locomotive all the time, he could do much better than
he does. But he does pretty well at that.

Mr. Edmunds is known all over this part of Virginia for his
ability to play tunes with a locomotive whistle. He puffs along
between Newport News and Richmond, playing "Auld Lang
Syne" at one crossing and "Lead Kindly Light" at the next, and
practices between crossings on "The Old Spinning Wheel." He
almost drives people crazy.

"If I had my own engine all the time, I could get the whistle just right, and could keep in practice," Mr. Edmunds says. "But we work out of a pool, and may have a different engine every night. Once in a while the whistle will be just right, but sometimes you get a whistle the devil himself couldn't play a tune on."

*

Mr. Edmunds has been a railroader all his life. He was born at Wytheville, in southwestern Virginia, and started firing on the railroad when he was seventeen. That was thirty-three years ago. He's been an engineer for twenty-six years. He works for the C&O. In the summer he throttles the potato train between here and Richmond—every night a whole trainload of nothing but potatoes.

He was smashed up in a wreck in 1912. His engine was standing still, and he was out oiling it, when another one came along, jumped the track, and smacked into him.

Mr. Edmunds has been playing tunes with the whistle ever since he can remember. It isn't as easy as it sounds, either. It takes a lot of practice to do it right, and most engineers can't do it at all. But Mr. Edmunds is so good that for the last three years the city fathers of Newport News have had him get an engine out in the yards and play tunes on New Year's Eve, at midnight. You could hear it a mile away, and the whole city listened.

Unfortunately, Mr. Edmunds has the habit of practicing his art at night, and when he's going through a town. A lot of people can't appreciate it. He's always getting stern typewritten memos from the company, saying they've had some more complaints, and if he doesn't cut it out they're going to fire him. So he lays off till the fuss blows over, and then starts playing again. Once in a while he gets a fan letter.

Once, several years ago, he was steaming through a Virginia village on a Sunday night, playing "In the Sweet Bye and Bye" on his locomotive whistle. He heard later that the preacher in the church stopped the choir, and they all listened till the engine was out of hearing.

Mr. Edmunds has a natural ear for music. He plays the piano, and doesn't know one note from another. He also plays the French harp like nobody's business, and says he's not bad on the Hawaiian guitar. . . .

*

Firemen don't mind engineer Edmunds playing with the whistle, he says. In fact, most of them like it. They'll say: "Come on, now, you haven't played for a long time. Let's have a tune."

His standbys are "The Old Oaken Bucket," "Sweet Bye and Bye," "Auld Lang Syne," and "Missouri Waltz." I forgot to ask him if he plays "The Wreck of the Old 97." He can't do much with jazz music. The most recent piece he has touched is "The Old Spinning Wheel." He played that for me on the harmonica, too. He can really make it hop on the harmonica.

February 13, 1936

FRED COCK, HARBOR PILOT

NEWPORT NEWS, VIRGINIA—During the World War, a German submarine torpedoed and sank the Diamond Shoals lightship, off the coast of Norfolk, Virginia.

The submarine skipper put the distressed American sailors into a boat, handed them a Norfolk newspaper of the day before, and sent them safely ashore. How the submarine captain got that newspaper was one of the mysteries of the war.

A couple of years later, one of the regular harbor pilots here was easing a German freighter across Hampton Roads into her berth. Suddenly the German skipper, standing on the bridge beside him, said: "I was in Norfolk during the war."

The pilot, amazed, said: "How did you get to Norfolk during the war?"

"Why, I sank the Diamond Shoals lightship," the skipper replied. "We pulled in close to Virginia Beach the night before, and I came ashore in a small boat, and went to a movie in Norfolk. After the movie I rowed back out to the sub, and the next morning we torpedoed the lightship. Sure, I remember giving them the Norfolk newspaper."

*

Of course, a harbor pilot doesn't bump into a yarn like that every day, but the pilots do meet a lot of interesting people. Take Captain Fred Cock, for instance. He's been meeting ships from across the oceans out at Cape Henry, and guiding them through the Hampton Roads channels into their berths at Norfolk and Newport News, for forty-six years.

He's been on so many ships and knows so many captains he couldn't begin to count them. And yet he's been across the ocean only once. That was in 1900, when he went to Europe on a vacation. He never has been to sea as a sailor. He still lives in the house he was born in, at Hampton.

It takes a staff of forty-two pilots to move the fifteen hundred ships in and out of Hampton Roads each year. Few of the pilots have ever been to sea. Most of them, like Captain Cock, started right here as apprentice pilots. They are turned out at any hour of the night, and in all kinds of weather, to bring ships in. But they have pretty nice jobs at that. They're off three or four days between each trip, and if they behave they have lifetime jobs.

*

Captain Cock is sixty-two, and has snowy hair. But he's still bringing them in on his turn. Right now he's sitting at a desk in the pilot's office, directing the others. But it's just while somebody is sick. He doesn't like desk jobs.

He's a huge, jolly man, and when he speaks he yells. He kids everybody, and when pilots' wives call up to ask when their husbands will be home, he tells them they're stuck on a mud bank and won't get off for a week.

During the war, but before we got into it, Captain Cock was taking his turn out at Cape Henry one morning when a German submarine, the *Deutschland*, showed up to be piloted up the bay to Baltimore. Some people might not have known what to do, but Captain Cock sent her right up to Baltimore, just as the skipper wanted. He was called on the carpet for it; but he told them the submarine skipper had papers as a commercial vessel, and the papers were made out correctly, so who was he to be stopping a ship with proper papers? He was right, too. The sub fueled at Baltimore, and was allowed to take to the sea again. Two British and one French cruiser were waiting for her at Cape Henry, but they never saw her leave.

*

When Captain Cock started piloting ships into Hampton Roads, most of them were sailing vessels. He hasn't seen a sailing ship in three years. Nobody else thinks so, but Captain Cock believes sailing ships will come back. He says steam vessels are getting too expensive to operate, and there's a lot of cargo that isn't in that big a hurry.

The ice has been pretty bad in Hampton Roads this winter, but nothing like what it was in the past. Three times during Captain Cock's career it has been so cold that he walked on the ice from shore to his ship. He's been lucky about bad weather. In fact, the piloting force in Hampton Roads has lost only one man in its entire history. He was one of the pilot's crew, who drowned when their small transfer boat capsized one stormy night.

The little finger on Captain Cock's right hand is gone. I had visions of some adventurous struggle with a storm-bogged freighter, or maybe even a fight with an East Indian skipper. "No," said Captain Cock. "Years ago I was monkeying with my rowboat at home, and stepped on a stick, and it flew up and mashed my finger against the boat."

February 14, 1936

TENNESSEE

AHEAD OF THE NIGHT
IN A MOUNTAIN VILLAGE—Falling snow is a beautiful thing almost anywhere. But when snow comes falling on a dark day down into the deep and narrow valleys of the Cumberland Mountains—as it does frequently and with an awful immensity—there is about it not only beauty but a strange fearfulness.

Somehow you feel that snow and low clouds and mountains and darkness are all coming down upon you, and this is the end of everything, and there will never be sunlight or another day.

*

The Cumberland Mountains start in central Tennessee and run northeastward up through the corner of Kentucky and on into Virginia. In a car you can make a circle and touch all three states in one afternoon and never be out of the Cumberlands.

They are beautiful, even in the leaflessness of winter. They are not immense, like the Rockies; nor regimented in strips, like the Blue Ridge; nor equipped with vast vistas, like the San Jacinto in California. They are indeed none of these, but a terrific serration, like measles.

*

The valleys are narrow, very seldom more than a city block wide at the bottom. The hills rise sharply on either side. They are covered with trees, and great ledges of rock strata protrude.

The valleys are crooked. You can't see far in the bottom of a Cumberland valley, for it always makes a turn just a little way ahead. Usually there is a stream in the valley, and the road winds along the stream; you see hillside corn patches, and log cabins and old barns, and now and then you pass through a village.

Always in the Cumberlands you must raise your head to see
the sky, for all around, everywhere, are peaks. But in snowtime
the peaks are missing. They vanish in gray mist that reaches
down their sides and propels itself across the valleys to the other
peaks, making a ceiling that closes you in.

*

The snow starts in Virginia. For a few minutes it falls timidly,
feeling its way. The big wet flakes float down slowly, and they
stand out sharply against the dark background of forested hillside.

Then it becomes a cold encompassing flood. Where there
were two flakes, now there are thousands. Half the atmosphere
must be snow. The flakes change direction, from vertical to
horizontal, and come head-on like rushing atoms.

Swiftly as a tropical dusk, the light goes out of the valleys.
Twilight comes in midafternoon. Mountain cabins are dim
things through a downward-sliding screen. Trees and hillsides
and sheds and fences accumulate a covering of gray. And you
feel the darkness, as surely as you feel the cold.

And you know the foreboding, the sense of an impending end
to all things. Through your mind run, over and over, the dark
lines: "The shades of night were falling fast, when through an
Alpine village passed, a youth . . ."

Men chop wood in their barnyards, frantically, as though
stopping a leak in a dike. Horses stand in fence corners, tails to
the snow, but ears alert, as if listening for doom around the
bend. Workmen speed homeward, before it is too late. Life
rushes to get in ahead of the night. Soon there is no movement
in the valley—only the snow, and lonesomeness, and a feeling
of being all alone in a land of strange forces, and an intuition
that something will happen.

You don't imagine some specific things that might happen,
nothing so material as a wreck or a murder, but something
unreal and vaguely sinister. You want to speed, faster and faster.

*

That's what a blizzard in a Cumberland mountain valley does
to a tenderfoot. The people there, I suppose, don't feel that way
about it at all.

And in my own case, of course, nothing happened. I am here
tonight in the room of a little inn, in a mountain village, and I
feel so superior and safe. The radiator sizzles and the electric

lights shine. Snow and darkness and doom can't come in here. But it was a narrow escape—from fear.

December 26, 1935

"A Fox Has Never Got Away from Me"

OZONE, TENNESSEE—You've never heard of J. W. Hickey, trapper, fur tanner, and superbusinessman of Ozone, Tennessee? Then let me tell you about him.

We were driving down across Tennessee toward Alabama, and we got up in the Crab Orchard Mountains, where it is rough and woodsy, and snowy, and we began seeing little places along the road, right out there in the open, where men were selling fox furs.

They'd have a pole stuck in the ground, with a crossbar on it, and a dozen or so fox furs hanging from the crossbar. We saw eight or ten of these places in a couple of miles, and even though I've been all around the country, I'd never seen anything like that before.

So we pulled up at the next one, and a man came out of a log cabin across the road, and I said to him, "I don't want to buy any furs, but I'm a newspaperman and I'd like to find out what this roadside fur business is about."

Whereupon the man said: "Well, sir, you can write that J. W. Hickey of Ozone, Tennessee, was the first man to sell furs on the roadside, absolutely the first man. . . ."

"J. W. Hickey," I said. "Is that so?"

"Absolutely the first," the man said, and then in a lowered tone: "*I* am J. W. Hickey!"

*

Mr. Hickey is forty-five, and has shot forty-eight wild turkeys in his life and six deer. He wears a big square fur cap, made of muskrat furs. He wears corduroy pants wrapped down into leather boots, with overshoes over them. It snowed seven inches here the day before we came through.

Mr. Hickey was born here in these mountains. He farmed and trapped a little, as they all do. Then one day he signed up for a correspondence course in fur-cutting and taxidermy from a school in Omaha. "But you can leave that out," Mr. Hickey said. "That might sound sort of funny."

After he learned to cure his own furs, he started selling them on trains. I thought he meant selling them to passengers on trains, but Mr. Hickey meant that he rode on trains from one town to another, and then got off and sold the furs in town. "Banks were the best places," he says. "You go into a bank with a bunch of furs, and everything stops."

That was eighteen years ago. Mr. Hickey has been at it ever since. But it wasn't until about six years ago, when a new highway went through here, that he got the roadside idea. He has five stands now, and a few other fellows have a couple apiece. The competition nearly worries him to death, but he's still the biggest.

*

Mr. Hickey has a line of traps of his own, and he also buys from the mountaineers for fifty miles around. He catches about fifteen foxes a year himself, and buys about a hundred and fifty grays and four hundred reds from the other trappers.

The day I was there he had caught six skunks and one fox toe. "But I found his tracks in the snow," he said, "and I'll get him tomorrow. You can put in your piece that a fox has never got away from me. Never a one."

Mr. Hickey also finds such things as possums, coons, weasels, mink, and rabbits in his traps. And if he's anything like me, when I used to be a trapper, he occasionally finds a good big tomcat.

*

Mr. Hickey starts trapping and curing skins during the middle of November. He and his wife and one daughter and son-in-law work like blazes all winter long, curing fox furs. It takes so long to run his traps sometimes that he gets behind and then has to work far into the night on his furs.

He can take a raw skin and have it ready to go around a woman's neck in six days. He has labels bearing his name that he attaches to each fur. "There's a Hickey label around some woman's neck on the streets of every big city in this country," he says. "You just watch the labels." . . .

Mr. Hickey has seven fine children, and he's made enough money selling fox furs to build himself a big new house. He sells about three furs a week at each stand. And then people way off somewhere will see the label on some friend's neckpiece, and write him for one. He has sent them to every state in the Union.

At the roadside, you can get a good gray fox for ten or twelve dollars. You might get a not-so-nice one for seven dollars. Red foxes run from fifteen to twenty dollars. Mr. Hickey also has a few assorted mink skins and dyed lynx cats hanging around, but foxes are his specialty.

Personally, I wouldn't know a fox skin from a polar bear's, but the Girl who rides with me said Mr. Hickey had some fine furs there.

I was climbing into the car. "If you scatter my name all over the country," Mr. Hickey said, "maybe I'll send you a present."

I'm scattering.

December 26, 1935

MISS ALICE AND HER SCHOOL

ROGERSVILLE, TENNESSEE—The schoolhouse is fifteen miles from a town, out near Stone Mountain, at the end of Little Poor Valley.

It's made of logs. It isn't finished yet. Two rooms are occupied now, but when it's all done there will be five, and an auditorium. There are seventy-eight mountain boys and girls here, all of them poor, most of them ragged, many in overalls, even girls.

But what a school! You've heard of these modern private schools in the cities whose object is to encourage the child to think, and use his individuality, instead of making him a copyist. Well, they're doing the same thing in this log school back in the Tennessee mountains. I shouldn't say *they're* doing it; I should say *she's* doing it—Miss Alice Sturm, I mean.

*

Six-and-a-half years ago, Miss Alice, as she's known, showed up down here from Cleveland. She had a master's degree, and a set of personal circumstances that forced her permanently into these parts. So she nosed around and discovered twenty-five children who had never been to school, because there wasn't a school near enough.

Miss Alice started a school. She held classes every afternoon in an old empty store. She had forty pupils—twenty-five kids and fifteen parents. She had a mother and seven children who couldn't read or write.

In 1930 the county made it an official school. Miss Alice has been the teacher ever since, and she's a lot more than teacher. She's an entrepreneur. She has fought and harangued and begged and bustled about until she has achieved this fine log school. They don't know when it will be finished. The school,

like all the people, needs money terribly. But they're doing
mighty well with what they have.

*

When we walked up on the porch, the teacher came out and
got us. As we went inside, children rushed up with chairs for
us. A little boy jumped up and put more coal on the stove.

It didn't look like any schoolroom I ever saw. A mountaineer
workman was up on a scaffold, mud-cementing between the logs
in the wall. A mountaineer mother, school-visiting, was sitting
at a table with her hat and coat on, just watching. Boys in the
back of the room were sawing and pounding, at their manual
training.

There were about forty children, most of them girls. Some of
them were dressed nicely enough, but many were ragged. Their
shoes were worn out, and it was cold and snowy outside.

Miss Alice sat down and told us about the school. Right out
loud, with the children listening, just as if we were at home. The
teacher wasn't on edge, and the children weren't scared, as in
my school days when visitors came. They sat and looked at us,
their faces friendly, and eager and proud.

*

Miss Alice told a girl to get something. She brought a stack
of cardboards, each with a watercolor Christmas scene on it. We
looked and admired. That started a flood. Other children
brought theirs for us to see. I'll bet we looked at two hundred
Christmas scenes. They were excellent.

Then we saw compositions. Each was done up in a folder,
with the author's name on the front. Beautiful handwriting
inside—and outside such scrollwork as you never saw.

The girls showed us a bookstand the boys had made. We saw
beautifully colored maps. The children know about [the war in]
Ethiopia back in these hills.

These kids are smart. They like to learn. Miss Alice makes
learning something to be eager for, instead of a task. The children are free in the schoolroom. They talk to each other when
they want to. They walk around. Noise doesn't bother them.
They are at home here. If they want to write their names with
great curlicues on the end, that's all right. If they want to draw
Santa skinny, that's all right. For all Miss Alice knows, maybe
Santa is skinny.

The kids adore Miss Alice. And the funny part of it is, she's
no young squirt with a bunch of newfangled ideas, either. But

she has a lot of common sense. You can tell by looking at her from a quarter of a mile away that she's a schoolteacher.

*

The children from the other room came in and piled along the wall. Then the whole bunch sang a song for us. Seventy-eight of them, ragged and proud to be performing. Then a stunted little ragamuffin in overalls, with a little old-mannish face— malnutrition, the teacher whispered to us—stood up in front and, grinning at us, sang "Jesus Loves Me."

As we were leaving, there were two little girls with holly and mistletoe. They had slipped out back on the hillside and picked it for us. You have to have a hard heart, like mine, to stand the hospitality of Little Poor Valley.

December 27, 1935

IS FRANK MURPHY CRAZY?

MEMPHIS—Being a roving reporter teaches you one thing: he who laughs too long and loud at other people is liable to get sand in his mouth.

The more you travel around and see all sorts of people, the less inclined you are to stand up on a dais and look down at anybody, and laugh at him. Because he may be looking up, laughing at you.

Take this story about Frank Murphy, for instance. A few years ago, when I was smart guy and knew everything, I could have written a mighty clever piece about Frank. But today I hardly know what to write, for at the moment I still haven't figured out whether it's Frank who's crazy, or me—or maybe both of us.

*

Frank Murphy is an old man—seventy-six, he says. He is tall and thin, and not very clean, and he has a bushy gray beard, and gray eyes that stare out through horn-rimmed spectacles. His wife died fifty years ago. He hasn't anybody in this world.

Frank Murphy is a squatter. He lives just behind the city dump, right on the bank of the Mississippi. His home, and everything he has, and his whole livelihood, come out of the city dump. He culled old auto hoods out of the dump, and pounded them out flat, and built himself a mansion of them.

It isn't one of those wobbly shantytown shacks, either. It's straight and solid. His doors close snugly. His windows are tight. No rain or wind can get in. His house doesn't lean. It has four small rooms, and is fairly clean, and so full of homemade furniture and sundry trinkets you can hardly move around.

Murphy comes pretty close to being self-sufficient. He doesn't ask anything of anybody. He makes his own living, and no man has to help him. He gets old tin pans and kettles out of the dump and repairs them. He takes pieces of steel and files them down into butcher knives. All these things he peddles to housewives. "If they're too poor to buy them, I just give them away," he said. When he has enough for a few days' groceries, he doesn't peddle anymore. For he has many other things to do. He has a lot of painting and inventing to do, for instance.

He has something that's going to be a perpetual-motion machine. He showed it to us. It's just the rim of an old Ford steering wheel. He keeps it hanging on a nail in the ceiling. He has the whole thing figured out, except the one little item of how to keep it going. But things have a way of coming to him in the night, and he'll wake up with it some morning, he says. He's going to let me know.

But his housepainting is what captivated me. His house is daubed all over—not solid, or striped, but just daubed, like a speckled chicken, and in every color of the rainbow. I asked him why he painted it that way. He said so strangers would think he was crazy and wouldn't come near. But it worked out just the opposite. People came nosing around just to look at it.

He does his painting at night. He used to paint in the daytime, but then he stumbled into this night-painting idea a short time ago. He paints in the dark so he can't see what he's doing. Then the next morning he jumps up and runs out to see what it looks like. "And every time," he said, "I think it looks pretty." I thought it did, too.

"Do you want to see my house change color?" he asked. I said sure. So he ran back into the house, and after a while the panel alongside the front door started sliding back and forth, and sure enough it was changing color. There were slats in front of the panel, and right behind the slats he had painted the panel a different color, so that when he slid the panel back and forth, you could see the part behind the slats. He's going to put a little windmill on the roof, and hook it up through some Rube Goldberg arrangement to the panel, so that the wind will keep the panel going back and forth all the time, and won't strangers think that's funny?

He has a picture of Joan Crawford hanging on his porch. And in the house he has a self-portrait he did by looking into the mirror. Up by the window are a couple of great big slingshots. When people get to nosing around, he lets them have it, and they jump and never know where the rock came from.

Frank is a little weird about details. He says he's been living here "four or five years, ever since 1916." He comes from the "old country," from an island off the coast of Iceland. He thinks he has a son, but hasn't heard of him in fifty years.

So there you are. There are a lot of laughs in Frank's place, but I didn't laugh any.

After all, why not paint in the dark? It looks a lot better than some daytime painting I've seen in art galleries. And how many of us could make something, or paint something, and then when we sneaked out next morning to see how it looked, always have it look pretty to us? And am I laughing at the old Ford steering wheel that's going to be a perpetual-motion machine? I am not. There are a lot of things that would surprise me more than to find that wheel going around and around by itself one of these days. And what's wrong with making your house change color? I'll bet *you* can't make your house change color.

I wonder, yes I wonder very much, if when I'm seventy-six years old I will be able to build a house with my own hands, and paint pictures that look pretty to me, and have time pass pleasantly, and have to depend on no man in this world for company or the necessities of life. And if I should find myself so blessed, I'll consider myself a hell of a long way from being crazy. Wouldn't you?

June 15, 1936

JOHN CLAYBROOK AND SON

MEMPHIS—The most overpowering thing I have ever seen in a human being is the determination of John Claybrook to make his son exactly like himself.

John Claybrook is a Negro. He is a self-made man. He is rich. He is proud. He is somewhat pious. He considers himself the outstanding example of what a hardworking, right-living Negro can do in this world.

He owns twelve hundred acres of land across the river in Arkansas, and various logging contracting companies, and has a town house in Memphis, and deals with all the biggest banks here.

When he was a child he ran away from his home in Florence, Alabama, and started working on the docks. He knew as soon as he started that he was going to succeed. He knew he was a better man than other men. He knew he worked harder, gave his employer more. And if he didn't get a raise, he quit and went elsewhere. Never in his life has he made a change for the worse. Always it has been upward.

John married when he was twenty. He had never been to school, so his wife taught him his ABCs. He can't read or write very well today, although he can sound out a piece in the paper if there's no one around to read it to him. But figures? Ah, figures are terms for money, and figures came easily for him. He can do figures in his head. He never has to think twice to toss the numerals of a transaction around in his mind.

John Claybrook was born to save his money. Prodigality to him is a sin. He went into the logging business for himself. He acquired land. His savings grew into a pile, and the pile into a fortune. But his wealth put no flossy ideas in his head. He lives well today, but without color or display.

Middle age approached, and his money, and his piety, and his pride in his own success accumulated with his years. Then his wife died, and he married again. He was past forty-five when his only son was born. I don't know whether it was an obsession right from the start or not, this determination to shape his son in his own image. I imagine it just sort of grew on him. But today it is overwhelming.

The boy is twenty now. John is sixty-six. He is still as sound as an oak tree. He can still do a day's cotton chopping in the field, although he seldom does. He devotes his time to overseeing, and to the multifarious task of making the son worthy of the father.

The boy was inclined to be a little wild. He liked fun, and didn't care for work. John sent him away to school, in Alabama. But that didn't last long. John made him wash his own clothes at school, to teach him frugality. The other boys would say, "If my dad were as rich as yours, I wouldn't be washing my own clothes." John heard about that. So that's what a boy learns at school?

John took him out before it was too late. That was four years ago. He brought him back to the Arkansas farm, and put him to work in the fields. He paid him regular hired hand's wages, and made him drink out of the same water jug the hands used, so he wouldn't get the idea he was better than hired hands.

But that wasn't all. John evened things up for the boy. In school he had been crazy about athletics. So John built him a stadium on the farm, and bought him a ball team—actually bought him a baseball team. The whole thing cost him three or four thousand dollars. That pro ball team is known all over the South today. Five of the players work on John's farm. The others are just straight ballplayers, hired by John.

That worked for a while. But the boy was wild. His father was a straitjacket, always teaching him, always telling him something, always disciplining him. They couldn't get along. Four times in four years they have broken up, and the boy left home. But each time he has come back. A year or so ago he got married. The boy asked his father about it. John didn't know the girl. He told the boy to bring her over from Memphis.

The three of them sat on the porch all evening, and talked about it. "If you're the right girl for John, it would make me happier than anything in the world," John Sr. told her. "But how do I know you're the right girl?" They talked and talked. Finally, he gave his consent. "But remember this," he told her. "You're marrying John Claybrook, Jr., and not John Claybrook, Sr. You won't live on my money. You'll live on what he makes."

It didn't work. John is getting his son a divorce soon. That is one of the many blows he has had to take. But the boy is starting to come around. He's showing an interest in the farm. He's developing. John has started to take him around to the banks in Memphis, to introduce him to his bankers. He has started to teach him to think like a businessman.

The fight isn't over yet. But John Claybrook sees enough progress to encourage him. A little incident full of meaning happened the other day. John told me about it. He and his wife had left the plantation over Sunday for a little trip. They got back, unexpectedly, about two o'clock Sunday afternoon. All the hands, of course, had Sunday off.

"We drove up in the driveway," John said. "We thought the boy would be dressed up and sitting on the porch. But he wasn't. I looked around, and finally I saw him. He was out in the field. He had on his overalls, and he was down on his knees, scratching the ground with his hands, to see how the cotton was coming up. It made me so happy I just had to shed tears, right there."

June 18, 1936

THE STORY OF CASEY JONES' LAST RIDE

MEMPHIS—I suppose the most famous railroad engineer who ever pulled a throttle was John Luther Jones, better known as Casey.

Nearly everybody in America has sung that song—how Casey "mounted to his cabin with his orders in his hand, and took his farewell trip to that promised land."

Casey Jones was a real person who was actually killed in a train wreck. His widow is still alive, and so is his fireman, who went through the wreck with him.

I've just had a long talk with Casey's fireman. His name is Sim Webb. He's a colored man who lived here in Memphis at the time of the wreck and who lives here today.

The wreck happened at Vaughan Station, in Mississippi, nearly thirty-seven years ago, at eight minutes till four, just before daylight, on the morning of May 1, 1900.

Sim Webb can tell you the exact minute of nearly every mile of that last wild ride of Casey's. He has told it so many times that he reels off stations and minutes and speeds with the sureness of a mental calculator.

Sim was twenty-six at the time, and Casey Jones was thirty-two. Sim had been firing for Casey only four months. They were pulling a fast passenger train, on a run of a hundred and eighty miles from Memphis to Canton, Mississippi.

They were due out of Memphis at eleven-thirty P.M., but on that fatal night the connecting train was delayed and they were an hour and a half getting out. But "Mr. Casey" was in high spirits that night, so Sim poured on the coal, Casey bent the throttle back, and they boiled south through the night, making up time. So fast did they go that when they hit the freight a hundred and seventy-six miles out of Memphis, with just twelve miles to go, they were running only two minutes behind time.

Somewhere around a quarter to four, with the cab a bedlam of noise and rushing air, and the miles clicking off every fifty seconds or better, Casey looked at his watch, and stood up and yelled across the boiler top to Sim. He said, "Sim, the old girl's got her high-heeled slippers on tonight." Those were his last words.

The wreck wasn't Casey's fault. It was the fault of the freight train that had taken the siding, leaving several cars sticking out onto the main line.

"We were going around a double-S curve," Sim Webb said.

"We had taken the curve on Mr. Casey's side, and then we swung around so the curve was on my side.

"All of a sudden I saw a caboose ahead of us. Mr. Casey couldn't see it from his side. I jumped up and yelled, 'Look out, we're gonna hit something!' I never heard him say anything. I just know he stood up, and I heard him kick the seat out from under him.

"I grabbed the handrail and swung myself down and out of the cab. I held to the rail till I was almost down to the ground, and then let go. Just missed a cattle gate by that far. I hit the ground at seventy-five miles an hour. When I woke up I was in the hospital.

"The engine went clear through the caboose, through a car of corn, through a car of hay, and stopped in a car of lumber. The engine stayed on the track. It was stripped clean—cab and everything stripped off. They found Mr. Casey's body in the clear, lying on the ground by the back trucks. Every bone was broken. Mr. Casey was a fine man."

*

As soon as he was out of the hospital, Sim went back to firing on the same run. He went through another bad wreck in 1918. It was during flood time, and a trestle gave way and the locomotive toppled off and fell on its side into the river.

The engineer was thrown clear, but Sim went under with the engine. Somehow he managed to fish his way out of the cab, and to the top. He had a cigar stub in his mouth when they left the tracks, and it was still in his mouth when he came up.

His family kept at him to quit the railroad, so in 1919 he gave in and became a bricklayer. In his new, safe trade a wall caved in on him, covered him with six feet of rock, broke his leg, and put him in the hospital for two months.

Sim Webb is sixty-two now. He is tall and slender, and his skin is light brown. His kinky hair is grayish, but his face is thin and young-looking. His English is excellent—he doesn't even have the Negro accent. He is a happy, good-natured man.

Casey Jones' widow lives at Jackson, Tennessee, about eighty miles from here. Last November, Sim happened to be up there, so he went around to see her. "I was just going to stay a minute," he said, "but we got to talking about railroads and old times, and she kept me there two hours."

Sim said, "I made a mistake quitting the railroad, but I'm too old to get back on. I've done pretty well, though. I've seen hard times, but I never turn down anything honest, and we've managed to get along."

I asked Sim if he was a religious man. He misunderstood and thought I said a *careless* man. He said, "Well no, I wouldn't say I was a careless man. I've got my faults, yes sir, I've got my faults. I'll take a drink now and then, and I'm not perfect.

"But I go to church, and I've got three grown daughters and one of them has thirteen children, and I've still got the same wife I started out with. That's something to write about. We've never had but one quarrel. It was my fault. I was young and I got to liking some of the girls at the other end of the line, and she found out about it. But that's the only time we've ever had a sharp word. And it's going on thirty-nine years now."

January 29, 1937

A FORMER SLAVE REMEMBERS

KNOXVILLE, TENNESSEE—William Andrew Johnson is a happy old man with a distinction. He is, so far as he knows, the only living ex-slave of a President. He's mighty proud of it.

William is seventy-nine. He was freed when he was still a boy, yet his whole attitude toward life was molded by the fact that he was born into slavery.

I sat in the back of a Knoxville restaurant and had a long talk with William. He has all his faculties, despite his age. He hears well and sees well, and his mind works quickly. He is good-humored and feels kindly toward everything.

"My mother was a good-looking woman," William said. "Her owner sold her at a big auction at Greeneville, Tennessee. She looked around the crowd of buyers before the auction started, and she saw Andrew Johnson and liked his looks.

"So she went up to him and asked him if he wouldn't buy her. He bid her in for five hundred dollars. And he bought my uncle, her brother, for five hundred forty dollars.

"I hadn't been born yet when that happened. I was born into slavery under Andrew Johnson. When I was little, Mr. Andrew used to hold me on one knee and my sister on the other, and he'd rub our heads and laugh." William chuckled to himself when he told me that.

"One day Mrs. Johnson called us all in and said we were free now. She said we were free to go, or we could stay if we wanted to. We all stayed.

"I was only seven when Mr. Andrew was President, and I never went to Washington with him. But after he came back from Washington I was with him all the time. I slept right in the same room with him. He was elected senator, but he died before he could get back to Washington. He died in 1875, when I was seventeen.

"I used to sit by the side of his bed day and night. He was paralyzed on one side. He would reach over with his good arm and take hold of his wrist and say, 'Is that your hand, William?' And I'd say, 'No, Mr. Andrew, that's your own hand.' You see, he couldn't feel his own hand."

When Andrew Johnson died, he left a house and some land to his ex-slaves, and there they lived until William's mother died. William came to Knoxville many years ago. He never married, and he has no relatives at all now. He has made his living mostly as a cook, and even today at seventy-nine he cooks in a restaurant here. Andrew Johnson's granddaughter, Mrs. Margaret Johnson Patterson, comes down from Greeneville occasionally. And first thing, she always comes into the restaurant where William works, and he cooks her a meal just the way she wants it, and then comes out and serves it to her himself.

William has seen some hard times. A few years ago, a Knoxville reporter who knows him well wrote a story saying it looked as if William would have to go to the poorhouse. The woman who owns the restaurant where he works threw a fit. William quoted her as saying, "Do you think I'd ever let that old man go to the poorhouse? William needn't worry about the poorhouse as long as I'm here."

"White folks have been awful good to me," William said. I asked him if he wasn't better off when Andrew Johnson owned him than since then. He said, "Yes, we were mighty well off then. But any man would rather be free than be a slave. Some of us had fine masters, and we were better off. But some had awful masters."

*

William had a keen disappointment last spring. President Roosevelt came to Knoxville to dedicate Norris Dam. William got it into his head that he wanted to shake hands with the President and tell him he was once a slave of a President. William thought President Roosevelt might be agreeable to shaking hands with him.

So he went to some of his white friends—some big men in the

Chamber of Commerce—and asked them if they would fix it up. They told William they would try, but they didn't think anything could be done. Later they reported back that such a thing was impossible. William was upset about it.

Of course it wasn't impossible at all. William should have known better than to ask a Chamber of Commerce man. He should have asked a newspaperman. If my idea of the President is correct, the whole thing would have been as simple as this: a reporter would have told the President that William wanted to shake hands with him, and the President would have said sure, and they would have brought William up, and the President would have pumped his old brown hand and given him a big smile, and in all this world there wouldn't have been a happier or prouder mortal than William Andrew Johnson, the old slave man.

February 3, 1937

POSTSCRIPT: *President Roosevelt read Pyle's column about William in the* Washington Daily News *and arranged to have the old man brought to Washington, where the former slave shook the President's hand, received the keys to the city, had a private talk with the President, and received from Roosevelt a handsome walking stick. Pyle told his readers it was "the happiest I've ever inadvertently made anybody."*

MOONSHINE

NEWPORT, TENNESSEE—The way the government interferes with private business is enough to drive a fellow crazy.

The government moved into these parts and bought a lot of hilly land. Then they signed a paper and proclaimed a proclamation making this land into the Great Smoky National Park, thereby ruining the finest settlement of moonshiners in the United States of America.

Cocke County, in southeastern Tennessee, for twenty years has produced more moonshine than any other county in America. Even with this newfangled government interference, they say Washington still lists it as the moonshiningest county in America.

We didn't get to see any stills in operation, for naturally nobody knows where any are when a stranger's around. But at least they didn't consider us important enough to start setting off the dynamite.

That was the old signal system back in prohibition days. It's still the signal system. One man lies along the one road that leads into the moonshining hills. When a suspicious car goes past, he jerks out his dynamite, throws it into the road, and off she goes.

You can hear the boom for miles around. And a minute or two after the first explosion, great dynamite blasts start going off in the timbered hills, one after another, until the air is so full of noise you can't talk.

That is the signal that carries to the farthest ridge of the highest mountain, and it means "Look out! The revenuers are coming."

*

Newport, the county seat of Cocke County, is a modern little city much like any other modern little city in America. But some fifteen miles away, in the foothills of the Great Smokies, lies what they call the Cosby Section. Cosby is on the map, but you could hardly call it a town. It's just a few houses strung along several miles of road, with a country store or two, and a post office in an old one-room shack. But the Cosby Section bears the honor of being the moonshine capital of America.

Back in prohibition days, hundreds of stills were hidden around the mountain slopes. The agents sometimes captured as many as thirty stills and seventy-five men in one day. Moonshine was selling for twenty dollars a gallon. A thousand gallons—twenty thousand dollars' worth—went over the mountains in trucks every night to Asheville. And Asheville was the small end of the market. Even more than that went to Knoxville, and on up to Kentucky.

But the old days are gone. Repeal, and the new national park, and tighter restrictions on moonshiners' supplies, have pretty well shot the business. Moonshine is down to two dollars a gallon. But still Cocke County holds its lead. The boys told me there were thirty-six stills running in the Cosby section the day of our visit. . . .

*

The moonshine distilled in the mountains today isn't so hot. It's made mostly from sugar, and it will knock your head off. In Knoxville, the Negroes and poor whites drink it almost exclusively. The Negroes call it Splo, which is undoubtedly short for "explosive," and you can get a half pint for fifteen cents.

The famous old mountain corn whiskey, which many a connoisseur still claims is better drinking liquor than the bonded stuff, has almost gone out of existence. It simply takes too long to make, and there is not a market for such a high-class product.

There are anachronisms, here in the hills. For Cocke County, the moonshine capital of the world, just this year voted to keep the county dry! And in the nearby metropolis of Knoxville, prohibition still prevails. A man who wants a drink gets it by the whisper-and-sneak method. . . .

October 15, 1940

REVENUER'S REUNION

COSBY, TENNESSEE—I went into the Cosby moonshining section with a man who has sent scores of its residents to the penitentiary.

He is J. Carroll Cate, until recently high sheriff of Knoxville. For eleven years, from 1921 to 1932, Carroll Cate was with the Internal Revenue Service in this district—in other words, a revenuer.

You'd think a man who had put scores of people behind bars wouldn't be coming back to his old haunts without a little shaking of the knees and a swallow or two in his throat. No such conception of Carroll Cate's return could be further from the truth. I rode all day with Cate, and his visit was actually like a homecoming. People he had sent to prison came out and shook hands and laughed and talked over old times.

We spent most of the day with a former moonshine runner whom Cate had run down and wrecked at seventy miles an hour on a gravel road. Both of them were hurt, and the moonshine runner served two terms in the pen. He is one of the nicest fellows you ever met, and he and Cate are, and have always been, good friends.

We stopped at the home of a woman who was once known as Queen of the Moonshiners. She insisted that we stay for lunch, and said she'd scare up a chicken somewhere and cook it for us. She hadn't seen Cate for a long time, and they were always on opposite sides of the legal fence, but I heard her say to him: "Everybody always liked you up here. You played square with us."

*

This day in the moonshining country gave me a new conception of honor. For one thing, the bulk of the moonshiners aren't criminals at all. They're violating a law, of course, but, as they say, how else can you make a living up here? And you don't find vicious criminals who have genuine respect and friendship for the men who are sending them to the penitentiary right and left.

Later I asked Carroll Cate how he could be on such friendly terms with these people. He said it was partly their sense of the inevitability of things, and partly because he had never double-crossed them. In the old days, he'd meet a fellow on the street who he knew was running moonshine. But, of course, he had to catch him at it. And the fellow took the attitude "Well, catching me is your job, and if you can catch me then it's just my tough luck and your good luck, and no hard feelings about it."

But the main thing, according to Cate, was to tell the truth when the case came to court. If you testified to something the men knew was a lie, just to get a conviction, then your name was mud.

*

We sat alongside the road in Cosby for an hour, talking with people who had been moonshiners or liquor runners. They were complaining that the Cosby was almost dried up. "Practically everybody's in the penitentiary," they said. . . .

There are three federal agents stationed in this district now. The people refer to them by their first names. "They're pretty nice fellows," they say.

There's been only one agent who was really hated. He was one of their own, who turned deputy against them. They say he killed a man. He doesn't live around here now. The people say in their gentle way, "We don't like him very well around here." I'd hate for the mountain people to say gently of me that they just didn't like me very well. I'd spend the rest of my life in California.

Most of the moonshiners started poor, and are still poor. But there are some people in Cocke County today who made big money on moonshine, and saved it, and are among the county's richest people. Repeal, of course, dealt an awful blow to the industry. But the law of late has dealt further blows. They scared the storekeepers into making everybody who buys an excessive amount of sugar sign for it. And the moonshiners won't put their names down in the book, where the revenuers will see it. So they can't get sugar. So they don't make so much moonshine. . . .

October 16, 1940

Uncle Steve and the Bear

GATLINBURG, TENNESSEE— . . . Uncle Steve Cole lives on at his old home place, right in the Great Smokies National Park. He is a typical mountain man of the old school, the kind who lives right and does right.

I dropped in one afternoon to talk with him. Uncle Steve lit a fire, and sat down beside it and began spitting into the fireplace. He wasn't chewing tobacco, but he spit into the fireplace anyhow.

Uncle Steve has killed more bears than any man in these mountains. He says so himself, and others say so, too. He hasn't the remotest idea how many he has killed. But he has killed bears with muzzle-loaders, modern rifles, deadfalls, clubs, and axes, and he even choked one to death with his bare hands. I got him to tell me that story.

He and a neighbor went out one night. The dogs treed a bear. Uncle Steve took a half hour to tell it, but the essence of it was that they built a fire, the bear finally came down the tree, Uncle Steve stood there until the bear's body was pressing on the muzzle of the gun, and then he pulled the trigger. "I figured I couldn't miss that way," Uncle Steve said.

He didn't miss, but the shot didn't kill the bear. It ran fifty yards or so, and then the dogs were on it. And the first thing Uncle Steve knew the bear had clenched its great jaws right down on a dog's snoot, and was crushing it to pieces.

Now Uncle Steve's gun was an old-fashioned, sawed-off, muzzle-loading hog rifle, and he didn't have time to reload it. So to save the dog, he just rushed up to the bear from behind, put his legs around it, and started prying the dog's snoot out of the bear's mouth. "And before I knew what happened," said Uncle Steve, "the bear let go of the dog, and got my right hand in his mouth, and began a-crunchin' and a-growlin' and a-eatin' on my hand.

"One long tooth went right through the palm of my hand, and another went through the back of my hand. There wasn't nothin' for me to do but reach around with my left hand for the bear's throat. I got him by the goozle and started clampin' down. Pretty soon he let go. Then I just choked him till he was deader'n four o'clock." Uncle Steve spat into the fireplace.

Mrs. Cole was sitting on the bed, listening. Nobody said anything for a minute. Then Mrs. Cole chuckled and said, "Four o'clock ain't dead." Uncle Steve didn't dignify her quibble with an answer. He just spat into the fireplace again.

October 28, 1940

GEORGIA

SAVANNAH'S WAVING GIRL

SAVANNAH, GEORGIA—One night several years ago I was on a boat going down the Savannah River to the sea. About halfway down, when we passed a lighthouse, I noticed that somebody was swinging a lantern on shore, and the ship gave a couple of whistle blasts in reply.

I asked the captain about it, and he said it was the famous waving girl. He said she lived at the lighthouse with her brother, and had waved at every ship, day and night, for forty years. He said the legend was that when she was young her sweetheart went to sea and never came back, and she started waving at every ship so that if he should ever return, she would be the first to greet him.

The captain said that sailors all over the world knew about her. Later, on other ships and in other ports, I found that was true. Sailors from Cape Horn to Nome, and east and west, too, know of the waving girl of Savannah. Few have ever seen her close up, though.

*

When I got to Savannah this time, I thought I'd drive down the river and try to see this almost-mythical woman. I inquired how to get there, but was told she wasn't there anymore, that she had "retired" five years ago.

I finally found her in a little cottage under big trees on the road to the Isle of Hope, down on the salt flats out of Savannah, toward the sea. Her name is Florence Martus. She's sixty-seven now, and lives there with her brother George, who is seventy-five. They invited me in, and we three sat around their wood stove, talking about the cold weather up north, and in Savannah, too.

I'd half expected to see a mystical, unreal sort of person, legendlike even in personality, but Miss Florence is ordinary flesh and blood, quite matter-of-fact. She is very small and weathered, and her white hair is cut short like a man's, only in front it's longer and curled up across her forehead. She had on a brown sweater.

"Is it true that you never missed waving at a single ship in forty years?" I asked her.

"Yes," she said, "I guess it is. Even longer than that. How long were we there, George?"

"Forty-four years," George said, sucking at his pipe. Brother George was the lighthouse keeper, and sister Florence kept house for him. Just the two of them, on Elba Island, in the Savannah River, for forty-four years.

"Weren't you ever sick, and missed some?" I asked.

"No," she said, "I was never too sick to get up when one was coming."

"How did you know when one was coming at night? Didn't you ever sleep?"

"Oh, I could always hear them," she said. "It didn't bother me any to get up in the night. I got plenty of sleep. There wasn't much else to do."

I said, "Now please don't mind my asking this, but is that legend true about your sweetheart going away and never coming back? Is that why you waved at ships?"

"Oh, that old stuff!" she said. She said it sort of testily. She didn't say whether it was true or not, and I couldn't tell from her tone. "Why, I was born and raised right down at the mouth of the river, and we knew all the local tugboat and schooner captains, and it was only natural that I should wave at them when they passed. And then I just got to waving at everybody."

*

For forty-four years, day and night—a towel by day, a lantern by night. Maybe fifty thousand ships, maybe even more, were saluted by the waving girl of Savannah. And in all that time, not a single ship ever failed to salute her in return, with its whistle.

Then, five years ago, George was seventy and had to retire. The old couple didn't make any fuss about retiring. They'd rather have stayed, but it's the rule to retire, so what could they do? Brother and sister moved into Savannah. But they couldn't stand it there. "You feel cooped up when you've been out like us all your life." So they moved out onto the salt flats, where they could have more room.

They're half a mile from the water. They don't have a boat.

They'd like to have one, but it would cost too much to keep it. They have four beautiful collie dogs, and they live just like any other old couple who haven't anything to do. Their hearts are on the river, and in the lighthouse, but there's another man there now, a younger man. They've never been back to the island.

*

During all those forty-four years Miss Florence kept a diary and a log book. She wrote down what she thought and did every day, and listed every ship that passed—its name, where it was from, what kind it was, and so on. The ledger filled four big volumes.

The day they left the island and moved into town, Miss Florence sorted out her stuff. "The young people nowadays," she thought to herself, "don't want to read any of this old junk. It'll just collect dust." She threw it in the fire! The daily record, for forty-four years, of one of the most legendary figures of the Seven Seas, kept in her own hand, gone up in smoke in two minutes.

I said to her, "If I knew you better, I'd give you a great big kick."

She laughed and said, "Well, I guess you ought to."

February 18, 1936

IN SOUTHERN GEORGIA— . . . There must be lynchings down here that Northerners never hear about, and that never get in the annual compilations.

I met a white man who told me that yesterday afternoon he was asked to go along on a lynching party. He went, but when he got there the lynching was already over. I looked and looked, but there was never a word about it in the local papers. . . .

February 17, 1939

FLORIDA

LEANING TOWERS OF POVERTY ON THE ROAD TO FLORIDA
JACKSONVILLE, FLORIDA—All down the coast, all the way from Norfolk to the Florida line, you are driving through a swamp.

There are, I would be willing to bet, at least six billion snakes in these swamps. They are all asleep right now, thank heavens.

Now and then the road picks out a solid stretch, and runs along with fields and trees and dry land on either side, but that is the exception. Mostly the road is built up on a grade, and on both sides are dark forests, filled with a thick, ominous under-brush, standing in foul, silent water. Once in a while the forests disappear, and there is a tall, brown, swordlike grass, stretching level and far like a prairie wheat field. But you know that under-neath it is water, and it makes you shudder.

The towns look like small towns most anywhere. But in the country, the shacks are old. Ninety percent of the country popu-lation along the coastal road must be colored.

In the Carolinas the shacks are mostly of clapboard, never painted. Some of them have two stories, with only one room on each floor, and they're taller than they are wide. They invariably lean. I never saw so many leaning towers of poverty anywhere.

On a Sunday afternoon you meet droves of Negroes, walking along the highway, going home from church. They are dressed up and look happy. The Negro country churches are always big barnlike affairs, unpainted, with huge uncurtained windows. They sit on pillars of brick, and you can see under them. They seem lonesome and cold, in drab contrast to the heat and emo-tion of Negro worship that goes on inside them.

One little old colored woman was walking along the road, with a dozen big sticks of firewood balanced on her head. A string was tied around the wood. She stopped and turned clear around, but the load of wood never even teetered.

A few years ago, the road in Georgia was lined with turpen-tine camps. You would see hundreds of trees with wide notches cut in them, and little cans hanging on the side, to catch the sap. Now there are only three or four such places. The turpentine business in on the bum.

When you cross into Georgia, a big black-and-yellow sign tells you that if you're a vagrant, and are caught, you'll do time on Georgia's chain gangs. You see colored men in bunches, all in black-and-gray stripes, working on the roads. Hard-looking characters, in sheepskin coats, with rifles under their arms, stand looking at them.

North Florida is the same as Georgia. You wouldn't know the difference, except for the elaborate arch across the highway out in the wilderness there, saying FLORIDA. Even Jacksonville, thirty miles below the line, isn't what we picture Florida to be. It has some palm trees, and a lot of hotels, but otherwise it's like other cities. You don't get the Hollywood Spanish effect, or the droves of idle, bathing-suited money spenders, that you get farther south.

Everybody here thinks and talks about the Florida Canal.* In one of the taprooms, painted on the mirror back of the bar, is a big signing saying TRY OUR ROOSEVELT CANAL SPECIAL—A PICK-ME-UP—15 CENTS.

More people are coming to Florida this year, they say, than in any year since 1929. The newspapers run big stories about how trains from the north are running in six sections, getting people out of the cold. A story in one paper had a headline saying IT'S A LONG, LONG WAY TO CALIFORNIA. The story told about a family in Wisconsin who started to California, got snowbound within a few miles of home, and had been stuck right there for a week.

Because they didn't even get out of Wisconsin, it seems to me they'd have been snowbound even if they had been starting for Florida, but, of course, the Florida papers don't see it that way.

February 20, 1936

THE GREEKS OF TARPON SPRINGS

TARPON SPRINGS, FLORIDA—The manager of the Sponge Exchange took me aboard one of the little boats just in from the sponge banks, tied up at the dock.

The manager was a Greek. All the men on the boats were Greeks. In fact, there are more Greeks than native Americans in Tarpon Springs—about eighteen hundred of them.

This is the center of sponge-fishing in America. It's the biggest sponge center in the world. Sponges come only from here and the Mediterranean. The Greeks have been fishing for Mediterranean sponges for two thousand years. It was only natural they should get into the business here. . . .

The boat we went on was a little sailing schooner, about fifty feet long, with an auxiliary diesel motor. It was one of a dozen or so tied up at the block-long wharf. Men were sitting on the slippery wet deck, with buckets of water and piles of sponges all

*The canal was to meet the same fate as the Quoddy project in Maine: it was canceled, in March 1936, amid a flurry of controversy.

around them. They wore boots and had big rubber aprons over their laps.

A man would take a raw sponge off the pile, trim off the rough edges with a big knife, dip it into the bucket of water, and throw it over to another pile. They were talking with each other in Greek. Most of them speak little English.

The boat smelled like mushrooms, the way mushrooms smell out in the woods, among the dead leaves, after a warm spring rain. The manager told me the smell is healthy, for the sponges are full of iodine and phosphorus.

A sponge, of course, is an animal. You can actually see it breathing. A sponge as we know it is just the skeleton left after the jellylike body has been washed away. The sponge fastens itself to submerged coral rocks, and grows about half an inch a month. I saw one sponge on the boat that had grown onto a huge oyster shell. The oyster was still in it, too. The original sponge is covered with a dark skin, like a hornet's nest. When they scrape this off, the sponge is a brownish gray. Those pretty ones you see in stores have been bleached.

*

There are about seven hundred men in the sponge industry here. The rest of the eighteen hundred Greeks are their families. There are about a hundred boats fishing for sponges. Each boat carries from four to ten men. They are out sometimes as long as two months. They sometimes go fifty miles from shore, and work all the west coast of Florida, from Key West to Apalachicola. A few of the boats still "hook" sponges, with long poles, but that is slow and old-fashioned. Most of the boats, since 1905, carry divers.

The divers wear regular rubber diving suits, with helmets. They walk around the bottom and pull sponges off the rocks and put them in big sacks, which are then hauled to the top. The divers work from thirty to a hundred and twenty-five feet down. A diver is good for only about ten years.

They have trouble getting divers now. The young men, like young men everywhere, are drifting away from their fathers' business. The young Greeks won't go diving for sponges. They go out into the world and get educations and better jobs. A few young men keep coming from Greece, and they become sponge divers.

A diver earns about two thousand dollars a year. A common member of the crew makes seven or eight hundred dollars, which isn't much, but they live very cheaply. The pay depends on the catch. The owner of the boat takes a certain percentage. The rest is divided among the crew, in shares. The divers get the most—three shares. The cook gets a share-and-a-half.

*

When a boat gets a load, it comes in, and the sponges are put in a stall in the sponge exchange. This is merely a big courtyard, with a one-story brick building around three sides of it. The building is divided into dozens of small rooms or stalls, facing on the courtyard, with iron bars for the front wall.

Every Tuesday and Friday morning the sponge market is held. Great crowds gather. Buyers offer sealed bids for each batch. One day's sponge sale will run from fourteen to fifty thousand dollars. They have sold twenty million dollars' worth of sponges here in the last thirty years.

The Greeks here are a fine-looking people. Some of the daughters are classically handsome. Even the common sailors are courteous and pleasant, and say a few words of broken English to you, which you can hardly understand.

The little waterfront section is a dramatic place on sponge-market day. Dozens of boats tied up, painted white and red and blue, with banners flying, and men in boots and colored blouses and red rags on their heads. And the older men, the merchants, strolling around, with a massiveness and a dignity in their faces that the people of few nations can match.

March 3, 1936

CLEWISTON, FLORIDA— . . . Here in the Everglades, at two points less than twenty miles apart, the student of sociology has all the case history he needs.

At one end are the well-cared-for laborers in the company-controlled villages of a big business concern [U.S. Sugar Corporation]. At the other are the shifting migrants of the vegetable fields.

Migrants—most of them Negroes—are living in shacks, huts, lean-tos, trailers, just as the Okies live in California.

There has already been a stir about bad conditions around Belle Glade and Pahokee, the two vegetable towns of Lake Okeechobee. Farm Security Administration investigators have reported vile living conditions. The State Board of Health has issued a warning that if things aren't cleaned up, a quarantine on vegetables may result.

I'm glad I'm not a sociologist, for I wouldn't know what to make of life in the Everglades.

At one end is cleanliness, steady pay, good houses, good schools, and decency. But that is all wrong, you see, for a big, rich company is doing it. It is insidious—the workers are coerced with comforts, deluded and exploited under the guise of good living. It is terrible, and we must do away with it and get back to individual freedom.

And twenty miles away we *have* individual freedom. We have filthy shacks, piecework, and a lack of sanitation that borders on depravity. We have your little landlord pocketing his exorbitant rent for pigpens filled with humans. We have a floating population the police class as "the scum of the earth," and the Health Department shudders to think about. We have, in short, a Florida version of *The Grapes of Wrath*.

According to the sociologist, the *Grapes of Wrath* situation is intolerable. According to the professional defenders of individual liberty, the company villages are intolerable. The government is building two big camps for the unfortunate migrants, and the Republicans say such pampering of the poor is intolerable. It seems to sum up to the simple conclusion that no matter what you do, it's wrong.

April 24, 1940

Key West's Passive Resistance

KEY WEST, FLORIDA—This faraway little city is going through one interesting transition. It doesn't know whether it is going to become another Palm Beach, a Coney Island, or a public charge, or just stay the way it always was. And worst of all, it doesn't know which of these it *wants* to become.

Key West seems almost a foreign land. It is far away from the body of the United States; it is closer to Havana than to Miami. You hear Spanish spoken on the streets. Many of the people have the Latin look about them.

There doesn't seem to be much pride here, but there is great smugness. The people certainly are unlike those in any place I've ever been. Romantics see them as picturesque, or quaint; realists would call them backward. There are bright exceptions, of course.

Newcomers say it is awfully hard to get anybody here to do any work. There is jealousy among the select, and sewing-circle gossip among all.

The Army and Navy used to have big establishments here. But a few years ago they moved out, keeping, however, all the choice waterfront land. Then came the hurricane of 1935, washing away the last direct communication between Key West and the world. That was the final little noise to disturb Key West's sleep.

For the last three years the twelve thousand inhabitants were kept going largely by WPA.* The town was flat broke. People stopped paying taxes. WPA even had to collect the garbage.

*

During this time, somebody "discovered" Key West, the last outpost of solitude in America. Last July, the new Overseas Highway was opened. Key West was again directly connected with the world. The highway received a great deal of publicity. The tourists of America became Key West–conscious.

This winter, they are coming by the thousands. That is the transition. Once tourists have discovered a town, something is bound to happen. Even if the tourists throw it over and stop coming in a couple of years, the place will never be quite the same again.

What will happen here nobody knows. Key West doesn't know how to take it. Neither do the tourists. It is fun to sit here and watch it.

There is little here for the average tourist. The town itself is fairly drab. What it needs most is ten thousand gallons of white paint. The beaches are sparse, and poor; the government owns practically all the waterfront.

The staying and eating facilities are meager. On a recent weekend when there were at least five thousand tourists in town, it took us two hours to get a meal in a restaurant. There are several bars, open gambling, two carnivals, a regular and a miniature golf links—and that's all the tourist entertainment there is in Key West.

Tourists by the thousands come, look around, and go away disappointed. I've talked with dozens of them. A day or two was enough for them. Key West wasn't like what they thought. They'd go back to Miami for their vacations.

Those who dream of Key West's becoming another ultra-flossy Palm Beach have reckoned without the fundamental necessity for such a development—lots of capital, freely spent. And those

*Works Progress Administration. A New Deal agency that provided work relief for millions of Americans during the Depression.

who dream of Key West's becoming another low-priced, over-run tourist mecca have reckoned without the passive resistance of the Key West native—he will not toil, build, paint, nor create anything to attract the tourist and make him happy.

*

Already this winter, tourists by the thousand are going home and advising their friends not to come to Key West. In a few years, I believe the Key West rage will be over. A few score, or maybe a hundred, outsiders will make themselves simpatico. They will overlook the faults, and fall in love with it because the conchs are slow, the place is quiet, and the weather ideal.

They will buy old Negro houses, and remodel them, with private gardens behind and furnishings inside. They will fish a little, and gather in intellectual groups at the bars in the evenings. They will rest and read and paint and write and think.

I believe Key West will become a combination of Santa Fe, New Mexico, and Carmel, California. It will become a "colony," and like all such places it will soon have a majority of residents who are quietly retired on Army pensions, railroad stock, or government bonds.

I don't know why I'm doing all this analyzing. It's probably wrong, and I'll never be able to come here year after year, as I wish I could. For Key West has one heavenly thing: heat. And to me, that is everything. . . .

January 23, 1939

EXQUISITELY FINE BRUSHWORK

SILVER SPRINGS, FLORIDA— . . . Silver Springs is a small body of water in central Florida. It connects with a river that wanders more than two hundred miles to the sea. There are saltwater fish that have swum the two hundred miles upstream, and liked it so well they stayed.

Surrounding the little lake (about two blocks square) are all kinds of curio stores, restaurants, concessions, and whatnot. But don't let this fool you. The main attraction is under the water, where they've left nature alone.

You go out over the lake in glass-bottomed boats. There are seats along each side of the boat, and a sort of manger in the middle. You lean on the manger rail and look straight down through the bottom of the boat.

When you get in, the thick growth of underwater reeds is

right up against the glass, the water is that shallow. But you haven't gone fifty feet until suddenly the floor of the lake drops off, like a precipice, and you are staring into a vast hole more than fifty feet deep.

The water is as clear as air. You can see through it almost as if there were no water there. You see fish swimming around; you see an old dinosaur backbone; you see an old sunken Spanish boat; you see a few empty whiskey bottles. The colorings and formations in these holes are fantastic beyond description. People around you burst out with expressions of awe.

There was one old lady on our boat who had taken the ride every year for nineteen years, and there was a man who had been bringing his family here for four years, and waiting in the car while they made the boat trip. But this time they wouldn't go without him, so he grudgingly came along. He was the most enthusiastic one in the bunch. "What I've been missing!" he said. . . .

I believe Carlsbad Caverns and Silver Springs are the two outstanding spots of small, fantastic natural beauty in the United States. I don't mean to include them with such gargantuas as the Grand Canyon or Mount McKinley. Those are colossal and bold, while these are exquisitely fine brushwork. Carlsbad Caverns is best, of course, but in its way Silver Springs is just as fantastic.

Silver Springs has the exaggerated colored beauty of a Walt Disney epic. Down there you see mountains and glaciers and snowstorms in puppet fashion. And it's all natural—man hasn't monkeyed with it. You see dark-blue catfish so big you could hardly lift one. You see water reeds so violently colored that you say there just can't be such colors.

The ride in the glass boat takes an hour. A Seminole Indian runs it, and explains what you're seeing. He stops the boat over every beautiful cavern, and lets you look. You probably aren't half a mile from the dock during the whole trip, and never more than a hundred yards from shore. . . .

*

Silver Springs is not a national park. It is privately owned. The owner, and the two men who lease and operate the boats, are making themselves a pocketful of money. But it's honest money. I have yet to meet a person who wasn't overpleased at what he saw through the eyes of a fish at Silver Springs.

February 16, 1939

ALABAMA

BIRMINGHAM, ALABAMA—They call Birmingham the Magic City. I asked if that was because they make so many almost-magic things out of steel here.

They said no; it was because the city had grown so fast. In less than seventy years it has grown from nothing to almost a quarter of a million.

Birmingham, unlike most Southern cities, has no Civil War history. It wasn't even here then. It is Southern, but without the beloved Southern traditions.

It is the Pittsburgh of the South. All the ingredients are right here—iron ore, coal, and whatever that other thing is it takes to make steel.

Why, there's one mountain right alongside, covered by the city's finest residential section, which they say is practically all iron ore. Some far day, I suppose, it will all be chewed up by the machines—Beauty versus the Beast.

Birmingham is, I believe, the most beautiful industrial city in America. The downtown is neat and modern, and the residential sections are superb. There are hills and mountains all around. And up on the hillsides, on winding streets and back among trees, are the homes—homes ranging from ones you and I might buy on the installment plan on up to the great castles of the millionaires.

I have talked with many people whose business brought them temporarily to Birmingham, and here they stay, buying homes, expecting to remain forever.

The only thing I don't like about Birmingham is that when you blow your nose in the morning you wonder if you haven't been out cleaning chimneys in your sleep. . . .

March 3, 1939

EVENING AT VESTAVIA

BIRMINGHAM, ALABAMA—There is a man in Birmingham who lives by himself in a Roman temple on top of a mountain.

He isn't crazy. He just has a hobby, and it happens to be Roman history. He likes to surround himself with things

Roman. So ten years ago he bought twenty acres right on the top of Shades Mountain, fifteen miles from downtown Birmingham, and built a home.

Instead of building a house to resemble a temple, he built a temple and then fixed it up inside like a house. The temple is round, and those who make jokes like to say that George B. Ward lives in a silo. But George Ward's temple is no more like a silo than a cigaret, which is also round.

*

George Ward, now getting down the other side of life, is one of Birmingham's very first citizens. He was born in Birmingham, and has always lived here. He was mayor for ten years. He is a partner in a bond-brokerage house, and still goes downtown every day. He has been a civic leader most of his life. But his obsession for Roman history makes him a "character."

He made his home a replica of the Temple of Vesta. He calls his place Vestavia. Vesta was the goddess of the hearth fire, which was tended by the Vestal Virgins. . . .

*

The stone for Vestavia came right out of Shades Mountain. The temple has three stories and a basement, and rises fifty-eight feet above the ground. A fourteen-foot-wide porch circles it just below the top, and twenty large columns run down to the porch on the ground floor. That gives it the temple effect, and keeps it from looking like a lighthouse.

Inside there is just one room on each floor. Each room is round, and twenty-eight feet across. The first floor is a beautiful living room. The second floor, reached by a circular staircase, is the bedroom. It has a huge fireplace, two great canopied beds, and a bathroom. Ward has never finished the third floor inside. He doesn't need the space.

*

I spent an evening with George Ward in Vestavia. We walked about his grounds, just after dusk, looking down from the mountaintop far into the valleys below, watching the lights flicker, shrinking from the vicious night wind that sweeps the peak, shouting over the wind and the loud radio music that comes out of a tree in the yard, seeing the lighted pools and shrubbery and statues and models of Rome that pepper Vestavia's grounds.

And inside the temple, we sat before the immense fireplace, in easy chairs, in a city atmosphere of comfort, talking. Robert, a Negro boy, stood permanently just in the rear—to answer his master's questions when master couldn't remember something, to tend the hearth fire, to fill our glasses, to bring books from the shelves.

*

Ward says he is not a rich man, despite what people think. He points to three small marble statues. "Those are real, from Italy," he says. "And all the rest around here are cheap imitations."

Ward has a great white head of hair, and wears horn-rimmed glasses. When he blinks his eyes, he does it hard, and his eyebrows blink, too. He is just a little deaf. He looks straight ahead when he talks.

He is a lonesome man among his splendor. I know he is, because he told me so, and because I could tell he enjoyed my being there. He is unmarried. He is alone but for his three colored servants and his five little dogs. He has read about everything there is to read about what he's interested in. After a good many years, it gets lonesome on a mountaintop at night—especially, I imagine, in a temple. He draws in more and more. I'm afraid he sits at night and wonders.

*

Ward has shelf after shelf of books about the Roman Empire. He has read them all. He can answer the most minute question about Roman history. He thinks Caesar was the greatest of all men, and he puts Napoleon next. Militarists are his heroes. He thinks Mussolini the greatest man of our time. He thinks Italy's move into Ethiopia is all right. He thinks the Ethiopians should be saved from themselves. He says the reason I hate militarists is that I am young.

Vestavia is the showplace of Birmingham, and Ward is generous with it. Occasionally he throws it open to the public. One day for whites, another day for colored. He used to give grand parties, and dress his colored boys in armor, holding spears. Others would sweep great fans over the guests' heads. The colored boys thought it was swell. So did the guests.

*

When I left Vestavia to go down the mountain that night, I did not leave like an ordinary person leaving an ordinary place. No. One servant drove my car, two others followed in another car—a Roman escort down from Shades Mountain in the dark.

December 28, 1935

POSTSCRIPT: *George Ward died in 1940. A hobby, Pyle wrote, "has a way of running out. You play it for a long time, and then its power to beguile you begins to fade, and finally you have to pretend to play, so as not to be ashamed of the thing to which you once threw your passions.*

"George Ward was a wonderful man. Birmingham wouldn't be what it is today if he had not lived. And yet I feel positive that he died lonely within himself. We could feel his lonesomeness reaching out the last time we visited him in his Empire. Now it is all over."

THE OFFICIAL CHAPLAIN OF BIRMINGHAM

BIRMINGHAM, ALABAMA—As soon as you land in Birmingham you hear of Brother Bryan. Everybody knows him. He is a tradition.

He has a brick church of orthodox appearance, not far from downtown. But people don't think of him so much as a preacher. They think of him as the one man who lives the way the rest of us profess to live, but don't.

I went out to see Brother Bryan. He is getting old now, and you might say a little childish. But he is no crank. He is an educated, sincere man. He's merely explosive, vociferous, and emotional.

I found him in his little study, with its linoleum on the floor and its coal stove. "Oh, God bless you, God bless you," he shouted. "I'm so glad you came. You boys are so good to me. You and the radio boys. You're so good to me. . . ."

Brother Bryan started to cry. He is a big, tall man with a white beard, and very old; and when he cries he screws his face up like a baby and runs his big hands through his white hair.

It frightened me at first, but in the next half hour Brother Bryan cried and laughed so many times, each time so suddenly and heartily, that I kept getting behind with my sympathetic facial expressions, and would still be looking solemn when Brother Bryan was roaring with laughter.

Brother Bryan pushed me down in a rocking chair, and pulled another one up right in front of me. Then he started telling me how wonderful people are. Brother Bryan is a very enthusiastic man. For each person he loves, I got a hard slap on the hand, or a pound on the knee, or a punch in the shoulder.

Brother Bryan loves everything and everybody. I doubt if he has had an unkind or selfish thought in half a century. He even loves me. "Oh, Simmons," he yelled. "Come here. We've got a new friend."

*

Brother Bryan (his initials are J.A.) was born in South Carolina, graduated from Princeton in 1889, studied Hebrew and
Greek, and can still speak in Yiddish. He has been in Birmingham forty-four years. He has a wife and six grown children.
Two of them are in the ministry—one in Baltimore, one a missionary in Japan.

Despite his age, Brother Bryan's activities would make a football player feel like an invalid. He preaches forty times a week,
sometimes more—twice a day in his own church, twice a day on
the radio, usually a couple of times at noon somewhere in Birmingham. And every night he drives out into the country to
preach.

People call him, as you would a doctor, to come and preach.
He drives sometimes as far as a hundred miles, and back again
that night. He never charges anything except gasoline money.

He has a nice sedan, which he paid for by selling pictures of
himself. His driver is a fine-looking, one-legged boy he is sending through college.

"I even get calls from Texas," Brother Bryan says. "But I can't
go that far. I can't leave the sick people, and my funerals. I
average a funeral a day. And, oh, there are all kinds of sick
people I have to go see."

He told me how he would preach in stores and barns around
Alabama, and people would get interested and build a church.
He said he went out just the other day where they were building
a country church, and it was full of volunteer carpenters up on
scaffolds, and "the ceiling was so beautiful"—Brother Bryan
started to cry—"that ceiling was so beautiful, and all those men
up there"—he pointed—"building that beautiful church"—sob,
sob—"and I knew they were all bootleggers, but I didn't care"—
sob, sob—"it was so beautiful."

*

Brother Bryan is the official chaplain of Birmingham. He was
so well known and so good that everybody called him chaplain
anyhow, so the city just made it official.

There are thousands of stories about him. He's always giving
away his overcoat to some poor cold man. Brother Bryan has no
money, for the simple reason that he gives away every cent he
gets. "I led my class at Princeton, and now I ain't got a penny!"
Brother Bryan roars with laughter.

He feeds about sixty people a day in the basement of his

church. He runs out of money, but food of some kind is always rounded up.

Brother Bryan believes in prayer. He believes that if he asks God for something, God will send it. He told me how he didn't have any coffee for the poor men one day, and so he prayed, and when he got back to his study there were eight pounds of coffee on his desk.

"Do you know who brought it?" I asked him.

"Yes, it was a farmer out here in the country," he roared, and laughed and pounded me on the back.

December 30, 1935

RAID IN A BONE-DRY STATE

MOBILE, ALABAMA—"But what about reformers?" I said to my Mobile friend. "What about the professional bluenoses? Don't they ever make a fuss?"

"Why," said my friend, "if a reformer ever stuck his head up in Mobile they'd run him out of town before sundown."

We were sitting in a restaurant eating lunch. It wasn't a doggy restaurant at all. It was just a couple of jumps ahead of a greasy spoon, but the food was all right. There were booths along one side, and we were in one of them. Along the other side was a bar, with bottles of whiskey pyramided before the mirror, and a bartender in white mixing drinks, and a couple of men drinking at the bar.

"This place has been a bar for seventy years, I guess," my friend said. "And it has never closed. Never closed a single day during prohibition. Never locked its doors or worked behind a curtain. Alabama is one of two bone-dry states left in the Union. Kansas is the other. No beer or wine, even. But you see how much attention we pay to it.

"People in Mobile won't stand for any monkeying with their liberties. Why, there hasn't been a liquor conviction here since I can remember, and with everything running wide open. They can't even get a liquor jury here. Haven't had one for two years. The jurors simply tell the judge they'll acquit the defendant no matter what the evidence, so they just can't get a jury, and nobody is ever tried.

"Sure, we have raids. But they're the funniest things you ever saw. The officers come in and take a bottle or two, just enough for evidence so they can collect their raiding fee, and that's all there is to it. Nobody ever has to go to court or pay a fine or anything."

Men kept coming in, and having a drink, and going out again. Most of them were ordinary-looking people, but there were one or two with big noses and twinkly eyes swaying at the bar. We were paying so little attention that we didn't even notice at first when the five men walked in. A couple of them were big fat men—looked like politicians.

Some of them walked into the back room, and a couple of others walked around behind the bar, took flashlights out of their hip pockets, and started opening cabinet doors. That's when we first noticed them.

When I looked at my friend, he was about to explode. "It's a raid," he practically shouted in a stage whisper. "Boy, this is wonderful. They don't raid this place once in a month. Now you can say you've seen a raid in Alabama."

One of the big fat men took a bottle of whiskey out of one cabinet, and set it on the bar. It had only about four drinks left in it. One of the weaving blokes at the bar looked at it greedily.

"You working here now?" the fat man asked the bartender in a friendly voice.

"Yeah," said the bartender. "Let the boss off as easy as you can, will you?" He meant by that not to take too much of the boss' whiskey.

The fat man turned and started looking behind other cabinet doors. The swaying old soak at the bar kept looking at the bottle. Suddenly he made up his mind. He reached over, unscrewed the cap, poured a big drink, and downed it. Then he looked around, as if he expected applause. He got it.

The onlookers shouted and laughed. "Now you can say you've had a drink of government liquor," one fellow yelled at him. The soak was beaming. "I've been waiting for that for years," he said. The officers paid no attention.

Finally they were through. That one half-empty bottle was all they took—that and one case of beer. They took a case off the top of a stack of about thirty cases piled at the back of the room. The big fellow took some papers out of his pocket, and put them on the bar, and took out his pencil and signed his name at the bottom. Then he took the bottle of whiskey, and another fellow took the case of beer, and they said so long, and all walked out.

The spectators stepped up to the bar. The bartender opened a cabinet door, one that had been looked into with a flashlight a minute before, and took out a bottle of whiskey and started pouring drinks. Everybody laughed.

March 6, 1936

How the War Between the States Really Ended

MOBILE, ALABAMA—This is a story of the last battle of the Civil War. It was fought here in Mobile Bay, in 1905, some forty years after you thought the war was over. It was told me by a friend, and he says the story is true.

Steven Quayle, we shall call him, was a Mississippian of gentle birth and scholarly parts. He went north in search of adventure and fortune. He worked in many Northern cities, and being frequently appalled at the coarseness of climate and bleakness of manners, he longed at times for gentler scenes.

At length he adopted a routine. He would work diligently for six months, and then for the next half year, with his savings, travel on the magic carpet of strong liquors.

He would move physically, too, and always, of course, southward. It was during one of these periods that he found himself in Mobile, where he slept in the park. At dawn he wandered to the waterfront. He was penniless, and lank of food. He sat down on a bench to watch the spectacle of sunrise over Mobile Bay.

Shortly a small boat came across the waters, a rowboat. It tied up, and the oarsman came ashore. He gave good morning to Steven, and sat down to talk. Now Steven had a courteous manner that would make the courtiers of the old French courts look like stumblebums. Poor or rich, drunk or sober, he was of the school of chivalry.

The newcomer, it developed, was of the same school. His polished manners also knew no bounds. Gracious conversation began. They exchanged confidences. It rapidly developed that Steven was the son of a Confederate general. And by an odd coincidence, the man from the rowboat was, too. Companionship grew.

Steven told how he had fled north to wrest his fortune from the damnyankees. The other man had been even more thorough. He had spurned the very continent where such things as Appomattox could happen. He had preempted an island off the mouth of Mobile Bay, and lived there alone. He was an unreconstructed Rebel, and had built himself a hermitage. Once a month he rowed ashore for supplies, liquid and staple. This happened to be the morning.

Eventually the saloon and ship chandlery, before which they were sitting, opened. Our man invited Steve to join him in a little something. Steve explained his position, and our man became his enthusiastic host from then on. They filled themselves and also the demijohn the oarsman had brought along. Eventually they loaded it into the boat, and left for their island—for by now Steve had been invited to spend a month, and had accepted.

They alternately rowed and paused to sample the john. Above the rowing and the sampling was the hum of erudite conversation, confined largely to the War Between the States and its intolerable ending. In the midst of this, Steve espied a smudge of smoke on the horizon. They sat and watched. Soon the vessel was nearly abreast. And then the two friends recognized her as a battleship, flying the hated flag of the United States of America.

Now, it seems the man from the island always placed a fowling piece in his boat when he set out upon a trip. Steve, eyes agleam, seized the rifle and dropped a load across the bows of the battleship, calling upon her, in a loud voice, to heave to. The gun's pop attracted no attention whatever. Steve reloaded and fired at the foredeck, and then at the bridge. He drew attention that time.

The battleship hove to in a hurry, a gig was swung down, and a rough bosun's mate placed the men in the rowboat under arrest and took them to the battleship. Steve demanded that they be taken before the captain. This was done. The Confederates demanded immediate surrender of the battleship.

Now this, I understand, is all in the records of the Navy Department in Washington. I am sorry I have not had access to those records, so that I might give you the name of a captain in the United States Navy who possessed not only rich manners and a quick command of a situation, but also a sense of humor.

The captain invited the Confederates to be seated. He politely offered them cigars. With courtliness he begged for a discussion of terms before he should turn over his sword. Three bottles of champagne were ordered up and served. The conversation was heavy with elegance, and gradually became lightened by a certain bonhomie that grows between respected adversaries. It ended with the drawing of a formal truce, right there in the captain's cabin, between the Confederate States of America and the United States of America.

This treaty of peace was signed and sealed in duplicate. Under its terms, the battleship was allowed to proceed to Mobile, but not to sail near their island. The captain was permitted to retain his sword. The captain escorted the Confederates on deck. They were piped over the side with all the dignity that naval formality can bestow, and assisted into their rowboat, which they found almost dangerously loaded with cases of champagne and other ardent beverages.

A launch was waiting to tow them back to their island, and at a signal it shoved off. Steve stood in the forepeak of the dory, seized the old fowling piece, which had been restored to him, and fired a salute. The battleship fired a salute in return.

Thus ended the last battle of the War Between the States. The year, you'll recall, was 1905.

March 21, 1939

IT'S SMALL AND DISGUSTING BUT IT'S AMERICA

CRUMLY'S CHAPEL, ALABAMA; WESTWOOD, ALABAMA—No, that isn't a typographical error. The place I'm writing this from really has two names. The whole town is split up and mad over it. And since I am just a frail youth and do not like to get into fights, I'm datelining this column with both names.

When I first heard the story it sounded awfully funny. But when I got here and nosed around, I saw there wasn't anything funny about it.

This is a village of about a thousand people, some ten miles from Birmingham. It is made up mostly of schoolteachers, middle-salaried commuters, and a few farmers. It has a store and a church and a school and graveyard. The community is as old as Birmingham.

It has always been called Crumly's Chapel. That is because the first man through here was named Crumly, and the first church was Crumly's Chapel. There wasn't any town then, but when a town grew up it just continued to be called Crumly's Chapel.

Last fall some of the more modern elements thought it would be nice to call the village Westwood. They said the town never had a name in the first place, and also that if you tell people you live in Crumly's Chapel they think you live in a church. The majority of the town was for Westwood. A small but persistent minority was for Crumly's Chapel. So the fight started. And since November the following things have happened:

—Westwood road signs put up by the Highway Department have been tarred and feathered.

—A Crumly Chapel School sign was smeared with tar. The sign was taken down next day, so the town school now has no name at all.

—The Parent-Teacher Association is split over the thing. Neighbors won't speak to each other. Families are divided, even mother against son. Some residents are in the phone book under Westwood, others under Crumly's Chapel.

—A deacon, after passing the plate at church one Sunday morning, found a threatening note among the nickels and dimes.

—Two relatives, out fox-hunting, got into an argument over the name, and one wound up getting his teeth knocked out and the other getting stabbed. The case is still in court.

—Four scurrilous letters were received by people on the Westwood side. One was to the postman, who turned it over to the United States Postal Inspectors.

*

It was my intention to talk with both sides. For the Westwood side, I was directed to Mrs. Graydon Newman, whose husband teaches school and practices law on the side. Mrs. Newman herself is a relief teacher. The Newmans are what the Crumly's Chapel faction calls "squatters," or newcomers. They've only been here sixteen years, and hardly know their way down to the crossroads.

You never saw anybody nicer than Mrs. Newman. While the baby kept crawling around and untying my shoelaces, she told me their side of the story. She could see the funny side of it, and even said that some of the old families on the other side were the most accommodating people in the world till this thing came up.

I went to the other side, the Old Steelers side. It was then I knew that this was as grim as a Kentucky feud, that there was raging hatred in it, and that outsiders weren't welcome. "You'll have to go farther than this to get any talk," one man said. He was very suspicious and tried to find out who sent me to him. I was actually sent by somebody who has nothing to do with the feud, but because he wasn't talking I wasn't either, so I never told him. We parted with stiff courtesy, and not much of it.

I tried another of the Crumly's Chapel side. This man and I talked on the front porch. A woman came out. I spoke, but she didn't. She sat listening, giving me the old fish eye. "I won't allow you to print anything about this business," the man said. When I told him he was getting a little out of his field, he said, "Well, you won't get any talk from us."

You couldn't call them downright discourteous. They didn't order you off the premises. But they made it pretty plain that the sooner I got, the better it would be.

*

Small-town hatreds like this, verging on civil war, have happened all over the country—over a man shooting a neighbor's dog, over one kid's slapping another, over a dead relative's will, over which farmer was first in line at the grain elevator, over hiring a new preacher. It's small and disgusting, but it's America. And I suppose we might as well get used to the idea that people are going to be mean and ornery at certain times of the moon.

Where this one will end, nobody knows. There's tension in the air. If the residents would only listen to me, I could settle the whole thing. Why not compromise, combine the two names, and call the place Crumwood?

March 4, 1939

POSTSCRIPT: *I couldn't resist calling long-distance information. The AT&T operator tried her best, but she had no listings for a Crumly's Chapel, Alabama, no listings for a Westwood, Alabama. "How about* Crumwood, *Alabama?" I asked. "One moment, sir." Silence. "Nothing, sir—no Crumwood, Alabama, either." A search of the index of my* Rand McNally Contemporary World Atlas *was equally unfruitful: no Crumly's Chapel, no Westwood, no Crumwood.*

A SELFLESS NEGRO SCIENTIST HOLDS THE KEY

TUSKEGEE, ALABAMA—In this job of roving over the world I have met a few human beings so selfless as to be almost Utopian spirits.

But never have I met a man who towers above Dr. George W. Carver in nobility or intelligent greatness. He is one of the greatest men in the South. He is a scientist. He is a Negro.

Dr. Carver is getting old now, and has been sick. When I went to see him he was sitting behind a desk, hunched over almost in a half-moon. He shook hands weakly, and apologized for not getting up. He said the doctors made him rest every little while, and that he could talk only a few minutes. His voice was a tiny

thing, sharp and high. I had the feeling that my interview would
be short and futile.

Now I don't know whether this is a little trick of Dr. Carver's
or not. But trick or no, we got to talking, and the first thing I
knew he was sitting up, and his voice was strong. And within
five minutes we were out in the laboratory, and he was showing
me things and walking rapidly around like an enthusiastic
young athlete.

*

Dr. Carver was born in Missouri, apparently during the Civil
War. Night riders stole his parents and sold them at auction. He
never saw them again. But Amos Carver, the white plantation
owner, was good to the little boy. He gave him his own name,
which was customary in those days. George Washington
Carver, the Negro boy became.

He rose out of nothing into greatness. When he grew up, he
went to school in Iowa. He specialized in science, and rapidly
earned his degrees. Then he turned southward, to his own people. Forty-two years ago he came to Tuskegee Institute, the
South's famous Negro school. He has been here ever since—a
lifetime.

Dr. Carver has been a dark prophet—in the dark. He has
worked like an inspired man for forty-two years to help the
South. He has worked for the *whole* South, black and white.

His work has been of the soil, and of the things that grow
from it. Forty years ago he was preaching the dangers of erosion. He has tried to tell poor farmers how to improve their
land, but only a few would heed. And all through the forty-two
years he has also been working in his chemical laboratory. He
is a man of real standing in the scientific world. It seems impossible that he could have done so much even in forty-two years.

For he has found dozens of uses for almost every plant that
grows in the South. His discoveries of practical commodities
that can be made from sweet potatoes and peanuts run into the
hundreds. It would take two columns just to name them.

*

The government has called the South the nation's foremost
economic problem. The South as a whole resents that. The rich
people, who don't do much about it, resent it. And the poor
people, who are both unable and loath to do anything about it,
resent it even more. . . .

The South is fundamentally rural. Except for a steel city like

Birmingham, and a few textile towns, the whole heart and soul of the South springs from its soil. And the soil and its tillers have sunk to a point that is not pretty. Much of the South is Tobacco Road. And it needn't be so. The whole deep South could be, relatively, what Mobile's famous Azalea Trail and Natchez's gardens are. Just transfer the luxuriance of the flowers into the lives of the people. It can be done.

And I believe that for all the talk and wrinkling of administration brows over what to do, the whole fountain of Southern reconstruction lies right here in the laboratory of this humble Negro scientist—Dr. George W. Carver.

*

It seems to me that some farseeing force could take Dr. Carver's discoveries as a base, and rebuild a new, varied, and prosperous South around them. It would take money and intelligence. The money might sprout from the federal government, as money has a way of doing. The intelligence can come from the Southerners, if they would form themselves into a great sweeping movement to do better by themselves.

If farmers would rebuild their soil and open their minds to something besides cotton, if industry would set up factories to manufacture the things that Dr. Carver knows can be made from the varied plants of the South, if it would be done in an organized and forceful way, then it seems to me that within twenty, forty, fifty years the old, old South could again become the nation's garden spot, and no longer either Tobacco Road or that foremost economic problem.

March 7, 1939

A VENERABLE LIFE DRAWS TO A CLOSE
TUSKEGEE, ALABAMA—Dr. Carver has lived a lifetime on the underside of racial prejudice, and taken it in silent grace. He has been ignored by intelligent white men, and run out of towns by ignorant ones.

But he will not discuss these things. His colored assistant says Dr. Carver will not speak of them even to him. He passes them over. He is a giant of tolerance.

Dr. Carver has no relatives. He has no money. He has turned down scores of job offers—even one from Thomas A. Edison. All of his discoveries have been given freely to the world.

I had read that Dr. Carver was seventy-eight. I asked him

about it. He said, with sadness and futility in his voice: "I don't know. I was born into slavery. I was chattel, the same as the cows and pigs. We were all chattel. They didn't keep records of us. I don't know how old I am."

Dr. Carver has never married. For forty-two years he has lived on the campus of Tuskegee Institute, in his own apartment in one of the dormitories. He gets up at four every morning. For two hours he works at his books and calculations in his room. He eats breakfast at six, then goes to the laboratory. He is in bed by nine-thirty P.M.

Like many scientists, he has been careless in his eating. Often he forgets to eat at all. And if they didn't watch him, he'd revert to a slave's diet of fat meat, meal, and molasses. He has anemia now. He is very tall, and his clothes hang loosely on what has been a large frame. His hair is short, curly, and gray. I believe he looks older than seventy-eight.

Dr. Carver is extremely religious. He does not smoke, swear, or drink. On the other hand, he doesn't bring pious phrases into his conversation, and he sees no quarrel between science and religion. . . .

The variety of Dr. Carver's genius seems unlimited. Right now he spends most of his time experimenting with the use of peanut oil on polio cases. And once more he runs into prejudice. Not only prejudices against Negroes, but a stern "hands off" from the medical world. He is not a physician; therefore he must not presume to try his hand at medicine.

Nonetheless, he has massaged paralyzed muscles with some forty different oils, and found peanut oil the best. He thinks he has had some success in re-enlivening atrophied muscles.

*

During most of Dr. Carver's life at Tuskegee he never allowed himself an assistant; he never felt there was one he could trust to share his work. Then four years ago along came a fine-looking young colored man from West Virginia, just out of Cornell. For four years now this young man has been Dr. Carver's assistant. They work side by side in the laboratory.

His name is Austin W. Curtis, Jr. He is proud of the honor. His position is something akin to a young lawyer becoming the private secretary of a Justice Holmes. Last summer Austin Curtis made an auto trip through Missouri, where Dr. Carver was born.

I asked whether he found any of the white Carvers still living.

Yes, he did—three. They were all farmers, all very old, and they were out plowing. They stopped their teams and leaned on the fence to talk to Curtis. The youngest was seventy-two, and the oldest eighty-four. They had all played with Dr. Carver as boys. Curtis said they all seemed proud to remember him.

Dr. Carver himself has never been back to Missouri since he came to Tuskegee.

*

After talking with Dr. Carver, I sat for a long time with Curtis. When finally I went to say goodbye, Dr. Carver was in his laboratory, hard at work, He wiped his hands on his white apron, and came out. He hoped so much that I would come back and see his new museum when it is finished. He said he was no good at names, but he'd remember my face.

I am not especially emotional, but when I said goodbye to Dr. Carver I could hardly speak for the lump in my throat.

It all seemed to flare up vividly before me—the whole picture of all he has done, this vast lifetime of good now coming to a close, all the broadness and tolerance of his mind, all he has given and the little he has received.

When I come back, he may be gone. The news of his death may not even make the Northern papers. And of those who read it only a few will know, or care.

March 8, 1939

POSTSCRIPT: *Dr. Carver died January 5, 1943, in his dormitory apartment at Tuskegee Institute. Notice of death did run in Northern papers. The* New York Times *carried a column-and-a-half obituary on January 6. The* Times' *obituary contained additional information on Carver's early years, gleaned from biographical facts he had supplied* Who's Who:

Carver said he was "born of slave parents on a farm near Diamond, Grove, Missouri, about 1864; in infancy lost his father and was stolen and carried into Arkansas with mother, who was never heard of again; was bought from captors for a race horse valued at three hundred dollars and returned to former home in Missouri."

The Times *reported: "Because he was a puny boy who got his growth late, he was allowed to run around as a household pet without being put to heavy work. Outdoors he learned about trees, shrubs, and insects and liked to paint and draw them. In the kitchen he picked up much knowledge of cooking and of canning fruits and vegetables which later was to serve his people. In the parlor he learned something of music.*

"Until he was almost twenty he did not learn to read and write. That came after he grew up suddenly and struck out for himself. He had seen education at close quarters in a white household and felt he could use it. He worked his way through high school in Minneapolis, Kansas, and later through Iowa State College of Agriculture and Mechanic Arts.

"He was graduated there with the degree of Bachelor of Science in Agriculture in 1894, at the age of thirty, and was immediately made a faculty member in charge of the college greenhouse and the bacterial laboratory work in systematic botany. Two years later he had earned the degree of Master of Science and made the acquaintance of Booker T. Washington, who then was bringing the Tuskegee Institute in Alabama to notice.

"He went to Tuskegee in 1896. . . ."

THE FSA AND COFFEE COUNTY

ENTERPRISE, ALABAMA— . . . This is a New Deal story, so if you don't like the New Deal you won't see any sense in it.

When the government took a hand here in 1935, six out of ten schoolchildren in the county had hookworm. Every other baby died at birth. One mother in every ten died in childbirth. The average mentality was third-grade. One out of ten adults couldn't read or write. Three fourths of the farmers were tenant farmers. Most of them had never been out of debt in their lives. They averaged only one mule to three families.

And this is in Coffee County, which stands third among all the counties of Alabama in the value of agricultural products. These figures are not the scandalous revelations of some smart Brain Truster* from the North. They are from a survey made by Southerners. Sure, you'll find wealth and grace and beautiful homes in the South, homes as pretty and people as fine as anywhere in the world. But you drive the back roads, and you won't see one farm home in a hundred that would equal the ordinary Midwest farmhouse.

*

Coffee County has become a sort of experimental station in Alabama. Not by design, especially, but because the government people and the local agencies got enthusiastic, and it just grew up under them.

*Roosevelt's inner circle of academic advisers, who helped write New Deal legislation and run New Deal agencies, was sometimes called his brain trust.

Federal, state, and county agencies all have a hand. To prevent overlapping, they are coordinated under a council, with the county school superintendent as chairman. They say it's the only thing of its kind in America.

These agencies cover most everything from typhoid shots to fruit-canning. They're like the agencies in your home territory, only the need is greater and I suspect they are a bit more enthusiastic. The work is climaxed in the Farm Security Administration, which actually owns thousands of acres of land and plants these down-and-out farmers on its acres.

I wish there were something to call these things besides "projects." The idea of a project makes the farmers contemptuous, makes Republicans snort with rage, brings sneers from the townspeople. A project is Brain Trust—experimenting, regimenting people.

What they're doing here isn't a project, anyway. They aren't setting up a "settlement." Nobody is forced to do anything. The six hundred farmers on FSA are scattered over a county twenty-five miles square. What they're doing is simply a general and wide-stretching process—starting almost from zero—of trying to get people to living better.

March 16, 1939

SOUTHERN FOLKWAYS

ENTERPRISE, ALABAMA—When I was a boy, the professional horse trader, country peddler, and patent-medicine show were just going into the twilight.

But in the deep rural South they flourish. There are half a dozen mule skinners in every community—men who trade mules with the poor farmer, and skin him every time, you may be sure. The farmers have a passion for trading, like small boys, and about the only thing they have to trade is a mule.

One man around here, through government help, got a good team of mules. But a mule skinner got him. The man traded his team for a younger one, and gave the skinner forty dollars to boot. The government man raised Cain. "What in hell did you do that for?" he asked.

"Well," the tenant said, "he told me that if I'd keep them all summer and feed them up, he'd trade back in the fall and give me twenty-five dollars to boot."

"And it never occurred to you, did it," said the government

man, "that after feeding them all summer and trading back, you'd still be fifteen dollars behind?"

No, it hadn't occurred to him.

*

Patent-medicine salesmen reap harvests down here. One can get a crowd around him, do a few pea-shell tricks or some magic with dollar bills, then haul out his phony medicine and leave town with fifty or sixty dollars of people's hard-earned money. And before he leaves he'll make every customer in the crowd hold up his hand and say he's satisfied.

I've heard of one big landlord who has more than a hundred families sharecropping for him. They're treated so badly that a third move every year.

This landlord sells fertilizer to his tenants. Under the rental agreement, they are to pay half and he is to pay half. The price he puts on it is thirty dollars a ton. Consequently the tenants pay him fifteen dollars a ton. That sounds fair enough—except that the landlord buys the fertilizer in the first place for fifteen dollars a ton. At four tons per family, it's a nice profit of six thousand dollars a year. But in fairness, the local people tell me that fewer than half the landlords are like that. . . .

*

When the government tried to talk one backward tenant into moving to a decent place, he said no; he wouldn't move because his grandfather had once owned all this land. In two generations the family has gone from comparative wealth to grinding poverty.

His ragged children sitting on the porch had sores all over their legs. The government man suggested taking the little girl down to the doctor. The man said, "Naw," as soon as he could get four dollars he'd take her back over the hill to a doctor who had fixed her up before. It was a Negro "witch doctor," who used potions of manure and weird incantations.

*

It is part of the new program to get all rural families to equip their places with sanitary toilets. That is the only way hook-worm can be stamped out. The approved toilet consists of a pit in the ground, sealed on top with concrete, and a riser with a lid on it. The riser costs four dollars and fifty cents—the farmer can build the rest himself. The response has been fairly good. But one day a county official went out on an inspection tour of these modern Chic Sales.* He went into one, lifted the lid—and the whole pit was full of hay! It had never been used from the day they put it in. The whole family, women included, preferred to go out behind the barn.

*

You grain farmers around Indianapolis who read this, you beet farmers in Colorado, you citrus farmers in California—I don't believe you can possibly conceive of what life is like for half the farmers in the South.

A young man and woman marry. They are of sixth-grade education, and steeped in the hopelessness and listlessness of one-mule, sharecropping, debt-owing farming. Their parents can't help them, so they go to a supply merchant for "furnishing," and start life in debt. Thereafter, the girl gets pregnant as soon, and as frequently, as possible.

They live on fat meat and cornmeal, three meals a day. She never heard of a women's club. The house is filthy, and stays that way. She carries her littlest baby down to the fencerow, lays him down, and works in the field.

She knows only a few neighbors. Maybe twice a year she comes to town. She doesn't read anything, and they have no radio. They use coal-oil lamps, and the floors are bare. Likely as not they don't even have a privy. The children are half naked, and covered with sores. Soon she is old, and her sickly brood goes out to repeat the process. She chews snuff, spits at the fireplace, hits the wall, and there it stays for posterity. Her mark in life. . . .

March 17, 1939

SCOURGES OF THE SOUTH
ELBA, ALABAMA—I had heard of hookworm, but I never knew exactly what it was. Because it is the worst scourge of Coffee County, and probably of most of the far South, I looked into it a little.

It is actually a tiny worm that you can just barely see with the naked eye. It moves in a sort of cycle through the bodies of human beings, wasting them away. Children get it from going barefooted. It gets in the skin between the toes, starts an infec-

---

*Named for the humorist Chic Sales, who, according to the *Dictionary of American Slang,* "wrote a widely circulated catalogue of outhouses, a satirical booklet."

tion, gradually spreads through the system, and winds up in the intestines.

Here the worm multiplies by the hundreds, feeding, sapping the blood. It could eventually kill, but instead it so weakens your system that something else—pneumonia, whooping cough, diphtheria—takes hold and carries you off.

You can tell a hookworm victim by his paleness, a ghastly corpselike white in the face. He becomes listless, lifeless, ambitionless, just sick all over, till he finally does nothing but sit on the old porch in a daze and let life roll by.

Hookworm is curable, and very quickly. You eat a light supper, no breakfast, and then take some capsules the doctor gives you. This medicine dislodges all the hookworms. You follow that in about three hours with a big laxative.

But, walking barefooted, you're soon infected again—that is, unless there is a sanitary toilet available. The farmers call hookworm infection the "ground itch." They have all kinds of home remedies for it, but all too few will do anything modern about it.

*

Pellagra is caused by too few vegetables in the diet. It causes sores, and bloating, and is a horrible disease. It majors in the South. There would be no pellagra, especially among farmers, if they had the ambition to provide themselves with vegetables. Vegetables grow wonderfully in the South, but the average tenant farmer in Coffee County has no garden. They're becoming increasingly garden-conscious, though. There is a movement on to get women to can vegetables.

I stopped by one of the FSA homes. It was an old house remodeled into a comfortable bungalow. Half a mile down the dirt road you could see the medieval shack where the family used to live. The women took me out to the shed where she keeps her canned stuff. There in the meat-and-meal South it was like an oasis in neat rows, shelf after shelf.

Last year she canned three hundred and fifty quarts of vegetables, fruits, and meats. She has twenty-nine different vegetables canned. They've been eating real meals all winter. I asked her if she ever canned anything before this program started. She said no. I asked why. She said she just wasn't interested, she guessed. Down here, where the growing season is long and things flourish, half the people have starved themselves sick because they weren't interested.

*

Half the rural South is sick—I mean physically sick—and what can you expect of sick people? If you felt continually lousy, would you care whether you were honest or not, whether you got out of debt, whether you had what people call "character"? I'll bet you wouldn't.

W. L. McArthur, who is county head of the Farm Security Administration, has simple ideas about rehabilitation of the South. He says the first thing to do is get the people well again, get the disease out of them, get them eating properly. The other stuff can come later.

They've made wonderful progress in just three years. The nurses are responsible for dropping infant mortality from fifty-five percent to nineteen percent last year. And deaths of mothers at childbirth have fallen from just under ten-and-a-half percent to just over six-and-a-half percent.

But it will take generations to educate poor people to *want* to be well. They've been used to feeling rotten too long to change overnight. One of the government men here said the FSA couldn't tolerate a farmer who was a perpetual drunk, but he said down in his heart he couldn't blame the guys for taking a few snorts.

"My God!" he said. "The only time in their lives they ever feel halfway human is when they get a couple of shots of bad liquor in them."

March 18, 1939

An Affliction Called "Sorryness"

ELBA, ALABAMA—They have a way of using the word "sorry" down here that I've not heard in other parts of the country.

A listless, no-good, poor-paying fellow is known as sorry. You can be poor without being sorry. You're sorry when you lack character.

Of Coffee County's forty-two hundred farmers, six hundred are now under the Farm Security Administration. The FSA sets them up on decent land, in a new or remodeled little house, gives them a small loan for getting started, and then supervises them.

They don't hand out much on a silver platter. For instance, they don't put bathrooms in the houses. As McArthur, the county FSA head, says: "Lots of them won't even use privies now; what would they do with a bathroom? Wait till they get healthy and out of debt and grow up to a bathroom; then they can put one in themselves."

He's also strict about debts. The government is getting back most of the money it lends these farmers. Those who are just plain sorry, and won't try to make a crop, are kicked out. As McArthur says, "When you put a premium on sorryness, you might as well quit."

*

One out of seven farm families in this county is now on government land. I asked how many really were in need of this kind of help. The answer was at least half. Probably half of that half are too sorry to get any good out of such help. But what I mean is that only half the farmers are doing well enough to live at all decently.

There is no real money now in Southern farming. If a fellow is straight, keeps his place clean, has a car and enough to eat, and sends his kids through grade school, that's all any farm can produce here now.

They tell me that Southern farmers can get really well off in only three ways: by inheriting a lot of land; by being scrooges, and denying their families everything worth living for; or by skinning somebody out of it.

*

Probably half the land in Coffee County is washed away, not fit for raising anything. They feel that reforesting and terracing will bring much of this back. "But it's not submarginal land that puts us in our sorry shape," one man told me. "It's submarginal *people.*"

And when you get down and mix in it, you can't say it's wholly caused by cruel landlords, by sharpster supply merchants, or by erosion. You can't blame any individual, least of all the poor people themselves.

As McArthur says, all landlords aren't bad. In fact, many Southern farmers are better off under a capable and interested landlord than they would be on their own land. And he says you can't blame the supply merchant, either—the store owner who carries the people on credit and keeps them always in debt and reaps his high profit.

There are some bad supply merchants who skin people and become well-off in the process. But there are some good ones, too. They carry people who don't pay them for years, people who would otherwise starve. And they take an awful chance. Many and many a supply merchant has gone broke in this county. No, it's a combination of the landlord and the supply merchant and poor land and low prices and sickness and ignorance—in other words, it's the whole system.

I haven't gone much into detail about what the government has done here, because it's much the same as in other places where they're trying to recreate human beings. But they're trying, through a thousand little pinpoints of practical education, to change the system. It's a thankless job, for the system down here is as much a part of a man as his arm.

It will take generations to get the rural South raised above its system. Sorryness is a disease that America hasn't paid much attention to before now. It will take a long time to purge it.

*

Maybe I get too worked up about things like this. Sometimes I think maybe a fellow should just shut his eyes and drive fast.

Last night, I went to see a movie called *St. Louis Blues.* Dorothy Lamour was in it, and it was set on the Mississippi and was very romantic and full of the lovely old things of the South. I came away thinking that maybe my recent pieces were all wrong, and that Hollywood is right. I should have made Coffee County romantic, and full of guitars, and happy, happy Negroes, and sweeping bows to the ladies.

Maybe I should, I don't know. But Hollywood has never seen all the pale dead people walking slowly around the red clay countryside.

March 20, 1939

* * *

BILOXI, MISSISSIPPI— . . . One day we were eating a late lunch in a hotel coffee shop in Montgomery, Alabama. A young man came in. He was about twenty-five, tall and thin, and just a little stooped. He was nicely dressed, but there was a haunted look about him. We heard him ask one of the waitresses for the manager. She directed him back to the kitchen. In a minute he came back out, hung up his hat, sat down at the counter, and said: "Well, it *can* happen here. I just want a bowl of soup."

He ate it, thanked the waitress again and again, and walked out.

After he left, our waitress said to us, "He was nice-looking, too, wasn't he? Just down on his luck, I guess." She said they didn't have very many come in like that, asking for something to eat, but whenever one did, they always fed him.

So it can happen here. . . .

March 24, 1939

MISSISSIPPI

THE WORK OF SAD OLD WOMEN

BILOXI, MISSISSIPPI—The finest compliment I can pay the Biloxi shrimp-canning factories is to say that after going through one, I believe I could still eat a shrimp.

Biloxi has the biggest concentration of shrimp canneries in America. It has ten of them. They are called factories, which might lead you to believe shrimp are manufactured. But they aren't, I assure you.

Shrimp are caught with nets on the bottom of the Gulf, sometimes as far as fifty miles from shore. A shrimp boat carries only two men, and they are out three and four days. Those two men have to lower and raise the big nets all by themselves.

As soon as the shrimp are caught they must be put on ice, or they'll spoil. When the boat is full it comes in and ties up at the cannery dock, and a man in boots with a shovel scoops the shrimp out onto a wire conveyor belt. This belt carries the shrimp up into the factory. Here two men stand on either side of a trough, watching the shrimp go by. If they see a bad one—and they're trained to spot them at a glance—they grab it and throw it into a bucket.

I was standing at this trough talking with the government inspector. "If two men can't catch all the bad ones, I put on two more men," he said. "And if they can't get 'em all, I put on two more. When there are so many bad ones eight men can't handle them, I just condemn the whole boatload."

Government inspection is something new in shrimp canning, only a year and a half old. It isn't compulsory even now, but forty of the fifty factories in the United States have them. The inspectors say the stuff that was canned before that was shocking but that now everything is sanitary.

*

Removing the shells is the biggest job. A woman has a pile of shrimp on the table before her. She grabs a shrimp, takes off its head, slips the meat out of the shell. She drops the meat into a bucket, and tosses the head and shell over into a long slanting trough, filled with running water. This carries the refuse outside the building, and drops it back into the water, where fish eat it.

All the picking, as they call it, is done in one big room, at two long tables. Sometimes as many as two hundred people are working there, all standing, jammed elbow to elbow. Most of them are middle-aged or elderly women. There are some boys, and some small children. They all look sad and bleak, like the rows of miners' gray houses on Pennsylvania hillsides.

Some of the women wear men's coats and have shawls around their heads. It is damp, and often cold, in there. They come to work at four in the morning, and many's the time they are still there at six that evening. They work by the piece, so much a bucketful. It seemed to me a disagreeable way of making a very poor living. . . .

*

The bucketsful of shrimp meat go by conveyor belt to another part of the factory. They stand in big buckets of brine for fifty minutes, to harden them. Then they're blanched, or boiled, in big vats, for ten minutes. Then they go over another conveyor belt, where girls eye them closely, pick out little blades of grass, little rocks, broken pieces of shrimp.

Then to the canning table. Girls stuff them into cans by hand. A tablet of salt is dropped on top. The cans slide under a spray. The result is brine. A machine puts a cap on, and seals the can. Then comes another boiling—several hundred cans in a big iron basket, lowered into a vat. The inspector has the key to time and temperature control—no less than ten minutes. This kills the last lurking germ. Then a cold-water dip, and then to the crating department, and the trains.

Sixty million shrimp every year, in this one factory alone! I suppose eventually it gets to be just like sixty million grains of corn is to a corn sheller, but to me they'll always be sixty million shrimp having their heads snapped off by sad old women.

March 18, 1936

BILOXI, MISSISSIPPI—This is a legend about islands and buzzards. All along this Gulf Coast, a mile or so from shore, are long, narrow islands. They are almost like beads on a string, all about the same length and width. One of the islands just off Biloxi is called Ship Island. It was inhabited by Spaniards, but smallpox or something swept through, and most of the people died.

They were buried on the island, in the shallow sand. Years passed. And then came a great storm. The wind blew and the waves washed the island, disinterring the dead. Buzzards did the rest.

So enraged were the remaining residents by this viciousness of storm and fowl that they all packed up to leave. But the old padre had a solution. He said he would consecrate the island against buzzards. And so he did.

And to this day, they tell me here, there is not a buzzard on Ship Island. You can go out and see for yourself. Captain Bill Reed, who told me about it, says he has had a standing offer for years of twenty-five dollars to anyone who can show him a buzzard on Ship Island.

They infest all the other islands. They swarm over them by the hundreds, and swoop down to take anything that dies. Yet a cow can die on Ship Island and lie there forever without attracting a buzzard. They say a buzzard will not even fly over Ship Island. . . .

March 24, 1939

LOUISIANA

A Fighting, What-the-Hell Sort of City

NEW ORLEANS—Some people say of this fabulous spot that it is "the city of the psychological souse."

They say that when you get within a hundred miles you begin to feel a little drunk on just the idea of New Orleans, and that with every turn of the wheel you get a little drunker, and that when you get here you're completely out of control—blotto on romance and sentiment and freedom, a spiritual binge.

That is true. Anything you may say about New Orleans, good or bad, is true. There never was a city anywhere, I suppose, like it. It is a fantastic, hypnotic, mystic sort of place.

The first time I ever came here, I "got" the place in a minute. It was what I wanted it to be. It was everything I had heard about it. But I couldn't put a finger on it. So this time I have been pinning people down. "Tell me what it is about New Orleans," I say to them. "How are the people different? What is in their hearts? Just exactly what is the psychology of New Orleans, or the spirit, or whatever you call it?"

People scratch their heads, and feel around for words, and give examples, only to say no, that isn't it. So it's like music, or the wind. You can't see it, you can't put it in a bottle, you can't hang clothes on it, but it's there all right. It's there pounding in your temples and singing in your heart.

*

People care a little less in New Orleans. They're born to a what-the-hell attitude. They grow up to take a chance. They have a heritage in them, and they're hardly conscious of it. They have a heritage of hot blood mixtures, of warm weather and great rainfall, of pirates and buccaneers and revolutionists, of great wealth and great poverty, of battles and heroes and grand ladies, and balconies and iron lace and ships from far corners, and haughtiness and dignity and carousal.

The spirit of New Orleans is a spirit of pleasure. And it's just as strong in the shotgun cottages of the poor suburbs as in the shuttered homes of the proud Creoles. Maybe stronger. The people of New Orleans believe devoutly in their right to drink, dance, gamble, make love, and worship God.

People grow up drinking. Saloons are everywhere. A drunk is never arrested unless he's harming other people.

People grow up dancing. In the winter there are probably more dances here than anywhere in the world. The youngsters start making love early, and being happy.

People grow up to take a chance. New Orleans will fight for its right to gamble. Every night hundreds of people—common, ordinary people—take their dollar or two or three, and go shoot the works.

*

And what is the cause of it all? Just circumstances, I guess. There was a mixture of French and Spanish, a combination of teeming temperaments. New Orleans was nearly a hundred years old before it had American residents in it.

There was its location, which made it rich, which made it the greatest port in the South, and which even today keeps it the second port in America. Whenever a population rises around deep water and docks and ships from far away, there is a tang and a color about it.

Its location did something else, too—it bred a spirit of struggle, a back-to-the-wall psychology. New Orleans for two hundred years has fought harder against water than most cities ever fought in a war. The city is surrounded by water. The flooding Mississippi constricts it on three sides, and Lake Pontchartrain stands guard on the other. Swamps are beneath and terrific tropical rainfall overhead. New Orleans has been a city overwhelmed by water.

Its location has also made it a fighting city. It fought the Indians, and the British, and the North, and the French and Spanish fought each other, and it has always been an outpost hotbed for revolutionaries.

And there is the climate. Southern Louisiana is warm. Things grow quickly. Men move slowly. It is hot, and there is time for pleasure. After a few generations it gets in the blood, and becomes part of you, like getting hungry.

New Orleans hungers for pleasure, and has it, and let him beware who tries to interfere.

March 7, 1936

THREE SCENES FROM A FANTASTIC CITY

NEW ORLEANS—A French restaurant, far back in the Vieux Carré, the Old Quarter. Tourists don't go there. There is no reason why anybody would, for that matter, because it isn't a very good restaurant, and there's no atmosphere, and the food is just so-so. But you get an awful lot of it for a quarter.

You have ordered black coffee. Finally a startled-looking waiter arrives with it. He sets it down. He looks at the coffee, and then at you, and you look at him, and his mouth opens and he stands there like that, and finally he says:

"Why, I put milk in it."

That's what happened. He put milk in it.

So he tries again, and this time he comes back and sets the cup down, and looks at you, and then at the coffee, and then at you, and he seems to become sort of frightened at himself, and paralyzed, and finally picks up the cup and starts back with it, and says, "I guess I'll have to drink it myself." He has put milk in it again.

You'll think it's a lie, but it isn't: he had milk in it when he came back a third time. He never said a word that time. He just set it down, looked at it, picked it up, and started back again, as if he knew all the time he would find milk in it when he looked.

He made a fourth trip. But it was a demitasse. He began explaining ten feet away. "I've only got half a cup. I'm sorry but this is all the coffee there is. I used it all up making that damn coffee and milk."

*

High above the altar in the Church of the Immaculate Conception on Baronne Street she stands, the white marble Virgin, with two circles of light behind her. At her feet are three very old silver candlesticks, fancifully molded, with deer and little boys and birds in trees.

Men and women of New Orleans kneel in silence and cross themselves. Very few of them know the stories of the Virgin and the candlesticks.

The Virgin was sculpted by craftsmen of Lyons for Empress Marie Louise, wife of Napoleon. On her shoulder appeared a little black spot, one of those streaks that sometimes show up in marble. Marie Louis, empress, would have no Virgin with a black spot. Any Virgin for Marie Louise must be as white as snow. She refused her.

So the pious women of New Orleans heard about it, chipped in and bought the lovely figure, brought her over the ocean, and there she is today, high above the altar, black spot and all.

And the candlesticks—no one knows how old they are, not even Brother Peter, who has been the sacristan for fifty years. But he knows something that happened to them once. It was during the Civil War. Northern troops were in New Orleans. There was looting. Two officers came into the church and carried off the candlesticks.

The Jesuit priest saw them, and followed. He trailed them to their barracks. Then he hotfooted it to the headquarters of General Benjamin Butler, the Union commander. "Is it the practice of the North to loot the altar of the House of God when they make war?" he demanded. Said General Butler, "What the hell are you talking about?"

So the priest told him what the hell he was talking about, and General Butler swore a very large oath, and ordered the two officers before him. "Sure we took them," they said. "Everybody is taking things."

General Butler ordered them into their best uniforms. And
with an armed guard they carried those candlesticks down the
main street and back into the church, and apologized to the
priest. And there they are today.

*

An old, old house in the Vieux Carré, behind the ancient
Cathedral of St. Louis. In this house an old lady died the other
day. A very old lady, a Creole of sentiment and strong blood and
tenderness for the little things she loved.

She died at ninety-eight. She was born there, she died there,
and only three nights of her entire ninety-eight years had she
slept outside of that house. She always listened for the lovely
soft bells of the Cathedral of St. Louis. She had never married.

The night she died, two friends called to commiserate with
her brother, who lived with her. They offered restrained, sad
words. The old man put his arms around the two of them. He
was not sad.

"Do not grieve, my dear friends," he said. "Her death was a
beautiful death."

"How can death ever be beautiful?"

"Let me tell you," he said. "At five minutes till nine she called
to me. 'François,' she said. 'François, pour me a little glass of
brandy.'

"So I got a bottle of brandy forty-eight years old, and I poured
her a glass, and put one arm behind her and lifted her up, and
held it for her, and she sipped it in slow sips, and rested a little
between sips.

"And then at nine, the cathedral bells began ringing, and she
sat up with my arm around her and listened to the bells, and just
as they stopped, she smiled and lay back down and she was dead.

"My dear good friends, how could anything be more beautiful
than that? With the taste of good brandy in her mouth, and the
sound of the bells in her ears, and a smile on her face—is that
not beautiful?"

March 9, 1936

*After serving as governor—and near-dictator—of Louisiana, during
which time he did a great deal for the state's poor and modernized its roads,
Huey Long, or the Kingfish, as he called himself, arrived in Washington
as a United States senator in 1932.*

*His populist outspokenness and outright opportunism soon caused him
to split with President Roosevelt, whom Long saw as doing too little for*

*America's poor. Shortly after becoming a senator, Long created the Share
Our Wealth Society, which proposed to redistribute American wealth
among all Americans, instead of allowing it to be concentrated among an
elite few. This had enormous appeal to millions of Americans in the midst
of the Depression, and Long's following grew—so much so that Roosevelt
came to consider Long capable of diverting enough votes from the Demo-
crats in the 1936 election to put the Republicans back in the White House.*

*Long, together with the ultra-right-wing Father Charles Coughlin—the
"Radio Priest," as millions of listeners knew him—and Dr. Francis
Townsend, who had yet another popular scheme for redistributing the
country's wealth, represented restless constituencies that spurred Roosevelt
to move the New Deal leftward. Long was murdered the night of September 8, 1935, by Carl Weiss, a young doctor who thought Long a tyrant and
who believed his father-in-law had been wronged by Long's political
organization. Weiss himself was killed by Long's bodyguards.*

*Roosevelt won the 1936 election, and soon the popularity of Dr. Town-
send and Father Coughlin began to decline, as more and more of their
followers detected fascist leanings in their ideas.*

A Giant of Some Kind

BATON ROUGE, LOUISIANA—The spirit of Huey Long hovers over
Louisiana. You feel him in the air; you are conscious of him
always.

In Louisiana they never say Huey Long was shot, or murdered. They say he was assassinated. After hearing it awhile you
get the flavor of martyrdom, and Huey Long begins to take on
the aura of a Lincoln.

*

I came up to Baton Rouge just to see Louisiana's capitol. It is
always referred to as the monument Huey built for himself, and
I had the impression it was something garish and altogether too
grand. It's big, all right. You see it for miles before you get to
Baton Rouge, a white shaft alone in the sky. It is thirty-four
stories high, a startling thing, and beautiful.

Its beauty grows as you get closer. It sits on a rise, at the north
edge of town, and all around it for at least a block on each side
are landscaped gardens—grass, shrubs, flowers, fir trees, and
winding walks. The effect is serene.

A hostess takes you through the capitol itself. . . . Behind the
elevators, off a little hallway, are the governor's offices. The
guide takes you back there, and suddenly stops and says, "That's
the door there. That's the one Senator Long came out of when

he was assassinated. He fell right there. The assassin stood by that pillar there." . . .

*

As you leave, you stroll along the winding walks down through the vast gardens, down into a slightly sunken valley, all grassed and sprouting with shrubbery. Down in the middle the walks converge amid a cluster of small fir trees and bushes. And there, in the center of the grounds, about a hundred yards in front of the main capitol doors, rests Huey Long.

There is just a block of concrete, about ten feet across, with one corner of the square pointing toward the capitol. The block rises only about six inches from the sidewalks. It is ordinary pavement concrete—not even a glazed finish. There is no statue, or railing, or anything.

On each of the four corners sits a flower pot or a tall basket, containing fresh flowers. And right in the center is a marble marker about two feet high, looking quite common and temporary, and chiseled on it are these homely words:

> HUEY P. LONG
> 1893–1935
> *"Sleep on dear friend*
> *And take your rest*
> *They mourn the most*
> *Who loved you best."*

That is all. Here lies the King. The immense living monument he built for himself looks down upon the simplicity of the grave. You stand and wonder. Was he a good man, or was he bad? Was he great, or was he a fraud?

You don't know. But I'll tell you this: as you stand there before that plain concrete over the body of the dead King, you know that he was a giant of some kind, and you feel a pull at your heart, and the swaying of destinies, and a lonesomeness through all Louisiana now that he is gone.

March 17, 1936

raveler's
lotes

"A fellow can't even have a good local illusion anymore."

DRIVING

The Pyles returned to Washington for a brief rest in late June of 1936. The travel column was almost a year old, and Pyle, always fond of travel facts and figures, shared a few with his readers.

WHY HURRY?

WASHINGTON— . . . In almost twelve months of roving, I have driven twenty-nine thousand miles. My arms never get tired, even on rough roads. But being a skinny fellow, I do get to hurting where I sit down, and I think I'll have to get an air cushion to sit on.

The farthest we've driven in one day is five hundred and seventy miles—from a ranch in the center of Arizona clear into Los Angeles. I'll never do that again. There are people who can knock off seven hundred miles a day, but I can't, and don't want to. A friend of mine claims to have driven from Los Angeles to Washington, D.C., in three days and eight hours. I think he should have his driver's license taken away.

When I first started this roving assignment, I would clip along at seventy miles an hour. I remember once, on a long, straight road out in Arizona, the speedometer got up to eighty. When I saw it, it almost scared me to death. Even though I have always driven cautiously, I finally figured that seventy miles an hour was too much for a day-in, day-out traveling diet. Even if you're careful, the law of averages will catch up with you.

So I have gradually slowed down. On this last four-month trip, which included Mexico, my speedometer never passed fifty-five, and it was that high only a few times. Usually, on a straight road, the speedometer stands at forty-eight. After all, why should I hurry? I'm not going anyplace especially, as they say, and I've got all day to get there. . . .

In west Texas, a couple of months ago, a car passed us going sixty. The road was gravel, and very rough. In a few minutes we came upon the car, sitting crosswise of the road, looking as though a shell had hit it. It had turned over twice at sixty miles an hour, right in the middle of the road. The only injury to the driver was a scratch where his garter went around his leg.

He had just bought the car three days before. He was a salesman for a biscuit company. He had a big box of badges—the kind little boys pin on their coat lapels—advertising his cookies. They were scattered all over the highway. The man laughed and said: "Well, the boss can't say I don't spread advertising."

A few days later, in New Mexico, we came across a car hanging by two wheels over the edge of a cliff. The driver, another traveling salesman, had simply gone to sleep. He admitted it. We were afraid to try to pull the car back up, for it looked as though if you blew on it, it would fall over the cliff. So we got a towline onto each end, and while one car pulled sidewise toward the road, another pulled him forward, and out.

A fellow does get awfully sleepy driving, especially right after lunch on a hot day. . . . Once we stopped on the desert, for me to take a little nap. I have never heard such intense quiet as there was on the desert that day. That Girl who rides with me was reading a newspaper. This sounds incredible, but the desert stillness was so acute that the slight rustling of her paper made so much noise I couldn't get to sleep, as sleepy as I was. I never said anything to her about it, and I hope she doesn't read this.

June 23, 1936

CARS

It was time to trade the Ford coupe in for a new car, a 1936 Dodge convertible.

THE PARTING

WASHINGTON—Goodbye to you, my little old car. In a few minutes I must drive you away for the last time. Trading you off, selling you down the river for a shiny new hussy, just because you're old and crippled. I feel like a dog.

You look so old and weak, sitting there ready to go away. I know; you're thinking of the things we've been through together. You've never let me down, have you? And you're thinking that I just can't turn on you now. I hate it, I sure hate it, but I suppose I'll let you go.

We were both so proud that first day we marched down the road together three years ago. Remember how you purred, and how gently I drove you because you were mine and I didn't want to hurt you?

You're only a piece of machinery. But I've always felt as if you were human, and I've treated you that way. Remember how I've worried over you, and understood your little peeves, and eased you along when you felt bad, and almost never punished you?

Remember up there in Canada last fall, how some strange malady attacked your steering gear, and you could hardly bear to turn a corner, and it took every ounce of my strength to steer you around the mudholes and through traffic? But every time we'd get within yelling distance of a garage, you remember what you'd do? You'd pull yourself together, and when the mechanic would get in to test you, you'd steer like a feather. You used to burn me up with that kind of stuff.

And remember how you used to lean over to one side, like a tired horse that shifts its weight? And I'd look at your springs and fuss around and worry and get mad, but there wasn't anything wrong with you at all, except you'd be leaning over to one side. Just for the fun of it, I suppose.

Remember that time down in south Texas when you just up

and died, cold as a turkey? And I raised your hood, and after seeing the engine was still there I didn't know what to do next, so I just got back in and stepped on the starter, and you laughed and started right up. Remember that? We did take a hunk of dirt as big as a walnut out of your gas pump at the next town. But you did it just to scare me, didn't you?

You've been good to me, too. Don't think I don't appreciate it. That night we got home from six thousand miles in Canada, you recall. You'd taken a beating up there, on those rough roads. How you stood it all, I don't know. But you did, and remember when we pulled up in front of the apartment that night, with the trip ended, and just as I turned off the switch your front springs broke in two, and let your body down on the tires? You brought me home before you gave up, didn't you?

You've seen a lot of country that most cars don't see. And you've had some pretty full experiences for an automobile. Remember that blizzard in Mississippi? Yes, in Mississippi, of all places. How we drove all day through snow and freezing mud, and it just didn't seem possible you could keep on pulling. And how when we got into Brookhaven that night the garage man said you had four hundred pounds of frozen mud under your fenders, and it was sticking out behind for two feet?

And remember your long ride on the boat? I can see you now, sitting out there on top of that deckload of lumber, covered with a canvas. Six thousand miles you made on that boat, without moving a muscle. Pretty soft, wasn't it?

And do you remember that time the whole gearshift lever came right out in my hand? And when I put it back in everything was mixed up, and reverse was high gear, and low was second, and I had to call a garage to get you straightened out? I'll bet you chuckled a week over that.

And you remember that time in Los Angeles when somebody tried to steal you? But you didn't want to travel with anybody but me, did you? You wouldn't let them in, even if they did break your door handle off. You were swell about that.

But you know the thing I love you most for? The time we hit that hole in Mexico at fifty miles an hour. You showed what was in you that day. You took it standing up, and you stayed up.

You've been twelve thousand feet above sea level, and eighty feet below sea level. You've seen twenty below zero and a hundred and ten in the shade. And you've been through cloudbursts and snowstorms where I couldn't even see your radiator cap.

You've complained and whined and groaned, but you've always kept on going, haven't you?

We've ridden so far together, and we've been to such funny places, and we've been so close to tragedy, and things have looked pretty dark for us, but somehow we always came home together, didn't we?

So there you sit, waiting to go. If I were rich I'd turn you out to pasture, like a horse. But I'm not rich. And you must know there is a futility in all companionship, and days of parting come and they are always like ashes, and I'm putting on my hat to come down and drive you away. Try not to hate me for it, won't you?

We must go for the last ride. Goodbye to you, my dear little car.

June 29, 1936

WASHINGTON— . . . The [Dodge] was new when we started, and we've brought it back after sixteen thousand miles with not a scratch on it. In a San Francisco garage they knocked a big dent in a front fender, and then denied they did it, and wouldn't do anything about it. But a few nights later a garage in Santa Barbara—where I stored the car for the night—pounded the dent out and didn't charge anything for it, in fact didn't even mention they had done it. . . .

*

. . . We drive a convertible coupe. Two dealers tried to talk me out of buying it, saying the top would rattle. But I insisted, and I'm glad I did.

The car has been over thousands of miles of unbelievably rough roads, but the top does not rattle. In the summer it is wonderful to have the top down. Makes you feel like big stuff. And in the winter the convertible top seems as tight and cozy as a regular coupe. We have a heater, and never suffer from cold.

February 8, 1937

ROADS

WASHINGTON— . . . The best-marked city for a tourist to get through, in my opinion, is Pueblo, Colorado. The best-marked

state is Iowa. Kentucky is among the poorest. Ohio, a rich state,
has terrible main highways. The wildest drivers on the roads
have Illinois tags.

June 24, 1936

THE PRICE
OF TRAVEL

WASHINGTON—Living prices throughout the country are amaz-
ingly uniform, except for a few extremes. Day-in-and-day-out
living is a little cheaper in the West than in the East. I have
found Los Angeles the cheapest place in the country to live, and
Washington, D.C., the highest.

All through the West you can get a good lunch for thirty-five
to fifty cents, and it's only in the flossiest hotels that dinner goes
as high as a dollar. Ordinarily you can get an excellent dinner
for from fifty to eighty-five cents. . . .

February 10, 1937

PROVIDENCE, RHODE ISLAND— . . . We've been taking it in the neck
ever since we got back from the West this spring, and I'm getting fed up with it. Unreasonable prices reached a sort of hyster-
ical peak coming down through the vacation belt of New York
State, but they're bad all over the East.

It's got so you can't get into even a dump of a hotel for less
than five dollars. There isn't one tourist camp in fifty you'd keep
a chicken in. Tourist camps are getting better in the East, and
now and then you hit a dandy, but they're hard to find.

The food problem is just as bad, if not worse. You can't even
economize at a hash house these days. Hash houses apparently
have two proprietors, who collaborate on the menu. The one
who makes out the list of meals thinks his customers are named
Slats or Butch. The other one, who puts down the prices, has
got it in his head all the customers are named Rockefeller. The
result is unsatisfactory.

I'm not much of an eater, but now and then a fellow has to
have some beefsteak to keep his ribs apart. On half the menus

we see, they don't even have steaks. And when you do see one, it's never less than a dollar. A decent one costs a dollar fifty.

I've squandered a great deal of the company's time trying to figure this thing out. We're supposed to be in a depression now. People are short on money. I don't know of anybody who has had a raise in the past year. When I was in college Professor Phillips used to tell us something about supply-and-demand. If people haven't got any money, then prices go down, he said.

So here are the prices. And here are the people paying them. Just drive from Lake Champlain to New York City some weekend, and you'll find yourself in a traffic jam for two hundred and fifty miles.

Millions of people, and apparently every one able and willing to pay a dollar fifty for a steak, with the country going to hell. I wish I'd listened a little harder to Professor Phillips fifteen years ago. Maybe I could understand it better now.

September 6, 1938

AMERICAN MANNERS AND MORALS

LOS ANGELES— . . . I went one morning into a little coffee shop in Carmel, and gave the waitress my breakfast order—orange juice, one egg medium-boiled, crisp bacon, dry toast, and coffee.

The girl then took the menu, looked at it, and said, "That would be Number Three, but Number Three is a poached egg. You can't substitute."

So I said, gaily but politely, "Well, I don't care whether it's Number Three or Number Twenty-seven. I'm not trying to substitute. I'm just ordering what I want."

And the girl said, "But the cook won't boil one egg. He'll poach one, but not boil one."

So I said, "Well, a man can get one boiled egg if he's willing to pay for it, can't he? How much is the breakfast I ordered if you make it à la carte?"

So the girl, looking extremely doubtful, disappeared into the kitchen to find out. In a little while she came out. She looked a little scared, and said, "The cook won't boil one egg under any circumstances, for any price!"

And so I left, my vexation completely overshadowed by my admiration for such man.

November 7, 1939

TACOMA, WASHINGTON— . . . Many younger people in the East have never seen a silver dollar. But until recently they were practically compulsory in the West.

I remember my first trip to Seattle, twenty years ago, when a restaurant actually refused to take a dollar bill. They haven't been that finicky in recent years, but still the silver dollar was predominant. If you handed over a ten your change was in silver, and you went around thereafter all dragged down on your money-pocket side.

But now silver dollars are getting scarce, even out here. They say the government has quit making them. Even when you do get silver in change, they usually ask if you'd prefer paper.

Before long the cartwheel will follow the buffalo, and we'll have them only in museums. . . .

January 20, 1942

COASTING DOWN THE COAST— . . . Gadding about the country as I do, my fine New England sensibilities are continually outraged by the great American yen to carve, paint, whittle, write, or scratch your name, address, and the date on anything available at every national sightseeing place.

But the final curse upon American taste seems to me to have been perpetrated at the lovely old San Juan Capistrano mission, halfway between Los Angeles and San Diego.

This mission was built in 1776. It is gentle, and dignified, too, and quiet and peaceful in the garden under the sunlight or in the shade of the graceful arches. In the main garden is an old, old cactus plant, of the prickly pear type, grown quite tall and with large thick fronds, smooth and green.

The sun was so bright that I didn't notice at first, but when I looked closely there they were, covering the leaves like worms—hundreds and hundreds of names scratched into the green skin with knives or pins.

Not an inch of a single leaf was left uncarved. Among the

names was that of an Army colonel. Had his rank and everything carved on, just as if he were signing the Articles of
War. . . .

December 30, 1936

MIAMI— . . . When you see these tens of thousands of vacationers
taking it easy in Florida, you wish they'd at least have the grace
to shut up about it costing them so much to take care of the ten
million bums (to them) who are disgracing our country by being
out of work. . . .

April 1, 1940

MIAMI— . . . This evening, on the way back from dinner, I came
to a narrow sidewalk wide enough for only two people. A young
fellow and his girl were coming toward me, so I stepped off into
the street, between two parked cars, to let them by.

As they passed I looked up in a friendly way, more or less
automatically, to acknowledge the fellow's thanks. But he didn't
thank me. Didn't even look at me. Just walked past as though
he were an express and I were the freight train.

An incident like that would be impossible in a Latin country.
Down there they don't scrape and palaver, as many of us think
they do. Their courtesy isn't oily. It is quiet and natural—but
never forgotten. You don't ever step aside for anybody in Latin
America without being thanked for it, and graciously.

And out in the country, in the mountains or in the jungle, the
most frequently used word among the peons is *gracias.* But of
course they're backward and don't know any better. . . .

April 2, 1940

ST. PETERSBURG, FLORIDA—Human nature certainly is queer.

Today we were eating lunch in a small restaurant where the
winter visitors eat. Four women, neither young nor old, sat at
a nearby table.

They haggled a long time over the check, just to make sure
that none paid a cent more than her share. Then they carefully
laid out their tips. The poorest-looking of the women sat next
to us. The poorest-looking, and the kindest-looking.

They rose to go. The fat, healthy-looking woman was the last
to leave. She fussed around the table after the others, casually
glancing to see that no one spied. And then she snatched the

dime tip her poor-looking friend had left, slipped it into her pocketbook, and marched forward and out. . . .

April 18, 1940

CLEWISTON, FLORIDA— . . . The South is full of Negro phrases that are strange to Northern ears. For instance, when the maid knocks on my door in the morning and I say "Yes?" she invariably replies from outside: "It ain't nobody but me."

She is just a girl, but she says it in the most wan and worn-out tone, centuries of age hanging from it. I think it's one of the most wonderful things I ever heard. I've got so I wait for her just as you wait for the mailman. Waiting to hear, from outside the door, that profoundly touching little epic of humility:

"It ain't nobody but me."

April 23, 1940

DENVER— . . . If you send a telegram to a man in Denver, and put "love" on the end of it, Western Union won't read it over the telephone if a female answers.

We sent a wire to some relatives here, addressed it to the head of the house, said we'd arrive the next afternoon, and put "love" at the end, as most people do. Our relatives almost didn't get it.

Western Union called up, and when a woman answered the phone, they refused to read it. So Mrs. Jones (who guessed what the telegram was anyway) called Mr. Jones at his office downtown, and he called Western Union, and they read it to him.

They told him they'd had so much trouble lately with messages from sweeties getting into the hands of wives, they just had to stop reading them to women over the phone.

January 25, 1936

ABOARD SS LURLINE—I have noticed there is always a little crowd at the back rail, looking down onto the afterdeck below. Finally I went to see what the attraction was.

You wouldn't guess. It was the rich passengers in first class, standing at the rail and watching the passengers down in cabin class having a good time.

The cabin-class passengers have a couple of decks of their own, but they're not allowed up on our decks. Neither are we allowed on their decks—except by special pass between ten and twelve, and two and four P.M.

Cabin class isn't steerage, by any means. Cabin class has a fine dining room, and social halls and a swimming tank, and a lot of nice things. It's merely a little cheaper, and it permits a sharp line of distinction to be drawn between humans—something which Americans decry but most certainly demand. . . .

December 4, 1937

FROM THE
TRAVELER'S
VIEWPOINT

WILLIAMSTOWN, MASSACHUSETTS—As we drive along on our travels, we have mentally divided American sectional architecture into what we think is good and bad. Here are our selections:

GOOD—New England houses (and even barns); the pillared mansions of the Old South; the Santa Fe adobe of the Southwest; the log lodge of the Western mountains; the Spanish of southern California (although we might yield a few points there under stiff argument).

BAD—The awful rows of "company houses" in the industrial and mining cities of both East and West; the shacks of the poor South; the brownstone fronts left over from the last century; and, most hideous of all, the plain, square, double-decked, packing-box monstrosity of the flat Midwest and Canadian farming countries. . . .

October 1, 1938

LOS ANGELES— . . . We spent one night on the way out at a deluxe tourist camp at Flagstaff, Arizona. Some of you may remember reading about it before. We spent several days there two years ago.

It is called Arrowhead Lodge, and I believe it is the nicest place we've ever stayed outside of a hotel. We thought so then, and we still think so two years later.

Well, the other night when we got in we were admiring the furniture all over again. It is dark and rustic, and very fitting to the high, wooded beauty of Flagstaff's setting.

We said to ourselves, "You have to come out here to find stuff like this. They couldn't do anything like this anyplace but out here in the West."

Which would have been all right if That Girl hadn't up-ended a wooden bench, read the trademark, and discovered that it was made in Martinsville, Indiana. A fellow can't even have a good local illusion anymore.

May 5, 1941

WASHINGTON— . . . This business of constant wandering grows on a fellow. It gets in the blood, and you don't want to stop. I am a better wanderer now than when I started nearly two years ago. . . .

The happiest I am at any time on a long trip is when we have been laid up several days in one place and then finally one morning we pack up, check out, fill up with gas, and light out into open country. . . .

. . . [S]everal times I have awakened in the night and been unable to remember where I was. To find out, I would have to go back in my mind to the last distinctive place we stopped, and then come on up geographically to where we were. It only takes a few seconds. It never occurred to me just to let it go, and go back to sleep. . . .

When we first started out, there were times when I'd have that terrible "lost" feeling. We'd stop in a ratty hotel in a gloomy town in some thinly populated and dreary part of the country, and at dusk I'd feel alone, and foreign, and blue. But I never feel that way anymore. . . .

February 18, 1937

LAS CRUCES, NEW MEXICO—The county-courthouse situation in America has always had an awful fascination for me. I doubt if anything in this country's history has been so consistently ugly and unimaginative as its county courthouses.

From coast to coast, most of them are just alike. Most of them are square, cupolaed, standing straight-mouthed and old-fashioned in a shabby town square. . . .

I don't see how it has been possible for architects over the last fifty years to stick so tenaciously to a pattern of utter bleakness. . . .

April 8, 1938

AFTON, MINNESOTA— . . . The other night in a little hotel in a South Dakota village, the woman at the desk—the owner, I assume—gave me key 29½ and I carried my bags upstairs and started hunting my room.

I couldn't find 29½ but I did find a 29, so I put the bags down in the hall and went downstairs and told the woman what I'd found.

She said, "Yes, twenty-nine is your room. The key is to the bathroom. That's twenty-nine-and-a-half. There isn't any key to the room itself."

So I went back up and went in, and then I got to puzzling over that key-to-the-bathroom business. After a while it got the best of me, so I went back down and said, "What's the point in my having a key to the bathroom, and none to my main door?"

She just smiled and said, "Well, a person sort of likes to have a key to his bathroom sometimes."

I saw I was whipped. So I went back up and locked the bathroom door and then went out to supper, leaving my room unlocked. . . .

August 3, 1936

EUREKA, CALIFORNIA— . . . When we stop a day or two in a hotel for me to write up my pieces, I always have to leave finished columns and parts of columns lying around when I go out to eat.

I always feel a little self-conscious about it, because I know the maid will be in to clean up, and I've never known whether maids read what they see lying around or not.

Well, they do. For in Gold Beach, the other day, the maid came in while I was out, and right out of a clear sky she spoke to That Girl as follows: "Say, I didn't get to finish reading that column on Newport yesterday. I sure do like the way he writes. Has he got any more around I could read?" . . .

October 10, 1939

WASHINGTON— . . . People also often ask, "Don't you get into some awfully bad hotels?" The answer is yes. But probably no more than one out of twenty hotels, even in the tiny towns, is really terrible.

In a little less than two years of traveling we have stopped in about three hundred hotels. I recall only three that were absolutely dirty. In quite a few places the hotel owner appeared to be running a cockroach ranch in our bathroom, yet we have never encountered a bedbug.

The worst trouble with hotel rooms is the excuseless lack of taste. I can't understand how a hotel manager can be in the business and still not realize how important to a traveler's happiness are such things as a bed reading light, a floor lamp, an easy chair, fresh wallpaper, and clean curtains. Too many hotel rooms are furnished by men with bare souls. . . .

February 6, 1937

ON THE ROAD BACK— . . . Above all things, I hate hotels that have those spring handles on the water faucets—the kind where, if you let go, the water stops.

Have you ever tried to hold some tooth powder in the palm of your left hand, and a toothbrush in your right hand, and then see what you've got left to turn the water faucet with while you hold the toothbrush under it? . . .

January 6, 1936

SOME PEOPLE'S DOGS

Jerry Pyle often sent accounts of her travels with Ernie to friends around the country. One frequent recipient of Jerry's often-discursive letters was Elizabeth Shaffer, whose husband, Ed, was editor of Scripps Howard's Albuquerque Tribune. Here Jerry responds to a letter from Mrs. Shaffer bearing the news that recently one of the Shaffer children had been bitten by a dog. "Lord, you must have been worried," Jerry wrote from Toledo on April 20, 1937. She continued:

. . . I'm more and more incensed with the ill-bred dogs people have. Twice on this trip our evenings have been ruined by little yapping leapers whose owners haven't sense enough to train them. We were invited to breakfast Sunday morning with people I used to be nuts about—but they've acquired a queer little beast, of the family of weasel, who has burroughing propensities (or is it proclivities?). He also uses his teeth to good advantage—

never quite breaking the skin—just sort of sharpening them upon certain human bones, wrist bones preferred, tho gloves and pocket books he would gladly use as substitutes. I love good dogs, but when something a cross between a snake and a ferret wriggles and wiggles all over you for a couple of hours—even while you're trying to get a cup of coffee down—and when you realize that that something is listed in the dog book as a dog— you know you can never again make the general statement that you love dogs. . . .

The
Dust
Bowl
Revisited

ansas and Oklahoma
ay 1939

"We stopped in the town of Forgan, Oklahoma. If there ever was a town to make you sick, it is Forgan. No ghost town of the mining regions ever looked ghostlier."

A PARTIAL RECOVERY
GARDEN CITY, KANSAS—The Dust Bowl is better—in spots.

Today when we drove through the dust country a high wind was blowing. It roared against the side of the car until you could hardly talk. Yet there wasn't a speck of dust. Water was standing in the roadside ditches. The land was moist from last night's rain. The Dust Bowl has had an abundance of rain this spring.

If it keeps up, there will be a crop this year. *If* it keeps up. . . .

It doesn't take long for the land to dry and the earth to start rolling through the air. Take last night, for example, just before the rain. The wind whipped up to sixty miles an hour. A California family, in a brand-new Buick, got caught in the storm.

They were badly frightened. They had never seen a dust storm before. They didn't know what was happening to them. They came plowing through. And when they drove into a garage here, their windows were mottled by the sand, and there wasn't any paint left on their brand-new Buick. That's what a little drying sunshine, and a little puff of wind, can do to the Dust Bowl.

Around Garden City things look infinitely better than they did when we came through three years ago. At that time the country was like a graveyard—denuded, gray, almost vulgar in its pitiful nakedness. I spent an evening at the home of the local newspaper editor. His new brick bungalow lay filtered with fine seeping silt, and the windows were sealed with surgical tape.

But now, around Garden City you see green fields of wheat and alfalfa. Dozens of herds of nice-looking cattle graze in these fields. There is a prosperous look. Garden City itself seems to be a booming little city.

*

Friends have asked me to write and tell them whether man is making any progress against nature in the Dust Bowl. Is the government's hope of terracing and crop rotation and deep-growing grass restoring the blanched and useless plains?

The best answer I can give is—yes, in spots. It seems to me if it were possible for the government to have this entire wind-blown area, and control the management of every foot of it, then the Dust Bowl could be conquered. But nature itself is inconsistent and spotty in its ravaging of the dust country, and science must follow suit in its treatments. The government has done wonders in some places. In others, there seems to be no progress at all.

We stopped in the town of Forgan, Oklahoma. If there ever was a town to make your heart sick, it is Forgan. No ghost town of the mining regions ever looked ghostlier. Two-thirds of the store buildings in town are empty. The vacant windows are dusty, and kids have scrawled pictures on them with chalk. The movie is boarded up. Unpainted and empty houses straggle back from the highway.

Dust has killed Forgan. It likely will never recover. Just a few years ago, the town's population was six hundred. Now it is two hundred. Nearly everybody is on relief. Many of those four hundred who have left went to Beaver, the county seat, so they could be nearer their relief checks. I talked to one young fellow, just two years out of high school.

He told me that every boy in his graduating class, except himself, is now on relief. He would be, too, except for his pride, and the fact that his father has a job. The young man picks up a week's work here, and few days' there. He manages to get along. But he said he could no more hope to get married and raise a family than he could hope to flail his arms and fly. He would like to go away, but how?

Morale seems to have ebbed low in this section. One man told me that if the land were suddenly to be restored tomorrow the people wouldn't farm it. They like relief too well. I think he is too pessimistic about it, but that's what he said. But that question will have to remain a hypothetical one, for you can look around you and see that this land won't be restored tomorrow, or in a thousand tomorrows.

In some parts, a little-known weed has taken hold in the last couple of years, and serves well to hold the earth in place. But this cure is as bad as the disease. If you plant a crop now, this weed overwhelms the crop.

I don't know much about farming, despite the fact that I was born and raised on a farm. But it seems to me that a stretch just south of Garden City is the answer. That's where they are raising cattle on wheat and alfalfa. Maybe it wouldn't be necessary to evacuate all this country, and sweep it into one great grassy pasture for vast-range grazing. Maybe it could be done by each little farmer turning cattle onto his fields. One man, say, grazing twenty head of cattle on his richly intensified crop of alfalfa—instead of one great cattle baron, grazing thousands of head over half an unfenced state.

They do it that way in the Argentine. The great range and the cowboy are almost no more there. The cattle are fattened in small fields, on alfalfa and green crops. Maybe we could make the far Midwest a great cattle country again, under a different system. . . .

May 3, 1939

Home Report

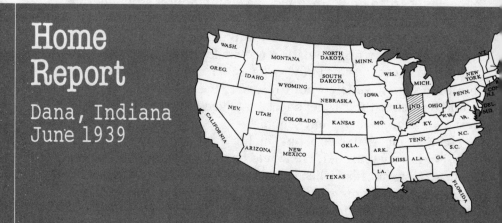

Dana, Indiana
June 1939

"Nature is afoot again in our farmed and paved and tractored country. I don't know what it is. The farmers don't know what it is. There is a new birth of something."

WATCHING THE COWS AND CHICKENS

DANA, INDIANA— . . . It has been a year since I was last at home. I was immensely pleased at the change in my mother. The change in her face, I mean. Her face has filled out again, and has color in it, and is almost the same as it was before her first stroke.

It is natural for people to remark on how well she is looking. But my mother doesn't like that. It makes her mad. "I'm no better and no worse," she says. "I feel exactly the same as I've felt for three years, and there's no sense in saying I look better."

And what she says is true. Outside of her looks, there has been little change. She is semiparalyzed, and can get around only with help. . . .

In the late afternoon, her chair is moved out onto the concrete cistern top east of the house, and she sits there with her back to the road. "I'd lots rather watch the cows and chickens than the people passing on the road," she says.

The folks in our neighborhood are still kind and thoughtful

of my mother. Hardly ever does one of the clubs or lodges meet but that they send her a box of gifts.

There was a time after each stroke when my mother couldn't speak. But she can speak now, very slowly, until she gets tired. Then her words play tricks on her. It is her greatest disappointment and frustration, when I am home, that she can't get said all she wants to say. When I leave she cries, and says, "I didn't get to talk to you."

She is able to ride in the car, but doesn't go every day, because it is too hard to get her into the seat. She enjoys riding around, although she gets frightened easily.

We were out driving, and when I decided to turn around, I backed up into a neighbor's driveway. There was a rise, and the back end of the car was tilted up. My mother grabbed the door-handle and started to whimper.

"Why, what's the matter?" I asked. "We're all right. You were never afraid of anything."

"I know," she said, "but I'm not well like I used to be. I get scared so easy. Storms nearly drive me crazy. I just can't help it." . . .

. . . When I am home, my mother never asks me about any of the places we have been. I asked her if she would like me to send her a big map of the United States so they could keep track of us wherever we went. She said, "No." And she said, "Whenever you're going to fly, don't let us know about it till after you've gotten there."

Occasionally my mother gets a rash of the giggles. It usually happens when they come to the most difficult point of lifting her into the car. And then it gets so funny that my father and Aunt Mary get to laughing, too, and they just have to cease operations and hold her up till the giggling is over.

I haven't figured out yet just what causes these giggles, but I believe it is her acute sense of the ridiculous—a woman like her having to be helped around is just too ironic. It's swell to be able to laugh about it.

June 5, 1939

DANA, INDIANA—At last my mother has a little dog. For a long time she has wanted one. She loves dogs anyhow, and now that she has nothing to do but sit all day, she would like to have a dog for company.

But the family verdict seemed to be "No." I never could find out why. It was none of my put-in, so I didn't go around looking for a dog. But then a week ago Saturday night, Fate took a hand. Somebody left a dog in our front yard. It was a very queer occurrence.

The folks heard a man out in the yard, whipping a dog. It was dark and they couldn't see. But they heard the man go away, and then the whipped dog came to the house. Officially, it is here on just a temporary basis. My father says the dog can't stay; my mother says she wants the dog to stay. She told me she wanted a collar and chain for it, so when we went to town yesterday I got a collar and chain.

I really didn't mean to take any hand in it, but I guess that collar and chain had some bearing. For my father hasn't said anything more about sending the dog away. And this morning I saw him petting it, and teaching it to stand on its hind legs to ask for candy.

*

. . . As I said before, no verdict has been given on whether or not the dog shall stay at our house. But if you want a tip from a stableboy who knows a little bit about how these things go, I'd put my two dollars on the proposition that the William C. Pyle household has a dog permanently in its midst.

June 6, 1939

POSTSCRIPT: *The dog—"part collie and part just dog"—did stay with Pyle's parents. Mrs. Pyle named her Snooky. Pyle's column about the largely unspoken tussle between his parents drew several reader letters. "I HOPE you KEEP that dog," an Indianapolis woman wrote Mrs. Pyle. A San Diego reader, also a woman, wrote a scorching invective against the mild-mannered Mr. Pyle in her letter to Mrs. Pyle. "Am surprised that your husband even questioned your having a dog when you wanted one," she wrote. "Anyone in your condition should have anything she desires to make her life happier, and those about her should be delighted to get it for her." Nor did this reader spare Ernie, much as she enjoyed his daily column. "Ernie said 'it was none of my put-in.' I beg to differ with him there. If your mother desires anything and you can have a hand in getting it for her, it is definitely your 'put-in,' regardless of what any other member of the family says. You know the mother is the head of the house."*

"I JUST FELT LIKE HELL"

DANA, INDIANA—I don't know what it is, but Nature is pulsing this spring, and there is a thriving of life in the country around our home.

The grass and the trees have never seemed so beautiful to me, so fresh and so green. The spirea bushes are out in a wild white, and if you weren't hot with spring warmth, you'd swear the bushes were covered with snow.

All the animal and bird life is growing, too. Half a dozen wild rabbits play in our front yard. Any time of the day you can see little rabbits sitting all around the old gravel pit up by the barn, grown up now in short grass.

In all my early years in this neighborhood I never saw a fox. But they say the country is thick with them now. They go right up to the edge of Dana, and set the dogs wild.

Never were quail so abundant. And, as I walk through the country, it seems to me the grass and the bushes are alive with birds. Birds I've never seen before. Birds I don't know the names of. New birds in our country. I don't know what it is.

There are more rats. And more cats, too. Enemies flourish side by side. Trees and bushes bloom and bugs and things by the thousands buzz and fly around. At night I cannot read in bed for the hard-shelled bugs roaring at the screen, trying to reach the light.

Nature is afoot again in our farmed and paved and tractored country. I don't know what it is. The farmers don't know what it is. There is a new birth of something.

*

The groundhogs are thick this spring. All our neighbors are bothered with them. At our house there are three big dens of them on the hillside up beyond the barn. Outside their dens, they have piled up mounds of fresh sand from their burrowings.

My mother said, "Ernest, why don't you go borrow Jack Bales' gun and see if you can't kill some of those groundhogs while you're home."

So I drove over to Bales' house. Nobody was home, but I went in anyway, as neighbors out here do, and got Jack's little .22 rifle, just a single-shot gun. I took it home and loaded it and walked up toward the barn with it under my arm. Groundhogs are nasty things, and I don't like them.

*

I went sneaking around behind the barn on tiptoe, like an Indian. Even the chickens and the birds seemed not to notice me, and give the warning sound. I peeked around the corner of the barn—and there it was, sitting out there in the middle of the

barnlot, right out in the open. I was between the groundhog and
its hole.

I took two steps out from the barn, and the groundhog saw
me. It stood motionless for a second, puzzled, as though it could
not conceive of being cut off from its den. Then it ran swiftly,
at right angles, toward the old barn.

I shot across the fence. It was a good forty yards, and I had
no idea of making a hit. But as the gun cracked the groundhog
rolled. It gave me a thrill, I can't help but admit. It rolled once,
and landed on its feet again, running.

But this time it ran straight toward me. Instinct, I suppose.
Instinct and hurt and numbing fright drove it toward its den,
man in the way or no man.

I had an extra cartridge in my fingers, and it took me only a
second to reload. I had the sight dead on it when it was within
ten feet of me, and was pressing on the trigger. And then the
groundhog staggered.

I never fired the second shot. The groundhog fell once to the
right. It pulled itself up and fell once to the left. It kicked twice.
It wasn't a yard from my feet when it twitched out its last
breath. I stood there looking, fascinated and horrified, as it died.

My father came, and said, "Well, that's good. You'll have to
bury it now."

So I got the spade and dug a deep hole in the bottom of the
old gravel pit, and tied a string around the dead groundhog's leg,
and dragged it into the hole, and covered it up. It was hard
digging. The groundhog was chubby, and there would soon
have been young ones. I tramped the earth down hard over the
filled hole.

*

Last night just before bedtime I went outdoors. Our country
is very quiet, and very dark, in the nighttime. I had a feeling of
something up toward the barn. It sounds foolish. But there was
a life less, and I had taken it. One pulse in that virile flowering
of nature around our country this spring had stopped beating.

Sure, a groundhog is no good, and ought to be killed. But
there was a home in the hillside without a tenant. Maybe a
groundhog enjoys living, too. I could feel a presence in the
darkness . . . a guilt and a sadness . . . a spirit kicking pitifully
at my feet . . . eyes looking up, and slowing glazing. . . .

No, I didn't run into the house. And I didn't blubber and cry.

I merely stood there in the dark for a long time thinking about it, out there under the maple trees, and I just felt like hell.

June 8, 1939

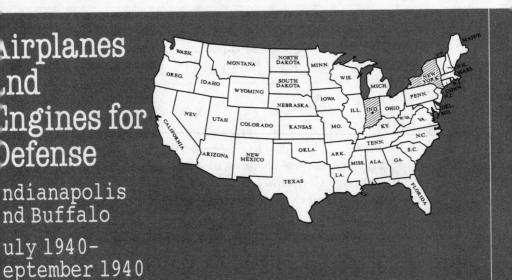

Airplanes
and
Engines for
Defense

ndianapolis
nd Buffalo

uly 1940–
eptember 1940

"Here you have our present national-defense picture all under one roof—its impetus, its urgency, its industrial genius, its terrific difficulties, and at last its accomplishments."

It was becoming harder for Pyle not to write about what was on everyone's mind—the war in Europe and the war in the Pacific. Though still isolationist, many Americans now assumed it was just a matter of time before the United States was drawn in. "In 1940," the playwright Robert E. Sherwood wrote some years later, "I used to read Ernie's pieces with great admiration but also with a kind of anger that anybody who was so obviously a fine observer and reporter could be so utterly indifferent to what was going on in the world. He seemed to mention every-

thing that he saw and felt except the fact that there was a war on and it was daily getting closer to us." The following series marked Pyle's first attempt to come to terms with America's response to the threat of events overseas.

ENGINES FOR DEFENSE

SWEPT FORWARD IN A GIGANTIC FLOOD

INDIANAPOLIS— . . . [T]oday I've been wandering deep within the Allison airplane-engine plant. Allison makes engines only for the government. Consequently, you don't get inside unless the government gives its permission. That comes to very few non-technical men.

My permission came from the War Department in Washington, subject to further approval by Wright Field, the Air Corps inspectors at the plant, and the Allison company itself. Somehow I ran the gamut. There came to me, from Lord knows where, four separate copies of a telegram authorizing the visit.

The hour and the day were set. I drove out to the plant. At the outer gate you have to convince a uniformed guard that your business is genuine. Then he shows you where to park. You enter a small lobby. You sign up at the desk, behind which sits a guard. You never get beyond that lobby unless somebody from inside, who knows all about you beforehand, comes out and gets you. And even then you have to wear a badge.

All this to-do about getting in didn't annoy me a bit. The things that are happening inside the Allison walls these days are vital, and I don't feel short-tempered when someone takes pains to make sure I'm not a fifth columnist. . . .*

*

The Allison Engineering Company has a long history—a long, thin history like a stem, which suddenly blossomed out on top into a great flower. It goes back to the early days of the Indianapolis Speedway. Jim Allison was one of the speedway founders, and his shops in those days made and remade speed

*An undercover subversive working to weaken a country from within.

cars for the great five-hundred-mile race. The plant today sits not far from the speedway.

After the war, Allison kept going by rebuilding thousands of old Liberty engines for the government—beefing them up with stronger parts and better bearings. And when the Liberties were all gone, Allison kept itself going by making superior bearings for other airplane engines. Even today it supplies the vital crankshaft bearings for nearly all our airplane engines.

When this country was having its fling with dirigibles, back in the early thirties, Allison was commissioned by the Navy to build a dirigible engine, one that you could run either forward or backward, like a boat engine. The death of American dirigibles left Allison stuck with its dirigible engine—yet that very engine was the father of today's magnificent Allison motor.

We come on up through the thirties. Jim Allison was dead. General Motors had bought out the company, and it had become the Allison Division of GM. In the mid-thirties it was still largely an experimental shop, but one now with plenty of capital.

Although the Army had no liquid-cooled airplane engines in regular use, it still kept experimenting. It gave occasional small orders to Allison, and kept trying them out. Each change in design brought a bigger and bigger engine—and one closer to perfection.

And then, just a little more than a year ago, the lid was off. An Army contract was awarded that justified Allison's rapidly expanding. Finally, after years of trying and pushing, suddenly the dam was taken away, and the Allison company was swept forward in a gigantic flood. No one knows where or when it will stop.

The Army wants more and more engines. A year ago Allison began building what is probably the most modern engine plant in the world. The foundation wasn't in until a bigger one was demanded. The first tool machine wasn't set in until it had to be moved to make room for others. Engine builders mingle side by side with workmen setting up new machines that have just arrived. A whole new wing is ready for tooling. And orders for more widening may come tomorrow. Everything is in a liquid state of expansion.

Here within the walls of the Allison plant you have our present national-defense picture all under one roof—its impetus, its urgency, its industrial genius, its terrific difficulties, and at last its accomplishments. Allison today is by far the biggest thing in Indianapolis—and, in a sense, one of the really big things in America.

July 27, 1940

INDIANAPOLIS— . . . These Allison airplane engines are of twelve cylinders, in two banks of six, placed in a V. They are rated at eleven hundred and fifty horsepower—almost a hundred horsepower for every cylinder.

You cannot but be impressed by the power that is packed into that little space. The best example I know is a contrast with the generating room of the Allison plant. In there are great diesel engines, driving electrical generators. These engines are the same kind that drive our streamlined trains and many of our submarines.

They stand twice as high as your head and are long and wide. Each one would fill two good-sized rooms. And yet all that bulk and metal and noise is producing exactly the same amount of power that the little Allison airplane engine is—an engine so small that they pack five of them into the cabin of an Army transport plane and fly them away to plane factories.

There are three great engine-building plants in America—the Wright plant at Paterson, New Jersey; Pratt & Whitney at Hartford, Connecticut; and Allison here. The first two produce radial air-cooled motors, the kind you ride behind on nearly every airline in the world today. For many years air-cooled motors have completely dominated, and liquid-cooled engines have been struggling back through experimental stages. Allison today is the only company making liquid-cooled engines for airplanes under our defense program. Three big companies— Lockheed, Curtiss, and Bell—are building their latest fighting planes for the government around Allison engines.

The advantages claimed for liquid-cooled engines are: (1) their frontal area is smaller—hence through streamlining you can get greater speed with less power; and (2) because of controlled cooling, they will run longer at high speed.

You notice I didn't say "water-cooled." No, water wouldn't do at all in these engines. Water boils at two hundred and twelve degrees, and these engines run hotter than that. They use a solution called ethylene glycol—almost the same as Prestone— that boils at three hundred and eighty-seven degrees.

The cooling of this engine can be controlled by the pilot, through the speed with which the fluid is forced around the cylinders. And even more remarkable than that, the temperature of each individual cylinder can be controlled. . . .

July 29, 1940

No What-the-Hell Attitude Here

INDIANAPOLIS— . . . The plant is just a vast space with a roof over it. You stand at one side and can barely see the opposite wall, it is so far away. There are no partitions.

And in that space, filling it almost completely, are row after row after row of machines. It is all comparatively peaceful. Parts don't fly past your ears on overhead carriers, as in an auto plant. Most pieces are so small that men can lift them.

There is no great sense of movement, for nine tenths of the job is tiny precision work of boring and measuring and fitting. There is an almost uncanny lack of sound and fury. The tooling machines were what got me. Machines like lathes in a tool shop. Machines as high as your waist, and longer than a room. Machines two stories high. Machines that drill upside down. Machines that drill a hundred holes at once. Machines that bore a pinpoint hole clear through the length of a steel rod.

The quantity of these machines is almost beyond comprehension. There are literally hundreds of them, row upon row, like big dull soldiers. Heavy, gray-painted, they stand in formidable lines across the whole area.

They are tremendously expensive. All big complicated tool machines are. But many of these were designed solely for this job, and took more than a year to build. If you said twenty-five thousand dollars was the average price you wouldn't be crazy. And there are hundreds of them.

The machines are all so new that the paint on them is still bright and unscarred. If it weren't for the steel shavings and the boring oil that flows around the drills, you might think the whole thing is a display at the World's Fair.

*

At nearly every machine stand two men. Why? Because one is running it, and the other is learning. Right here is being conducted one of the biggest educational processes in Indiana.

There weren't enough men in Indianapolis who knew how to run these complicated machines. So Allison had to take what it could get and train the rest. It has hundreds of employees who weren't worth a dime the first two months. The training still goes on.

I had heard that Allison wasn't taking on men of military age, because of fear they would all be drafted in case of war. But that was untrue. It looked to me as though ninety percent of the workmen were in their twenties. So I asked about it. And they said you have to take young men, because only the young mind is agile enough to learn these machines quickly. But Allison is worried about it, and does wish that older minds didn't slow up a bit.

You see almost no foreign-looking faces in the Allison plant. Indianapolis itself is somewhere around ninety-five percent native-born. And most all of Allison's four thousand men come from Indianapolis.

You sense an immediate difference in this plant from other large factories. . . . All through the intricate process of building an airplane engine, every man's job is so vital, so ticklish, so dignified with importance, that the workmen take a living interest in what they are doing. I never saw one hangdog, what-the-hell look on a workman's face.

And the plant executives say that when an engine is finally carted off the end of the assembly line, it isn't like some fellow twisting the last nut and thinking lanquidly, "Well, there goes the eight millionth goddam sedan."

Instead, that engine is an individual with personality, it is something almost alive, and a part of every man is in it, and he feels it. . . .

July 30, 1940

INDIANAPOLIS— . . . We stood watching them hook up a new engine in one of the test rooms. The various parts of that engine had been weeks in the making. Thousands of men, millions of dollars, worlds of knowledge and experience and care and patience, had gone into that engine. It was as perfect a mechanical thing as man could create.

Now for seven hours it runs, and five men sit at a desk outside the test room, looking through a window and watching their instruments and checking down thousands of reactions of that one engine.

Each test stand is a huge room, more than two stories high. Its walls are immensely thick, and it is heavily soundproofed.

Opposite the propeller, the walls are reinforced with steel beams and extra thickness, just in case the prop should come off. When you look through the window at that violently roaring engine inside, its maniacal power puts a chill into you, and you can feel the import of its heavy throbbing clear down to the bottom of your stomach.

You can lift one foot off the floor, and that leg trembles and vibrates from the pulsations in the air. If you go down into the basement room adjoining the engine, you cannot hear the loudest shout right in your ear. Inspector Joseph R. Volmer, having a pencil but no paper, wrote words on the palm of his hand in lieu of conversation.

This first seven-hour test is called the "green run." When it is over, and the engine cools, it is hauled back into the factory and taken completely apart. Once more, every tiny piece goes through the most microscopic tests. Any part that shows the slightest strain is replaced. And the engine is built up again, for three more hours of running before it is ready for shipment.

This final tearing down and assembling is where Allison and the Army use their strictest caution against sabotage. All this work is done in a separate room. That room is continually locked. Nobody can enter except the men working there. Even the general manager couldn't get in without a lot of red tape. We stood and looked through the heavy wire that forms the inside wall of it, but we didn't go in.

Every workman in that room is known down to the most intimate detail of his life, past and present. For sabotage in these last few hours might not show up for weeks—and then fatally.

August 1, 1940

INDIANAPOLIS— . . . The one thing I would like to do in this series is to disarrange the placid American belief that because we have appropriated five billion dollars for defense, this defense exists today, or will next month or next Christmas or next spring.

You'd simply have to go through what is probably the finest plant of its kind in America, and see the slow and meticulous processes of the whole thing, to realize what's ahead.

For instance, this Allison plant took more than a year to get going. When you go through, you can't believe it could have been built in a year, or even three years. And these huge expensive machines, in ordinary times, are delivered six months be-

hind the order given. Now they are running eight months behind.

As one executive described it, you have to have a machine to
make a certain part. Such a machine doesn't exist. They have to
design a pattern for it. It takes so many thousand hours of work
to complete that pattern.

A pattern is a small thing. You can appropriate twenty million dollars for it, but you can't put twenty million men around
it and finish it in half an hour. It's so small only five men can
get around it. So it takes months to build it.

Nature won't let them go any faster. And during those
months our defense mass production on that certain product
must wait. It's nobody's fault at all. It's the way things are. But
the point is, we all ought to realize it.

August 2, 1940

AIRPLANES FOR DEFENSE

BUILDING THE CURTISS P-40
BUFFALO, NEW YORK—When you start in at one end of the vast
Curtiss-Wright airplane factory here, you cannot see to the
other end, it is so far. Furthermore, you see nothing at first that
even remotely resembles an airplane.

You see only rows of machines, grinding and punching bars
of steel and sheets of metal. In the far distance you are conscious
of hundreds of men bending over workbenches.

As you walk on down the broad aisle you gradually come
upon men drilling holes in flat sheets of blue metal. And then,
farther down, these sheets begin to go together and are riveted
to each other, and pretty soon you see that a wing is being built.

When you finally get into the wing-building line, you see not
one but scores of wings, each a little more advanced than the
last, and with a group of busy workmen hovering around each
one.

The Curtiss P-40 plane is essentially in only three parts—the

engine, the wing, and the fuselage. The Allison engine comes
from Indianapolis, boxed in a crate. The wings and fuselage are
built here, but their building is altogether separate. The two
never meet until they have been trundled ten miles on a trailer
to the Buffalo airport.

*

To go back to the beginning, most of the plane enters the
factory in the form of thin, flat sheets about twelve feet long.
They are aluminum-colored, and come from around Pittsburgh.
First these sheets are dipped in a chemical solution that turns
them blue. This is merely a protective surface, to save the metal
from serious scratches if a drill slips.

Next these pieces are cut, on huge machines, into various sizes
and lengths, all preconceived to fit into certain parts of the wing
or fuselage. Then they are drilled. The edge of every sheet of
metal in that plane is riveted to the next one at intervals of about
an inch. There are seventy-seven thousand rivets in a P-40 plane.
That takes one hundred and fifty-four thousand holes.

As far as I could see, none of these was drilled by a machine
that bores hundreds of holes at once. The drilling is done by
men, using electric hand drills. They do pile about a dozen
sheets on top of each other, and drill the same hole through all
of them at once. But that one operation is about as near to the
automobile version of mass production as I saw.

*

When the sheets are drilled, they go to the wing-building line.
One piece of metal has been curved and shaped to form the
leading edge of a wing. This becomes the foundation. It is laid
in a long wooden jig, or cradle. Workmen gather around, with
their drills and their rivets. Piece by piece—by the insertion of
metal spars, crosspieces, and flat sheets of outer skin—they build
the wing upward. It is almost like building a house.

You can walk down the line in the forenoon, and if you pass
again in the afternoon, and your memory is good, you can see
how any certain wing has grown while you were away.

The fuselage is put together in very much the same way.
Workmen build it up piece by piece, as though they were building the framework of a house. It is actually in four sections—
two top, two bottom. Then these are bolted together, and then
the skin, or outer wall, is riveted on. Now the fuselage is moved
out into another huge room—big and light in comparison with
the main factory, which seems rather dark.

Out here the fuselages sit a few feet apart, in long row after long row. Movable workbenches and ladders surround each one. And here begins the slow and vastly skilled process of installing the engine and all the instruments.

You might say that up to this point it has just been carpenter work. But from here on the craftsmen come in. The instruments in a modern fighting plane may cost as much as the engine, and the two of them together are likely to exceed the cost of the rest of the plane. It is this vast final-assembly room that you see in rotogravure pictures of airplane factories—fuselages lined up as far as you can see.

I don't know the actual production figures of the Curtiss-Wright factory, but I know that I was surprised and struck by the large number of fuselages almost ready to go out the back door as finished products. A plane is a big, complicated, and expensive thing. And when you see in one room a hundred of them getting the last finishing touches, you're seeing a lot of airplanes.

My only trouble was that I'd climb all over one, and gaze at the maze of expensive instruments in the cockpit, and admire the intricacy of the engine, and the beauty of the finish on the fuselage, and then I'd think—all these wonderful and laborious things, all this labor and genius, and two months from now it may be lying in the English countryside, utterly and completely wrecked, forever.

September 20, 1940

BUFFALO, NEW YORK— . . . An airplane makes almost as much noise being built as it does in one of those roaring power dives. The Curtiss-Wright factory is so noisy you can barely talk to a companion by shouting. It's all that damn riveting, and on top of that there is the loudspeaker system. It has outlets all over the plant, so the phone operators can call various foremen and executives to the phone. Somebody is being called almost all the time. . . .

When the plant slows down for lunch, the silence is something akin to heaven. During the time there are fewer calls over the loudspeaker—so they put on phonograph records, and the grim factory that makes man-killing machines with such fury then scintillates and reechoes with sweet music. While I was there they kept playing "Sweet Leilani." . . .

*

There has been much talk of getting our various military industrial plants moved away from the coasts and borders, deep into the interior, just in case of invasion. But Buffalo isn't worried about its location. For they figure that if any enemy ever actually got down the St. Lawrence as far as Montreal, then Buffalo wouldn't be any more vulnerable than Cincinnati or St. Louis. . . .

*

Curtiss-Wright, like Allison in Indianapolis, does a pretty thorough check-up job on all new employees. There have been no spy or sabotage scares here in several years. I don't know whether there are FBI men in the plant, but I suspect there are.

Buffalo has a much larger percentage of foreign-born than Indianapolis. But even that doesn't worry the Curtiss-Wright people especially. . . .

To tell the truth, I don't see how it would be possible for any serious sabotage to take place here, anyhow. Inspection, as in all such plants, is meticulous. When a part leaves one division, it is inspected just before leaving. And that same part is again inspected when it arrives in the next division. The Air Corps alone has twenty-eight inspectors in the plant, in addition to all the factory inspectors.

I saw one undercowling for a motor sitting on the floor. On it was written in red crayon SECOND TRY—STILL NO GOOD. The inspector who wrote it sounded mad.

Consequently, with such a fine-toothed inspection system, and everybody on his toes about everybody else, and with an airplane factory by nature not subject to great explosions or catastrophes, it seems to me almost impossible for fatal flaws to be hidden in an individual plane, or for the flow of production itself to be seriously hindered.

September 23, 1940

Washington
November 1940

"In the mid-twenties, Washington
was without animation, except that
produced by bathtub gin and
Maryland rye. But today ideas and
ideals charge the atmosphere.
Thousands of important men have
posterity by the hair."

A City Bursting with Self-Importance

washington—We still like Washington very much, although it
is not the Washington we came to twenty years ago. It surges
and teems now, whereas then it poked along.

The city has doubled in population since we came here. People, bent on missions, swarm about you in hordes. There is a
different personality to the street crowds. A whole new spirit
has taken hold—a spirit of crusade, of importance, of vital men
doing vital things.

Colorful phrases rise up to describe Washington and its teeming thousands. Jokes are made about it, as they are about Los
Angeles. Out in Los Angeles, they say, all those people are just
living off each other. Here in Washington, they say, they're all
saving the world from each other. There must be more world-
savers and civilization-retrievers in Washington than in any city
in the world.

There are a hundred and forty-five thousand people working for the government today in Washington. That's twenty thousand more than a year ago, fifteen thousand more than in 1918. As in most businesses, the bulk of them are clerks. They carry out policy, but they do not set it. They are people with jobs.

But the upper crust of that hundred and forty-five thousand are important. Their importance runs a scale of many degrees, but they have one thing in common—they are all important to themselves. You can spot them everywhere. They're huddled, they're prepondering, they're discussing. They have a mission, and that mission is to save humanity. And the astounding part of it is that they may succeed.

A few years ago these world-savers were called the Brain Trust, and the Inner Circle. But now circumstances and events have broadened their exclusive club. The circle is so big you can no longer encompass it with a few names. Not that they all have the President's ear, or that he even knows them. But they are here, devoutly performing. The Washington circle today takes in hundreds who are just as inspired as Rex Tugwell or Tommy Corcoran* ever were.

*

In the mid-twenties, Washington was without animation, except that produced by bathtub gin and Maryland rye. People just worked in the government. Nobody was saving anything from anybody. And I doubt that civilization moved much in Washington between 1922 and 1932.

But today ideas and ideals charge the atmosphere. Thousands of important men have posterity by the hair. Great deeds are done daily, and also little deeds that seem like great deeds. Humanity is being saved. And all through Washington there is animation. Wherever the path, or whatever the goal—you can't say that civilization is standing still. Why, just stand on a Washington street late some afternoon and you'll see civilization as she streaks by.

*

Washington has changed much in appearance in these last five years. Today I was riding with some friends, and remarking on so many things being different. And one friend who has been here all the time said, "Why, I don't see that anything has changed."

*Tugwell was one of the original Roosevelt Brain Trust. Corcoran was a Harvard-educated attorney and Roosevelt administration insider who helped draft key New Deal legislation.

And just as he said it the car did a sort of nosedive, and we went roaring down a concourse and into a tunnel, and I thought our end had come. But it was just a brand-new underpass, right downtown, carrying traffic under Thomas Circle. It wasn't there the last time I looked. It almost scared me to death.

Lots of streets have been widened. The beautiful old trees have gone with the widening. Occasionally downtown I get lost for a moment, because the same old street is so different. New buildings are everywhere. It would take me a year to get them all placed. Bureaus that used to be small, homeless affairs now have huge, beautiful mansions of their own.

And even so, there simply isn't room enough in Washington—not room enough in offices, homes, streets, or sidewalks. All the needs have grown too fast. Just take the expansion of the British government's business here as an example. The British have the largest embassy in town. They have rented other buildings to house the overflow. All year they have had a whole floor, set up as offices, in the Willard Hotel. And now they have just taken over an entire apartment house.

Over in Virginia, building along the main roads has been heavy for miles out of town. So changed are the main highways from ten years ago that we didn't realize where we were until we had almost reached the city.

And despite all this, it is amazing how quickly you fall back into familiarity with what's remembered of the old, and acquire an ease with the tempo of the new. Yesterday I saw the waitress who served up our coffee in 1924, and she looked just the same. Tomorrow, who knows, I might be on a white horse rescuing a portion of civilization myself.

Might, but probably won't.

November 15, 1940

REMINISCING

WASHINGTON—This old carcass is now going on its sixth fantastic year of just busting constantly around the country and writing a daily column about it. I have decided to spend a week reminiscing and summing up. It isn't an anniversary, and I'm not getting ready to die or resign. It's just a whim.

When we started I weighed one hundred and eight pounds, had two bad colds a year, felt very tired of an evening, and was scared to death of meeting strange people. But now, after five-

and-a-half years and a hundred and sixty-five thousand miles of travel, I weigh one hundred and eight pounds, have two bad colds a year, feel tired of an evening, and am afraid of people. Travel, indeed, is broadening. . . .

We have traveled by practically all forms of locomotion, including piggyback. We have been at least three times in every state in the Union. We have been to every country in the Western Hemisphere but two.

We have stayed in more than eight hundred hotels, have crossed the continent exactly twenty times, flown on sixty-six different airplanes, ridden on twenty-nine different boats, walked two hundred miles, and put out approximately twenty-five hundred dollars in tips.

*

The reason we do all this is simple. We do it to make a living. That is accomplished by writing a thousand words a day for the Scripps-Howard Newspapers, and some others, too.

In five years these columns have stretched out to the horrifying equivalent of twenty full-length books. Set in seven-point type they would make a newspaper column three quarters of a mile long. The mere thought of it makes me sick to my stomach.

People often ask me how we stand all this travel. Well, it has its compensations. You don't have to make your own beds. You don't have to buy coal. You can make new friends and go on before they find out how dull you are. You don't have to get up at four A.M. and milk the cows. And then, too, lots of people write us nice letters, and there are even fanatics who thrill me by vowing that there is a certain quality in my writings that on some days actually makes sense.

In five years of sending my columns into Washington from odd spots all the way from Nome to Asunción, not a single column has ever been lost. Once I went for five months without seeing my own column in print. And among fatal statistics—two men whom I interviewed have died before the columns about them were published. We have no figures on the number who have died of shock after seeing themselves in print. . . .

*

But this job has created one distinction nobody can take away from me. And that is that I am probably the only solvent person in America (and I don't mean *too* solvent) who literally has no home, no place to hang his hat, no base to go back to and start away from.

We have worked up a whole new continent-wide list of intimate friends, and we consequently keep up a personal correspondence with about three hundred people.

In these years we have worn out two cars, five sets of tires, three typewriters, and pretty soon I'm going to have to have a new pair of shoes. I love to drive, and never get tired of it, but on long days I do get to hurting on the bottom.

Where this wandering business will get us, or where it will all end, I have no idea. So far as I know, it is only an interlude in my life. Five-and-a-half years ago my boss in Washington got tired of my pestering him about the travel idea, so he said, "Oh, all right, go on and get out. Try it a little while as an experiment. We'll see how it turns out."

From that day to this he has never mentioned it again. That's all right with me, for I was never one to rush into hasty decisions, either. But if they don't make up their minds about my future within the next fifteen or twenty years, I'm going to begin to wonder.

November 16, 1940

Home Again

Dana, Indiana and Albuquerque
April 1941

"Little pictures of my mother raced across the darkness before my eyes. Pictures of nearly a lifetime. Pictures of her at neighborhood square dances long, long ago, when she was young and I was a child."

"When you sit out here in the silent vastness of the desert, so remote from turmoil, you feel that the ghostly rustling of a falling bomb can be only something that you dreamed once in a nightmare."

Pyle spent part of December 1940 and January, February, and March of 1941 in Britain reporting on the German air offensive against various cities. His mother died of cancer while he was in London. Unable to attend her funeral, he traveled to Dana immediately upon his return to the United States.

His pieces about his mother and her many strokes had touched millions of readers. One man had written to him from Denver in the summer of 1939, "Your [recent] column about your mother touched me very much. My newspaper, soliciting, and life experience [have] taught me that back of a worthwhile man is a great mother. My own mother . . . and my father were killed when I was four. When I was sixteen I was through high school and set adrift. . . . Even at my age, forty-six, I find myself wishing I had a mother."

Pyle had always considered himself fortunate to have had a strong, loving mother. Now it was time to say goodbye.

PICTURES OF A MOTHER'S LIFETIME

DANA, INDIANA—My father met me at the train in Indianapolis. When we shook hands there were no tears in his eyes, and I was glad.

When we drove up the lane to the farmhouse my Aunt Mary came rushing out onto the front porch. She did not cry, and I was glad.

Then the dog Snooks came running up, but she was timid and afraid, as though she could not make up her mind. There seemed no life in her, and she was sad and lost.

The little dog Snooks was the only one who let on, and her loneliness cut me as deeply as though she had shed tears. For Snooks spoke in her wordless aimlessness the void that my mother left behind her when she went away.

*

One drear evening in London, just at dusk, when outlines become soft and begin their slow blending with the final blackness of night, a friend and I started out to dinner.

We were walking down the Strand, brushing past the late pedestrians hurrying for home before blackout and bombers could catch them. We had gone about two blocks when we heard hurrying footsteps behind us. We turned, and saw that it was a little bellboy from my hotel.

The lad's name was Tom Donovan, and he was the one who had showed me my room on that first strange night months before when I had arrived in London. I had always been fond of him, for his face was so bright and eager, and his manner so nice, and all his little actions so thoughtful.

"This telegram just came for you, sir," he said. "I thought maybe I could catch you." I thanked him and he started on back.

There was barely light enough to see. I stepped over to the curb, out of people's way, while I read the telegram.

"What is it?" my friend asked. "More good news from home?"

"Read it," I said, and went on ahead. When he caught up he

said, "I'm sorry," and we walked on toward Leicester Square. The London night grew quickly darker, and we spoke no more as we walked.

It was the cablegram that told me that my mother, far away in Indiana, had come to the end of her life.

*

That night in London, back in my room alone, it seemed to me that living is futile, and death the final indignity. People live and suffer and grow bent with yearning and bowed with disappointment, and then they die. And what is it all for? I don't know.

I turned off the lights and pulled the blackout curtains and went to bed. Little pictures of my mother raced across the darkness before my eyes. Pictures of nearly a lifetime. Pictures of her at neighborhood square dances long, long ago, when she was young and I was a child. Pictures of her playing the violin. Pictures of her doctoring sick horses, of her carrying newborn lambs into the house on raw spring days.

I could see her when she drove our first auto—all decorated and bespangled—in the Fourth of July parade. She was dressed up in frills, and she won first prize and was awfully proud.

And one midafternoon when I was nine—the first day I ever drove a team in the fields all by myself. She made many trips to the field that day, to bring me bread and butter and sugar spread on it—and to make sure I hadn't been run over by the harrow. I could see her, there in the London darkness, as she came out toward that Indiana field more than thirty years ago.

The sirens sounded and the *groan-groan-groan* of the engines came, and the far guns began to roll off their symphony like sad distant thunder on a hot prairie night.

I could see her on bitter winter days in the old familiar woolen hood, with her nose red from cold, and wearing a man's ragged coat fastened with a horse-blanket pin.

I could see her as she stood on the front porch, crying bravely, on that morning in 1918 when I, being youthful, said a tearless goodbye and climbed lightly into the neighbor's waiting buggy that was to take me out of her life.

Pictures of a lifetime. Pictures of her in worry and distress, pictures of her in anger at fools or injustice, pictures of her in gaiety, pictures of her in pain. They were all as clear and vivid as if I were there again on the prairies where I was born.

The pictures grew older. Gradually she became stooped, and toil-worn, and finally white and racked with age, but always spirited, always sharp.

I wondered if she could hear the guns now, wherever she was, and what they meant to her if she could.

*

On the afternoon that I was leaving London, I called little Tom Donovan, the bellboy, to my room. My bags were packed. One by one the floor servants had come in, and I had given them farewell tips.

But because I liked him, and more than anything else, I suppose, because he had shared with me the message of finality, I wanted to do something more for Tom than for the others. And so I started to give him a pound note.

But a look of distress came over his face, and he blurted out, "Oh, no, Mr. Pyle, I couldn't." And then he stood there so straight in his little English uniform, and suddenly tears came into his eyes, and they rolled down his cheeks, and he turned and ran through the door. I never saw him again.

*

On that first night I had felt, in a sort of detached bitterness, that because my mother's life was hard, it was also empty. But how wrong I was.

For you need only have seen little Tom Donovan in faraway London wretched at her passing, or the loneliness of Snooks, or the great truckloads of flowers they say came from all over the continent, or the scores of Indiana youngsters who journeyed to her both in life and death because they loved her, to know that she had given a full life. And received one, in return.

April 10, 1941

GOODBYE, MOTHER

DANA, INDIANA—One winter night a few years ago I was sitting in the dark cabin of a westbound airplane high over the rolling hills of southern Ohio.

Word had come that afternoon that my mother had had a second stroke, and that she might not live. I had taken the first plane from Washington that went toward Indiana.

I had flown many thousands of miles before, but never had I flown in an emergency. And for the first time I felt the full significance of what aviation science had given me and others like me, suddenly faced with the need for desperate hurry.

Perhaps I felt it too much, for my flight through the night to my mother's bedside took on a touch of drama for me, and I built up the scene of my homecoming in my own mind somewhat as though I were seeing it on a screen. They had said my mother might not live, but somehow I felt that she would live till I got there. For I felt that she wanted to live to tell me something.

I was proud of myself in those days. I don't mean that I was big-headed, or thought I was better than anyone else. I was looking at myself more by the standards of those who stay at home in the neighborhood than by any specific accomplishments.

Only you who have come from the intimate confines of a Midwestern farm community can know in what fear parents live of their children bringing shame and disgrace upon them. I was an only child. All that my parents had was centered in me. I was young when I went away. They sacrificed to send me to school. I had gone from there on into the world, and my visits home, though regular, were brief and far apart.

In twenty years my mother had not seen me a total of two months. But I had been good about writing, in later years I had been able to send a little money, but best of all I had never brought disgrace upon my parents. They had never seen me jobless or loafing, they had never had to swallow the bitter pill of gossip that their son was worthless, and I had never been in jail or mixed up in scandal.

And so, thinking of these things, I pictured in my mind my return to my mother's bedside. I saw her lying there; I saw myself rush in and take her hand. I could hear her whisper, just in her last moments, "I am proud of you." And dreaming thus, I felt the warm self-glorification of good people who have forced the gratitude of others.

*

A car met me at Indianapolis that dramatic night, and rushed the seventy-five miles through the night to the maple-hidden farmhouse where I had spent my youth. My mother was conscious, but she could not speak. I did not know until later that she didn't realize who I was.

I stayed on and nursed her for many days. I took the night shift, so that my father and Aunt Mary could get their sleep. For long hours, after all the routine sickbed duties were attended to, I would sit on the edge of her bed, and sometimes she would reach out for my hand with her one good hand, and she would hold it tight, but she could not speak.

And finally she would drop off to sleep, and then I would sit in the sitting room with the light turned dim and my feet up on the base-burner, where I could see through the door to her room.

My father and Aunt Mary were usually up at five in the

morning, and then I would turn in. I had been there almost a week, and one cold morning had been in bed barely an hour, when Aunt Mary came in and awakened me. She was excited. "Your mother has just realized you are home," she said. "She wants to see you. Get up and come in quick. She can say a few words."

So I jumped out, threw on my bathrobe, and went to her room. Her worn face went into a small smile as I came in, and her eyes shone. She reached out her hand for mine, and I sat on the side of her bed, and she squeezed my hand almost until it hurt.

It was a long time before she could say anything. Her words came with great effort, and I had to lean over and listen closely to make them out. And what my mother said, there so white in her bed, laboring to produce each whispered word, was this: "Are—you—proud—of—me?"

In that one blinding moment, I knew that I had come too late. I knew that inside, I had always been too late. A great choking self-hatred swept over me, and I could only squeeze her hand, give her a slap on the knee, and say, "You bet I'm proud of you."

And then I ran to my own room and, I think for the first time in more than twenty years, lay on my bed and wept.

*

I went alone yesterday to the graveyard, and stood in the sharp wind over my mother's grave, with its flowers put there on a recent day when I was across the ocean.

And as I stood there it seemed to me that she and I were all alone in the world, and I could speak to her, and there was only one thing I could say to her, and that was: "Too late, Mother. You waited a lifetime for it, and I couldn't tell you. But I was, always. You know I was."

It was brief. I could not bear it. I got in the car and put on my dark glasses and drove to town and got a loaf of bread for supper, and drove home with it as though I had not been anywhere special and nothing had happened.

In whatever mystic form it may have been, we had had our final communion. Beyond that lies only ritual. I will never go again to my mother's grave. Others may not understand why. But she does.

April 10, 1941

POSTSCRIPT: *The above touched John Sorrells, executive editor of Scripps Howard Newspapers, who wrote Pyle: "Only one who has lost his mother*

*after he has reached manhood, and has thus been able to really appreciate
her, can understand clearly what the passing of your mother meant to
you. I lost my mother just a few years ago, and only then did I realize
the meaning of 'too late.' In the last years of her life, I tried to do things
to add to her comfort, and to her happiness. Possibly I succeeded in both,
but it was far too late to do what I fear I never was able to do, much
as I wanted to do it—to get over to her how much she meant to me. What
a swell audience she had been. What a grand sport. Oh hell—a hundred
things that she meant which I never, somehow, could tell her."*

*Pyle flew to Albuquerque to see Jerry and their new house, finished while
he was away.*

FINER THAN ANY WORDS

ALBUQUERQUE, NEW MEXICO—Maybe the sun never sets on the
British Empire, but it sure sets on us out here in the desert.

It sets once a day, as regular as can be. And it sets in a manner,
and with a flair and a splendor, that makes you feel sorry for
people with just ordinary sunsets.

We have a window that looks to the west. Across our vista is
a dark, slanting line, so sharp and even that you can hardly
believe it is nature's line. It is the rim of the mesa on the far side
of the Rio Grande Valley.

In the far beyond—sixty miles on toward the setting sun—
there rises old Mount Taylor, all snow-covered now, and as clear
and clean as though you were holding it at arm's length.

And then, just as the sun is on the horizon, and its gold
radiates upward onto the hanging clouds above, and that
unearthly long line of the mesa rim turns into a silhouette as
though cut from black paper, then you see something from my
chair in the west window that is big, something that is finer than
any words.

*

It is so quiet out here just at dawn. I don't know what, but
something awakens us each dawn—the silence, or the gentleness, or something. And we get up, and watch the light come
softly over the great Sandias just to the east of us, and it is the
most perfect hour of the day.

The little birds from the sage-filled mesa come twirping out
at daylight, and they come over into our as-yet-unseeded yard,
and they peck in the fresh earth, and waddle around and sing

and have a wonderful time. Peace seems to be over everything at dawn and at sunset.

*

All this is here for us to relish, so lively and beautiful and serene. But when I sit in our west window at sunset it is past midnight in London, and the guns are going and the bombers are raising hell and my friends of yesterday are tense and full of a distracting excitement—peering, listening, alert to death and the sound of death.

When you sit out here in the silent vastness of the desert, so remote from turmoil, you feel that the ghostly rustling of a falling bomb can be only something that you dreamed once in a nightmare. It has no truth in it. . . .

April 15, 1941

POSTSCRIPT: *Pyle's Great Britain columns were published in book form in* Ernie Pyle in England, *for which he wrote a brief epilogue based on the column above. "Day and night, always in your heart, you are still in London," he wrote. "You have never really left. For when you have shared even a little in the mighty experience of a compassionless destruction, you have taken your partnership in something that is eternal. And amidst it or far away, it is never out of your mind."*

ALBUQUERQUE, NEW MEXICO— . . . A year or so ago I wrote about the mysterious and anonymous person who had been sending my mother a weekly postcard from San Diego.

It has been going on now for about two years. At home they have no idea who does it. Neither have I. The handwriting is unfamiliar. It is doubtless a reader of this column, whom none of us knows personally.

And since my mother's death, the postcard has continued to come, with its simple cheery little note about the weather or the scenery or something—to my father.

April 18, 1941

POSTSCRIPT: *The cards continued to come. By December of 1943, Pyle had already covered the war in North Africa and Sicily and was soon to travel to mainland Italy—and the cards continued to come addressed to "Ernie Pyle's Father." "We must have more than two hundred of them by now," Pyle wrote during a visit to Dana. "We still don't know who sends them. Just somebody good, that's all we know."*

he
ve
ar

s Angeles and
n Diego; Nebraska

ril—
gust 1941

"There is a migration of
Midwesterners in general toward
California right now that is as big
as and maybe will be bigger
than the famous mass movement of
Oklahoma Dust Bowlers a few years
ago. It is caused by the defense
boom, by the rumors of
almost-certain jobs waiting in this
paradise land."

THE DEFENSE BOOM

Americans were still largely isolationist in the spring of 1941, though public opinion was gradually shifting toward war.

After much debate, Congress had in March passed President Roosevelt's Lend-Lease Act, which allowed the President to provide war matériel to England and other nations whose defense was vital to the United States. Thus began the Battle of the Atlantic, as German ships and submarines sank or damaged American vessels conveying or escorting Lend-Lease shipments across the ocean.

Behind Lend-Lease was a peacetime economy that had all the markings of a wartime one. The Depression wasn't over yet, but the mood of the country said it was. The economy was booming. Employment opportunities for skilled workers were abundant, while many of the unskilled still had no work. The boom was "a very mixed blessing," Geoffrey Perrett has written. "For every problem it solved, it appeared to create two more."

JOBS IN PARADISE

LOS ANGELES—On the way out here I am sure we passed a hundred cars from Oklahoma, and quite a few from Missouri and Louisiana.

"What is this thing?" I thought to myself. "A new Okie trek?" So I inquired around, and that's exactly what it is, a new Okie trek. There is a migration of Midwesterners in general toward California right now that is as big as—and maybe will be bigger than—the famous mass movement of Oklahoma Dust Bowlers a few years ago.

It is caused, of course, by the defense boom, by the expansion of the great airplane factories out here, by the rumors of almost-certain jobs waiting in this paradise land.

These new migrants have a name. They aren't called just Okies. They're called Aviation Okies. Because, almost without exception, they are drawn by visions of work in the airplane factories.

*

It is almost impossible to get definite statistics on migration into California. But the auto figures show that more migrants came in from the Midwest in January and February than in any similar two months, even at the height of the last great trek.

For many of them, it is going to be just as pitiful an experience as the other great movement was. Many get jobs, but the number who don't is frightening.

I have an acquaintance [actually his good friend Paige Cavanaugh] who works for the State Employment Service, interviewing people who register for jobs. They come there after they've been turned down everywhere else. They come past his desk, and scores of others like his, all day long. And he says that nearly ninety percent of them are from Oklahoma.

Almost none of them have been through the eighth grade. They have no skills. They are just good, gentle people who haven't had much of a chance in life. They have been farmhands, or laundry workers, or delivery-wagon drivers, or helpers in a dairy. They've been making from ten to fifteen dollars a week, and getting along on it. But they quit their jobs back home in hope of better things, and here they are.

This friend of mine is somewhat sentimental, and he says it is terrible to sit there and talk to them, one after the other, seeing how helpless they are, and knowing how dismal their future is going to be. But at that, they're better off than were the Dust Bowl Okies, who had nothing, who had simply been scourged out of their normal existences by nature and changing times.

This new bunch is, on the average, younger; they have better cars, and better clothes. Most of them have a little money, and they aren't, yet, so full of despair.

*

It is true that the airplane companies are taking on thousands and thousands of workers. But they have stiff tests for intelligence and ability, and the fellow with little schooling and no experience at the trade doesn't have a chance.

Friends tell me Los Angeles is full of trade schools that draw the Midwesterners here. Some are long-established and legitimate, but others are fake, fly-by-night schools, sprung up to skim the cream from a good thing. They send handbills throughout the Midwest; they advertise in magazines and country papers. They even send bush-beaters on tour to drum up recruits.

They are careful not to guarantee aircraft jobs upon completion of their course, but they do strongly intimate that there will be openings. The prospect pays so much down, the balance to come out of his wages after he gets his big-paying job. Of course the school is set up to clear itself on the first payment, never even expecting the rest to be paid.

I saw a jobless man whose only reference was a mimeographed To Whom It May Concern letter from a trade school, saying that the bearer, whose name had simply been written in the blank space, was a man of superlative character, unusual skill, and absolute integrity, an all-around good bet. They must put out thousands of such letters. It didn't mean a thing to a prospective employer, yet the poor gullible fellow was as proud of it as though it had been a medal for bravery.

But the most despicable thing about these schools is that they appeal to the patriotism of small-town boys from the flat states. They say that Uncle Sam is crying for them out there, that it is a young man's duty to drop everything and come on out, that it is the way he can do his part to defend America against peril.

Social workers and employment-agency people will tell you it is common to find men completely puzzled by the cold shoulder they've received when they actually quit their jobs and came out under the impression they were doing their patriotic duty.

*

My friend says the hardest thing for him to bear is that all these wretched, homesick, helpless people of little knowledge still carry the mildness of the cattle country in their manner. They speak slowly and without much bitterness. No matter what you say to them, you never get a rough answer back. Maybe, someday, they will all inherit California.

May 7, 1941

BOMBERS ARE THE MAIN THING
LOS ANGELES—The airplane factories of America have become so big and efficient it's enough to make an aviation old-timer sit down and weep. I can remember when an airplane factory consisted of a shed and ten men. But out here I've just seen two factories that work twenty-five thousand men each.

There are eight big airplane plants in the Los Angeles area. They employ about eighty-five thousand men. By midsummer they will be up to a hundred and twenty-five thousand, maybe even a hundred and forty thousand.

Two of the eight plants are brand-new, unbelievably immense and modern to a fantastic degree. They are just now getting started. One company alone is hiring a thousand men a week.

Airplanes will probably never come rolling from an assembly line every few minutes the way autos do, but just the same they're rolling out the bombers from here in an amazing manner. Surely by this fall southern California will be producing at least a fourth of Mr. Roosevelt's famous fifty thousand a year.*

When you visit one of the big aircraft plants, it's just like going to a movie studio. They look about the same from the outside, it's just as impossible to get in without an appointment, you can't find a place to park at either, and the halls are equally full of pretty girls.

Everything has grown so fast I don't see how one keeps track of it. A friend and I were conjecturing the other evening about the probable plight of poor Donald Douglas, the president of Douglas Aircraft. Unless he's superhuman, the thing must surely have gotten entirely away from him. I'll bet he could walk though his factory today and see things he never heard of before. He's paying more than twenty-five thousand men, and probably most of them wouldn't know him if they met him on the street. . . .

*

There are three Douglas plants. The home plant is in Santa Monica, which is really the west end of Los Angeles, not far from the sea. You're never actually out of the city when you drive from downtown Los Angeles to Santa Monica, although it's about twelve miles.

At Douglas they're still making a few of the big silver transports that have become almost synonymous with airline travel the world over, but very few indeed. For the government has control now, and Douglas turns out a transport for a commercial line only when the Army gives its reluctant approval. There are about nine transports in the plant, for Pan American Airways and Northeast Airlines. That's all.

Bombers are the main thing. They are two-motored light bombers, and very powerful. They've already started making a name for themselves in the English skies. They have a tricycle

---

*The President had appeared before a joint session of Congress on May 16, 1940, and requested "vast sums to mechanize and motorize the Army . . . and funds for fifty thousand planes a year." Isolationism may have been the prevailing sentiment among Americans, but the prevailing reality in Europe was a stark one: Denmark, Norway, Holland, Belgium, and France had all fallen to the Nazis in the month and a half preceding Roosevelt's speech.

landing gear, with one wheel right out under the nose, and they land and taxi level, instead of being cocked up at an angle. This gives them a strange and vicious appearance. When you see one crawling along the runway it resembles a huge doodlebug all bristled up and ready to jump at something.

We spent several hours walking through the factory, and probably saw less than half of it. There is no confusion in this great plant. There is considerable noise from the automatic riveters, but not nearly so much as at the Curtiss fighter plant I visited last fall in Buffalo.

Men work mostly in small teams, building one section of a wing, or one side of a fuselage, or installing wires and cables and tubing. The plant is light and airy, and the work is clean. The men mostly wear brown duck pants and shirts, although there's no rule about it.

The idea at Douglas is not to let any part of the plane get too big until the final stage of assembly. Hence the wings are made in fairly small sections, and not assembled until the plane reaches the last of the assembly lines.

I asked over and over, in the various factories, just how much time elapsed from the first lick of work until a completed plane rolled out onto the runway, but there's no answer to that because nobody knows exactly where the work begins. Actually, it starts in a hundred different departments. In one department they might punch out certain curved flanges for a thousand planes. All through the plant men are working on things that don't even remotely resemble an airplane. It is only when all the hundreds of pieces hit that final assembly line that you could really guess what they are building.

May 12, 1941

LOS ANGELES— . . . Up until the very last stage the planes are painted a greenish yellow. As you stand up on a balcony overlooking the factory floor, the entire factory becomes a field of yellow beneath you.

This yellow stuff is merely a protective surfacing, to keep the metal from being scratched. When the ship is finished, this coloring is taken off and the real paint is sprayed on.

The planes for Britain and for our own Army are camouflaged before they leave the factory. The color is a dull greenish-brown, with gray on the belly and gray under the wings. One plane we saw was a lush jungle green. It was headed for the Dutch East Indies, where the jungles are a deep green.

*

At every plant I visited there was an immense amount of work outdoors. The factories all are crowded, so the assembly line just continues out into the open. Both at Douglas and at Lockheed you can walk for block after block alongside planes being finished under the beautiful California sun. At night they work outside under huge floodlights. And there are even spare-part and storage rooms in tents out behind the hangars. That gives you a feeling of great urgency, a feeling that all these planes are being rushed for the war. . . .

*

The installation of the tubing and wiring in a modern warplane is so complicated and intricate that I don't see how they ever get the right things connected together. You'll see the inside of a plane with literally hundreds of wires and tubes hanging out of the walls. The workmen call this stuff spaghetti, and that's exactly what it looks like. . . .

*

Few of the factories have any special protection against bombing. In fact, the only one is the new Douglas plant at Long Beach, which is equipped for blackout, has its power stations buried underground, and has tunnels between the auto park and the factory that could be used as air-raid shelters.

But the older plants have nothing. They look vulnerable to me. Of course, the Army and Navy claim they won't let an enemy within a thousand miles of the coast, and civilians can't conceive of the enemy trying, anyhow. But that's what Chamberlain* couldn't conceive of, either.

May 13, 1941

LOS ANGELES—A birth-certificate epidemic has swept the country. You can hardly buy a chocolate soda out here these days without a birth certificate.

It's caused by the government order that no aliens shall be employed on aircraft defense work. And to prove you're not an alien, you have to show a birth certificate. I have a friend who went to an aircraft factory the other day for a job. He took his

*Neville Chamberlain, the British prime minister who favored appeasing Germany, Italy, and Japan in the 1930s. He resigned in 1940 and was replaced by Winston Churchill.

passport, his World War Army discharge, and an affidavit from his father. But he didn't have a birth certificate. They wouldn't even let him fill out an application.

There are several million Americans like me, born in the little places, who have never had a birth certificate. They just didn't follow the practice back in those days, so now some of us are in a mess. It's possible to get some kind of delayed certificate, but it takes a lot of corresponding and affidavit-taking and notary-swearing. You can't do it overnight, by any means. They say birth-certificate lawyers have now hung out their shingles, promising to get you a certificate for fifty dollars or so. . . .

LOS ANGELES—The aircraft companies are really getting the cream of young American manhood.

It is very confusing to job-hunters. They see ads in the papers, they read about the thousands being taken on, about the shortage of men and so on—and then when they go for a job, they don't get a tumble.

The reason is simply that most people aren't up to the standards the aircraft companies have set. The qualifications are set so high that the supply of workers is already becoming limited. . . .

Here is the score at Lockheed. Each week, twenty-five thousand people apply for jobs. Of the twenty-five thousand, only five thousand ever get upstairs to take the test. Of that five thousand, only a thousand are good enough to get jobs with Lockheed. . . .

*

To get a job at Lockheed a fellow has to be so superior that it led a friend of mine to say, "Well, that's all right from Lockheed's standpoint, but my God, what's to become of all the people who aren't the cream of the crop? There's more milk in this world than there is cream. Isn't there any place today for an ordinary man?" . . .

May 15, 1941

Life in the boom towns wasn't pleasant. "Look at a town like San Diego: it spent the late 1930s happily thinking it was growing so fast it would double its population and reach three hundred thousand inhabitants by 1960," Geoffrey Perrett has written. "Before 1941 was over, San Diego had its doubling in population—and critical shortages of gas, water, electric-

ity, housing, transportation, schools and sewers. In boom towns it was impossible to escape the congestion and the strain it placed on nerves, courtesy, goodwill, and the simple decencies of life. All hope of comfort, convenience, silence, cleanliness, and privacy had been abandoned. On the frontier such things might have counted for little, but frontier sensibilities were a thing of the past."

HOUSING FOR DEFENSE WORKERS

SAN DIEGO, CALIFORNIA—There has been a lot of talk in various places about the government throwing up gigantic new defense industries, bringing in thousands of people to run them, yet providing no places for these new people to live.

Here in San Diego, for instance, men are actually driving eighty miles a day to work. Homeowners are buying double-decked bunks, putting them in their garages, and renting them out to aircraft workmen.

The greatest congestion is in the area around the aircraft plants. It seems single men don't like to travel far to work, so they are jammed up as many as four in a room in rooming houses near the plant. But the government is doing something about it here. It is, in fact, building the biggest governmental housing project in America.

It is creating a whole new city just outside of San Diego—yet within the city limits—a city of three thousand houses, which will hold at least ten thousand people. It is up on the mesa above San Diego, and you can see a long way from there. The place, so far, is called the Kearny Mesa project.

It wasn't started until last February. When ground was broken, it was absolutely untouched mesa, covered with high bush and lousy with sidewinder rattlesnakes. Today the houses stretch almost as far as you can see. The first families have already moved in. Building goes steadily on. More than three thousand men are working on it.

The rattlesnakes, incidentally, are putting up a fight for their domain. They tell me there have been ninety workmen in the hospital this spring with rattlesnake bites.

*

This new city will be two-and-a-half miles long, a mile and a half wide. It will have parks and playgrounds and churches. It will have two elementary schools and one junior high school. It will have stores at each end and in the middle.

It is six miles from downtown San Diego, and there will be bus service. The whole thing is costing a little under ten million dollars. The contract calls for completion within three hundred working days, which means by midwinter.

The houses are permanent—not of the semipermanent Army-cantonment type. They are compact and furnished with all modern contraptions. No two houses of the same design are put side by side. They sit back from the street with ample lawn space. Two or three years from now, when grass and trees and shrubbery have their way, the city will be nice to look at.

There isn't a house with a garage in this new city. Cars will have to stand out, the idea being, apparently, that when people start buying these houses after the war, they can build their own garages.

For after the war the government intends to sell the whole thing—not by the individual house, but to private companies able to take over large sections of four hundred to five hundred houses. They, in turn, will sell them to individuals. These three thousand houses will be rented now only to men doing defense work—which here means largely the workers at Consolidated Aircraft.

*

The houses are of three sizes—one-, two-, and three-bedroom. The rental rate will not be based on size, but upon the occupant's wages.

The size of the house a workman gets depends not on his salary but on the size of his family. A man can't get a big house just because he can afford it. If you're married, but childless, you get only a one-bedroom house. Some other fellow might get a three-bedroom house and pay less rent than you do, simply because he has a big family and is making less.

When this new city is finished, the government intends to put up no more permanent houses. But that doesn't mean it has shut its eyes to future housing needs here, for it has set the private building industry of San Diego a quota of forty-five hundred new houses within the next six months, in addition to regular normal building, which already has run over twenty-three hundred houses this year.

If, within six months, private industry doesn't appear to be making its quota, then the government will move in with collapsible houses. They may be metal or composition—whatever they are they'll be thrown up quickly, and taken down when the war is over. . . .

On top of all this, the Navy has two huge projects to house twelve hundred families, which will help relieve the pressure on city housing. Totaling it all, homes are being created in San Diego this year for about thirteen thousand families.

That seems like an awful lot. Yet—before the summer is over Consolidated Aircraft will take on some eighteen thousand new men, and they will have to come from outside. Right there you have a surplus of five thousand men and their families with no place to live.

May 28, 1941

HEADED EAST

CROSSING NEBRASKA— . . . [A]s far as I can see in traveling around the country talking to people, the public polls are right—the people are against going to war.

That, of course, is all right, if the majority says so. What isn't all right (at least with me) is our smugness about it. In the past few months I have seen the following incident duplicated a half-dozen times throughout the country.

We go to some big public celebration, such as a Fourth of July parade, five thousand miles from the nearest bomb. The Army puts a group of two-month draftees in the parade. They march by in good order and look pretty nice. The flag passes and everybody stands up. The announcer cracks over the loud-speaker, "Boy, if old Hitler could just see this!" We all cheer wildly, ripple our muscles, picture Hitler shaking in his boots, sit back down, nod knowingly to each other, and go back to eating our beautiful popcorn out of a sack. . . .

August 5, 1941

At War in the West

San Francisco
December 1941

"It is impossible for hands or minds to lie in easy composure during days like these."

"I have been struck, most of all, with the average man's apparent placidity toward the war," Pyle wrote from San Francisco in October 1939.

"And by that I don't mean indifference. For everybody is interested in the war. But their conversation is all so objective, as though the war were something in a book. I have yet to hear anyone speak passionately about it."

This was all the more true on the West Coast, Pyle wrote, because "California is so far away from Europe, and so close to the Orient. Those who think deeply out here about the war usually have an Oriental angle on it."

A little over a year later—on December 7, 1941—Japanese planes attacked the American Navy at Pearl Harbor. No longer did President Roosevelt have to seek ways to impress upon his countrymen the importance of the United States' taking a hand in what was happening in Europe and Asia. American isolationism vanished with the first news bulletin from Pearl Harbor. The United States declared war on Japan the next day; three days later Germany and Italy declared war on the United States.

Pyle had been on an extended leave from his job, caring for Jerry, who had suffered an emotional breakdown. He went back to work immediately, traveling from his home in Albuquerque to San Francisco.

A FEELING OF DRASTIC URGENCY

SAN FRANCISCO—The long rest is over. All long rests are over, for everybody. A new vitality is abroad in our land, and even those of us who are wan and frail sense in ourselves an overpowering compulsion to flail and strike around, doing something.

For four months this column and its author have lain in hibernation. In a way it was a sweet repose, and we discovered that it is pleasant not to work or worry or feel the surge of worldly things. But war changes all those feelings. It makes for restlessness, and an eagerness to be up and about. Hence this column, a month ahead of the planned date, comes back to life.

We are under no illusion that there is anything this space can contribute to the great force that America must now have. But we do know that the faintest of us must be active now, even if only for ourselves. It is impossible for hands or minds to lie in easy composure during days like these. Even mine must scramble anxiously back to work. For me, as for millions of others, things did not turn out as they had been planned.

Some six weeks ago That Girl grew definitely better, and I knew that sooner or later I must be on my way. We laid out an itinerary. We decided upon a winter roaming around the Orient—the Philippines, Hong Kong, Chungking, the Burma Road, Rangoon, Singapore, and the Dutch East Indies.

All arrangements were made. The red tape was vanquished. Out came the old passport, and on its traveled pages there was more ink of many colors. Final things were done at home—bags packed, money drawn, vaccination certificates looked up, letters written, bookings made, priorities for travel confirmed.

I was booked to leave San Francisco for Manila on the Clipper of December 2—the week before the new war came. But at the last minute my seat was taken away by the Army, to make room for supplies urgently needed in the Far East. Then I found passage to Honolulu by boat, expecting to catch a later Clipper there. But once again the Army parried my thrust. It commandeered the entire boat. As a last resort, I was arranging on a Saturday to cross the Pacific on a bomber. And then, next day, came that shocking Sunday at Pearl Harbor.

Automatically everything was off. I was still in Albuquerque. All that Sunday was a daze. The news was too horrible. Albuquerque took it hard, for in the Philippines there are two thousand New Mexico boys. The jitters began to take hold of people.

Monday was just the same. I don't remember what I did. I only remember that all that day people were talking, talking, talking, and that nobody knew what he was saying or thinking. And just after dark came the then-frightful rumor that two

Japanese carriers were off San Francisco, and that the entire coast was to be blacked out.

That was enough for me. San Francisco was definitely someplace to go, something you could tie your emotions to. So I went to the phone and asked how soon I could get a plane. They said at five the next morning.

Even the flight was warlike. When we left Albuquerque before dawn we had clearance from the Army only as far as Dagget, California. We were over Dagget by eight A.M., and still no clearance. So we waited up there over the bare Mojave Desert, waited in gigantic circlings in the air until word did come.

Then they cleared us to Palmdale, and again over Palmdale we circled and circled, waiting on the war. Finally they ordered us on, but we did not land at the great air terminal in Burbank. No, we went down in a pasturelike place many miles away, and they took us on in by bus. The Army was running things now.

Late that afternoon we did get to San Francisco. The sun was shining, and I'll always remember the thousands of sea gulls sitting alongside the runway as we landed.

There were two odd little coincidences for me in this arrival in bomb-expectant San Francisco. For one thing, it was exactly a year to the day from my arrival in London. For another, San Francisco did have an alarm and a blackout that night, and I slept serenely through it, just as I had slept through my first real air raid on my first night in London.

So now we are in San Francisco, looking with deep curiosity into the hours ahead. Nothing has happened here yet, but only an ostrich would declare that nothing ever will. We shall wait a little while and see.

San Francisco is exciting these days. For there is suspense here, and wonderment of what the night will bring, and a feeling of drastic urgency. Several times I've heard these words, said not in braggadocio but more in fateful resignation:

"Well, if it comes it'll be bad here, but I guess we can take it, too."

Yes, I guess we can.

December 15, 1941

NOTES

FRONT QUOTES

vii   "Not so many years ago": Daniel J. Boorstin, *The Image: Or What Happened to the American Dream* (New York: Antheneum, 1962), p. 115.

vii   "Highways have made": Phil Patton, *Open Road: A Celebration of the American Highway* (New York: Touchstone, Simon and Schuster, 1987), page 13.

INTRODUCTION

xviii   "I reckon I got to light out": Mark Twain, *The Adventures of Huckleberry Finn*, Henry Nash Smith, ed. (Boston: Houghton Mifflin, 1958), p. 245.

xix   "The wind of futility": Pyle column, 23 September 1935.

xxii   "almost without exception": letter from Frank R. Ford to Will and Maria Pyle, 10 June 1936, Indiana State Museum, Indianapolis.

xxii   "too-heavy grist": letter from Don E. Weaver to Ernie Pyle, 30 May 1938, Manuscripts Department, Lilly Library, Indiana University, Bloomington.

xxii   "gentle wholesomeness": cable from John Sorrells to Lee Miller, 16 February 1938, Lilly Library.

xxiv   "sorry to read": anonymous letter to Ernie Pyle, 16 June 1932, Lilly Library.

xxiv   "Please don't forget": letter from C. H. Harrington to Ernie Pyle, 17 June 1932, Lilly Library.

xxiv   "alcoholic insanity": interview with Richard Hollander by David Nichols, Dana, Indiana, 3 July 1976.

xxv   "a Mark Twain quality": quoted in Lee G. Miller, *The Story of Ernie Pyle* (New York: Viking, 1950), p. 53.

xxvii   "Am I glad": letter from Ernie Pyle to Edward and Elizabeth Shaffer, 15 May 1937, private collection of George Shaffer, Albuquerque, New Mexico.

xxviii   "the richest vein of ore": Pyle column, 24 November 1937.

xxix   "American roads have": Patton, p. 14.

xxx   "I hope that you may": letter from Blanche Hunter to Maria Pyle, 11 June 1939, Indiana State Museum.

xxx   "intelligent and friendly": Pyle column, 5 August 1941.

xxx   "Of course, characters" etc.: Pyle column, 5 November 1935.

xxxi   "But we had engagements": Pyle column, 28 November 1939.

xxxi   "Stability cloaks you": Pyle column, 11 October 1938.

xxxi   "I haven't had": letter from Ernie Pyle to Paige Cavanaugh, 4 June 1937, Lilly Library.

xxxii   "I find that": letter from Walter Morrow to Ernie Pyle, 31 May 1938, Lilly Library.

xxxii   "[Readers say], 'Ernie talks' ": letter from Lee Hills to Ernie Pyle, 31 May 1938, Lilly Library.

xxxiii   "We must print": letter from Edward J. Meeman to Ernie Pyle, 6 June 1938, Lilly Library.

xxxiii   "[Alaska is] too damn cold": letter from Ernie Pyle to Paige Cavanaugh, 4 June 1937, Lilly Library.

xxxiii   "One of their own": quoted in Lee G. Miller, *The Story of Ernie Pyle* (New York: Viking, 1950), p. 123.

xxxiv   "OHIO SERIES BY ERNIE PYLE": cable from Midwestern Scripps Howard editors to George B. Parker, 7 June 1938, Lilly Library.

xxxv   "We fled San Diego": letter from Ernie Pyle to Paige Cavanaugh, 26 October 1939, Lilly Library.

xxxv   "I know it must sound awful": quoted in Miller, p. 120.

xxxv   "I'd gaily take a little": *ibid.*

xxxvi   "panicky": letter from Ernie Pyle to Paige Cavanaugh, 26 October 1939, Lilly Library.

xxxvi   "just quietly make": *ibid.*

xxxviii   "We have worked up": Pyle column, 16 November 1940.

xxxviii   "I'm just a pawn": letter from Jerry Pyle to Elizabeth Shaffer, undated, 1936, George Shaffer.

xxxix   "during some of their years": Miller, p. 69.

xxxix   "I *can't* give you a child": quoted in *ibid*, p. 185.

xxxix   "We are wandering people": Pyle column, 13 July 1940.

xl   "I've talked with Albuquerque": letter from Ernie Pyle to Paige Cavanaugh, 19 March 1942, Lilly Library.

xli   "agonizing and cruel": Miller, p. 188.

xli   "The doctors all say": letter from Ernie Pyle to Paige Cavanaugh, 23 March 1942, Lilly Library.

xli   "has been in Christ-awful shape": letter from Ernie Pyle to Paige Cavanaugh, 5 May 1942, Lilly Library.

xlii   "under the impression" and "I feel that if I": letter from Ernie Pyle to Jerry Pyle, 8 May 1942, Lilly Library.

xlii   "Darling—I am taking off": Letter from

Ernie Pyle to Jerry Pyle, 18 June 1942, Lilly Library. — 266

xliii   "I don't like that idea": letter from Ernie Pyle to Paige Cavanaugh, 18 August 1937, Lilly Library. — 266

"Being on the move": citation misplaced. — 266

xliv   "seemed more like something": Pyle column, 8 April 1941 — 268

xlvi   "wrung and drained": Ernie Pyle, *Brave Men* (New York: Henry Holt, 1944), p. 464.

xlvi   "My spirit is wobbly": Pyle column, 5 September 1944.

EDITOR'S NOTE

li   "In five years": Pyle column, 16 November 1940.

PART-TITLE QUOTE

1   "I have no home": Pyle column, 16 January 1939

HOME COUNTRY

11   "Dana is a pretty town": Pyle column, 16 January 1939

THE EAST

49   "The sudden cutting off": *New York Times*, 12 July 1936.

NEW DEAL WASHINGTON

58   Footnote: "survive the Depression": Robert S. McElvaine, *The Great Depression: America, 1929–1941* (New York: Times Books, 1984), p. 155

THE MIDWEST

104   "I swear the reporters": quoted in Miller, p. 66.

THE WEST

129   "old-time prospector" etc.: Pyle column, 4 June 1936.

135   "worked up a sort of mania": Pyle column, 15 September 1936.

140   "tall, graying" etc.: Pyle column, 2 September 1939.

146   "Seattle is a mighty fine place": letter from Ernie Pyle to Will and Maria Pyle, 30 March 1922, Indiana State Museum.

FAR NORTH COUNTRY

192   "In 1900, [Pantages] became": Pierre Berton, *The Klondike Fever: The Life and Death of the Last Great Gold Rush* (New York: Knopf, 1958), p. 424–425.

THE SOUTHWEST

212   "In the seventeen years" etc.: Pyle column, 27 April 1939.

214   ". . . [Y]ear by year": Pyle column, 25 April 1939.

255   "an instant hit": Miller, p. 53.

266   "The Hales haven't caught" etc.: Pyle column, 18 November 1939.

266   "Their house and filling station": Pyle column, 6 April 1942.

266   "not once did we leave": quoted in Miller, p. 115

268   "The Teec Nos Pas column": letter from Ernie Pyle to Edward Shaffer, 30 June 1939, George Shaffer.

THE SOUTH

306   "the happiest I've ever": Pyle column, 5 November 1940.

325   "has a way of running out": Pyle column, 26 November 1940.

337   "born of slave parents": quoted in *New York Times*, 6 January 1943.

A TRAVELER'S NOTES

368   "Lord, you must have": letter from Jerry Pyle to Elizabeth Shaffer, 20 April 1937, George Shaffer.

HOME REPORT: JUNE 1939

374   "part collie and part just dog": Pyle column, 6 June 1939.

374   "I HOPE you KEEP that dog": letter from Blanche Hunter to Maria Pyle, 11 June 1939, Indiana State Museum.

374   "Am surprised your husband": anonymous letter to Maria Pyle, 10 June 1939, Indiana State Museum.

AIRPLANES AND ENGINES FOR DEFENSE

377   "In 1940 I used to read": quoted in Miller, p. 322.

HOME AGAIN

393   "Your [recent] column": letter from Robert M. Campbell to Ernie Pyle, 8 June 1939, Indiana State Museum.

398   "Only one who has lost": letter from John H. Sorrells to Ernie Pyle, 7 March 1941, Lilly Library.

400   "Day and night": Ernie Pyle, *Ernie Pyle in England* (New York: Robert M. McBride, 1941), p. 228.

400   "We must have": Pyle column, 10 November 1943.

THE DEFENSE BOOM

402   "a very mixed blessing": Geoffrey Perrett, *Days of Sadness, Years of Triumph: The American people 1939–1945* (New York: Coward, McCann & Geoghegan, 1973), p. 174.

405   Footnote: "vast sums": William E. Leuchtenburg, *Franklin D. Roosevelt and the New Deal, 1932–1940* (New York: Harper & Row, 1963), p. 300.

408   "Look at a town": Perrett, 174–175.

AT WAR IN THE WEST

412   "I have been struck": Pyle column, 24 October 1939.

BIBLIOGRAPHY

Allen, Frederick Lewis. *Only Yesterday: An Informal History of the 1920s.* New York, 1931.
——. *Since Yesterday: The 1930s in America, September 3, 1929–September 3, 1939.* New York, 1940.
——. *The Big Change: America Transforms Itself, 1900–1950.* New York, 1952.
Atherton, Lewis. *Main Street on the Middle Border.* Bloomington, Ind., 1954.
Banks, Ann, ed. *First-Person America.* New York, 1980.
Bird, Caroline. *The Invisible Scar.* New York, 1966.
Boorstin, Daniel J. *The Image: Or What Happened to the American Dream.* New York, 1961.
Corn, Joseph J. *The Winged Gospel: America's Romance with Aviation, 1900–1950.* New York, 1983.
Fuller, Wayne E. *RFD: The Changing Face of Rural America.* Bloomington, Ind., 1954.
Garraty, John A. *The Great Depression.* New York, 1987.
Hobson, Archie, ed. *Remembering America: A Sampler of the WPA American Guide Series.* New York, 1985.
Leuchtenburg, William E. *The Perils of Prosperity, 1914–32.* Chicago, 1958.
McElvaine, Robert S. *The Great Depression: America, 1929–1941.* New York, 1984.
——, ed. *Down and Out in the Great Depression: Letters from the Forgotten Man.* Chapel Hill, N. C., 1983.
Manchester, William. *The Glory and the Dream: A Narrative History of America, 1932–1972.* 2 vols. Boston, 1973.
Patton, Phil. *Open Road: A Celebration of the American Highway.* New York, 1986.
Peeler, David P. *Hope Among Us Yet: Social Criticism and Social Solace in Depression America.* Athens, Ga., 1987.
Perrett, Geoffrey. *Days of Sadness, Years of Triumph: The American People 1939–1945.* New York, 1973.
Robertson, James Oliver. *American Myth, American Reality.* New York, 1980.
Stott, William. *Documentary Expression and Thirties America.* New York, 1973.
Susman, Warren I. *Culture as History: The Transformation of American Culture in the Twentieth Century.* New York, 1984.
Terkel, Studs. *Hard Times: An Oral History of the Great Depression.* New York, 1970.

INDEX

ABOUT THE EDITOR

DAVID NICHOLS lives in Fort Wayne, Indiana, with his wife and three daughters. This is the second volume of Ernie Pyle's pieces he has edited. *Ernie's War* appeared in 1986.